COINS OF ENGLAND

AND
THE UNITED KINGDOM

34th Edition

SPINK
LONDON

A Catalogue of the Coins of Great Britain
and Ireland
first published 1929

Standard Catalogue of British Coins
Coins of England and the United Kingdom
34th edition, 1999

© Spink & Son Ltd
5 King Street, St James's
London SW1Y 6QS

Typeset by Data Layout Ltd, 136 Tooley Street, London
Printed in Great Britain by
Cromwell Press
Trowbridge
Wiltshire

ISBN 1 902040 06 6

CONTENTS

CONTENTS

APPENDICES:

PREFACE

This, the new 1999 edition of Seaby's Standard Catalogue of British Coins: Coins of England and the United Kingdom, has again been updated by the numismatic specialists at Spink.

Firmly established over the past 60 years or more as the most handy guide to current market trends, we feel we are now making more and more improvements from one new edition to another.

This is the second year it has been revised and published by Spink, and, as with last year's edition, it incorporates many changes.

All prices and texts have been carefully checked to ensure they reflect current market conditions. New illustrations have been added where necessary, whilst some of those that have been used for a number of previous editions have now been replaced with better ones, often of coins in stock at the time of rewriting.

No less than five completely new maps have been prepared to replace the single map which had been included in past editions.

For this new edition the whole of the Roman Britain section has been rewritten for us by David Sear, the author of so many of our books, and whose masterful new work: *The History and Coinage of the Roman Imperators 49-27BC* is in the press as this Preface is being written.

Peter Clayton, Expert Advisor (coins and antiquities) Treasure Valuation Committee, has contributed a totally up to date summary of the concept of "Treasure Trove" and the law relating to it, the new Treasure Act.

We would particularly like to thank the following members of the Coin Department at Spink for their work on this edition of the Catalogue: Antony Wilson (Celtic, Hammered coins, and the new maps), May Sinclair (Hammered coins), Steve Hill and Mark Rasmussen (Milled coins) and Geoff Kitchen (Modern coins). More especially we are grateful to the many collectors who have taken the time to contact us with suggestions, corrections and who have contributed invaluable help in their own particular series.

The cover has been designed for us by Paul Sharp, and the coins illustrated on the cover were in stock whilst this edition was in production.

INTRODUCTION

Arrangement

The arrangement of this catalogue is not completely uniform, but generally it is divided into metals (gold, silver, copper, etc) under each reign, then into coinages, denominations and varieties. In the Celtic section the uninscribed coins are listed before the dynastic coins; under Charles II all the hammered coins precede the milled coinage; the reign of George III is divided into coins issued up to 1816 and the new coinage from 1816 to the end of the reign; and under Elizabeth II the decimal issues are separated from the pre-decimal (£.s.d.) coinages.

Every major coin type is listed though not every variety. We have endeavoured to give rather more coverage to the varieties of relatively common coins, such as the pennies of Edward I, II and III, than to the very much rarer coins of, for instance, King Offa of Mercia.

Values

The values given represent the range of retail prices at which coins are being offered for sale at the time of going to press and **not** the price which a dealer will pay for those coins. These prices are based on our knowledge of the numismatic market, the current demand for particular coins, recent auction sale prices and, in those cases where certain coins have not appeared for sale for some years, our estimation of what they would be likely to sell at today, bearing in mind their rarity and appeal in relation to somewhat similar coins where a current value is known. Values are given for two grades of preservation from the Celtic period onwards and three to four grades of preservation for coins of the 17th to the 20th century.

Collectors normally require coins in the best condition they can afford and, except in the case of a really rare coin, a piece that is considerably worn is not wanted and has little value. The values given in the catalogue are for the exact state of preservation stated at the head of each column and bearing in mind that a score of identical coins in varying states of wear could be lined up in descending order from mint condition (FDC, *fleur de coin*), through very fine (VF) to *poor* state. It will be realized that only in certain instances will the values given apply to particular coins. A 'fine' (F) coin may be worth anything between one quarter and a half of the price quoted for a 'very fine' (VF); on the other hand, a piece in really mint condition will be valued substantially higher than the price quoted for 'extremely fine' (EF). The designation BV has been adopted for coins whose value on the market has yet to exceed its bullion value. Purchasing sovereigns, catalogued as BV, will attract a dealers' premium.

We emphasize again that the purpose of this catalogue is to give a general value for a particular class of coin in a specified state of preservation, and also to give the collector an idea of the range and value of coins in the English series. The value of any particular piece depends on three things:

Its exact design, legend, mintmark or date.

Its exact state of preservation; this is of prime importance.

The demand for it in the market at any given time.

Some minor varieties are much scarcer than others and, as the number of coins issued varies considerably from year to year, coins of certain dates and mintmarks are rarer and of more value than other pieces of similar type. The prices given for any type are for the commonest variety, mintmark or date of that type.

The Scope

Coin collecting, numismatics, is a fascinating hobby. It requires very little physical exertion and only as much mental effort as one wishes or is able to put into it at any time. There is vast scope and boundless ramifications and byways encompassing not only things historical and geographical, but also touching on economics, metallurgy, heraldry, literature, the fine arts, politics, military history and many other disciplines. This catalogue is solely concerned with British coinage from its earliest times right up to date. From the start the beginner should appreciate that the coinage of our own nation may be seen as a small but very important part of the whole story of world currency.

The first coins, made of electrum, a natural alloy of gold and silver, were issued in western Asia Minor (Lydia) in the later seventh century B.C. Over the next century or so coinage of gold and silver spread across the Aegean to mainland Greece, southwards to the eastern Mediterranean lands and eventually westward to the Greek colonies in southern Italy, Sicily (Magna Graecia) and beyond. The coins of the Greeks are noted for their beautiful, sometimes exquisite craftsmanship, with many of the coin types depicting the patron deities of their cities. Coins of Philip II of Macedon (359-336 B.C.), father of Alexander the Great, circulated amongst the Celtic peoples of the Danubian Basin and were widely copied through central Europe and by the Gauls in France. Gold Gaulish staters were reaching Britain around the beginning of the first century B.C. and the earliest gold to be struck in the island must have been produced shortly afterwards. Although their types and designs copy the Apollo head and racing charioteer of Philip II's gold coins, they are stylistically much removed from the original representation and very individually Celtic in concept.

The coins of the Romans cover some seven centuries and include an enormous number of different types that were current throughout a major part of the civilized world from Spain to Syria and from the Rhine in the north to the Sudan in the south. The Roman province of Britain was part of this vast empire for four hundred years from AD 43 until the early fifth century. Innumerable Roman coins have been recovered from sites in this country, most being made of brass or bronze. Many of these are quite inexpensive and very collectable. In recent years many hoards of gold and silver coins have been found, usually by use of metal detectors.

Following the revival of commerce after the Dark Ages, coinage in Western Europe was virtually restricted to silver until the thirteenth century, though gold was still being minted in Byzantium and in the Islamic world. In the Middle Ages many European cities had their own distinctive coinage and money was issued not only by the kings but also by nobles, bishops and abbots. From the time of the later Crusades gold returned to the West, and the artistic developments of the Renaissance in the fifteenth century brought improved portraiture and new minting techniques.

Large silver crown-size thalers were first minted at Joachimsthal in Bohemia early in the sixteenth century. The substantial shipments of silver coming to Europe from the mines of Spanish America over the next couple of centuries led to a fine series of larger coins being issued by the European states and cities. The larger size allowed greater artistic freedom in the designs and the portraits on the coins.

Both Germany and Italy became unified nation states during the later nineteenth century, thereby substantially reducing the number of mints and coin types. Balancing the reduction in European minting authorities were the new coins that were issued by the independent states of South and Central America. Since the 1950s many new nations have established their independence and their coinage provides a large field for the collector of modern coins.

It can be seen that the scope for the collector is truly vast, but besides the general run of official coinage there is also the large series of token coins—small change unofficially produced to supplement the inadequate supply of authorized currency. These tokens were issued by merchants, innkeepers and manufacturers in many towns and villages in the seventeenth, eighteenth and nineteenth centuries and many collectors specialize in their local issues.

Some coins have designs of a commemorative nature; an example being the Royal Wedding crown of 1981, but there are also large numbers of commemorative medals which, though never intended for use as coinage, are sometimes confused with coins because they are metal objects of a similar shape and sometimes a similar size to coins. This is another interesting field for collectors as these medals often have excellent portraits of famous men or women, or they may commemorate important events or scientific discoveries. Other metallic objects of coin-like appearance that can be confusing for the beginner are reckoning counters, advertising tickets, various other tickets and passes, and items such as brass coin weights.

Minting processes

From the time of the earliest Greek coins in the late seventh century BC to about the middle of the sixteenth century AD, coins were made by hand. The method of manufacture was simple. The obverse and reverse designs were engraved or punched into the prepared ends of two bars of bronze or iron, shaped or tapered to the diameter of the required coin. The obverse die, known as the *pile,* was usually spiked so that it could be anchored firmly into a block of wood or metal. The reverse die, the *trussel,* was held by hand or grasped by tongs.

The coin was struck by placing a metal blank between the two dies and striking the trussel with a hammer. Thus, all coinage struck by this method is known as 'hammered'. Some dies are known to have been hinged so there would be an exact register between the upper and lower die. Usually a 'pair of dies' consisted of one obverse die (normally the more difficult to make because it had the finer detail, such as the ruler's portrait) and two reverse dies. This was because the shaft of iron bearing the reverse design eventually split under the constant hammering; two reverse dies were usually needed to last out the life of the obverse die.

Some time toward the middle of the sixteenth century, experiments, first in Germany and later in France, resulted in the manufacture of coins by machinery.

The term 'milled', which is applied to all machine-made coins, comes from the type of machinery used – the mill and screw press. With this machinery the obverse die was fixed as the lower die and the reverse die brought down into contact with the blank by heavy vertical pressure applied by a screw or worm-drive connected to a cross bar with heavy weights at each end. These weights usually had long leather thongs attached which allowed a more powerful force to be applied by the operators who revolved the arms of the press. New blanks were placed on the lower die and the struck coins were removed by hand. The screw press brought more pressure to bear on the blanks and this pressure was evenly applied, producing a far better and sharper coin.

Various attempts were made during the reigns of Elizabeth I and Charles I to introduce this type of machinery with its vastly superior products. Unfortunately problems associated with the manufacture of blanks to a uniform weight greatly reduced the rate of striking and the hand manufacture of coins continued until the Restoration in 1660, when Charles II brought to London from Holland the Roettiers brothers and their improved screw press.

The first English coins made for circulation by this new method were the silver crowns of 1662, which bore an inscription on the edge, DECVS ET TVTAMEN, 'an ornament and a safeguard', a reference to the fact that the new coins could not be clipped, a crime made easy by the thin and often badly struck hammered coins.

The mill and screw press was used until new steam-powered machinery made by Boulton and Watt was installed in the new mint on Tower Hill in London. This machinery had been used most successfully by Boulton to strike the large 'cartwheel' two- and one-penny pieces of 1797 and other coins, including 'overstriking' Spanish *eight-reale* pieces into Bank of England 'dollars' since the old Mint presses were not able to exert sufficient power to do this. This new machinery was first used at the Mint to strike the 'new coinage' halfcrowns of 1816, and it operated at a far greater speed than the old type of mill and screw presses and achieved a greater sharpness of design.

The very latest coining presses now operating at the Royal Mint at Llantrisant in South Wales, are capable of striking at a rate of up to 800 coins a minute.

Condition

One of the more difficult problems for the beginner is to assess accurately the condition of a coin. A common fault among collectors is to overgrade and, consequently, to overvalue their coins.

Most dealers will gladly spare a few minutes to help new collectors. Many dealers issue price lists with illustrations, enabling collectors to see exactly what the coins look like and how they have been graded.

Coins cannot always be graded according to precise rules. Hammered coins often look weak or worn on the high parts of the portrait and the tops of the letters; this can be due to weak striking or worn dies and is not always attributable to wear through long use in circulation. Milled coins usually leave the Mint sharply struck so that genuine wear is easier to detect. However a x5 or x10 magnifying glass is essential, especially when grading coins of Edward VII and George V where the relief is very low on the portraits and some skill is required to distinguish between an uncirculated coin and one in EF condition.

The condition or grade of preservation of a coin is usually of greater importance than its rarity. By this we mean that a common coin in superb condition is often more desirable and more highly priced than a rarity in poor condition. Coins that have been pierced or mounted as a piece of jewellery generally have little interest to collectors.

One must also be on the lookout for coins that have been 'plugged', i.e. that have been pierced at some time and have had the hole filled in, sometimes with the missing design or letters re-engraved.

Badly cleaned coins will often display a complexity of fine interlaced lines and such coins have a greatly reduced value. It is also known for coins to be tooled or re-engraved on the high parts of the hair, in order to 'increase' the grade of coin and its value. In general it is better to have a slightly more worn coin than a better example with such damage.

Cleaning coins

Speaking generally, *do not* clean coins. More coins are ruined by injudicious cleaning than through any other cause, and a badly cleaned coin loses much of its value. A nicely toned piece is usually considered desirable. Really dirty gold and silver can, however, be carefully washed in soap and water. Copper coins should never be cleaned or washed, they may be lightly brushed with a brush that is not too harsh.

Buying and selling coins

Exchanging coins with other collectors, searching around the antique shops, telling your relatives and friends that you are interested in coins, or even trying to find your own with a metal detector, are all ways of adding to your collection. However, the time will come when the serious collector needs to acquire specific coins or requires advice on the authenticity or value of a coin.

At this point an expert is needed, and the services of a reputable coin dealer are necessary. There are now a large number of coin dealers in the UK, many of whom belong to the B.N.T.A. (The British Numismatic Trade Association) or the I.A.P.N. (The International Association of Professional Numismatists) and a glance through the 'yellow pages' under 'coin dealer' or 'numismatist' will often provide local information. Many dealers publish their own lists of coins. Studying these lists is a good way for a collector to learn about coins and to classify and catalogue their own collections.

The Standard Catalogue of Coins of England and the UK has been published since 1929. It serves as a price guide for all coin collectors. Spink also publish books on many aspects of English, Greek, Roman and Byzantine coins and on British tokens which serve as a valuable source of information for coin collectors. Our books are available directly from Spink or through reputable booksellers. Many branches of W. H. Smith, and other High Street booksellers, stock copies of *The Standard Catalogue*.

Numismatic Clubs and Societies

There are well over one hundred numismatic societies and clubs in the British Isles. For details of how to contact them see page 466. Joining one is the best way to meet fellow enthusiasts, learn about your coins and other series and acquire coins in a friendly and informative way.

Useful suggestions

Security and insurance. The careful collector should not keep valuable coins at home unless they are insured and have adequate protection. Local police and insurance companies will give advice on what precautions may be necessary.

Most insurance companies will accept a valuation based on *The Standard Catalogue*. It is usually possible to have the amount added to a householder's contents policy but particularly valuable individual coins may have to be separately listed. A 'Fire, Burglary and Theft' policy will cover loss only from the insured's address, but an 'All Risks' policy will usually cover accidental damage and loss anywhere within the U.K.

For coins deposited with a bank or placed in a safe-deposit box a lower insurance premium is usually payable.

Keeping a record. All collectors are advised to have an up-to-date record of their collection and, if possible, photographs of the more important and more easily identifiable coins. This should be kept in a separate place from the collection so that a list and photographs can be given to the police should loss occur. Note the price paid, from whom purchased, the date of acquisition and the condition of the coin.

Storage and handling. New collectors should get into the habit of handling coins by the edge. This is especially important as far as highly polished proof coins are concerned.

Collectors may initially keep their coins in paper or plastic envelopes housed in boxes, albums or special containers. Many collectors will eventually wish to own a hardwood coin cabinet in which the collection can be properly arranged and displayed. If a home-made cabinet is being constructed avoid using oak and cedar wood; mahogany, walnut and rosewood are ideal. It is important that coins are not kept in a humid atmosphere; especial care must be taken with copper and bronze coins which are very susceptible to damp or condensation which may result in a green verdigris forming on them.

From beginner to numismatist

The new collector can best advance to becoming an experienced numismatist by examining as many coins as possible, noting their distinctive features and by learning to use the many books of reference that are available. It will be an advantage to join a local numismatic society, as this will provide an opportunity for meeting other enthusiasts and obtaining advice from more experienced collectors. Most societies have a varied programme of lectures, exhibitions and occasional auctions of members' duplicates.

Those who become members of one or both of the national societies, the Royal Numismatic Society and the British Numismatic Society, receive an annual journal containing authoritative papers and have access to the societies' library and programme of lectures.

Many museums have coin collections available for study, although they may not always be displayed, and a number of museum curators are qualified numismatists.

ABBREVIATIONS

Archb.	Archbishop	l.	left
Æ	bronze	laur.	laureate
Æ	silver	*mm.*	*mintmark*
Ν	gold	mon.	monogram
Bp.	Bishop	*O., obv.*	obverse
BV	bullion value	p.	new penny, pence
cuir.	cuirassed	pl	plume
d.	penny, pence	quat.	quatrefoil
diad.	diademed	qtr.	quarter
dr.	draped	rad.	radiate
ex.	exergue	R., *rev.*	reverse
grs.	grains	r.	right
hd.	head	s.	shillings
i.c.	inner circle	var.	variety
illus.	illustration	wt.	weight

SOME NUMISMATIC TERMS EXPLAINED

Obverse	That side of the coin which normally shows the monarch's head or name.
Reverse	The side opposite to the obverse, the 'Tails'.
Blank	The coin as a blank piece of metal, i.e. before it is struck.
Flan	The whole piece of metal after striking.
Type	The main, central design.
Legend	The inscription. Coins lacking a legend are called 'mute' or anepigraphic.
Field	That flat part of the coin between the main design and the inscription or edge.
Exergue	That part of the coin below the main design, usually separated by a horizontal line, and normally occupied by the date.
Die	The block of metal, with design cut into it, which actually impresses the coin blank with the design.
Die variety	Coin showing slight variation of design.
Mule	A coin with the current type on one side and the previous (and usually obsolete) type on the other side, or a piece struck from two dies that are not normally used together.
Graining or reeding	The crenellations around the edge of the coin, commonly known as 'milling'.
Proof	Carefully struck coin from special dies with a mirror-like or matt surface. (In this country 'Proof' is *not* a term used to describe the state of preservation, but the method of striking.)
Hammered	Refers to the old craft method of striking a coin between dies hammered by hand.
Milled	Coins struck by dies worked in a coining press. The presses were hand powered from 1560-1800, powered by steam from 1790 and by electricity from 1895.

COINS AND TREASURE IN ENGLAND, WALES AND NORTHERN IRELAND

The concept of 'Treasure Trove', and the law relating to it has been radically changed since the Treasure Act came into force on 24 September 1997. The new Treasure Act (England, Wales and Northern Ireland) has been drafted to give greater protection to archaeological objects that are discovered, archaeological objects of gold or silver, and hoards of coins, and to ensure their proper reporting, recording and preservation as appropriate. Prior to the Act the law relating to Treasure Trove (as outlined in greater detail in the *Standard Catalogue* for 1998) originated from the twelfth century and the need of the King to augment his income from casual finds of gold and silver. As such, Treasure Trove was Common Law; although dating in essence from the reign of Henry II it can be traced back as 'Finders, Keepers' to Anglo-Saxon England. The law of Treasure Trove related only to England and Wales, as Scotland and Northern Ireland had their own laws relating to discovered antiquities and 'treasure'.

The old law of Treasure Trove required that any items of gold, silver or bullion that had been concealed had to be declared to the local Coroner. The law was administered under the Coroners' Act 1984. A Coroner could call a jury, and expert witnesses, to decide whether the original owner intended to recover his goods or had abandoned them. Where the original owner, in a case of intended recovery, or his heirs could not be traced, the items were declared to be Treasure Trove and the property of the Crown. The practice was to reward the finder – if they had acted promptly in declaring the items – with the full market value of all or any items that were required by the national collection or other interested museums. If any part was not required by a museum, then it was returned to the finder, not the landowner. Often an agreement had been reached previously between, say, the farmer and metal detectorist on the division of any finds or money involved. The market value was assessed by an independent Treasure Trove Committee, set up in 1977, which met quarterly and could call upon outside expert opinion for valuations.

The majority of finds declared to be Treasure Trove were invariably coin hoards, sometimes mixed with other items such as jewellery or plate. The annual report of the Treasure Trove Reviewing Committee of the Department of National Heritage (as it was then called) for 1995-6 recorded that 25 out of 29 Treasure Trove cases were coin hoards (one was mixed) spreading in date from Ancient British to Late Medieval.

The new Treasure Act now covers, in effect protects, a much wider range of material than came under the old law of Treasure Trove. Principally, it now includes objects that are not made of precious metals as previously specified, but which may have been found in association with such items; objects that were accidentally lost, or buried in a grave (which obviously shows no intent to recover), and all coin hoards.

The definition of 'treasure' specifies any object (excluding coins) that has at least 10 per cent of precious metal (gold or silver) and is at least 300 years old when it was found. Coins have their separate specification of requirement to be declared as 'treasure'. Single coins of any metal are not deemed to be treasure unless they have been found in a context with other items that come under the definition of treasure, or if there is sufficient evidence to show that the coin had been buried with intention of recovering it.

For coins to be declared treasure they have to contain at least 10 per cent of gold or silver and be part of the same find (i.e. hoard), and be at least 300 years old when found. Coins that have less than this requirement in terms of precious metal content are identified as treasure if there are more than ten such coins in the group and that, likewise, they were over 300 years old at the time of discovery.

For the purposes of the Treasure Act groups of coins to be identified as coming from the same find are: hoards that have been deliberately hidden; smaller groups of coins that have been accidentally lost, e.g. the contents of a purse, such as the small group of Roman 28 silver denarii in a bronze arm purse found in 1949 at the fort of Birdoswald on Hadrian's Wall. Current under Hadrian, they had been accidentally buried when the purse was put to one side and rampart-backing was piled against the fort wall. The original owner's expletives (in which language, Latin or local dialect ?) at the time of such a large loss must have been incredible to hear! The other major group recognised is that of votive or ritual deposits of coins, a prime recent example of which was the vast hoard of Celtic coins found at the temple site at Wanborough.

One of the great benefits of the new Act is the inclusion in the definition of 'treasure' objects found in the context of those items declared to be treasure. For example, this means that the pot in which, say, a hoard of coins had been found is, by its association, also declared to be treasure. This ensures that the whole group is kept together. In the past there have been some serious anomalies due to the separation of items found together but split under the law of Treasure Trove. A prime example of this was the Snettisham jeweller's hoard of 83 silver denarii, 27 bronze coins, over three dozen mixed silver rings, 100 loose carnelian intaglios, jeweller's tools and the pot itself – which were only kept together by the enlightened attitude of the finder and declared owners Wagg and Jex Ltd (and now displayed in the Weston Gallery of Roman Britain in the British Museum; see *Minerva*, May/June 1998, p. 55).

There are some other points to be aware of in the scope of the Act. It applies to all ownerless objects found in England, Wales and Northern Ireland that come under the definition of 'treasure'. It only applies to objects found after the Act coming into force on 24 September 1979 – it is not retrospective. Under the old law of Treasure Trove there were some exceptions other than the Crown in which rights were vested as a franchise holder. These franchises, which entitled the holders to prior claim to ownerless treasure, were held by the Duchies of Lancaster and of Cornwall, the Corporation of London and the City of Bristol. The mentioned franchise holders have confirmed that they intend to follow the normal system of paying rewards as previously.

There is a requirement that the finder report their find within 14 days of the discovery, or within 14 days of their realising that the object/coins come under the definition of treasure – this latter would, no doubt, be by virtue of the item/coins having been identified. The local coroner, museum or police should be notified in person, by letter, telephone or fax. The coroner will advise the finder to which museum or archaeological organisation their find should be delivered for examination. This will invariably be the local museum in the first instance, which will then pass a copy of the relevant documentation to the national museum – in England this will be the British Museum; in Northern Ireland to the Ulster Museum, and to the National Museum of Wales, Cardiff, for finds from Wales. There are standard receipt forms now available from the Department of Culture, Media and Sport (previously the Department of National Heritage). Full descriptions are required since, under the Treasure Act, liability for loss or damage is accepted, except in cases of proved negligence. Some museum receipt forms carry a denial of liability for loss or damage, and if one of these forms is used, that clause has to be deleted and signed by a responsible officer.

Obviously, and especially with finds of coins, the exact location of any find spot must remain confidential although the location and context of the find should be reported to the Sites and Monuments Record in case rapid archaeological response and assessment is required. An excellent example of the latter was the find of the great Roman Hoxne treasure on 16 November 1992 by Mr Eric Lawes which enabled rapid archaeological response by the Suffolk Archaeological Unit. Much valuable information regarding the circumstances of the hoard's deposition, as well as minute details relating to its containers, was recovered which would have otherwise been lost.

Many finds reported will clearly not be treasure and, in those instances, the coroner will give permission for them to be returned to the finder and their disposal will be a matter for the finder/owner. In this event, the objects or coins should be recorded by the local museum following their usual procedure for recording new finds. Treasure items that have been reported but for which no interest has been shown by a registered museum will normally be disclaimed by the Secretary of State and the information passed to the coroner and to the Sites and Monuments record. An inquest will now only normally be held when a registered museum has expressed interest. Now, the finder, landowner or current occupier of the land may attend the inquest. In a straightforward case there is no need for them to be summoned to attend. When a decision has been reached, if the item is not treasure it is returned to the finder. If it is declared to be treasure, then a valuation will be sought by the Treasure Valuation Committee from their panel of expert advisers. Such valuations are made available to interested parties before the Committee meets to make its decision. The Committee of five presently meets quarterly under the Chairmanship of The Rt Hon. the Lord Stewartby (himself a renowned numismatist). The interested parties, and this also includes any museum interested in acquisition, may make comments on the valuations obtained by the Treasure Committee and also submit their own evidence or alternative valuations before the Treasure Committee valuation is recommended. The assessed and agreed reward for treasure is paid when the Department of Culture, Media and Sport has received the appropriate sum of money from the museum, or museums if several are involved, who wish to acquire the treasure. The rewards are paid to the finder, although this can be to the landowner or occupier following defined guidelines. The reward can be withheld, or curtailed, where the proper procedure for reporting treasure has not been adhered to (as happened in 1979 with the Thetford Roman Treasure Trove, where an ex gratia payment was made to the finder's widow by the Treasury). When a find has been made by an archaeologist, or a person working in or for a museum, then a reward would not normally be payable (this was the case with the great Iron Age hoard of torcs found in recent years at Snettisham).

One of the last cases to be heard under the old law of Treasure Trove was held in April on a hoard of nearly 500 late Anglo-Saxon coins found early in September 1997, just before the Act came into force. The coins were found by two detectorists at Appledore, near Dungeness, Kent, buried in an earthenware pot (found in fragments). The majority of the coins were of the 'expanding cross' type of Edward the Confessor (1022-1066) and, since they were newly struck and of the 'heavy' type (no 'light' types being present), the date of deposition can be tied down to 1051-52. The majority of the coins came from local Kentish mints but the mints of Chester, Lincoln and York were also included. The coins were declared to be Treasure Trove.

The last Annual Report 1996-97 of the Treasure Trove Reviewing Committee (now replaced by the Treasure Valuation Committee) lists 35 cases of Treasure Trove, all of which save one were found by metal detectorists. The Rt Hon. Mark Fisher, Under Secretary of State for Culture, Media and Sport, commented that he was 'happy to take this opportunity to acknowledge the contribution made by responsible detectorists towards the understanding of our heritage.' He welcomed the passing of the Treasure Act as he believed that it would 'together with the pilot schemes for the voluntary reporting of all archaeological finds, provide detector users and archaeologists alike with an opportunity to make a fresh start to everyone's benefit.' In the eight months since September over 75 potential treasure finds have been reported, as against some 25 during the whole of the previous year. It should be noted by metal detectors users and potential reporters of treasure that there is no intention by the present Government, or of the European Union, to ban or otherwise restrict responsible metal detecting that is carried out with permission and within the law.

Analysis of the 1996-97 Report reveals that of the 35 cases, only four concerned objects, the remainder were all coin finds. The breakdown into categories show Celtic (11), Roman (8), Anglo-Saxon (4), medieval (5), and modern (3). One Celtic group and one Roman group was mixed: the former included a gold bracelet and a gold ring, the latter two gold rings and some silver scraps. Nine of the finds were returned wholly to the finders as not being required and in one instance the finders disclaimed their right to a reward.

Peter A. Clayton, FSA.
Expert Adviser (coins and antiquities), Treasure Valuation Committee

CELTIC COINAGE

The Celtic or Ancient British issues are amongst the most interesting and varied of all British coins. They are our earliest coins and are the product of a society that left no historical sources of its own. It is therefore often difficult to be specific about for whom, when or where they were produced. Despite only being used for approximately a hundred and fifty years they do provide a rich variety of designs and types in gold, silver and bronze. Collectors looking for a theme to concentrate on may find the coins of one tribe, an individual ruler or a particular phase in the coinage interesting.

Grading Celtic Coins

The majority of Celtic coins were struck by hand, sometimes resulting in a loss of definition through weak striking. In addition, the design on the dies was often bigger than the blank flan employed, resulting in the loss of some of the design. Coins with full legends are generally more valuable than examples with incomplete legends. Bronze coins in good condition (VF or better) and especially toned examples attract a premium. Factors that detract from a coins value are chips, scratches and verdigris on bronze coins. It is important to take into account these factors as well as the amount of wear on a coin when assessing its grade.

| Cunobelin Bronze Unit | Epatticus Silver Unit | Cunobelin Gold Stater |

Fine

Very Fine

Plated Coins

Plated gold staters, quarter staters and silver units are recorded for many known types. They vary considerably in the quality of their production and are usually priced at around a quarter of the substantive types value. Their exact purpose or relation to the type they copy is not fully understood.

References and Select Bibliography.

M   Mack, R.P. (1975) 3rd edition, The Coinage of Ancient Britain.
V   Van Arsdell, R.D. (1989), Celtic Coinage of Britain.
BMC   Hobbs, R. (1996), British Iron Age Coins in the British Museum.

de Jersey, P. (1996), Celtic Coinage in Britain. *A good general introduction to the series.*
Nash, D. (1987), Coinage in the Celtic World. *Sets the coinage in its social context.*

The layout of the following list is derived from the standard works by Mack, Van Arsdell and the British Museum Catalogue by Richard Hobbs. References are made to these works where possible, in the case of the last work it should be noted that the British Museum collection is not exhaustive, and therefore should not be used to assess the rarity of a coin. More detailed information than that given here can be gained from these works.

IMPORTED COINAGE

The earliest coins to circulate in Britain were made in northern Gaul (Belgica) and imported into the south-east of England from around 150 B.C. onwards. They were principally the product of two tribal groups in this region, the Ambiani and Suessiones. In Britain these types are known as Gallo-Belgic A to F. The first type Gallo-Belgic A is ultimately derived from the Macedonian gold staters (M) of Philip II (359-336 B.C.)

The reasons why they were imported are not fully understood. However, the context for their importation is one of close social, political and economic ties between Britain and Gaul. Within this cross-channel relationship they undoubtedly had various functions, such as payment for military service or mercenaries, in exchanges between the elite of each society: in cementing alliances for example, or as gifts in a system of exchange.

Numbers in brackets following each entry refer to numbers employed in previous editions of this catalogue.

GALLO-BELGIC ISSUES

GOLD

M	2	3	5	7

		F £	VF £
From c.150 B.C. – c.50 B.C.			
1	**Stater.** Gallo-Belgic A. (Ambiani). Good copy of Macedonian stater, large flan. Laureate head of Apollo r. R. Horse r. *M. 1; V. 10. (1)*	650	2000
2	Similar, but head and horse l. *M. 3; V. 12. (1)*	500	1500
3	B. (Ambiani). Somewhat similar to 1, but small flan and 'defaced' *obv.* die. R. Horse r. *M. 5; V. 30. (3)*	200	500
4	— Similar, but with lyre between horse's legs. *M. 7; V. 33. (3)*	225	525
5	C. (Ambiani), *Stater.* Disintegrated Apollo head. R. horse. *M. 26; V. 44. (5)*	200	400
6	**Quarter Stater.** Gallo-Belgic A. Similar to 1. *M. 2; V .15. (2)*	200	475
7	— Similar to 2. *M. 4; V. 20. (2)*	225	525
8	B. Similar to 3. *M. 6; V. 35. (4)*	150	320
9	— Similar. R. Two horses l. with lyre between legs. *M. 8; V. 37. (4)*	180	400
10	D. Portions of Apollo head R. A mixture of stars, crescents, pellets, zig-zag lines; often referred to as 'Geometric' types,(See also British 'O', S. 46.). *M. 37, 39, 41, 41a, 42; V. 65/7/9/146. (6)*	60	125

From c.50 B.C.

11

		F	VF
		£	£
11	**Stater.** Gallo-Belgic E. (Ambiani). Blank obv. R. Disjointed curved horse r., pellet below, zig-zag in exergue. *M. 27; V. 52, 54. (7)*	120	235
12	F. (Suessiones). Devolved Apollo head r. R. Disjointed horse r. With triple-tail. *M. 34a; V. 85. (8)*	200	375
13	Xc. Blank except for VE monogram at edge of coin, R. S below horse r. *M. 82; V. 87-1. (9)*	225	450

BILLON
Armorican (Channel Islands and N.W. Gaul, c.75-50 B.C.)

	14		15		
14	**Stater.** Class I. Head r. R. Horse, boar below, remains of driver with Victory above, lash ends in or two loops, or 'gate'. *(12)*			435	80
15	— Class II. Head r. R. Horse, boar below, remains of Victory only, lash ends in small cross of four pellets. *(13)*			30	70
16	— Class III. Head r., anchor-shaped nose. R. Somewhat similar to Class I. *(14)*			35	75
17	— Class IV. Head r. R. Horse with reins, lyre shape below, driver holds vertical pole, lash ends in three prongs. *(15)*			40	80
18	— Class V. Head r. R. Similar to last, lash ends in long cross with four pellets. *(16)*			40	85
19	— Class VI. Head r. R. Horse, boar below, lash ends in 'ladder' *(17)*			45	95
20	**Quarter Stater.** Similar types to above. *(18)*			50	110

20

CELTIC COINS STRUCK IN BRITAIN

Coin production in Britain began at the very end of the second century B.C. with the cast potin coinage of Kent (Nos 62-64). Inspired by Gaulish issues and ultimately derived from the potin coins of Massalia (Marseilles) in southern Gaul, the precise function and period of use of this coinage is not fully understood. The domestic production of gold coins started around 70 B.C., these issues are traditionally known as British A-P and are derived from imported Gallo-Belgic issues. Broadly contemporary with these issues are quarter staters, silver units, and bronze units. Recent work by John Sills has further enhanced our understanding of this crucial early period with the identification of two new British staters (Insular Belgic C or Kentish A and the Ingoldisthorpe type) and their related quarters and a Westerham quarter stater. The Insular Belgic C or Kentish A type derived from Gallo-Belgic C now becomes the first British stater.

EARLY UNINSCRIBED COINAGE

GOLD

20A   20B

		F	VF
		£	£
20A	**Stater.** Insuler Belgic C/Kentish A type. Devolved Apollo head r. R. Disjointed horse r, a rosette behind or in front, or both. *M. —; V. —; BMC —*	*Extremely rare*	
20B	Ingoldisthorpe type. Similar to last, as illustration. *M.—; V.—; BMC—* ..	*Extremely rare*	

21	British A. Westerham type. Devolved Apollo head r. R. Disjointed horse l. large pellet below. *M. 28, 29; V. 200, 202; BMC 1-32 (19)*	165	330
22	B. Chute type. Similar to 9 but crab-like object below horse. *M. 32; V. 1205; BMC 35-76. (20)*	145	235
23	C. Yarmouth type. Similar to 9 but star-like object in front of horse. *M. 31; V. 1220; BMC 78-85. (21)*	325	650
24	D. Cheriton type. Similar to Chute type but with large crescent face. *M. 33; V. 1215; BMC 86-128. (22)*	175	325
25	E. Waldingfield type. Annulet and pellet below horse. *M. 48; V. 1462; BMC — —. (23)*	*Extremely rare*	

26 27

		F	VF
		£	£
26	F. Clacton type 1. Similar to Westerham type but rosette below horse. M. 47; V. 1458; BMC 137-44. (24)	275	500
27	G. Clacton type 2. Similar but horse r., with pellet, or pellet with two curved lines below. M. 46, 46a; V. 30, 1455; BMC 145-79. (25)	260	480

28 30

28	H. North-East Coast type. Variety of 9, pellet or rosette below horse to r. M. 50, 50a, 51, 51a; V. 800; BMC 182-191. (26)	185	350
29	I. — Similar, horse l., pellet, rosette or star with curved rays below. M. 52-57; V. 804, 805, 807; BMC 193-211. (27)	175	325
30	J. Norfolk Wolf type. R. Crude wolf to r. M. 49; V. 610-1; BMC 212-16. (28)	225	475
31	— Similar but wolf to l. Usually base gold. M. 49a/b; V. 610-2/3; BMC 217-78. (28A)	90	200
32	L. Whaddon Chase type. R. Spirited horse r. of new style, various symbols below. M. 133-138a, 139a; V. 1470-6; 1485/7/9/93; BMC 279-343. (31)	175	350
33	— Plain. R. Horse r. With ring ornament below or behind. M. 140-143; V. 1498-1505; BMC 344-46. (32)	200	425
34	Lx. NorthThames group. Blank apart from reversed SS. R. Similar to last. M. 146; V. 1509; BMC 350. (33)	Extremely rare	
35	Lz. Weald group. Blank with some traces of Apollo head. R. Horse r., large wheel ornament below. M. 144-145; V. 1507; BMC 347-49. (36)	300	600

36

| 36 | Ma. Wonersh type. Crossed wreath design with crescents back to back in centre. R. Spiral above horse, wheel below. M. 148; V. 1520; BMC 351-56. (37) | 250 | 600 |

37 38

		F	VF
		£	£
37	Mb. Savernake Forest type. Similar but *obv.* plain or almost blank. *M. 62; V. 1526; BMC 361-64*	200	425
38	Qa. British 'Remic' type. Crude laureate head. R. Triple-tailed horse, wheel below. *M. 58, 60, 61; V. 210-124; BMC 445-58. (41)*	225	450
39	Qb. — Similar, but *obv.* blank. *M. 59; V. 216; BMC 461-76. (42)*	175	300
39A	**Quarter Stater.** Insuler Belgic C/Kentish A type. Similar to Gallo-Belgic D, but with rosette in field on obverse. *M. —; V.—; BMC—*	*Extremely rare*	
39B	Ingoldisthorpe type. Similar to last but with sperm-like objects in field. *M.—; V.—; BMC—*	*Extremely rare*	
39C	British A. Westerham type. Similar to last but of cruder style, or with L-shapes in field on rev. *M.—; V.—; BMC—*	*Extremely rare*	
40	British D. Cheriton type. Similar to Stater, large crescent face. R. Cross motif with pellets. *M. —; V. 143 var; BMC 129-136*	145	325
41	F/G. Clacton type. Plain, traces of pattern. R. Ornamental cross with pellets. *M. 35; V. 1460; BMC 180-1. (43A)*	175	350
42	H. Crescent design and pellets. R. Horse r. *M. —; V. —; BMC 192*	200	325
43	Lx. N.Thames group. Floral pattern on wreath. R. Horse l. or r. *M. 76; V. 234; BMC 365-370. (44)*	100	200

43 44 45

44	Ly. N.Kent group. Blank. R. Horse l. or r. *M. 78; V. 158; BMC 371-3. (45)*	100	200
45	Lz. Weald group. Spiral design on wreath. R. Horse l. or r. *M. 77; V. 250; BMC 548-50. (46)*	120	240

46 47 48

46	O. Geometric type. Unintelligible patterns (some blank on obv.). *M. 40, 43-45; V. 143, 1225/27/29; BMC 410-32. (49)*	60	125
47	P.Trophy type. Blank. R. Trophy design. *M. 36, 38; V. 145-7; BMC 435-44. (50)*	70	165
48	Qc.British 'Remic' type. Head or wreath pattern. R. Triple-tailed horse, l. or r. *M. 63-67; 69-75; V. 220-32, 36, 42-6, 56; BMC 478-546. (51)*	90	200
49	Xd. Head l. of good style, horned serpent behind ear. R. Horse l. *M. 79; V. 78; BMC 571-575. (11)*	225	450

SILVER

Units (unless otherwise stated)

50   52

	F £	VF £
50 Lx. Head l.or r. **R**. Horse l. or r. *M. 280, 435, 436, 438, 441; V. 80, 1546, 1549, 1555; BMC 376-382. (53)*	45	100
51 — Head l. **R**. Stag r. with long horns. *M. 437; V. 1552; BMC 383-7. (54)*	75	200
52 — **Half Unit.** Two horses or two beasts. *M. 272, 442, 443, 445; V. 474, 1626, 1643, 1948; BMC 389-400. (55)*	110	275
53 Lz. Danebury group. Head r. with hair of long curves. **R**. Horse l., flower above. *M. 88; V. 262; BMC 580-82*	100	225

54   54A

54 — Helmeted head r. **R**. Horse r. wheel below. *M. 89; V. 264; BMC 583 -592. (58)*	100	210
54A Cruciform pattern with ornaments in angles. **R**. Horse l., ear of crown between legs, crescents and pellets above, *M.—; V.—; BMC—*	80	175
55 — **Quarter Unit.** As last. *M. 90; V. 268; BMC 642-43. (59)*	65	125
56 — Head r. **R**. Horse r. star above, wheel below. *M. –; V. 280; BMC 595-601*	75	150
57 — Head l., pellet in ring in front. **R**. Horse l. or r. *M. –; V. 284; BMC 610-630*	85	175
58 — Serpent looking back. **R**. Horse l. *M. –; V. 286; BMC 631-33*	100	220
59 — **Quarter Unit.** Cross pattern. **R**. Two-tailed horse. *M. 119; V. 482; BMC 654-56. (56C). (Formerly attributed to Verica)*	45	125

BRONZE

60 **Unit.** Lx. Winged horse l. **R**. Winged horse l. *M. 446; V. 1629; BMC 401 (78)*	85	250
61 Chichester Cock type. Head r. **R**. Head r. surmounted by cock. *M. –; V. – BMC 657-59*	40	90

POTIN
(Cast Copper/Tin alloy)

62

	F £	VF £
62 **Unit.** Thurrock type.Head l. R. Bull butting l. or r. *M. —; V. 1402-42;* *BMC 660-666. (84A)*	40	100

63   64

| 63 | Class I type. Crude head. R. Lines representing bull *(Allen types A-L.)*
M. 9-22a; V. 104, 106, 108, 112, 114, 115, 117, 119, 120, 122, 123, 125,
127, 129, 131, 133; BMC 667-714. (83) .... | 30 | 80 |
| 64 | Class II type. Smaller flan, large central pellet. *(Allen types M-P.)*
M. 23-25; V. 135-39; BMC 715-23. (84) .... | 40 | 90 |

CELTIC DYNASTIC AND LATER UNINSCRIBED COINAGE

From Julius Caesars expeditions to Britain in 55/54 B.C. and his conquest of Gaul in 52 B.C. to the Claudian invasion in 43 A.D., southern Britain was increasingly drawn into the orbit of the Roman world. This process is reflected not only in the coins but also in what we know about their issuers and the tribes they ruled. Latin legends begin to appear for the first time and increasingly accompany objects and designs drawn from the classical world. A lot of what we know about the Celtic tribes and their rulers, beyond just their names on coins, is drawn from contemporary and slightly later Roman historical sources. A great deal however is still uncertain and almost all attributions to either tribes or historically attested individuals have to be seen as tentative.

The coin producing tribes of Britain can be divided into two groups, those of the core and those of the periphery. The tribes of the core, the Atrebates/Regni, Trinovantes/Catuvellauni and Cantii, by virtue of their geographical location controlled contact with the Roman world. Unlike the tribes of the periphery they widely employed Latin legends, classical designs and used bronze coinage in addition to gold and silver.

Following the Roman invasion of 43 A.D. it is likely that some coinage continued to be produced for a short time. However in 61 A.D. with the death of King Prasutagus and the suppression of the Boudiccan revolt that followed, it is likely that Celtic coinage came to an end.

TRIBAL/MINT MAP

Known Mints
1 – Camulodunum (Colchester)
2 – Verulamium (St. Albans)
3 – Calleva (Silchester)

ATREBATES AND REGNI

The joint tribal area of these two groups corresponds roughly with Berkshire and Sussex and parts of northern and eastern Hampshire. The Atrebatic portion being in the north of this region with its main centre at Calleva (Silchester). The Regni occupying the southern part of the region centred around Chichester.

COMMIUS
(Mid to Late 1st Century B.C.)

The first inscribed staters to appear in Britain, closely resemble British Q staters *(no.38)* and are inscribed 'COMMIOS'. Staters and silver units with an inscribed 'E' are also thought to be related. Traditionally this Commius was thought to be the Gaulish chieftain who Caesar refers to in *De Bello Gallico*, as firstly serving him in his expeditions to Britain and finally fleeing to Britain *c*.50 B.C. This attribution does however present chronological problems, and the appearance of a few early staters reading 'COM COMMIOS' suggests that the Commius who issued coins is more likely to have been the son of Caesar's Commius.

GOLD

65

		F £	VF £
65	**Stater.** Devolved Apollo head r. R. COMMIOS around triple tailed horse r., wheel below. *M. 92; V. 350; BMC 724-29. (85)*	600	1500

66   67

66	Similar, but 'E' symbol above horse instead of legend. *M. —;V. 352. BMC 730*	675	1700
67	**Quarter Stater.** Blank except for digamma. R. Horse l. *M. 83; V. 353-5; BMC —. (10)*	125	250

SILVER

69

69	**Unit.** Head l. R. Horse l. Mostly with 'E' symbol above. *M. —;V. 355; BMC 731-58. (57)*	35	100

70

	F	VF
	£	£

70   **Minim.** Similar to Unit. *M. —; V. 358-5; BMC 759-60* 25   55

TINCOMARUS or TINCOMMIUS
(Late 1st Century B.C. – Early 1st Century A.D.)

Successor to Commius and on his coins styled as 'COM.F' (son of Commius). Early coins of the reign like his predecessors are very obiviously Celtic in their style. However later coins exhibit an increasing tendancy towards Roman designs. Indeed Tincommius is recorded as a supliant king of the Roman emperor Augustus *(Res Gestae, xxxii)*, finally fleeing to Rome in the early 1st century A.D. The discovery of the Alton Hoard in 1996 brought to light gold staters with the new legend TINCOMARVS.

GOLD

71   73

71   **Stater.** *Celtic style.* Devolved Apollo head r. R. TINC COMM. F.
      around horse. *M. 93; V. 362; BMC —. (86)*   450   900
72   Similar but legend reads TINCOMARVS. *M. 94; V. 363;*
      BMC 761-765. (86)   750   1900
73   **Quarter Stater.** Spiral with pellet centre. R. Horse r. T above. *M. 81;*
      V. 366; BMC 781-797. (46)   110   200

74   75

74   TINCOM, zig-zag ornament below. R. Horse l. *M. 95; V. 365;*
      BMC 798-810. (87)   185   400
75   **Stater.** *Classical style.* TINC(O) on a sunk tablet. R. Horseman with
      javelin r. often with CF in field. *M. 96-98; V. 375-76; BMC 765-769. (88)*   250   550

76   77

	F £	VF £
76 COM.(F). on a sunk tablet. R. Horseman with javelin r. TIN in field		
M. 100; V. 385; BMC 770-774. (88)	250	550
77 **Quarter Stater.** TINC on a tablet, C above, A or B below. R. Winged		
head (Medusa?) facing. *M. 97; V. 378; BMC 811-826. (89)*	235	525
78 TIN on tablet. R. Boar l. *M. 99; V. 379; BMC 827-837. (90)*	125	250

79   83

79 COMF on tablet. R. Horse r. TIN around. *M. 101; V. 387;*		
BMC 838-841. (90)	125	275
80 — R. Horse l. TIC around. *M. 102; V. 388; BMC 842-851. (90)*	125	275
81 COM on tablet. R. Horse l. T above. *M. 103; V. 389; BMC 852-3. (90)* ..	120	265
82 COMF on tablet. R. Horse r. TINC around. *M. 104; V. 390;*		
BMC 854-879. (90)	120	265

SILVER

83 **Unit.** Laureate head r. TINCOM in front, V behind. R. Eagle stg. on		
snake. *M. 105; V. 397; BMC 880-905. (91)*	55	150
84 Laureate head l. R. Bull l. TINC around. *M. 106; V. 396;*		
BMC 906-910. (91A)	50	135
85 Laureate head r. R. Bull r. TIN(C) around. *M. —; V. 381;*		
BMC 911-925. (92B)	50	125
86 Facing head. R. Bull l. TINC around. *M. —; V. 370; BMC 926-29 (92)* ..	60	160

87   91

87 TINC in angles of cross, R. Lion l. *M. —; V. 372; BMC 930-45. (93B)*...	50	145
88 Star. R. Boy riding dolphin r. TINC in field. *M. —; V. 371;*		
BMC 946-977. (93C)	50	140
89 TINC around pellet. R. Lion l. *M. 106a; V. 382; BMC 978-80. (93)*........	60	160
90 Head l. TINCOMMIVS in front. R. Horse l. lyre above. *M. 131b; V. 473;*		
BMC —-. (92C) (Formerly attributed to Verica)	60	160
91 **Minim.** CF within two interlinked squares. R. Boar? r. TINC. *M. 118;*		
V. 383-1; BMC 981-82. (94)	100	220
92 As above but CO. R. Bull r. TI. *M. —; V. 383-5; BMC —-*	100	210

		F £	VF £
93	C inside box, box above and below. R. Bull r. TIN. *M. —; V. 383-7; BMC 983*	90	200
94	Cross, T? in angles. R. uncertain object. *M. 120; V. 483; BMC 984-85.* *(Formerly attributed to Verica)*	80	190

EPPILLUS

(Later 1st Century B.C. – Early 1st Century A.D.)

His reign is likely to have coincided with that of Tincommius's, who also claimed to be a son of Commius. Two coinages appear in his name, one for Kent and one minted at Calleva (Silchester, Hants.) in the northern part of the territory of the Atrebates and Regni. The coins of Calleva conform to the southern denominational structure of gold and silver with fractions of each, whilst the Kentish series is distinctly tri-metallic, replacing the silver minim with bronze. A joint coinage was issued by Eppillus and Verica. It is not understood if Eppillus held both territories simultaneously.

COINAGE STRUCK AT CALLEVA
GOLD

95   **Stater.** Devolved Apollo head r. R. EPPI COMMI F around horse. *M. —; V. 405; BMC —* ....   *Extremely rare*

96

96   **Quarter Stater.** CALLEV, star above and below. R. Horse r. EPPI. *M. 107; V. 407-08; BMC 986-1005. (95)*   110   250

           97   98

97	COMM F EPPILV, around crescent. R. Hound r. *M. —; V. 409; BMC 1006-1009. (95A)*	135	325
98	EPPI COMF in two lines. R. Winged horse r. *M. 302; V. 435; BMC 1010-15. (129)*	100	235

SILVER

           99   100

99	**Unit.** Crescent REX CALLE above and below. R. Eagle r. EPP. *M. 108; V .415. BMC 1016-1060. (96)*	35	95
100	Bearded hd. r. in wreath. R. Boar r. EPPI(L) F CO(M). *M. —; V. 416; BMC 1061-87. (96A)*	50	130

		F	*VF*
		£	£
101	Bearded hd. in pellet border. R. Lion r. EPP COMF. *M. 305; V. 417;* *BMC 1088-1115. (131)*.....................	50	130
102	**Minim.** Floral cross. R. Eagle r. EPPI. *M. —; V. 420; BMC 1116-17*.......	75	200
103	Spiral and pellets. R. Ram r. EPP. *M. —; V. 421; BMC 1118-20. (96C)* ...	80	220
104	Bulls head facing. R. Ram r. EPP. *M. —; V. 422; BMC 1121-24. (96D)* ..	80	220
105	Wreath pattern. R. Boar r. EPP. *M. —; V. 423; BMC —-*	75	200
106	Crescent cross. R. Hand holding trident. *M. —; V. 487; BMC —. (111C)*	75	200

KENTISH TYPES
GOLD

| 107 | **Stater.** COMF within wreath. R. Horseman l. EPPILLVS above.
 M. 300; V. 430; BMC 1125-26. (127).. | *Extremely rare* |

108   107

108	Victory holding wreath l., within wreath. R. Horseman r. holding carnyx, F EPPI COM below. *M. 301; V. 431; BMC 1127-28. (128)*.........	*Extremely rare*
109	**Quarter Stater.** Crossed wreaths, EPPI in angles. R. Horse l. *M. 303;* *V. 436; BMC 1129. (130)*.....................	140 350
110	COMF in pellet border. R. Horse r. EPPI. *M. 304; V. 437;* *BMC 1130-31. (130)*.....................	135 325

SILVER

| 111 | **Unit.** Head l. EPPIL in field. R. Horseman holding carnyx, EPPILL.
 M. 306; V. 441; BMC 1132. (131)............................. | 60 175 |

BRONZE

112	**Unit.** Bow cross, EPPI COMF around. R. Eagle facing. *M. 309; V. 450;* *BMC 1137-38. (134)*.....................	55 200
113	Bull r., EPPI COF around. R. eagle facing. *M. 310; V. 451;* *BMC 1139-41. (134)*.....................	50 200
114	Head l., EPPI in front. R. Victory l. holding wreath and standard. *M. 311; V. 452; BMC 1142. (133)*	60 220
115	Bearded hd. r., EPPI CF. R. Biga r. CF. *M. 312; V. 453; BMC —*	60 220

JOINT TYPES OF EPPILUS AND VERICA
SILVER

		F £	VF £
116	**Unit.** Head l. CO VIR in front. R. Victory, EP. *M. 307; V. 442;* *BMC 1133-34. (132)*........	125	350

117

| 117 | Head r. VIR CO in front. R. Capricorn l. EPPI COMF. *M. 308/a; V. 443;*
BMC 1135-36. (132)........ | 110 | 325 |

VERICA
(*c*.10.-*c*.40 A.D.)

The exact details of Verica's succession and relationship to Eppillus and Tincommius are not fully understood. However by *c*.10 A.D. it seems likely that Verica was the sole ruler of the southern region. His close contact with Rome, both political and economic, seen in the increasing use of classical designs on his coins, culminated in his flight to Rome in *c*.42 A.D. to seek assistance from Claudius.

GOLD

| 118 | **Stater.** COM:F on tablet. R. Horseman r. holding spear, VIR below.
M. 109; V. 460; BMC 1143-44. (97)........ | 200 | 400 |
| 119 | COM.F. on tablet, pellet in ring ornament above and below. R.
Similar to last. *M. 121; 461; BMC 1146-53. (97)* .... | 200 | 400 |

120   121

120	COM.F on tablet. R. Horseman r. holding spear, VIR above, REX below. *M. 121 var; V. 500; BMC 1155-58. (98)*	150	325
121	Vine-leaf dividing VI RI. R. Horseman r. with shield and spear. COF in field. *M. 125; V. 520-1; BMC 1159-73. (99)*	275	550
122	Similar, reads VE RI. *M. 125; V. 520-5/7; BMC 1174-76. (99)*	285	575
123	**Quarter Stater.** COMF on tablet. R. Horse l. VIR. *M. 111; V. 465;* *BMC 1177-78. (100)*	110	200

124

| 124 | COMF on tablet, pellet in ring ornament above and below R. Horse
r. VI. *M. 112; V. 466; BMC 1179-1206. (100)* .... | 100 | 180 |

		F £	VF £
125	COMF on tablet, pellet border. R. Horse r. VI above. *M. 113; V. 467; BMC 1207-16. (100)*	100	175

126   128

126	COM FILI. in two lines, scroll in between. R. Horse r. VIR(I) above. *M. 114; V. 468; BMC 1217-22. (100)*	140	280
127	VERI COMF, crescent above, star below. R. Horse r. REX below. *M. 122; V. 501; BMC 1223-36. (101)*	125	225
128	VERI beneath vine-leaf. R. Horseman r. with sword and shield, FRX in field. *M. 124; V. 525; BMC 1237-38. (102)*	250	600
129	COM, horseman r. R. Seated figure, VERICA around. *M. 126; V. 526; BMC 1239. (103)*	300	700
130	Similar to last. R. Laureate bust r., VIRI in front. *M. 127; V. 527; BMC 1240. (103)*	300	700

SILVER

131	**Unit.** COMF, crescent and or pellet in ring above and below. R. Boar r. VI(RI) below. *M. 115; V. 470/72; BMC 1241-1331. (104)*	30	85

132   133

132	VERICA COMMI F around pellet in ring. R. Lion r. REX below. *M. 123; V. 505; BMC 1332-1359. (105)*	40	120
133	COMMI F, horseman with shield r. R. VERI CA, mounted warrior with spear r. *M. 128; V. 530; BMC 1360-92. (106)*	40	125

134   137

134	Two cornucopiae, COMMI F. R. Figure seated r. VERICA. *M. 129; V. 531; BMC 1393-1419. (107)*	35	100
135	Bust r. VIRI. R. Figure seated l. *M. 130; V. 532; BMC 1420. (108)*	65	175
136	Naked figure l. R. Laureate bust r., COMMI F. *M. 131; V. 533; BMC 1421-49. (108)*	35	100
137	VERICA REX, bull r. R. Figure stg. l., COMMI F. *M. —; V. 506; BMC 1450-84. (108B)*	35	110
138	COMF, in tablet and scroll. R. Eagle facing, VI RI. *M. —; V. 471; BMC 1485-1505. (104A)*	30	90

		F £	VF £
139	VIRIC across field,ornaments above and below. R. Pegasus r., star design below. *M. —; V. —; BMC —. (104B)*	50	135
140	Head r. Verica. R. COMMI F., eagle l. *M. 131A; V. 534; BMC —. (108A)*	65	175
141	**Minim.** COF in tablet, R. Facing head (Medusa?), VE below. *M. —; V. 384; BMC 1506.(94A). (Formerly attributed to Tincommius)*	60	160
142	Head r. R. Horse r., VIRICO. *M. 116; V. 480; BMC —. (109)*	45	110
143	Pellet and ring pattern. R. Lion r. VIR. *M. 120a/c; V. 484; BMC 1514-17. (109)*	55	130
144	VIRIC reversed. R. Boar r. *M. —; V. 485; BMC 1518*	40	110
145	Cross. R. Trident. *M. —; V. 486-1; BMC —-*	60	150
146	Uncertain. R. Boar r. *M. 120b; V. 510-1; BMC —. (109)*	40	110
147	Crescent cross. R. Boar r. *M. —; V. 510-5; BMC 1521-23. (109)*	50	130
148	VIR VAR in tablets. R. Winged horse r. CO. *M. 120d; V. 511; BMC 1507-12. (109)*	45	125

149   150

149	Vine-leaf, CFO. R. Horse r. VERI CA. *M. —; V. 550; BMC 1524-25*	50	135
150	CF in torc. R. Head r. VERIC. *M. 132; V. 551; BMC 1526-33. (111A)*	40	110
151	Altar, CF, R. Bulls head facing, VERICA. *M. 120e; V. 552; BMC 1534-37. (109)*	55	145
152	Temple, CF. R. Bull r, VER REX. *M. —; V. 553; BMC 1538-41*	45	125

153   154

153	Cornucopia, VER COM. R. Lion r. *M. —; V. 554; BMC 1542*	45	125
154	Two cornucopiae. R. Eagle l. *M. —; V. 555; BMC 1543-58*	40	100
155	Floral pattern, CF. R. Lion r. *M.—; V. 556; BMC 1559-63. (111E)*	50	135
156	Sphinx r., CF, R. dog curled up, VERI. *M. —; V. 557; BMC 1564-68. (109B)*	40	110
157	VERI. R. Urn, COMMI F. *M. —; V. 559; BMC —-*	45	125
158	A in star. R. Bird r. *M. 316; V. 561; BMC 1569-71*	50	130
159	Urn, Rex. R. Eagle r., VERRICA COMMI F. *M. —; V. 563; BMC 1572-78. (109C)*	40	110
160	VIR inside tablet. R. Boars head r. *M. 117; V. 564; BMC 1579-81. (109A)*	40	120
161	Cross. R. bull l. *M. —; V. —; BMC 1582*	45	125
162	Boars head r., CF, R. Eagle, VE. *M. —; V. —; BMC 1583-86*	45	125

163

163	Head r, COMM IF., R. Sphinx, R VE. *M. —; V. —; BMC 1587-89*	40	115

	F	VF
	£	£

164 A in tablet. R. Boar r. VI CO. *M. —; V. —; BMC 1590* 60 150
The two following coins are possibly issues of Epatticus.
165 Bull r. R. Eagle with snake l. *M. —; V. 512; BMC 2366-70* 40 120
166 Bust r. R. dog r. *M. —; V. 558; BMC 2371-74* 40 110

CANTII

The Cantii who gave their name to Kent, occupied a similar area to that of the modern county.
Caesar considered this the most civilised part of Britain and the early production of potin units in
Kent can be seen as an indicator of this. A number of Kentish rulers for whom we have coins, appear
to be dynasts from the two neighbouring kingdoms, who were involved in struggles to acquire territory. Eppillus (see Atrebates and Regni) produced coins specifically for circulation in Kent and like
those of Cunobelin they circulated widely.

EARLY UNINSCRIBED
GOLD

167 **Stater.** Ly. Blank. R. Horse l. numerous ring ornaments in field.
M. 293; V. 142; BMC 2472. (34).. 275 600
168 Blank. R. Horse r. numerous ornaments in field. *M. 294; V. 157;*
BMC— (34) 250 550

169

169 Lz. Blank. R. Horse l., box with cross hatching below. *M. 84, 292;*
V. 150, 144; BMC 2466-68. (35) 300 700

170   171

170 **Quarter Stater.** Ly. Blank. R. Horse r., pentagram below. *M. 285;*
V. 163; BMC 2473-74. (45) 100 200
171 Blank. R. Horse r., 'V' shape above. *M. 284; V. 170; BMC 2475-77. (45)* 100 200
172 Lz. Blank. R. Horse l., 'V' shape above. *M. 85; V. 151; BMC 2469-70. (47)* 100 220

SILVER

173 **Unit.** Curved star. R. Horse r. Pentagram below. *M. 272a; V. 164;*
BMC—. (56) 65 200
174 Serpent torc. R. Horse r., box with cross hatching below. *cf Mossop 8;*
BMC 2478 .... 85 275
175 **Half Unit.** Spiral of three arms. R. Horse l. *M. —; V. —; BMC 2479* 60 175

BRONZE
176   **Unit.** Various animal types, R. Various animal types. *M. 295-96,*
316a-d; V. 154/167; BMC 2480-91. (80/141-44)..   70   250

DUBNOVELLAUNUS
(Late 1st Century B.C.)
Likely to be the same Dubnovellaunus recorded on coins in Essex (see Trinovantes / Catuvellauni).
The two coinages share the same denominational structure and have some stylistic similarities. It has
been suggested that Dubnovellaunus is the British king of that name mentioned along with
Tincommius as a client king in the *Res Gestae* of the Roman emperor Augustus.

GOLD

177

		F	VF
		£	£
177	**Stater.** Blank. R. Horse r., bucranium above, serpent like object below, DUBNOV[ELLAUNUS] or similar around. *M. 282; V. 169; BMC 2492-96. (118)*....................	250	575
178	— R. Horse r., but without bucranium and with wheel below. *M. 283; V. 176; BMC 2497-98. (118)*....................	300	700

SILVER
179   **Unit.** Winged animal r. R. Horse l., DVBNO. *M. 286; V. 171;*
BMC 2499-2501. (119)..   110   265

180

180   Winged animal l. R. Seated fig. l., holding hammer, DVBNO.
M. 287; V. 178; BMC 2502-03. (119).................................   120   275

BRONZE
181   **Unit.** Horse r. R. Lion l., DVBN. *M. 290; V. 166; BMC 2504-06. (122)*.   75   250
182   Boar l., DVBNO. R. Horseman r. *M. 291; V. 181; BMC 2507-08. (121)*.   70   220
183   Boar r., DVBNO. R. Eagle facing. *M. 289; V. 180; BMC 2509-10. (121)*   70   220

VOSENOS
(Late 1st Century B.C./ Early 1st Century A.D.)

Little is known of this ruler who issued coins in a characteristically Kentish style similar to those of Dubnovellaunus.

GOLD

		F £	VF £
184	**Stater.** Blank. R. Horse l., bucranium above, serpent like object below., [VOSE]NOS. *M. 297; V. 184; BMC 2511-12. (123)*	*Extremely rare*	

185

185	**Quarter Stater.** Blank. R. Horse r., VOSI below. *M. 298; V. 185; BMC 2514-15. (124)*	300	675

SILVER

186	**Unit.** Horse and griffin. R. Horse r., retrograde legend. *M. 299a; V. 186; BMC —. (125)*	175	450

"SA" or "SAM"
(Late 1st Century B.C./ Early 1st Century A.D.)

An historically unattested individual whose coins are stylistically associated with those of Dubnovellaunus and Vosenos. His coins have been predominantly found in north Kent

SILVER

187	**Unit.** Head l., R. Horse l., SA below. *M. —; V. —; BMC —*	150	425

BRONZE

187A	**Unit.** Boar l., R. Horse l., SA below. *M. 299; V. 187; BMC 2516-19. (126)*	125	300

187B

187B	Horse l., SAM below. R. Horse l., SAM below. *M. —; V. —; BMC —*	125	300

AMMINUS

(Early 1st Century A.D.)

Issued a coinage stylistically distinct from other Kentish types and with strong affinities to those of Cunobelin. Indeed it has been suggested that he is the Adminius recorded by Suetonius, as a son of Cunobelin. The enigmatic legend DVN or DVNO may be an unknown mint site.

SILVER

188

		F £	VF £
188	**Unit.** Plant, AMMINIUS around. R. Winged horse r., DVN. *M. 313; V. 192; BMC 2522-23. (136)*	140	300

190

190	A in wreath. R. Capricorn r., S AM. *M. 314; V. 194; BMC 2520-21. (137)*	140	300

BRONZE

189

189	AM in wreath. R. Horse r., DVNO. *M. —; V. 193; BMC — —*	150	325
191	**Unit.** Head r. R. Hippocamp r., AM. *M. 315; V. 195; BMC 2524. (139)*	125	285

TRINOVANTES AND CATUVELLAUNI

Occupying the broad area of Essex, southern Suffolk, Bedfordshire, Buckinghamshire, Hertfordshire, parts of Oxfordshire, Cambridgeshire and Northamptonshire, they are likely to have been two separate tribes for most of their history. The Trinovantes were originally located in the eastern half of this area, with their main centre at Camulodunum (Colchester). The original Catuvellauni heartland being further west, with their main centre at Verulamium (St.Albans). The whole area eventually came under the control of Cunobelin at the end of the period.

TRINOVANTES

ADDEDOMAROS

(Late 1st Century B.C.)

Unknown to history he appears to have been a contemporary of Tasciovanus. The design of his staters is based on the Whaddon Chase type (No.32) which circulated widely in this region.

GOLD

200

		F	VF
		£	£
200	**Stater.** Crossed wreath. R. Horse r., wheel below, AθθDIIDOM above. *M. 266; V. 1605; BMC 2390-94. (148)*	175	450

201   202

201	Six armed spiral. R. Horse r., cornucopia below, AθθDIIDOM above. *M. 267; V. 1620; BMC 2396-2404. (148)*	160	375
202	Two opposed crescents. R. Horse r., branch below, spiral or wheel above, AθθDIIDOM. *M. 268; V. 1635; BMC 2405-2415. (149)*	165	425
203	**Quarter Stater.** Circular flower pattern. R. Horse r. *M. 271; V. 1608; BMC 2416. (44)*	135	300
204	Cross shaped flower pattern. R. Horse r. *M. 270; V. 1623; BMC 2417-21. (44)*	125	275
205	Two opposed crescents. R. Horse r., AθθDIIDOM around. *M. 269; V. 1638; BMC 2422-24. (150)*	225	500

BRONZE

206	**Unit.** Head l. R. Horse l. *M. 274; V. 1615/46 BMC 2450-60. (77)*	40	95

DUBNOVELLAUNUS
(Late 1st Century B.C./ Early 1st Century A.D.)

Dubnovellaunus is likely to have been the successor to Addedomaros, with whom his coins are stylistically related. It is not clear if he was the same Dubnovellaunus who also issued coins in Kent (see Cantii) or if he is the same Dumnobeallaunos mentioned in the *Res Gestae* of the emperor Augustus c.AD14.

GOLD

207   208

		F	VF
		£	£
207	**Stater.** Two crescents on wreath. R. Horse l., leaf below, pellet in ring, DVBNOVAIIAVNOS above. *M. 275; V. 1650; BMC 2425-40. (152)*	190	450
208	**Quarter Stater.** Similar. *M. 276; V. 1660; BMC 2442. (153)*	135	260

SILVER

209	Unit. Head l., DVBNO. R. Winged horse r., lattice box below. *M. 288; V. 165; BMC 2443-44. (120)*	140	300
210	Head l., legend ?, R. Horse l. DVB[NOV]. *M. 278; V. 1667; BMC 2445. (154)*	50	120

BRONZE

211	**Unit.** Head l., R. Horse l., DVBNO above. *M. 281; V. 1669; BMC 2446-48. (154)*	55	130
212	Head r., R. Horse l. *M. 277; V. 1665; BMC 2461-65. (154)*	45	100

DIRAS
(Late 1st Century B.C./ Early 1st Century A.D.)

An historically unattested ruler, responsible for a gold stater related stylistically to Dubnovellaunus's.

GOLD

213	**Stater.** Blank. R. Horse r., DIRAS? above, yoke like object above. *M. 279; V. 162; BMC 2449. (151)*	*Extremely rare*

CATUVELLAUNI

TASCIOVANUS

(Late 1st Century B.C./ Early 1st Century A.D.)

The early gold coins of Tasciovanus like those of his contemporary Addedomaros are based on the Whaddon Chase stater. Verulamium (St.Albans) appears to have been his principal mint, appearing as VER or VERL on the coinage. Staters and quarter staters inscribed CAM (Camulodunum/Colchester) are known and perhaps suggest brief or weak control of the territory to the east. The later coins of Tasciovanus use increasingly Romanised designs. The adoption of the title RICON, perhaps a Celtic equivalent to the Latin REX (King), can be seen as a parallel move to that of his contemporary Tincommius to the south.

GOLD

214   217

		F £	VF £
214	**Stater.** Crescents in wreath. R. TASCIAV and bucranium over horse r. *M. 149; V. 1680; BMC 1591-1603. (157)*	250	500
215	— R. Similar reads TAXCIAV. *M. 150; V. 1682; BMC 1604-05. (157)*	265	525
216	— R. Similar reads TASCIOVAN above, CAM below. *M. 186/a;* *V. 1684; BMC 1606-07. (160)*	375	850
217	— R. Horseman r. helmeted and with carnyx, TASC in field. *M. 154-55/57; V. 1730-32; BMC 1608-1613. (158)*	240	500
218	Crescents in wreath, with V or VER in design. R. Similar to last. *M. 156-57; V. 1734-35; BMC 1623-24. (158)*	300	600

219   221

219	TASCIO(V) RICON in panel. R. Horseman l., wearing armour and holding sword and shield. *M. 184; V. 1780; BMC 1628-36. (161)*	475	1050
220	**Quarter Stater.** Floral design. R. Horse r. *M. —; V. —; BMC 1638-39...*	170	350
221	Crossed Wreath. R. Horse l. *M. 151; V. 1688; BMC 1651-53. (44)*	120	225
222	— R. Horse r., CAM. *M. 187; V. 1694; BMC 1640. (164)*	200	425
223	Similar, TASCI in wreath. R. Horse r., TASC. *M. 153; V. 1692;* *BMC 1641. (163)*	120	225

224 226

		F £	VF £
224	Similar, VERO in wreath. R. Horse l., TAS. *M. 152; V. 1690;* *BMC 1642-43. (163)*	200	400
225	TASCIO on tablet. R. Horse l. *M. 195; V. 1848; BMC 1646. (166)*	165	350
226	TASC on tablet. R. Horse l. *M. 185; V. 1786; BMC 1647-50. (165)*	100	200

SILVER

227	**Unit.** Head l. R. Horse r. *M. —; V. 1698; BMC 1654*	60	135
228	Cross and box. R. Horse r., VER in front. *M. —; V. —; BMC 1655*	70	185
229	Cross and crescent. R. Horse l., TASCI. *M. —; V. —; BMC 1665-57*	65	175
230	Bearded head l. R. Horseman r., TASCIO. *M. 158; V. 1745;* *BMC 1667-68. (167)*	70	200
231	Winged horse l., TAS. R. Griffin r., within circle of pellets. *M. 159;* *V. 1790; BMC 1660. (168)*	70	200
232	Eagle stg. l., TASCIA. R. Griffin r. *M. 160; V. 1792; BMC 1658-59. (169)*	75	225
233	VER in beaded circle. R. Horse r., TASCIA. *M. 161; V. 1699;* *BMC 1670-73. (170)*	75	225
234	— R. Naked horseman. *M. 162; V. 1747; BMC 1674-76. (171)*	100	245

235 238 242

235	Laureate hd. r., TASCIA. R. Bull l. *M. 163; V. 1794; BMC 1681-82. (172)*	70	190
236	Cross and box, VERL. R. Boar r. TAS. *M. 164; V. 1796;* *BMC 1661-62. (173)*	75	235
237	TASC in panel. R. Winged horse l. *M. 165; V. 1798; BMC 1664-65. (174)*	65	150
238	— R. Horseman l., carrying long shield. *M. 166; V. 1800;* *BMC 1677-79. (174)*	65	150
239	Two crescents. R. Winged griffin, VIR. *M. —; V. —; BMC 1666*	75	225
240	Head r., TAS?. R. Horseman r. *M. —; V. —; BMC 1669*	70	180

BRONZE

241

241	**Double Unit.** Head r., TASCIA, VA. R. Horseman r. *M. 178; V. 1818;* *BMC 1685-87. (190)*	135	400

		F £	VF £
242	**Unit.** Two heads in profile, one bearded. R. Ram l., TASC. *M. 167; V. 1705; BMC 1711-13. (178)*	70	200
243	Bearded head r. VER(L). R. Horse l., VIIR or VER. *M. 168; V. 1707; BMC 1714-21. (179)*	55	175
244	Bearded head r. R. Horse l., TAS. *M. 169; V. 1709; BMC 1722-23. (179)*	65	190
245	Head r., TASC. R. Winged horse l., VER. *M. 170; V. 1711; BMC 1688-89. (180)*	60	185
246	— R. Horseman r., holding carnyx, VIR. *M. 171; V. 1750; BMC 1724-27. (182)*	65	190

247

247	VERLAMIO between rays of star. R. Bull l. *M. 172; V. 1808; BMC 1745-51. (183)*	60	185
248	Similar without legend. R. Bull r. *M. 174; V. 1810; BMC 1752-55. (185)*	55	175
249	Similar. R. Horse l., TASCI. *M. 175; V. 1812; BMC 1709-10. (186)*	60	185
250	Head r., TASCIO. R. Lion r., TA SCI. *M. 176; V. 1814; BMC 1736-38. (188)*	55	175
251	Head r. R. Figure std. l., VER below. *M. 177; V. 1816; BMC 1739-44. (189)*	65	200
252	Cross and Crescents. R. Boar r., VER. *M. 179; V. 1713; BMC 1702-05. (191)*	65	200
253	Laureate head r. R. Horse l., VIR. *M. 180; V. 1820; BMC 1706-08. (192)*	60	185
254	Raised band across centre, VER or VERL below. R. Horse grazing r. *M. 183a; V. 1717; BMC —. (193)*	75	250
255	**Fractional Unit.** Animal r. R. Sphinx l. *M. 181; V. 1824; BMC 1760-61. (198)*	65	160
256	Head l., VER. R. Goat r. *M. 182; V. 1715; BMC 1765-68. (199)*	40	130
257	Head r. R. Boar r, *M. 183; V. 1826; BMC 1762-64. (199)*	40	130
258	Head l. R. Animal with curved tail. *M. 183b, c; V. 1822; BMC 1759. (200)*	40	125

ASSOCIATES OF TASCIOVANUS
(Early 1st Century A.D.)

Towards the end of his reign, a number of joint issues bearing his name and the name of either Sego or Dias appear. In addition coins similar in style to those of Tasciovanus appear with either the name Andoco or Rues. It has been suggested that these issues belong to a period of struggle following the death of Tasciovanus and are all rival contestants for the throne. Another theory is that they are associates or sub-kings of Tasciovanus responsible for areas within the wider territory.

SEGO

GOLD

259

	F £	VF £
259 **Stater.** TASCIO in tablet, annulets above. R. Horseman with carnyx r., SEGO. *M. 194; V. 1845; BMC 1625-27. (162)*		*Extremely rare*

SILVER

260

260 **Unit.** SEGO on panel. R. Horseman r. *M. 196; V. 1851; BMC 1684. (176)*	150	400

BRONZE

261 **Unit.** Star shaped pattern. R. Winged sphinx l., SEGO. *M. 173; V. 1855; BMC 1690. (184)*..	110	300

ANDOCO

GOLD

262

262 **Stater.** Crescents in wreath. R. Bucranium over horse r., AND below. *M. 197; V. 1860; BMC 2011-14. (202)*..	500	1250

		F £	VF £

263   **Quarter Stater.** Crossed wreaths, ANDO in angles. R. Horse l. *M. 198;*
     V. 1863; BMC 2015-17. (203)   135   350

SILVER

264

264   **Unit.** Bearded head l. R. Winged horse l., ANDOC. *M. 199; V. 1868;*
     BMC 2018. (204)   135   350

BRONZE

265

265   **Unit.** Head r., ANDOCO. R. Horse r., ANDOCO. *M. 200; V. 1871;*
     BMC 2019-20. (205)   75   200
266   Head r., TAS ANDO. R. Horse r. *M. 175a; V. 1873; BMC —. (187)*   80   235

DIAS
SILVER

267   268

267   **Unit.** Saltire over cross within square. R. Boar r., TASC DIAS.
     M. —; V. —; BMC 1663. (173A)   150   375
268   DIAS CO, in star. R. Horse l., VIR. *M. 188; V. 1877; BMC 1683. (177).*   125   325

BRONZE

269

269   **Unit.** Bearded head r., DIAS TASC. R. Centaur r., playing pan pipes.
     M. 192; V. 1882; BMC 1728-35. (197)   100   275

RUES
BRONZE

		F £	VF £
270	**Unit.** Lion r., RVII. R. Eagle. *M. 189; V. 1890; BMC 1691. (194)*	120	300
271	— R. Similar reads RVE. *M. 189; V. 1890-3; BMC 1692. (194)*	110	290

272   273

272	Bearded head r., RVIIS. R. Horseman r., VIR. *M. 190; V. 1892;* *BMC 1698-1701. (195)*	125	325
273	RVIIS on tablet. R. Winged sphinx l. *M. 191; V. 1895;* *BMC 1693-97. (196)*	120	300
274	**Fractional Unit.** Annulet within square with curved sides. R. Eagle l., RVII. *M. 193; V. 1903; BMC 1756-58. (201)*	120	275

CUNOBELIN
(Early 1st Century A.D. to c.40 A.D.)

Styled as son of Tasciovanus on some of his coins, Cunobelin appears to have ruled over the unified territories of the Trinovantes and Catuvellauni, with additional territory in Kent. His aggressive policy of expansion that involved members of family eventually lead to Roman concern over the extent of his power. Following his death just prior to 43 AD, the emperor Claudius took the decision to invade Britain.

During his long reign an extensive issue of gold, silver and bronze coins used ever increasingly Romanised designs. It has been estimated from a study of known dies that around one million of his gold corn ear staters were produced. His main centre and mint was at Camulodunum (Colchester) appearing as the mint signature CAMV. The names SOLIDV and AGR appear on a few coins associated with Cunobelin and are likely to represent personal names.

GOLD

280   281

280	**Stater.** Biga type. CAMVL on panel. R. Two horses l., wheel below, CVNOBELIN. *M. 201; V. 1910; BMC 1769-71. (207)*	725	1500
281	Linear type. Corn ear dividing CA MV. R. Horse r., branch above., CVN. *M. 210; V. 1925; BMC 1772-76. (208)*	200	425
282	— Similar, privy mark 'x' above a letter in *obv.* legend. *M. 210a;* *VA 1925-3/5; BMC 1777-81. (208)*	210	450

283   285

		F £	VF £

283   Wild type. Corn ear dividing CA MV. R. Horse r., branch above.,
    CVN(O). *M. 211/2; V. 1931/33; BMC 1784-92/1804-08. (208)*   190   400
284   — Similar, heart shaped object between horses forelegs. *M. 211 var;*
    V. 1931-3; BMC 1793. (208)   210   450
285   — Similar, privy mark pellet or pellet triangle above a letter(s) in *obv.*
    legend. *M. —; V. 1931-5/7/9; BMC 1797-1803. (208)*   200   225

286   288

286   Plastic type. Corn ear dividing CA MV. R. Horse r., branch above.,
    CVNO. *M. 203/13; V. 2010-1/3/5; BMC 1809-11/15-23. (208)*   190   400
287   — Similar, 'B' in front of horse. *M. —; V. 2010-7; BMC 1813. (208)*   225   475

289   290

288   Classic type. Corn ear dividing CA MV. R. Horse r., branch above.,
    CVNO. *M. 206-07; V. 2025/27; BMC 1827-31/33. (208)*   240   525
289   — Similar, horse l., lis like object above. *M. 208; V. 2029;*
    BMC 1834-35. (209)   525   1100
290   **Quarter Stater.** Biga type. Similar to 280. *M. 202; V. 1913;*
    BMC 1836/A. (210)   225   550

292   296

292   Linear type. Similar to 281. *M. 209; V. 1927; BMC 1837-42. (211)*   120   265
293   Wild type. Similar to 283. *M. —; V. 1935; BMC 1843-44. (211)*   110   250
294   Plastic type. Similar to 286. *M. 204; V. 2015; BMC 1846-48. (211)*   100   240
295   — Similar but corn ear dividing CAM CVN. *M. 205; V. 2017;*
    BMC 1845. (212)   135   275
296   Classic type. Similar to 288. *M. —; V. 2038; BMC —. (211)*   165   425

SILVER

299

		F £	VF £

299 **Unit.** Two bull headed serpents, inter twined. R. Horse l., CVNO.
M. *214; V. 1947; BMC 1856. (213)* 95 300
300 Curled serpent inside wheel. R. Winged horse l., CVN. *M. —; V. —;*
BMC 1857 .... 90 275
301 CVN on panel R. Horse l., (C)M. *M. 255; V. 1949; BMC 1858-59. (228)* 80 240
302 CVNO BELI on two panels. R. CVN below horseman r. *M. 216/7;*
V. 1951/53; BMC 1862. (215) 70 210
303 Head l., CAMVL. R. CVNO beneath Victory std. r. *M. 215; V. 2045;*
BMV 1863-65. (214) 85 250

304   305

304 Two leaves dividing CVN. R. Horseman r., CAM. *M. 218; V. 2047;*
BMC 1866-67. (216) 90 275
305 Flower dividing CAMV. R. CVNO below horse r. *M. 219; V. 2049;*
BMC1867A. (217) 90 275
306 CVNO on panel. R. CAMV on panel below griffin. *M. 234; V. 2051;*
BMC 1868-69. (218) 85 250
307 CAMVL on panel. R. CVNO below centaur l. carrying palm. *M. 234a;*
V. 1918; BMC —. (219) 80 240
308 CAMVL on panel. R. Figure seated l. holding wine amphora, CVNOBE.
M. —; V. —; BMC —. (219A) 85 250

		F £	VF £

309 Plant, CVNOBELINVS. R. Figure stg. r. holding club and thunderbolt
dividing CA MV. *M. —; V .—; BMC 1897. (219B)* 90 275
310 Laur. hd. r., CVNOBELINVS. R. Winged horse springing l., CAMV
below. *M. —; V. —; BMC —. (219C)* 90 275
311 CVNO on panel, wreath around. R. Winged horse r., TASC F. *M. 235;*
V. 2053; BMC 1870. (220) 70 210

312   313

312 Head r., CVNOBELINI. R. Horse r., TASCIO. *M. 236; V. 2055;*
BMC 1871-73. (221) 80 240
313 Winged bust r., CVNO. R. Sphinx std. l., TASCIO. *M. 237; V. 2057;*
BMC 1874-78. (222) 60 140

314   316

		F £	VF £
314	Draped female fig. r., TASCIIOVAN. R. Figure std. r. playing lyre, tree behind. *M. 238; V. 2059; BMC 1879-82. (223)*	75	225
315	Figure stg. l., holding club and lionskin., CVNO. R. Female rider r., TASCIOVA. *M. 239; V. 2061; BMC 1884-85. (224)*	70	200
316	Female head r., CVNOBELINVS. R. Victory r., TASCIO(VAN). *M. —; V. —; BMC 1883. (224A)*	75	225
317	Fig. r. carrying dead animal, CVNOBELINVS. R. Fig. stg. holding bow, dog at side, TASCIIOVANI. *M. 240; V. 2063; BMC 1886-88. (225)*	90	275
318	CVNO on panel, horn above, dolphin below. R. Fig. stg. r. altar behind. *M. 241/41a; V. 2065; BMC 1889-90. (226)*	90	275

319

		F £	VF £
319	CVN on panel. R. Fig. holding club walking r., CVN. *M. 254; V. 2067; BMC 1891-92. (227)*	80	240
320	CVN in wreath. R. CAM, dog? trampling on serpent r. *M. 256; V. 2069; BMC 1893. (229)*	100	300
321	Winged horse l., CVN. R. Std. fig. r. *M. 258; V. 2071; BMC 1896. (230)*	90	275
322	CVNO in angles of cross. R. Capricorn r., CVNO. *M. —; V. —; BMC 1898*	95	285

BRONZE

		F £	VF £
323	Head l., CVNO. R. Boar l., branch above. *M. 220; V. 1969; BMC—. (232)*	50	175
324	CVNOB ELINI in two panels. R. Victory std. l., TASC. *M. 221; V. 1971; BMC 1921-27. (233)*	40	120
325	Winged horse l., CAM. R. Winged Victory stg l., CVN. *M. 222; V. 1973; BMC 1938-43. (234)*	45	140

326

		F £	VF £
326	Bearded head facing R. Boar l., CVN. *M.223; V.1963; BMC 1904-05. (235)*	50	165
327	Ram-headed animal coiled up in double ornamental circle. R. Animal l., CAM. *M. 224; V. 1965; BMC —. (236)*	70	200
328	Griffin r., CAMV. R. Horse r., CVN. *M. 225; V. 2081; BMC 1909-12. (237)*	45	155

		F £	VF £
329	Bearded head l., CAMV. R. CVN or CVNO below horse l. *M. 226, 229; V. 2085/2131; BMC 1900-01. (238)*	45	140
330	Laureate head r., CVNO. R. CVN below bull butting l. *M. 227; V. 2083; BMC 1902-03. (239)*	50	175
331	Crude head r., CVN. R. Figure stg. l., CVN. *M. 228; V. 2135; BMC —. (240)*	50	165

332

332	CAMVL / ODVNO in two panels. R. CVNO beneath sphinx crouching l. *M. 230; V. 1977; BMC 1928-30. (241)*	45	155
333	Winged horse l., CAMV. R. Victory stg. r. divides CV NO. *M. 231; V. 1979; BMC 1931-34. (242)*	40	140
334	Victory walking r. R. CVN below, horseman r. *M. 232; V. 1981; BMC 1935. (243)*	50	165
335	Head l., CAM. R. CVNO below eagle. *M. 233; V. 2087; BMC —. (244)*	50	165

336   337

336	Head l., CVNOBELINI. R. Centaur r., TASCIOVANI.F. *M. 242; V. 2089; BMC 1968-71. (245)*	40	120
337	Helmeted bust r. R. TASCIIOVANII above, sow stg. r., F below. *M. 243; V. 2091; BMC 1956-60. (246)*	40	120
338	Horseman galloping r. holding dart and shield, CVNOB. R. Warrior stg. l., TASCIIOVANTIS. *M. 244; V. 2093; BMC 1961-67. (247)*	35	100

339

339	Helmeted bust l., CVOBELINVS REX. R. TASC FIL below boar l., std. on haunches. *M. 245; V. 1983; BMC 1952-55. (248)*	60	180
340	Bare head r., CVNOBELINVS REX. R. TASC below bull butting r. *M. 246; V. 2095; BMC 1944-51. (249)*	40	120
341	Bare head l., CVNO. R. TASC below bull stg. r. *M. 247; V. 1985; BMC —. (250)*	50	150

342 343

	F £	VF £

342 Head l., CVNOBELIN. R. Metal worker std. r. holding hammer, working
on a vase, TASCIO. *M. 248; V. 2097; BMC 1972-83. (251)* 40 120

343 Winged horse r., CVNO. R. Victory r. sacrificing bull, TASCI. *M. 249;
V. 2099; BMC 1913-19. (252)* 30 100

344 CVNO on panel within wreath. R. CAMV below horse, prancing r.
M. 250; V. 2101; BMC 1987-90. (253) 40 145

345 346

345 Bearded head of Jupiter Ammon l., CVNOBELIN. R. CAM below
horseman galloping r. *M. 251; V. 2103; BMC 1984-86. (254)* 60 180

346 Janus head, CVNO below. R. CAMV on panel below, sow std. r.
beneath a tree. *M. 252; V. 2105; BMC 1998-2003. (255)* 55 175

347

347 Bearded head of Jupiter Ammon r., CVNOB. R. CAM on panel below
lion crouched r. *M. 253; V. 2107; BMC 1991-97. (256)* 50 150

348 Sphinx r., CVNO. R. Fig stg. l. divides CA M. *M. 260; V. 2109;
BMC 2004-09. (257)* 45 150

349 Horse r. R. CVN below horseman r. *M. 261; V. 1987; BMC 1936-47. (258)* 60 180

350 Animal l. looking back. R. CVN below horse l. *M. 233a; V. 1967;
BMC— . (259)* 70 190

350A Ship, CVN below. R. Fig. r. dividing S E. *M. —; V. 1989; BMC 2010.* ... 110 325

"SOLIDV"

SILVER

351

		F	VF
		£	£
351	**Unit.** SOLIDV in centre of looped circle. R, Stg. fig. l., CVNO.		
	M. 259; V. 2073; BMC 1894-95. (231)	175	475

"AGR"

GOLD

| 352 | Quarter Stater. Corn ear dividing CAM CVN. R. Horse r., branch above., AGR below *M. —; V. —; BMC 1854*... | 250 | 600 |

353

| 353 | — R. Horse r., branch above., cross and A below. *M. —; V. —; BMC 1855* .... | 240 | 550 |

SILVER

| 354 | **Unit.** AGR inside wreath. R. Female dog r., AGR below. *M. —; V. —; BMC 1899* .... | 170 | 450 |

EPATICCUS

(1st Half 1st Century A.D.)

Epaticcus styled as a son of Tasciovanus on his coins, was most probably a brother of Cunobelin. The corn ear employed on his staters is similar to that of his brother's produced at Colchester. His coins appear in northern Atrebatic territory and conform to the area's denominational structure. It seems likely that Epaticcus's coinage reflects an incursion into Atrebatic territory by the Trinovantian/Catuvellaunian dynasty.

GOLD

355

| 355 | **Stater.** Corn ear dividing TAS CIF. R. Horseman r., with spear and shield. EPATI. *M. 262; V. 575; BMC 2021-23. (112)*............................... | *Extremely rare* |

SILVER

356　　　　　　　　　　　　357

		F £	VF £
356	**Unit.** Head of Hercules r., EPAT(I). R. Eagle stg. on snake. *M. 263/a; V. 580; BMC 2024-2268/2270-76. (113)*	25	55
357	Victory seated r. TASCIOV. R. Boar r., EPAT. *M. 263; V. 581;* *BMC 2294-2328. (114)*	35	85

358

358	Bearded head l., TASCIO. R. EPATI below lion r. *M. —; V. 582;* *BMC 2329*	110	250
359	EPATI inside panel. R. Lion r. *M. —; V. 583; BMC 2330. (114A)*	110	245

360　　　　　　　　　　　　361

360	**Minim.** EPATI. R. Boars head r., TA. *M. 264; V. 585; BMC 2331-46.* *(115)*	50	110
361	TA inside star. R. Winged horse r., EPA below. *M. —; V. 560;* *BMC 2351-57. (116)*	60	130
362	Helmeted head r. R. Horse r., E below. *M. —; V. —; BMC 2358-63*	65	145
363	EPATI. R. Winged horse r., cross below. *M. —; V .—; BMC 2365*	65	145

CARATACUS
(1st Half 1st Century A.D.)

Coins inscribed CARA have been traditionally associated with the historically attested son of Cunobelin, Caratacus the leader of British resistance against Rome. His coins appear in the same area as those of Epaticcus and he may have been his successor.

SILVER

364　　　　　　　　　　　　364A

364	**Unit.** Head of Hercules r., CARA. R. Eagle stg. on snake. *M. 265;* *V. 593; BMC 2376-84. (117)*	125	275
364A	**Minim.** CARA around pellet in ring. R. Winged horse r. *M. —; V. 595;* *BMC 2385-89. (117A)*	90	225

DUROTRIGES

(Mid 1st Century B.C. to Mid 1st Century A.D.)

The Durotriges inhabited West Hampshire, Dorset and adjoining parts of Somerset and Wiltshire. Their coinage is one of the most distinctive in Britain due to its rapid debasement. The disappearance of precious metals from the coinage should perhaps be linked to the declining trade between the south-west and western Gaul, following the Roman conquest of the Gaul. Hengistbury Head is the probable mint site of the cast bronzes. Coins inscribed CRAB have been traditionally associated with the tribe.

UNINSCRIBED

SILVER

		F	VF
		£	£
365	**Stater.** White Gold type. Derived from Westerham stater (no. 21). *M. 317; V. 1235, 52, 54, 55; BMC 2525-2731. (60)*	70	150

366   368

366	Silver type. Similar. *M. 317; V. 1235, 52, 54, 55; BMC 2525-2731. (60)*	50	100
367	Billon type. Similar. *M. 317; V. 1235, 52, 54, 55; BMC 2525-2731. (60)*	30	65
368	**Quarter Stater.** Geometric type. Crescent design. R. Zig-zag pattern. *M. 319; V. 1242/29; BMC 2734-79. (61). Quality of metal varies, obv. almost blank on later issues*	40	110

369

369	Starfish type. Spiral. R. Zig-zag pattern. *M. 320; V. 1270; BMC 2780-81 (61A)*	60	125
370	Hampshire Thin Flan type. Crude head of lines and pellets. R. Stylised horse l. *M. 321; V. 1280; BMC 2782-87. (62)*	70	140

BRONZE

371	**Stater.** Struck Bronze type. Similar to No.365-67. *M. 318; V. 1290; BMC 2790-2859. (81)*	20	45

372

	F	VF
	£	£

372   Cast Bronze type. Many varities, as illustration. *M. 322-70;*
V. 1322-70; BMC 2860-2936. (82)   30   85

"CRAB"

SILVER

373

373   **Unit.** CRAB in angles of cross. R. Eagle. *M. 371; V. 1285;*
BMC 2788. (145) .... *Extremely rare*
373A   **Minim.** CRAB on tablet. R. Star shape. *M. 372; V. 1286; BMC 2789.*
(146) .... *Extremely rare*

DOBUNNI

(Mid 1st Century B.C. to Mid 1st Century A.D.)

Dobunnic territory stretched over Gloucestershire, Hereford and Worcester and into parts of Somerset, Wiltshire and Gwent. The earliest Dobunnic coins are developed from the British Q stater, and have the distinctive tree-like motif of the tribe on the obverse. The inscribed coinage is difficult to arrange chronologically and it may be that some of the rulers named held different parts of the territory simultaneously.

UNINSCRIBED

GOLD

374   **Stater.** Plain except for tree-like object. R. Three tailed horse r.,
wheel below. *M. 374; V. 1005; BMC 2937-40. (43)*   275   600
375   **Quarter Stater.** Plain with traces of wreath pattern. R. Horse r.
M. 68; V. 1010-3; BMC 2942-46. (52)   135   275
376   Wreath pattern. R. Horse l., pellet in ring motifs in field. *M. 74; V. 1015;*
BMC 2949. (51)   125   225

SILVER

377 378

377 **Unit.** Allen types A-F/I-J. Regular series. Head r. R. Triple-tailed horse
l. or r. *M. 374a, b/75/76, 378a-384; V. 1020/45/49/74/78/95/1135/1137;
BMC 2950-3011. (63-64). Style becomes progressively more abstract,
from-* 30 80

378 Allen types L-O. Irregular series. Similar to last. *M. 377-384d;
V. 1170-85; BMC 3012-22. (63-64)* 40 95

INSCRIBED
The following types are not arranged chronologically.

ANTED
GOLD

379 **Stater.** Dobunnic emblem. R. ANTED or ANTEDRIG over triple
tailed horse r., wheel below. *M. 385-86; V. 1062-69;
BMC 3023-3031. (260)* 275 550

SILVER

380 **Unit.** Crude head r. R. ANTED over horse. *M. 387; V. 1082;
BMC 3032-38. (261)* 80 175

EISV
GOLD

381

381 **Stater.** Dobunnic emblem. R. EISV or EISVRIG over triple tailed horse
r., wheel below. *M. 388; V. 1105; BMC 3039-42. (262)* 600 1300

SILVER

382

382 **Unit.** Crude head r. R. Horse l., EISV. *M. 389; V. 1110;
BMC 3043-55. (263)* 65 150

INAM or INARA

GOLD

	F	VF
	£	£

383 **Stater.** Dobunnic emblem. R. INAM or INARA over triple tailed horse r., wheel below. *M. 390; V. 1140; BMC 3056. (264)* .... *Extremely rare*

CATTI

GOLD

384

384 **Stater.** Dobunnic emblem. R. CATTI over triple tailed horse r., wheel below. *M. 391; V. 1130; BMC 3057-60. (265)* 250 525

COMUX

GOLD

385 **Stater.** Dobunnic emblem. R. COMVX retrograde, over triple tailed horse r., wheel below. *M. 392; V. 1092; BMC 3061-63. (266)* 650 1450

CORIO

GOLD

386   387

386 **Stater.** Dobunnic emblem. R. CORIO over triple tailed horse r., wheel below. *M. 393; V. 1035; BMC 3064-3133. (267)* 375 750

387 **Quarter Stater.** COR in centre. R. Horse r., without legend. *M. 394; V. 1039; BMC 3134. (268)* 550 1200

BODVOC

GOLD

388

389

		F £	VF £
388	**Stater.** BODVOC across field. R. Horse r., without legend. *M. 395; V. 1052; BMC 3135-42. (269)*	650	1400

SILVER

389	**Unit.** Head l., BODVOC. R. Horse r., without legend. *M. 396; V. 1057; BMC 3143-45. (270)*	125	270

CORIELTAUVI

The Corieltauvi formerly known as the Coritani, occupied Lincolnshire and adjoining parts of Yorkshire, Northamptonshire, Leicestershire and Nottinghamshire. The earliest staters, the South Ferriby type, are developed from Gallo-Belgic C staters, and are associated with the silver Boar/Horse types. The distinctive dish shaped scyphate coinages have no parallels in Britain and stand apart from the main series. The later inscribed issues present a complex system of inscriptions. It has been suggested that some of the later inscriptions refer to pairs of names, possibly joint rulers or moneyers and rulers.

EARLY UNINSCRIBED

(Mid to Late 1st Century B.C.)

GOLD

390

393

390	**Stater.** South Ferriby type. Crude laureate head. R. Disjointed horse l., rosette or star below, anchor shape and pellets above. *M. 449-50; V. 809-815/19; BMC 3146-3179. (30)*	125	235
391	Wheel type. Similar, but wheel below horse. *M. 449c; V. 817; BMC 3180*	225	450
392	Kite type. Similar to 390, but diamond shape containing pellets above, spiral below horse. *M. 447; V. 825; BMC 3181-84. (29)*	200	400
393	Domino type. Similar to last, but with rectangle containing pellets. *M. 448; V. 829; BMC 3185-86. (29)*	200	400

394   395

	F £	VF £
394 Trefoil type. Trefoil with central rosette of seven pellets. R. Similar to 390. *M. 450a; V. 821; BMC —. (30A)*	*Extremely rare*	
395 North Lincolnshire Scyphate type. Stylised boar r. or l. R. Large S symbol with pellets and rings in field. *M. —; V. —; BMC 3187-93*	300	700

* chipped or cracked specimens are often encountered and are worthless

SILVER

![coin 396]

396

396 **Unit.** Boar/Horse type I.Boar r., large pellet and ring motif above, reversed S below. R. Horse l. or r., pellet in ring above. *M. 405-06, 451; V. 855-60, 864, 867; BMC 3194-3214. (66)*	65	165
397 Boar Horse type II. Vestiges of boar on obv. R. Horse l. or r. *M. 410, 452-53; V. 875-877; BMC 3214-27. (68)*	40	95

![coins 398 and 399]

398   399

398 Boar Horse type III. Blank. R. Horse l.or r. *M. 453-54; V. 884-77; BMC 3228-35. (69)*	30	65
399 **Fractional Unit.** Similar to 396-97. *M. 406a, 451a; V. 862/66; BMC 3236-3250. (67)*	50	110
400 Similar to 398. *M. —; V. 877-81; BMC 3251-55. (70/71)*	25	60
401 Pattern/Horse. Flower pattern. R. Horse l. *M. —; V. —; BMC 3256-57*	50	110

INSCRIBED

(Early to Mid 1st Century A.D.)
The following types are not arranged chronologically.

AVN COST

GOLD

			F £	VF £
402	**Stater.** Crude wreath design. R. Disjointed horse l., AVN COST. *M. 457; V. 910; BMC 3258. (286)*		475	1050

SILVER

403

403	**Unit.** Remains of wreath or blank. R. AVN COST, horse l. *M. 458; V. 914; BMC 3261-66. (287)*	40	95
404	**Fractional Unit.** Similar. *M. —; l V. 918; BMC 3267-68. (288)*	35	85

ESVP RASV

GOLD

405	**Stater.** Crude wreath design. R. Disjointed horse l., IISVP RASV. *M. 456b; V. 920; BMC 3269. (289)*	450	1200

SILVER

406	**Unit.** Similar. *M. 456c; V. 924; BMC 3272-73. (290)*	80	175

VEP

GOLD

407	**Stater.** Blank or with traces of wreath. R. Disjointed horse l., VEP. *M. —; V. 905; BMC 3274-75. (296)*	425	925

SILVER

408	**Unit.** Blank or with traces of wreath. R. VEP, horse r. *M. —; V. 963; BMC 3277-82. (297)*	65	140
409	**Half Unit.** Similar. *M. 464b; V. 967; BMC 3283-3295. (298)*	60	125

VEP CORF

GOLD

410

		F £	*VF* £
410	**Stater.** Crude wreath design. R. Disjointed horse l., VEP CORF. *M. 459, 460; V. 930/40/60; BMC 3296-3304. (291)*	375	825

SILVER

| 411 | **Unit.** Similar. *M. 460b/464; V. 934/50; BMC 3305-14. (292)* | 60 | 125 |

412

| 412 | Similar but VEPOC (M)ES, pellet in ring below horse. *M. —; V. 955; BMC —. (294)* | 70 | 150 |
| 413 | **Half Unit.** Similar. *M. 464a; V. 938/58; BMC 3316-24. (293/95)* | 50 | 120 |

DVMNO TIGIR SENO

GOLD

414

| 414 | **Stater.** DVMN(OC) across wreath. R. Horse l., TIGIR SENO. *M. 461; V. 972; BMC 3325-27. (299)* | 700 | 1550 |

SILVER

415

| 415 | **Unit.** DVMNOC in two lines. R. Horse r., TIGIR SENO. *M. 462; V. 974; BMC 3328-29. (300)* | 175 | 375 |

VOLISIOS DVMNOCOVEROS

GOLD

416

		F £	VF £
416	**Stater.** VOLISIOS between three lines in wreath. R. Horse r. or l., DVMNOCOVEROS. *M. 463/a; V. 978-80; BMC 3330-3336. (301)*	400	850

SILVER

417	**Unit.** Similar. R. Horse r., DVMNOCO. *M. 463a; V. 980;* *BMC 3339. (302)*	165	350
418	**Half Unit.** Similar. *M. 465; V. 984; BMC 3340-41. (303)*	95	210

VOLISIOS DVMNOVELLAUNOS

GOLD

419	**Stater.** VOLISIOS between three lines in wreath. R. Horse r. or l., DVMNOVELAVNOS. *M. 466; V .988; BMC 3342-43. (304)*	700	1550

SILVER

420	**Half Unit.** As last but DVMNOVE. *M. 467; V. 992; BMC 3344-46. (305).*	175	375

VOLISIOS CARTIVEL

SILVER

421	**Half Unit.** VOLISIOS between three lines in wreath. R. Horse r., CARTILEV. *M. 468; V. 994; BMC 3347-48. (306)*	200	425

IAT ISO E

SILVER

422	**Unit.** IAT ISO (retrograde)on tablet, rosettes above and below. R. Horse r., E above. *M. 416; V. 998; BMC 3349-51. (284)*	190	400

CAT

SILVER

422A	**Unit.** Boar r., pellet ring above, CAT above. R. Horse r. *M. —; V. —;* *BMC 3352*	*Extremely rare*

LAT ISON

GOLD

423

	F	VF
	£	£

423   **Stater.** LAT ISO(N) in two lines retrograde. R. Horse r., ISO in box
above, N below. *M.* —; *V.* —; *BMC* —. *Only recorded as an AE/AV
plated core, as illustrated*...   *Extremely rare*

ICENI

The Iceni centered on Norfolk but also occupying neighbouring parts of Suffolk and
Cambridgeshire, are well attested in the post conquest period as the tribe who under Boudicca
revolted against Roman rule. Their earliest coins are likely to have been the British J staters, Norfolk
Wolf type (no.30/31), replaced around the mid first century B.C. by the Snettisham, Freckenham and
Irstead type gold staters and quarter staters. Contemporary with these are silver Boar/Horse and
Face/Horse units and fractions. The introduction of legends around the beginning of the millennia
led to the adoption of a new obverse design of back to back crescents. The continuation of the
coinage after the Roman invasion is attested by the coins of King Prasutagus. Some of the
Face/Horse units (no.434) have been attributed to Queen Boudicca.

EARLY UNINSCRIBED
(Mid to Late 1st Century B.C.)
GOLD

424   424   425

424   **Stater.** Snettisham type. Blank or with traces of pellet cross. R. Horse
r., serpent like pellet in ring motif above. *M.* —; *V* .—; *BMC 3353-59*   250   525
425   Similar. Blank or with 3 short curved lines. R. Horse r., symbol above
more degraded. *M.* —; *V.* —; *BMC 3360-83*   220   500

426   427

		F £	*VF* £
426	Freckenham type. Two opposed crescents with stars or pellets in field. R. Horse r., various symbols in field. *M. 397/99; V. 620; BMC 3384-89. (38)*	185	400
427	Similar. Blank or with traces of pellet cross. R. Horse r., wheel or arch containing pellets above. *M. 400; V. 624; BMC 3390-95. (40)*	210	450

428

| 428 | Similar. Trefoil on cross design. R. Similar. *M. 401-03; V. 626; BMC 3396-3419. (39)* .... | 200 | 400 |

429   430

| 429 | **Quarter Stater.** Snettisham type. Wreath cross. R. Horse r. *M. —; V. —; BMC 3420-35* .... | 100 | 200 |
| 430 | Irstead type. Hatched box, wreaths at sides. R. Horse r. *M. 404; V. 628; BMC 3436-39. (48)* .... | 90 | 180 |

SILVER

431   432

| 431 | **Unit.** Boar / Horse type. Boar r. R. Horse r. *M. 407-09; V. 655-59; BMC 3440-3512. (72)* .... | 25 | 60 |
| 432 | Bury type. Head l. or r. R. Horse l. or r. *M. —; V. —; BMC 3524-35* .... | 65 | 150 |

433   433

		F	VF
		£	£
433	Early Face / Horse type. Celticised head l. or r. R. Horse l. or r. *M. 412/413a-c/e; BMC 3536-3555. (74)*	45	120

434   435

		F	VF
434	Face / Horse Regular type. Head r. R. Horse r. *M. 413/d; V. 790-94; BMC 3556-3759. (74). Attributed to Queen Boudicca by R.D. van Arsdell*	35	100
435	Early Pattern / Horse type. Cross of two opposed crescents. R. Horse l. or r. *M. 414-15; V. 675-79; BMC 3763-74. (75)*	20	45

436

		F	VF
436	ECEN symbol type. Two opposed crescents. R. Horse r. *M. 429; V. 752; BMC 4297-4325*	20	50
437	**Half Unit.** Boar / Horse type. Similar to 431. *M. 411; V. 661; BMC 3513-20. (73)*	25	60
438	**Fractional Unit.** Early Pattern / Horse type. Similar to 435. *M. 417/a; V. 681-83; BMC 3775-89. (76/A)*	35	70

INSCRIBED

(Early to Mid 1st Century A.D.)
The following types are not arranged chronologically.

CAN DVRO

SILVER

439

		F	VF
439	**Unit.** Boar. R. Horse r., CAN(S) above, DVRO below. *M. 434; V. 663; BMC 3521-23. (271)*	100	225

ANTED

GOLD

440

		F £	VF £
440	**Stater.** Triple crescent design. R. Horse r., ANTED monongram below. M. 418; V. 705; BMC 3790. (272)	400	900

SILVER

441

441	**Unit.** Two opposed crescents. R. Horse r., ANTED. M. 419-21; V. 710-11/15; BMC 3791-4025. (273)	25	60
442	**Fractional Unit.** Similar to last. M. 422; V. 720; BMC 4028-31. (274)	30	65

ECEN

GOLD

443

443	**Stater.** Triple crescent design. R. Horse r., ECEN below. M. —; V. 725; BMC 4032.	*Extremely rare*	

SILVER

443A	**Unit.** Two opposed crescents. R, Horse r., ECEN. M. 424; V. 730; BMC 4033-4215. (275)	20	50
443B	**Half Unit.** Similar to last. M. 431; V. 736; BMC 4216-17. (276)	25	60

EDN

SILVER

		F £	VF £
444	**Unit.** Two opposed crescents. R, Horse r., ED, E, EI or EDN. *M. 423, 425b; V. 734/40; BMC 4219-81. (277)*..	30	65

ECE

SILVER

445

| 445 | **Unit.** Two opposed crescents. R, Horse r., ECE. *M. 425-28; V. 761-66; BMC 4348-4538. (278-80)*.. | 25 | 50 |

SAENU

SILVER

| 446 | **Unit.** Two opposed crescents. R. Horse r., SAENV. *M. 433; V. 770; BMC 4540-57. (281)* .... | 45 | 110 |

AESU

SILVER

447

| 447 | **Unit.** Two opposed crescents. R. Horse r., AESV. *M. 432; V. 775; BMC 4558-72. (282)* .... | 50 | 125 |

ALE SCA

SILVER

| 448 | **Unit.** Boar r., ALE. R. Horse r., SCA. *M. 469; V. 996; BMC 4576* .... | 175 | 350 |

AEDIC SIA

SILVER

		F £	VF £
449	**Unit.** AEDIC in two lines. R. Horse r., SIA? below. *M.—; V.—;* *BMC 4581*	*Extremely rare*	

PRASUTAGUS

SILVER

450

450 **Unit.** Romanised head l., SUB RII PRASTO. R. Rearing horse r.,
ESICO FECIT. *M. 434a; V. 780; BMC 4577-80. (283)* 600 1300
This legend translates as "Under King Prasto, Esico made me", giving the name of both King and moneyer.

ROMAN BRITAIN

The systematic conquest of Britain by the Romans began in A.D. 43 when the Emperor Claudius (41-54), anxious to enhance his military reputation, authorized an invasion in which he personally participated, albeit in a purely symbolic role. The initial military contact between the two cultures had taken place almost a century before when Julius Caesar, during the course of his conquest of Celtic Gaul, led expeditions to the island in 55 and 54 B.C. Although no actual Roman occupation of Britain resulted from Caesar's reconnoitring campaigns commercial intercourse was certainly accelerated, as evidenced by the 'Romanization' of the British Celtic coinage in the final decades of its production.

The Claudian conquest, commencing in A.D. 43, brought about a complete change in the nature of the currency circulating in Britain and ushered in a period lasting more than three and a half centuries during which Roman coinage was the only official medium of exchange. Local copies of the money brought with them by the four legions of the invasion army began to appear at a very early stage, the most popular type for imitation being the well-known Claudian copper as with reverse type fighting Minerva. Some of these copies are well-executed and of a style not much inferior to the prototype, suggesting that their local minting may have been officially sanctioned by the Roman government in order to make good a shortage of currency in the newly-conquered territory. Other examples are of much poorer style and execution and are frequently well below the normal weight of a Claudian as (usually between 10 and 11 grams). These copies must have been issued unofficially and provide evidence of the huge demand for this type of currency in a population which had never before experienced the benefits of having base metal coins available for small everyday transactions.

In the decades that followed, the boundaries of the Roman province of Britannia were continually pushed further north and west until, under the celebrated Flavian governor Gnaeus Julius Agricola, the Roman army even penetrated to northern Scotland (A.D. 83/4). A few years later, under Trajan, the northern frontier was established along the Tyne-Solway line, a barrier made permanent by the construction of Hadrian's Wall following the emperor's visit to the province in 122. For a brief period in the mid-2nd century the frontier was temporarily advanced to the Forth-Clyde line with the building of the Antonine Wall, though this seems to have been abandoned early in the reign of Marcus Aurelius (ca. 163) when the Hadrianic barrier was re-commissioned and became the permanent frontier. The security thus provided to the now-peaceful province in the south facilitated urban expansion and the development of commerce. The new prosperity brought a flood of Roman coinage into the island-province and it was no longer necessary for shortages to be made good by large scale local imitation.

Until the mid-3rd century the production of Roman coinage remained the prerogative of the mint in the capital, with only occasional issues from provincial centres to serve short-term local needs. But with the deepening political and economic crisis in the third quarter of the century there was a dramatic decentralization of minting operations, with permanent establishments being set up in many important cities in the western as well as the eastern provinces. Britain, however, still remained without an official mint at this time and in the dark days of the 270s, when the separatist Gallic Empire to which Britain belonged was close to collapse, large scale production of imitative antoniniani (commonly called 'barbarous radiates') occurred in the province. The integrity and prestige of the Empire was, to some extent, restored by a rapid succession of Illyrian 'soldier emperors', until the situation was finally stabilized by Diocletian (A.D. 284-305) who established the tetrarchy system under which governmental responsibility was shared by four rulers. By the end of the 3rd century Britain had been reorganized into a civil diocese of four provinces: it had already been subdivided into Britannia Superior and Britannia Inferior almost a hundred years before, under Septimius Severus or Caracalla.

It was left to the colourful and enigmatic usurper Carausius (A.D. 287-293) to establish mints in Britain. It was, of course, vital for him to do so as his dominion was mostly confined to the island-province. Londinium (London) was his principal mint, with a secondary establishment at a place usually signing itself 'C' (probably Camulodunum, modern Colchester). After the downfall of Carausius' murderer and successor Allectus (293-296) Britain was restored to the central government, an event commemorated by the celebrated gold medallion of Constantius I showing the Caesar riding alongside the Thames approaching the gateway of the city of Londinium. At this point the mysterious 'C' mint disappears from the picture. Londinium, on the other hand, retained its status as an official mint under Diocletian's tetrarchy and its successors down to A.D. 325, when it was closed by Constantine the Great who regarded it as superfluous to his needs. In nearly four decades of existence as a Roman mint Londinium had produced a varied and extensive coinage in the names of almost all the emperors, empresses and Caesars of the period. It was destined never again to be active during Roman times, unless the extremely rare gold and silver issues of the late 4th century usurper Magnus Maximus, signed AVG, AVGOB and AVGPS, are correctly attributed to Londinium under its late Roman name of Augusta.

The termination of Roman rule in the British provinces is traditionally dated to A.D. 410 when the emperor Honorius, in response to an appeal for aid from his British subjects, told them to arrange for their own defence as best they might ('Rescript of Honorius'). In reality, the end probably came quite gradually. As the machinery of government ground to a halt and the soldiers stopped receiving their pay there would have been a steady drift of population away from the semi-ruinous cities and military installations to the countryside, where they could better provide for themselves through farming. Under these conditions the need for coinage would have been drastically reduced, as a primitive economy based on barter would largely have replaced the complex monetary economy of the late Roman period. In any case the supply of coinage from the Continent would now have dried up. The few monetary transactions which still took place were made with worn-out coins from earlier periods augmented by local imitations, production of which in Britain had resumed in the mid-4th century. Such was the pitiful end of the long tradition of Roman coinage in the remote island-province of Britannia. More than two centuries of 'Dark Ages' were to elapse before England's new rulers, the Anglo-Saxons, commenced the issue of gold thrymsas, the designs of many of which were based on late Roman types.

As Rome's Imperial coinage provided the currency needs of this country over a period of almost four centuries no representative collection of British coins is complete without some examples of these important issues. The following listing is divided into four categories: 1. Regular Roman issues, all of which would have been legal tender in Britain after A.D. 43; 2. Issues with types referring specifically to the province of Britannia, usually in commemoration of military campaigns in the north; 3. Official Roman coinage struck in Britain; 4. Imitations of Roman coins produced in Britain, all but possibly some of the earliest being of unofficial origin. The reference 'R.R.C.' is to the listing of the type in Michael Crawford's *Roman Republican Coinage* (Cambridge, 1974); and 'R.I.C.' to *The Roman Imperial Coinage* (London, 1923-1994, in ten volumes).

For more detailed collectors' information on Roman coinage, including a more comprehensive listing of types, the reader is referred to *Roman Coins and their Values* by David R. Sear (4th revised edition). A complete catalogue of silver issues may be found in the 5 volumes of *Roman Silver Coins* (H.A. Seaby and C.E. King) which provides a quick and convenient reference and is especially aimed at the collector. Gilbert Askew's *The Coinage of Roman Britain* (2nd edition) concentrates on those issues which are particularly associated with the Roman province of Britannia, but does not provide valuations. A more recent work on this subject is R. Reece's *Coinage in Roman Britain*. Newly published is David R. Sear's *The History and Coinage of the Roman Imperators, 49—27 BC* which is devoted to the vital two decades of transition from Republic to Empire.

The standard works on the coinages of the Roman Republic and the Roman Empire have already been mentioned *(Roman Republican Coinage and Roman Imperial Coinage)*. These monumental publications are essential to the advanced collector and student and their importance cannot be overstated. The British Museum Catalogues (3 volumes of Republican, 6 volumes of Imperial) are also vital. They contain superb interpretive material in their introductions and are very fully illustrated. A similar work is Anne S. Robertson's *Roman Imperial Coins in the Hunter Coin Cabinet*, in 5 volumes (volume 4 is especially important for the later 3rd century coinage). For more general reading we may recommend J.P.C. Kent and M. & A. Hirmer's *Roman Coins*, undoubtedly the most lavishly illustrated book on the subject; C.H.V. Sutherland's *Roman Coins;* and R.A.G. Carson's *Coins of the Roman Empire*. Finally, for a most useful single-volume work on interpretation and background information we would suggest A *Dictionary of Ancient Roman Coins* by John Melville Jones.

1. REGULAR ROMAN ISSUES

A token selection of the types of Roman coins which might be found on Romano-British archaeological sites. Many of the rarer emperors and empresses have been omitted and the types listed often represent only one of hundreds of variant forms which might be encountered.

		F £	VF £
451	**THE REPUBLIC: P. Aelius Paetus** (moneyer), 138 B.C. Æ *denarius*. Helmeted hd. of Roma r. Rev. The Dioscuri galloping r. R.R.C. 233/1....	20	50
	Although dating from long before the Roman conquest many Republican coins circulated well into the Imperial period and found their way to Britain where they are often represented in early hoards.		
452	**L. Thorius Balbus** (moneyer), 105 B.C. Æ denarius. Hd. of Juno Sospita r., clad in goat's skin. Rev. Bull charging r. *R.R.C. 316/1*	25	60
453	**Q. Antonius Balbus** (moneyer), 83-82 B.C. Æ *denarius*. Laur. hd. of Jupiter r. Rev. Victory in quadriga r. *R.R.C. 364/1*	20	55

454   456

454	**C. Calpurnius Piso** (moneyer), 67 B.C. Æ *denarius*. Laur. hd. of Apollo r. Rev. Horseman galloping r., holding palm-branch. *R.R.C. 408/1a*........	25	60
455	**Mn. Acilius Glabrio** (moneyer), 49 B.C. Æ *denarius*. Laur. hd. of Salus r. Rev. Valetudo stg. l., holding snake and resting on column. *R.R.C. 442/1.*	20	55
456	**Julius Caesar** (dictator), visited Britain 55 and 54 B.C., died 44 B.C. Æ *denarius*. CAESAR. Elephant r. Rev. Priestly emblems. *R.R.C. 443/1....*	75	150
456A	— Wreathed hd. of Caesar r. Rev. P. SEPVLLIVS MACER. Venus stg. l., holding Victory and sceptre. *R.R.C. 480/9*	300	700
457	**Mark Antony** (triumvir), died 30 B.C. Æ *denarius*. Galley r. Rev. LEG. II. Legionary eagle between two standards. *R.R.C. 544/14*	50	125

458   459

458	**Octavian** (triumvir), named Augustus 27 B.C. Æ *denarius*. Bare hd. of Octavian r. Rev. IMP. CAESAR. Trophy set on prow. *R.I.C. 265a.*	90	200
459	**THE EMPIRE: Augustus,** 27 B.C.-A.D. 14. Æ *denarius*. Rev. C. L. CAESARES AVGVSTI F COS DESIG PRINC IVVENT. The emperor's grandsons, Gaius and Lucius, stg. facing, with spears and shields. *R.I.C. 207.*	55	130
	Almost all the coins in the Roman Imperial series have a head or bust of the emperor, empress or prince as their obverse type. Therefore, in most instances only the reverses will be described in the following listings.		

		F £	VF £
460	Æ as. ROM. ET AVG. The altar of Lugdunum. *R.I.C. 230.*	50	125
460A	Æ quadrans. Obv. Anvil. Rev. Moneyers' inscription around large S. C. *R.I.C. 443.*	15	35
461	**Augustus and Agrippa,** general and designated heir of Augustus, died 12 B.C. Æ *dupondius.* Obv. Their hds. back to back. Rev. COL. NEM. Crocodile r., chained to palm-branch. *R.I.C. 159*..................................... *See also no. 468.*	55	140
462	**Divus Augustus,** deified A.D. 14. Æ as. PROVIDENT S. C. Large altar. *R.I.C. 81.*	60	150
463	**Tiberius,** A.D. 14-37. *N aureus.* PONTIF MAXIM. Livia (?) seated r., holding sceptre and branch. *R.I.C. 29.*	350	850

464   467

		F £	VF £
464	ÆR denarius. Similar. *R.I.C. 30.* .... *This type is commonly referred to as the 'Tribute Penny' of the Bible (Matthew 22, 17-21).*	70	150
464A	Æ *as.* Inscription around large S. C. *R.I.C. 44.*..	55	140
465	**Livia,** wife of Augustus, mother of Tiberius. Æ *dupondius.* Obv. Veiled bust of Livia as Pietas r. Rev. Inscription of Drusus Caesar around large S. C. *R.I.C. 43.*	120	325
466	**Drusus,** son of Tiberius. Æ *as.* Inscription around large S. C. *R.I.C. 45..*	65	165
467	**Caligula,** A.D. 37-41. Æ *as.* VESTA S. C. Vesta seated l. *R.I.C. 38.*........	85	225

468

		F £	VF £
468	**Agrippa,** grandfather of Caligula, died 12 B.C. Æ *as.* S. C. Neptune stg. l., holding dolphin and trident. *R.I.C. 58.* .... *See also no. 461 and under Category 4.*	50	150
469	**Germanicus,** father of Caligula, brother of Claudius, died A.D. 19. Æ *as.* Inscription of Caligula around large S. C. *R.I.C. 35.*	65	165
470	**Agrippina Senior,** mother of Caligula, died A.D. 33. Æ *sestertius.* S.P.Q.R. MEMORIAE AGRIPPINAE. Carpentum drawn l. by two mules. *R.I.C. 55.*	250	850

471   474

		F	VF
		£	£

471   **Claudius,** A.D. 41-54, initiated the conquest of Britain by his invasion in
A.D. 43. Æ *as*. LIBERTAS AVGVSTA S. C. Libertas stg. r., holding pileus.
R.I.C. 113. 55   140

471A   Æ *quadrans*. Obv. Hand holding scales. Rev. Inscription around large
S. C. *R.I.C. 85.* 15   35
See also under Categories 2 and 4.

472   **Nero Claudius Drusus,** father of Claudius, died 9 B.C. Æ *sestertius*.
TI. CLAVDIVS CAESAR AVG. P. M. TR .P. IMP. P. P. S. C. Claudius seated
l. on curule chair amidst arms. *R.I.C. 109.* 130   450
See also under Category 4.

473   **Antonia,** mother of Claudius, died A.D. 37. Æ *dupondius*. TI. CLAVDIVS
CAESAR AVG P.M. TR. P. IMP. S. C. Claudius stg. l., holding simpulum.
R.I.C. 92. 100   275
See also under Category 4.

474   **Nero,** 54-68, emperor at the time of Queen Boudicca's rebellion in Britain.
N aureus. SALVS. Salus seated l. *R.I.C. 66.* 450   1,050

475   Æ *denarius*. IVPPITER CVSTOS. Jupiter seated l. *R.I.C. 53.* 85   250

476   Æ *sestertius*. ROMA S. C. Roma seated l., holding Victory and parazonium.
R.I.C. 274. 100   350

476A   Æ as. S. C. Victory hovering l., holding shield inscribed S. P. Q. R. *R.I.C. 312.*   50   125

477   **Galba,** 68-69. Æ *denarius*. S.P.Q.R. / OB / C.S. within oak-wreath. *R.I.C. 167.*   90   275

478   **Otho,** 69. Æ *denarius*. SECVRITAS P. R. Securitas stg. l. *R.I.C. 10.*   200   500

479   **Vitellius,** 69. Æ denarius. CONCORDIA P. R. Concordia seated l. *R.I.C. 90.*   90   275

480   **Vespasian,** 69-79, commanded Legio II in the Claudian invasion of Britain
(43) and appointed Agricola to governorship of the province in 77/8. *N aureus*.
ANNONA AVG. Annona seated l. *R.I.C. 131a* 500   1,200

481

481   Æ *denarius*. VICTORIA AVGVSTI. Victory advancing r., crowning standard.
R.I.C. 52. 22   65

481A   Æ *dupondius*. FELICITAS PVBLICA S. C. Felicitas stg. l. *R.I.C. 554...*   40   100

482   **Titus,** 79-81 (Caesar 69-79). Æ *denarius*. TR. P. IX. IMP. XV. COS. VIII.
P. P. Thunderbolt on throne. *R.I.C. 23a* 40   120

483 485

	F £	VF £

483 **Domitian,** 81-96 (Caesar 69-81), recalled Agricola in 83/4 and abandoned the conquest of northern Scotland (ca. 87). Æ *denarius*. IMP. XIX. COS. XIIII. CENS. P. P. P. Minerva stg. l., resting on spear. *R.I.C. 140.* 22 55

484 Æ *dupondius*. VIRTVTI AVGVSTI S. C. Virtus stg. r. *R.I.C. 393.* 30 75

484A Æ *as*. MONETA AVGVSTI S. C. Moneta stg. l. *R.I.C. 354b*................... 30 75

485 **Nerva,** 96-98. Æ *denarius*. AEQVITAS AVGVST. Aequitas stg. l. *R.I.C. 13.* 40 100

485A Æ *as*. LIBERTAS PVBLICA S. C. Libertas stg. l. *R.I.C. 86*.................... 55 140

486 **Trajan,** 98-117, established the northern frontier in Britain along the Tyne-Solway line (ca. 100). Æ *aureus*. P. M. TR. P. COS. VI. P. P. S. P. Q. R. Genius stg. l., holding patera and corn-ears. *R.I.C. 347*. 400 900

487 490

487 Æ *denarius*. COS. V. P. P. S. P. Q. R. OPTIMO PRINC. Military trophy. *R.I.C. 147*. 22 55

488 Æ *sestertius*. S. P. Q. R. OPTIMO PRINCIPI S. C. Spes walking l., holding flower. *R.I.C. 519*... 40 150

488A Æ *dupondius*. SENATVS POPVLVSQVE ROMANVS S. C. Emperor advancing between two trophies. *R.I.C. 676*.. 25 65

489 **Hadrian,** 117-138, visited Britain in 122 and initiated the construction of a fortified frontier line (Hadrian's Wall). Æ *aureus*. HISPANIA. Hispania reclining l. *R.I.C. 305*... 500 1,100

490 Æ *denarius*. P. M. TR. P. COS. III. Roma stg. l., holding Victory and spear. *R.I.C. 76*. 25 60

491 Æ *sestertius*. COS. III. S. C. Neptune stg. r., holding dolphin and trident, foot on prow. *R.I.C. 632*.. 50 175

491A Æ *as*. FELICITATI AVG COS. III. P. P. S. C. Galley travelling l. over waves. *R.I.C. 719*. 40 100
See also under Category 2.

492 **Sabina,** wife of Hadrian. Æ *denarius*. IVNONI REGINAE. Juno stg. l. *R.I.C. 395a*. 40 100

493 **Aelius Caesar,** heir of Hadrian, 136-138. Æ *denarius*. CONCORD. TR. POT. COS. II. Concordia seated l. *R.I.C. 436*... 75 200

493A Æ *as*. TR. POT. COS. II. S. C. Spes walking l., holding flower. *R.I.C. 1067*. 50 130

| | F | VF |
| | £ | £ |

494   **Antoninus Pius,** 138-161, ordered the expansion of the Roman province
      to include southern Scotland and constructed the Antonine Wall on the
      Forth-Clyde line (beginning ca. 143). An uprising in northern Britain in the
      150s results in a permanent withdrawal to the Hadrianic frontier early in
      the next reign. *N aureus*. COS. IIII. Togate emperor stg. l., holding globe.
      R.I.C. 233b.   350   750
495   *Æ denarius*. PIETATI AVG. COS. IIII. Pietas stg. l. between two children,
      holding two more in her arms. *R.I.C. 313c.*   20   50

496

496   *Æ sestertius*. SALVS AVG. S. C. Salus stg. l. at altar, feeding snake.
      R.I.C. 635.   32   120
496A *Æ dupondius*. TR. POT. XX. COS. IIII. S. C. Providentia stg. l., pointing
      at globe at her feet and holding sceptre. *R.I.C. 2025.*   24   60
      See also under Categories 2 and 3.
497   **Antoninus Pius and Marcus Aurelius Caesar.** *Æ denarius*. Obv. Laur.
      hd. of Antoninus Pius r. Rev. AVRELIVS CAESAR AVG PII F. COS. Bare
      hd. of young Marcus Aurelius r. *R.I.C. 417a.*   50   120

498   501

498   **Divus Antoninus Pius,** deified 161. *Æ denarius*. CONSECRATIO.
      Four-storeyed crematorium of Antoninus Pius. *R.I.C. 436.*   24   60
499   **Diva Faustina Senior,** wife of Antoninus Pius, deified 141. *Æ denarius*.
      AETERNITAS. Aeternitas stg. l., holding globe and billowing veil. *R.I.C. 351.*   20   50
499A *Æ sestertius*. AVGVSTA S. C. Ceres stg. l., holding two torches. *R.I.C. 1120.*   30   110
500   **Marcus Aurelius,** 161-180 (Caesar 139-161), re-established Hadrian's Wall
      as the permanent northern frontier of the province, ca. 163. *N aureus*.
      PROV. DEOR. TR. P. XV. COS. III. Providentia stg. l., holding globe and
      cornucopiae. *R.I.C. 19*..   400   900
501   *Æ denarius*. PIETAS AVG. Priestly emblems. *R.I.C. 424a.*   24   60
501A — SALVTI AVG. COS. III. Salus stg. l. at altar, feeding snake. *R.I.C. 222.*   20   55
502   *Æ sestertius*. CONCORD. AVGVSTOR. TR. P. XVI. COS. III. S. C. Marcus
      Aurelius and Lucius Verus stg. face to face, clasping hands. *R.I.C. 826.*..   35   120
502A *Æ as*. HONOS TR. POT. II. COS. II. S. C. Honos stg. r. *R.I.C. 1271a.*....   30   75

		F £	VF £

503   **Divus Marcus Aurelius,** deified 180. Æ *denarius*. CONSECRATIO.
Eagle stg. r. on altar. *R.I.C. 272.*   28   70

504   506A

504   **Faustina Junior,** daughter of Antoninus Pius, wife of Marcus Aurelius.
Æ *denarius*. FECVNDITAS. Fecunditas stg. r., holding sceptre and child.
R.I.C. 677.   20   50
504A   Æ *sestertius*. HILARITAS S. C. Hilaritas stg. l. *R.I.C. 1642.*   30   110
505   **Diva Faustina Junior,** deified 175. Æ *as*. S. C. Crescent and seven stars.
R.I.C. 1714.   30   75
506   **Lucius Verus,** 161-169. Æ denarius. PAX TR. P. VI. IMP. IIII. COS. II.
Pax stg. l. *R.I.C. 561.*   25   65
506A   Æ *dupondius*. TR. P. IIII. IMP. II. COS. II. S. C. Mars stg. r., resting on
spear and shield. *R.I.C. 1387.*   30   75
507   **Lucilla,** daughter of Marcus Aurelius, wife of Lucius Verus. Æ *denarius*.
IVNONI LVCINAE. Juno stg. l., holding child in swaddling clothes.
R.I.C. 771.   25   65
507A   Æ *sestertius*. PIETAS S. C. Pietas stg. l., altar at feet. *R.I.C. 1756.*   35   120
508   **Commodus,** 177-192 (Caesar 175-177), major warfare on the British
frontier early in the reign; situation restored by Ulpius Marcellus in 184/5,
followed by unrest in the British legions. Æ *denarius*. LIB. AVG. IIII. TR.
P. VI. IMP. IIII. COS. III. P. P. Liberalitas stg. l. *R.I.C. 22.*   20   50

509   511

509   Æ *sestertius*. IOVI VICTORI IMP. III. COS. II. P. P. S. C. Jupiter seated l.
R.I.C. 1612.   35   110
509A   Æ *as*. ANN. AVG. TR. P. VII. IMP. IIII. COS. III. P. P. S. C. Annona stg. l.,
modius at feet. *R.I.C. 339.*   24   60
See also under Category 2.
510   **Crispina,** wife of Commodus. Æ *denarius*. CONCORDIA. Clasped hands.
R.I.C. 279.   30   75
511   **Pertinax,** January-March 193, formerly governor of Britain, ca. 185-7. Æ
denarius. PROVID. DEOR. COS. II. Providentia stg l., reaching up to star.
R.I.C. 11a.   250   550

512   513A

		F £	VF £

512   **Didius Julianus,** March-June 193. Æ *denarius.* CONCORD MILIT.
Concordia Militum stg. l., holding standards. *R.I.C. 1.* 375   850

513   **Clodius Albinus,** 195-197 (Caesar 193-195), governor of Britain (from
191/2) at the time of his imperial proclamation by his troops. Æ *denarius.*
MINER. PACIF. COS. II. Minerva stg. l. *R.I.C. 7.* 55   125

513A   — FIDES LEGION. COS. II. Clasped hands holding legionary eagle.
R.I.C. 20b. 75   175

514   516

514   **Septimius Severus,** 193-211, restored the frontier forts in northern Britain
following the downfall of Clodius Albinus; later repaired Hadrian's Wall,
and spent the years 208-11 in Britain campaigning in Scotland; divided
Britannia into two provinces, Superior and Inferior; died at York, February
211. Æ *denarius.* VIRT AVGG. Roma stg. l., holding Victory, spear and
shield. *R.I.C. 171a* 15   35

514A   — P.M. TR. P. XVIII. COS. III. P. P. Jupiter stg. l. between two children.
R.I.C. 240. 15   35
See also under Category 2.

515   **Julia Domna,** wife of Septimius Severus, mother of Caracalla and Geta,
accompanied her husband and sons on the British expedition, 208-211, and
probably resided in London during the northern campaigns. Æ *denarius.*
VENERI VICTR. Venus stg. r., resting on column. *R.I.C. 536.* 15   40

515A   — VESTA. Vesta stg. l., holding palladium and sceptre. *R.I.C. 390.* 15   40

516   **Caracalla,** 198-217 (Caesar 196-198), accompanied his father and brother
on the British expedition, 208-211, and led the final campaign in Scotland
in 210 during Severus' illness; made frontier dispositions before returning
to Rome and finalized his father's arrangements for the division of Britain
into two provinces. Æ *antoninianus (double denarius,* introduced in 215).
VENVS VICTRIX. Venus stg. l., holding Victory and resting on shield.
R.I.C. 311c 25   65

517   Æ *denarius.* PART. MAX. PONT. TR. P. IIII. Trophy with two captives at
base. *R.I.C. 54b.* 15   40

517A   — P. M. TR. P. XV. COS. III. P. P. Hercules stg. l., holding olive-branch
and club. *R.I.C. 192* 15   35
See also under Category 2.

		F £	*VF* £

518 **Plautilla,** wife of Caracalla. Æ *denarius*. PROPAGO IMPERI. Caracalla
and Plautilla clasping hands. *R.I.C. 362.* 25 65

519   522A

519 **Geta,** 209-212 (Caesar 198-209), accompanied his father and brother on
the British expedition, 208-211, and took charge of the civil administration
in London during the northern campaigns. Æ *denarius*. PRINC. IVVENTVTIS.
Prince stg. l. beside trophy, holding branch and spear. *R.I.C. 18.*............. 20 50
519A — FORT RED TR. P. III. COS. II. Fortuna seated l. *R.I.C. 75.* 25 65
See also under Category 2.
520 **Macrinus,** 217-218. Æ *denarius*. PROVIDENTIA DEORVM. Providentia
stg. l., globe at feet. *R.I.C. 80.* 30 75
521 **Diadumenian,** 218 (Caesar 217-218). Æ *denarius*. PRINC. IVVENTVTIS.
Prince stg. l., two standards behind. *R.I.C. 109.* 70 175
522 **Elagabalus,** 218-222. Æ *antoninianus*. MARS VICTOR. Mars advamcing r.
R.I.C. 122. .... 22 55
522A Æ *denarius*. P. M. TR. P. III. COS. III. P. P. Jupiter seated l., eagle at feet
R.I.C. 27. .... 15 35
523 **Julia Paula,** first wife of Elagabalus. Æ *denarius*. CONCORDIA.
Concordia seated l. *R.I.C. 211*... 40 100
524 **Aquilia Severa,** second wife of Elagabalus. Æ *denarius*. CONCORDIA.
Concordia stg. l., altar at feet. *R.I.C. 226*... 60 150
525 **Julia Soaemias,** mother of Elagabalus. Æ *denarius*. VENVS CAELESTIS.
Venus seated l., child at feet. *R.I.C. 243.* 30 75
526 **Julia Maesa,** grandmother of Elagabalus and Severus Alexander. Æ
denarius. SAECVLI FELICITAS. Felicitas stg. l., altar at feet. *R.I.C. 271.* 22 55
527 **Severus Alexander,** 222-235 (Caesar 221-222). Æ *denarius*.
PAX AETERNA AVG. Pax stg. l. *R.I.C. 165*.. 15 35
527A — P. M. TR. P. XIII. COS. III. P. P. Sol advancing l., holding whip. *R.I.C. 123.* 15 35

528

528 Æ *sestertius*. MARS VLTOR S. C. Mars advancing r., with spear and shield.
R.I.C. 635. .... 25 75

	F	VF
	£	£

529   **Orbiana,** wife of Severus Alexander. Æ *denarius*. CONCORDIA AVGG.
Concordia seated l. *R.I.C. 319.* 70   175

530   **Julia Mamaea,** mother of Severus Alexander. Æ *denarius*. VESTA.
Vesta stg. l. *R.I.C. 362* 20   45

530A   Æ *sestertius*. FELICITAS PVBLICA S. C. Felicitas stg. facing, hd. l.,
resting on column. *R.I.C. 676.* 30   85

531

531   **Maximinus I,** 235-238. Æ *denarius*. PAX AVGVSTI. Pax stg. l. *R.I.C. 12.*   20   45

531A   Æ *sestertius*. SALVS AVGVSTI S. C. Salus seated l., feeding snake arising
from altar. *R.I.C. 85* 30   85

532   **Maximus Caesar,** son of Maximinus I. Æ *denarius*. PRINC IVVENTVTIS.
Prince stg. l., two standards behind. *R.I.C. 3.* 50   125

533   **Gordian I Africanus,** March-April 238, governor of Britannia Inferior
late in the reign of Caracalla. Æ *denarius*. P. M. TR. P. COS. P. P. Togate
emperor stg. l. *R.I.C. 1.* 250   600

534   **Gordian II Africanus,** March-April 238. Æ *denarius*. VIRTVS AVGG.
Virtus stg. l., with shield and spear. *R.I.C. 3.* 250   600

535   **Balbinus,** April-July 238. Æ *antoninianus*. FIDES MVTVA AVGG.
Clasped hands. *R.I.C. 11.* 75   175

535A   Æ *denarius*. PROVIDENTIA DEORVM. Providentia stg. l., globe at feet.
R.I.C. 7. 50   125

536   **Pupienus,** April-July 238. Æ *antoninianus*. AMOR MVTVVS AVGG.
Clasped hands. *R.I.C. 9a* 75   175

536A   Æ *denarius*. PAX PVBLICA. Pax seated l. *R.I.C. 4.* 50   120

537   **Gordian III,** 238-244 (Caesar 238). Æ *antoninianus*. LAETITIA AVG. N.
Laetitia stg. l. *R.I.C. 86.* 12   25

538   Æ *denarius*. DIANA LVCIFERA. Diana stg. r., holding torch. *R.I.C. 127.*   15   30

538A

538A   Æ *sestertius*. AETERNITATI AVG. S.C. Sol stg. l., holding globe. *R.I.C. 297a.*   22   65

539

		F £	VF £
539	**Philip I,** 244-249. Æ *antoninianus*. ROMAE AETERNAE. Roma seated l. *R.I.C. 65.*	12	25
539A	Æ *sestertius*. SECVRIT. ORBIS S. C. Securitas seated l. *R.I.C. 190.*	22	65
540	**Otacilia Severa,** wife of Philip I. Æ *antoninianus*. PIETAS AVGVSTAE. Pietas stg. l. *R.I.C. 125c.*	15	35
540A	Æ *sestertius*. CONCORDIA AVGG. S. C. Concordia seated l. *R.I.C. 203a.*	25	75
541	**Philip II,** 247-249 (Caesar 244-247). Æ *antoninianus*. PRINCIPI IVVENT. Prince stg. l., holding globe and spear. *R.I.C. 218d.*	15	35
541A	Æ *sestertius*. PAX AETERNA S. C. Pax stg. l. *R.I.C. 268c.*	25	75

542   543

542	**Trajan Decius,** 249-251. Æ *antoninianus*. DACIA. Dacia stg. l., holding staff with ass's hd. *R.I.C. 12b*	12	30
542A	Æ *sestertius*. PANNONIAE S. C. The two Pannoniae stg., each holding standard. *R.I.C. 124a*	25	75
543	**Herennia Etruscilla,** wife of Trajan Decius. Æ *antoninianus*. PVDICITIA AVG. Pudicitia stg. l. *R.I.C. 58b.*	15	35
544	**Herennius Etruscus,** 251 (Caesar 250-251). Æ *antoninianus*. PIETAS AVGG. Mercury stg. l., holding purse and caduceus. *R.I.C. 142b.*	25	65
545	**Hostilian,** 251 (Caesar 251). Æ *antoninianus*. PRINCIPI IVVENTVTIS. Apollo seated l., holding branch. *R.I.C. 180.*	35	85
546	**Trebonianus Gallus,** 251-253. Æ *antoninianus*. FELICITAS PVBLICA. Felicitas stg. l., resting on column. *R.I.C. 34A*	12	30
546A	Æ *sestertius*. SALVS AVGG S. C. Salus stg. r., feeding snake held in her arms. *R.I.C. 121a.*	25	75
547	**Volusian,** 251-253 (Caesar 251). Æ *antoninianus*. VIRTVS AVGG. Virtus stg. l. *R.I.C. 186*	12	30
548	**Aemilian,** 253. Æ *antoninianus*. PACI AVG. Pax stg. l., resting on column. *R.I.C. 8.*	50	120
549	**Valerian,** 253-260. Billon antoninianus. FIDES MILITVM. Fides stg. r., holding two standards. *R.I.C. 241*	8	20
550	**Diva Mariniana,** wife of Valerian, deified 253. Billon *antoninianus*. CONSECRATIO. Empress seated on peacock flying r. *R.I.C. 6.*	45	110

		F £	VF £

551 **Gallienus,** 253-268, during whose reign Rome temporarily lost control over Britain when Postumus rebelled and established the independent Gallic Empire in 260. Billon *antoninianus*. VIRT GALLIENI AVG. Emperor advancing r., captive at feet. *R.I.C. 54.* 10 25

552

552	— DIANAE CONS. AVG. Doe l. *R.I.C. 176*..	8	20
552A	— SOLI INVICTO. Sol stg. l., holding globe. *R.I.C. 658*.......................	8	18
553	**Salonina,** wife of Gallienus. Billon *antoninianus*. VENVS FELIX. Venus seated l., child at feet. *R.I.C. 7.*	8	20
553A	— IVNONI CONS. AVG. Doe l. *R.I.C. 16*...	8	20
554	**Valerian Junior,** son of Gallienus, Caesar 256-258. Billon *antoninianus*. IOVI CRESCENTI. Infant Jupiter seated on goat r. *R.I.C. 13*.................	15	35
555	**Divus Valerian Junior,** deified 258. Billon *antoninianus*. CONSECRATIO. Large altar. *R.I.C. 24.*	12	30
556	**Saloninus,** 260 (Caesar 258-260). Billon *antoninianus*. PIETAS AVG. Priestly emblems. *R.I.C. 9*..	12	30
557	**Macrianus,** usurper in the East, 260-261. Billon *antoninianus*. SOL. INVICTO. Sol stg. l., holding globe. *R.I.C. 12*..	35	85
558	**Quietus,** usurper in the East, 260-261. Billon *antoninianus*. INDVLGENTIAE AVG. Indulgentia seated l. *R.I.C. 5.*	35	85
559	**Postumus,** usurper in the West, 260-268, founder of the 'Gallic Empire' which temporarily detached Britain from the rule of the central government, a state of affairs which continued until Aurelian's defeat of Tetricus in 273. Billon *antoninianus*. HERC. DEVSONIENSI. Hercules stg. r. *R.I.C. 64.*	12	30

560

560	— MONETA AVG. Moneta stg. l. *R.I.C. 75*..	10	25
560A	Æ *sestertius*. FIDES MILITVM. Fides stg. l., holding two standards. *R.I.C. 128.*	50	140
561	**Laelianus,** usurper in the West, 268. Billon *antoninianus*. VICTORIA AVG. Victory advancing r. *R.I.C. 9*..	110	275
562	**Marius,** usurper in the West, 268. Billon *antoninianus*. CONCORDIA MILITVM. Clasped hands. *R.I.C. 7.*	35	85
563	**Victorinus,** usurper in the West, 268-270. Billon *antoninianus*. INVICTVS. Sol advancing l. *R.I.C. 114*..	8	20

		F	VF
		£	£
564	**Tetricus,** usurper in the West, 270-273, defeated by Aurelian, thus ending the 'Gallic Empire' and the isolation of Britain from the authority of Rome. Billon *antoninianus*. LAETITIA AVGG. Laetitia stg. l. *R.I.C. 87*...........	8	20
	See also under Category 4.		
565	**Tetricus Junior,** son of Tetricus, Caesar 270-273. Billon *antoninianus*. SPES PVBLICA. Spes walking l., holding flower *R.I.C. 272*.................	8	20
	See also under Category 4.		
566	**Claudius II Gothicus,** 268-270. Billon *antoninianus*. IOVI STATORI. Jupiter stg. r. *R.I.C. 52*...	8	18
567	**Divus Claudius II,** deified 270. Billon *antoninianus*. CONSECRATIO. Large altar. *R.I.C. 261*........	8	20
	See also under Category 4.		
568	**Quintillus,** 270. Billon *antoninianus*. DIANA LVCIF. Diana stg. r., holding torch. *R.I.C. 49*..........................	18	45
569	**Aurelian,** 270-275, restored Britain to the rule of the central government through his defeat of Tetricus in 273; possibly began construction of the chain of 'Saxon Shore' forts on the eastern and southern coastlines. Billon *antoninianus*. ORIENS AVG. Sol stg. l. between two captives. *R.I.C. 63*.	10	25
569A	— RESTITVT. ORBIS. Female stg. r., presenting wreath to emperor stg. l. *R.I.C. 399*.	10	25
570	**Aurelian and Vabalathus,** ruler of Palmyra 267-272 and usurper in the East from 271. Billon *antoninianus*. Obv. Laur. bust of Vabalathus r. Rev. Rad. bust of Aurelian r. *R.I.C. 381*..............	25	65

571   574A

571	**Severina,** wife of Aurelian. Billon *antoninianus*. PROVIDEN. DEOR. Concordia (or Fides) Militum stg. r., facing Sol stg. l. *R.I.C. 9*.	18	45
572	**Tacitus,** 275-276. Billon *antoninianus*. SECVRIT. PERP. Securitas stg. l., leaning on column. *R.I.C. 163*.	15	35
573	**Florian,** 276. Billon *antoninianus*. LAETITIA FVND. Laetitia stg. l. *R.I.C. 34*.	30	75
574	**Probus,** 276-282, suppressed governor's revolt in Britain and lifted restrictions on viticulture in Britain and Gaul. Billon *antoninianus*. ADVENTVS PROBI AVG. Emperor on horseback l., captive seated before. *R.I.C. 160*........................	10	25
574A	— VICTORIA GERM. Trophy between two captives. *R.I.C. 222*...........	15	40
575	**Carus,** 282-283. Billon *antoninianus*. PAX EXERCITI. Pax stg. l., holding olive-branch and standard. *R.I.C. 75*......................	15	40
576	**Divus Carus,** deified 283. Billon *antoninianus*. CONSECRATIO. Eagle facing, hd. l. *R.I.C. 28*.	18	45
577	**Carinus,** 283-285 (Caesar 282-283). Billon *antoninianus*. SAECVLI FELICITAS. Emperor stg. r. *R.I.C. 214*......................	12	30

	F £	VF £

578 **Magnia Urbica,** wife of Carinus. Billon *antoninianus*. VENVS VICTRIX. Venus stg. l., holding helmet, shield at feet. *R.I.C. 343.* 60 150

579 **Numerian,** 283-284 (Caesar 282-283). Billon *antoninianus*. CLEMENTIA TEMP. Emperor stg. r., receiving globe from Jupiter stg. l. *R.I.C. 463....* 12 35

580 **Diocletian,** 284-305. Æ *argenteus*. VIRTVS MILITVM. The four tetrarchs sacrificing before gateway of military camp. *R.I.C. 27a (Rome).* 100 250

581 Billon *antoninianus*. IOVI CONSERVAT AVGG. Jupiter stg. l. *R.I.C. 162.* 10 25

582 Æ *follis*. GENIO POPVLI ROMANI. Genius stg. l. R.I.C. 14a *(Alexandria).* 10 30

582A — (post-abdication coinage, after 305). PROVIDENTIA DEORVM QVIES AVGG. Quies and Providentia stg. facing each other. *R.I.C. 676a (Treveri).* 22 65
See also under Category 3.

583 **Maximian,** 286-305 and 306-308, failed in his attempts to suppress the usurpation of Carausius in Britain. Æ *argenteus*. VICTORIA SARMAT. The four tetrarchs sacrificing before gateway of military camp. *R.I.C. 37b (Rome).* 100 250

584

584 Billon *antoninianus*. SALVS AVGG. Salus stg. r., feeding snake held in her arms. *R.I.C. 417.* 8 20

585 Æ *follis*. SAC. MON. VRB. AVGG. ET CAESS. NN. Moneta stg. l. *R.I.C. 105b (Rome).* 12 35

585A — (second reign). CONSERVATORES VRB SVAE. Roma seated in hexastyle temple. *R.I.C. 84b (Ticinum)* 12 35
See also under Category 3.
*[For coins of the usurpers **Carausius** and **Allectus** see under Category 3]*

586 **Constantius I,** 305-306 (Caesar 293-305), invaded Britain 296 and defeated the usurper Allectus, thus restoring the island to the rule of the central government; Britain now divided into four provinces and the northern frontier defences reconstructed; died at York, July 306. Æ *argenteus*. PROVIDENTIA AVGG. The four tetrarchs sacrificing before gateway of military camp. *R.I.C. 11a (Rome).* 110 275

587

587 Æ *follis*. GENIO POPVLI ROMANI. Genius stg. l. *R.I.C. 26a (Aquileia).* 12 35

587A — SALVIS AVGG. ET CAESS. FEL. KART. Carthage stg. l., holding fruits. *R.I.C. 30a (Carthage).* 15 40
See also under Category 3.

588

		F	VF
		£	£

588 **Galerius,** 305-311 (Caesar 293-305). A argenteus. VIRTVS MILITVM.
The four tetrarchs sacrificing before gateway of military camp.
R.I.C. 15b (Ticinum).. 100 250

588A — XC / VI in wreath. *R.I.C. 16b (Carthage)*........................... 150 400

589 Æ *follis*. GENIO AVGG ET CAESARVM NN. Genius stg. l. *R.I.C. 11b*
(Cyzicus)... 12 35

589A — GENIO IMPERATORIS. Genius stg. l. *R.I.C. 101a (Alexandria)*...... 8 25
See also under Category 3.

590 **Galeria Valeria,** wife of Galerius. Æ *follis*. VENERI VICTRICI. Venus
stg. l. *R.I.C. 110 (Alexandria).* 35 85

591 **Severus II,** 306-307 (Caesar 305-306). Æ *follis*. FIDES MILITVM. Fides
seated l. *R.I.C. 73 (Ticinum)*.. 35 85
See also under Category 3.

592 **Maximinus II,** 310-313 (Caesar 305-310). Æ *follis*. GENIO CAESARIS.
Genius stg. l. *R.I.C. 64 (Alexandria)*... 8 25

592A — GENIO POP. ROM. Genius stg. l. *R.I.C. 845a (Treveri)*.................... 8 20
See also under Category 3.

593

593 **Maxentius,** 306-312 (Caesar 306). Æ *follis*. CONSERV. VRB. SVAE.
Roma seated in hexastyle temple. *R.I.C. 210 (Rome)*....................... 10 30

594 **Romulus,** son of Maxentius, deified 309. Æ *quarter follis*. AETERNAE
MEMORIAE. Temple with domed roof. *R.I.C. 58 (Ostia)*...................... 35 85

595 **Licinius,** 308-324. Æ *follis*. GENIO AVGVSTI. Genius stg. l. *R.I.C. 198b*
(Siscia). 8 20

595A Æ 3. IOVI CONSERVATORI AVGG. Jupiter stg. l. *R.I.C. 24 (Nicomedia).* 8 20
See also under Category 3.

596 **Licinius Junior,** son of Licinius, Caesar 317-324. Æ 3. CAESARVM
NOSTRORVM around wreath containing VOT. / V. *R.I.C. 92 (Thessalonica).* 8 22

597 **Constantine I, the Great,** 307-337 (Caesar 306-307), campaigned with
his father Constantius I against the Picts in northern Britain, summer 306,
and proclaimed emperor by the legions at York on Constantius' death
in July; closed the London mint early in 325 ending almost four decades
of operation. Æ *follis*. GENIO POP ROM. Genius stg. l. *R.I.C. 719b (Treveri)*. 12 35

598 — SOLI INVICTO COMITI. Sol stg. l. *R.I.C. 307 (Lugdunum)*............. 6 18

598A Æ 3. PROVIDENTIAE AVGG. Gateway of military camp. *R.I.C. 153*
(Thessalonica)... 5 15

599　　　　　　　　　　600

		F £	VF £

599　— VIRTVS EXERCIT. Trophy between two captives. *R.I.C. 280 (Treveri).*　　12　　30

599A　Æ 3/4. GLORIA EXERCITVS. Two soldiers stg. either side of two standards.
R.I.C. 518 (Treveri). ....　　4　　12
See also under Category 3.

600　'**Urbs Roma**', after 330. Æ 3/4. Obv. Helmeted bust of Roma l. Rev.
She-wolf l., suckling twins. *R.I.C. 195 (Nicomedia).* ....　　5　　15

601　　　　　　　　　　604

601　'**Constantinopolis**', after 330. Æ 3/4. Obv. Helmeted bust of
Constantinopolis l. Rev. Victory stg. l., foot on prow. *R.I.C. 339 (Rome).*　　5　　15

602　**Fausta**, wife of Constantine I. Æ 3. SALVS REIPVBLICAE. Empress
stg. l., holding two children. *R.I.C. 459 (Treveri).* ....　　18　　45
See also under Category 3.

603　**Helena**, mother of Constantine I. Æ 3. SECVRITAS REIPVBLICE.
Empress stg. l., holding branch. *R.I.C. 38 (Alexandria).* ....　　18　　40

603A　Æ 4 (posthumous issue, 337-340). PAX PVBLICA. Pax stg. l. *R.I.C. 78
(Treveri)* ....　　10　　25
See also under Category 3.

604　**Theodora**, second wife of Constantius I. Æ 4 (posthumous issue, 337-340).
PIETAS ROMANA. Pietas stg. r., holding child. R.I.C. 43 (Treveri). ......　　12　　30

605　**Crispus**, eldest son of Constantine I, Caesar 317-326. Æ 3. CAESARVM
NOSTRORVM around wreath containing VOT. / V. *R.I.C. 68 (Aquileia).*　　8　　20
See also under Category 3.

606　**Delmatius**, nephew of Constantine I, Caesar 335-337. Æ 3/4. GLORIA
EXERCITVS. Two soldiers stg. either side of two standards. *R.I.C. 90
(Antioch)* ....　　18　　45

607　**Hanniballianus**, nephew of Constantine I, Rex 335-337. Æ 4. SECVRITAS
PVBLICA. River-god Euphrates reclining r. *R.I.C. 147 (Constantinople).*　　100　　250

608　**Constantine II**, 337-340 (Caesar 317-337). Æ 3. BEATA
TRANQVILLITAS. Altar inscribed VOT / IS / XX. *R.I.C. 312 (Treveri).*　　8　　20

608A　Æ 3/4. GLORIA EXERCITVS. Two soldiers stg. either side of standard.
R.I.C. 392 (Rome). ....　　4　　10
See also under Category 3.

609　**Constans**, 337-350 (Caesar 333-337), visited Britain in 343, the last
reigning emperor to do so. Æ 2. FEL. TEMP. REPARATIO. Soldier r.,
dragging barbarian from hut beneath tree. *R.I.C. 103 (Aquileia).* ....　　10　　30

609A   611B

	F £	VF £
609A — FEL. TEMP. REPARATIO. Emperor stg. l. on galley steered by Victory. R.I.C. 219 (Treveri).	10	30
609B Æ 4. VICTORIAE DD. AVGG. Q. NN. Two Victories stg. face to face. R.I.C. 195 (Treveri).	4	10
610 **Constantius II,** 337-361 (Caesar 324-337). Æ 3/4. GLORIA EXERCITVS. Two soldiers stg. either side of two standards. R.I.C. 85 (Cyzicus).	4	12
611 Æ siliqua. VOTIS / XXX. / MVLTIS / XXXX. in wreath. R.I.C. 207 (Arelate).	25	60
611A Æ 2. FEL. TEMP. REPARATIO. Emperor stg. l. on galley. R.I.C. 218 (Treveri)	10	30
611B Æ 3. FEL. TEMP. REPARATIO. Soldier advancing l., spearing fallen horseman. R.I.C. 189 (Lugdunum).	5	15

See also under Categories 3 and 4.

612   616

612 **Magnentius,** usurper in the West, 350-353, temporarily detached Britain from the rule of the legitimate Constantinian dynasty. Æ 1. SALVS DD. NN. AVG. ET CAES. *Chi-Rho* Christian monogram between Alpha and Omega. R.I.C. 34 (Ambianum).	75	175
612A Æ 2. FELICITAS REIPVBLICE. Emperor stg. l., holding Victory and labarum. R.I.C. 264 (Treveri).	15	40

See also under Category 4.

613 **Decentius,** brother of Magnentius, Caesar 351-353. Æ 2. VICTORIAE DD. NN. AVG. ET CAE. Two Victories supporting between them shield inscribed VOT. / V. / MVLT. / X. R.I.C. 146 (Lugdunum).	20	50

See also under Category 4.

614 **Vetranio,** 'usurper' in the Balkans, 350. Æ 2. CONCORDIA MILITVM. Emperor stg. l., holding two labara. R.I.C. 281 (Siscia).	50	125
615 **Constantius Gallus,** Caesar under Constantius II, 351-354. Æ 2. FEL. TEMP. REPARATIO. Soldier advancing l., spearing fallen horseman. R.I.C. 94 (Cyzicus).	15	40
616 **Julian II,** 360-363 (Caesar 355-360). Æ siliqua. VOT. / X. / MVLT. / XX. in wreath. R.I.C. 309 (Arelate).	25	60

	F	VF
	£	£

617   Æ 1. SECVRITAS REIPVB. Bull stg. r. *R.I.C. 411 (Siscia).*   45   140

617A Æ 3. VOT. / X. / MVLT. / XX. in wreath. *R.I.C. 108 (Sirmium).*   8   25

618   **Jovian,** 363-364. Æ 3. VOT. / V. / MVLT. / X. in wreath. *R.I.C. 426 (Siscia).*   12   35

619   **Valentinian I,** 364-375 (in the West), during whose reign the Roman province of Britannia was devastated by the simultaneous attack of hordes of invaders on several fronts (the 'Barbarian Conspiracy'); order eventually restored by Count Theodosius, father of the future emperor . *N̄ solidus.* RESTITVTOR REIPVBLICAE. Emperor stg. r., holding standard and Victory. *R.I.C. 2b (Antioch).*   100   250

619A Æ 3. GLORIA ROMANORVM. Emperor advancing r., dragging barbarian and holding labarum. *R.I.C. 14a (Siscia).*   5   15

619B

619B — SECVRITAS REIPVBLICAE. Victory advancing l. *R.I.C. 32a (Treveri).*   5   15

620   **Valens,** 364-378 (in the East). *Ȑ siliqua.* VRBS ROMA. Roma seated l. *R.I.C. 27e (Treveri).*   25   60

620A Æ 3. SECVRITAS REIPVBLICAE. Victory advancing l. *R.I.C. 42b (Constantinople)*   5   15

621   **Procopius,** usurper in the East, 365-366. Æ 3. REPARATIO FEL. TEMP. Emperor stg. r., holding standard and shield. *R.I.C. 17a (Constantinople).*   50   125

622   **Gratian,** 367-383 (in the West), overthrown by Magnus Maximus who had been proclaimed emperor by the army in Britain. *Ȑ siliqua.* VRBS ROMA. Roma seated l. *R.I.C. 27f (Treveri).*   25   65

623   **Valentinian II,** 375-392 (in the West). Æ 2. REPARATIO REIPVB. Emperor stg. l., raising kneeling female figure. *R.I.C. 20c (Arelate).*   10   30

623A Æ 4. SALVS REIPVBLICAE. Victory advancing l., dragging barbarian. *R.I.C. 20a (Alexandria)*   4   12

624   **Theodosius I,** the Great, 379-395 (in the East), son of the Count Theodosius who had cleared Britain of barbarian invaders in the reign of Valentinian I; the Emperor Theodosiua twice restored Britain to the rule of the central government, by his defeat of the usurpers Magnus Maximus (in 388) and Eugenius (in 394). *Ȑ siliqua.* CONCORDIA AVGGG. Constantinopolis enthroned facing, foot on prow. *R.I.C. 55a (Treveri)*   30   75

624A

624A — VIRTVS ROMANORVM. Roma enthroned facing. *R.I.C. (Aquileia) 28d.*   30   75

624B Æ 2. VIRTVS EXERCIT. Emperor stg. r., foot on captive, holding labarum and globe. *R.I.C. 24b (Heraclea).*   12   35

	F	VF
	£	£

625   **Aelia Flaccilla,** wife of Theodosius I. Æ 2. SALVS REIPVBLICAE.
Victory seated r., inscribing Christian monogram on shield set on cippus.
R.I.C. 81 (Constantinople). 25   65

626   627

626   **Magnus Maximus,** usurper in the West, 383-388, proclaimed emperor
by the army in Britain, invaded Gaul, and overthrew the legitimate western
emperor Gratian; possibly reopened the London mint for a brief issue of
precious metal coinage (Rudyard Kipling presented a rather fanciful
version of his career in "Puck of Pook's Hill"). *Æ siliqua.* VIRTVS
ROMANORVM. Roma enthroned facing. *R.I.C. 84b (Treveri).* 30   75
See also under Category 3.

627   **Flavius Victor,** son of Magnus Maximus, co-emperor 387-388. Æ 4.
SPES ROMANORVM. Gateway of military camp. *RIC 55b (Aquileia).*   40   100

628   **Eugenius,** usurper in the West, 392-394, recognized in Britain until his
defeat by Theodosius the Great. *Æ siliqua.* VIRTVS ROMANORVM.
Roma seated l. on cuirass. *R.I.C. 106d (Treveri).* 120   275

629   **Arcadius,** 395-408 (in the East, co-emperor with his father Theodosius I
from 383). *Æ solidus.* VICTORIA AVGGG. Emperor stg. r., foot on
captive, holding standard and Victory. *R.I.C. 1205 (Milan).* 90   225

629A   631

629A   Æ 2. GLORIA ROMANORVM. Emperor stg. l., holding standard and
shield, captive at feet. *R.I.C. 41 (Antioch).* 15   40

630   **Honorius,** 395-423 (in the West, co-emperor with his father Theodosius I
and brother Arcadius from 393), this reign saw the end of Roman rule in
Britain following a succession of usurpations in the province, culminating
in that of Constantine III against whom the Britons rebelled in 409;
Honorius' celebrated 'Rescript' of the following year instructed the
provincials to look to their own defence as he was no longer able to assist
them. *N solidus.* VICTORIA AVGGG. Emperor stg. r., foot on captive,
holding standard and Victory. *R.I.C. 1287 (Ravenna).* 90   225

630A   *Æ siliqua.* VIRTVS ROMANORVM. Roma seated l. on cuirass.
R.I.C. 1228 (Milan). 35   85

631   **Constantine III,** usurper in the West, 407-411, proclaimed emperor by the
army in Britain, but his authority rejected by the Romano-Britons two years
later, thus effectively ending 366 years of Roman rule in Britain. *Æ siliqua.*
VICTORIA AVGGG. Roma enthroned l. *R.I.C. 1532 (Treveri).* 125   300

		F	*VF*
		£	£

632 **Valentinian III,** 425-455 (in the West), during whose reign the Saxon
conquest of the former Roman province commenced, following the final
unsuccessful appeal of the Romano-Britons for help addressed to the general
Aetius in 446. *N solidus*. VICTORIA AVGGG. Emperor stg. facing, foot
on human-headed serpent. *R.I.C. 2010 (Ravenna)*. 125 300

632A Æ 4. VOT. PVB. Gateway of military camp. *R.I.C. 2123 (Rome)*. 25 75

2. ISSUES WITH TYPES REFERRING SPECIFICALLY
TO THE PROVINCE OF BRITANNIA

Struck in Rome, unless otherwise indicated. These usually commemorate military operations in the
northern frontier region of the province or beyond.

633   635

		F	*VF*
		£	£

633 **Claudius,** A.D. 41-54. AV aureus, celebrating the early stages of the
Roman conquest of Britain which commenced in A.D. 43. DE BRITANN
on architrave of triumphal arch. *R.I.C. 33.* 900 2250

634 *Æ denarius*. Similar. *R.I.C. 34.* 275 650

634A *Æ didrachm* of Caesarea in Cappadocia. DE BRITANNIS. Emperor in
triumphal quadriga r. *R.I.C. 122*.. 300 750

635 **Hadrian,** 117-138. Æ as, commemorating the restoration of order in the
province following a serious uprising (or invasion) in the north, probably
early in the governorship of Q. Pompeius Falco (118-122). BRITANNIA
PONT. MAX. TR. POT. COS. III. S. C. Britannia seated facing on rock.
R.I.C. 577a. 125 325

636 *Æ sestertius,* commemorating Hadrian's visit to the province in 122, when
he planned and initiated the construction of the northern frontier system
which bears his name. ADVENTVI AVG. BRITANNIAE S.C. Emperor
and Britannia stg. either side of altar. *R.I.C. 882.* .... *Extremely rare*

637

637 — BRITANNIA S. C. Britannia seated facing, foot resting on rock.
R.I.C. 845. .... *Extremely rare*

	F	VF
	£	£

637A   Æ *dupondius* or as. *Similar. R.I.C. 846.* .... *Extremely rare*

638   Æ *sestertius*, commemorating Hadrian's attention to the legionary garrison strength of the province, principally his transfer of *VI Victrix* from Germany in 122. EXERC. BRITANNICVS S. C. Emperor on horseback r., addressing gathering of troops. *R.I.C. 912* .... *Extremely rare*

638A   — EXERC. BRITANNICVS S.C. Emperor stg. r. on tribunal, addressing gathering of troops. *R.I.C. 913.* .... *Extremely rare*

639   **Antoninus Pius,** 138-161. *N aureus*, commemorating the conquests in Scotland by the governor Q. Lollius Urbicus (138/9-142/3) at which time construction of the Antonine Wall was begun. BRITAN. IMPERATOR II. Victory stg. l. on globe. *R.I.C. 113.* 600   1500

640

640   Æ *sestertius*. BRITANNIA S. C. Britannia seated l. on rock, holding standard. *R.I.C. 742* 400   1000

641   — BRITAN. IMPERATOR II. S. C. Helmeted Britannia seated l., foot on rock. *R.I.C. 743.* 450   1200

642   — BRITAN. IMPERATOR II. S. C. Britannia seated l. on globe above waves, holding standard. *R.I.C. 744.* 500   1400

643   — BRITAN. IMPERATOR II. S. C. Victory stg. l. on globe. *R.I.C. 719.* 175   450

643A   — BRITANNIA IMPERATOR II. S. C. Britannia seated l. on rock, holding standard. *R.I.C. 745.* 450   1200

644   Æ *as.* IMPERATOR II. S. C. Victory hovering l., holding shield inscribed BRI / TAN. *R.I.C. 732* 90   225

645   Æ *dupondius*, commemorating the quelling of a serious uprising in the north, ca. 154/5, necessitating the evacuation of the recently constructed Antonine Wall in Scotland. BRITANNIA COS. IIII. S. C. Britannia seated l. on rock, shield and vexillum in background. *R.I.C. 930.* 75   185

| | *F* | *VF* |
| | £ | £ |

646   Æ *as*. Similar. *R.I.C. 934*   60   150

Many specimens of this type are carelessly struck on inadequate flans.
Moreover, they have been found in significant quantities on Romano-British
sites, notably in Coventina's Well at Carrawburgh fort on Hadrian's Wall,
raising the interesting possibility that they may have been issued from a
temporary mint in Britain. The style of the engraving is quite regular,
indicating that even if locally produced these coins would have been struck
from normal Roman dies brought to Britain especially for this purpose.
See under Category 3.

647   **Commodus,** 177-192. Æ *sestertius,* commemorating the victories in
Scotland of the governor Ulpius Marcellus in 184/5. These were in
retribution for a major barbarian invasion several years earlier resulting
in serious damage to Hadrian's Wall, which had been temporarily overrun,
and the defeat and death of an unknown governor. BRITT. P. M. TR. P.
VIIII. IMP. VII. COS. IIII. P. P. S. C. Britannia stg. l., holding curved
sword and helmet. *R.I.C. 437.* ....   *Extremely rare*

648

648   — VICT. BRIT. P. M. TR. P. VIIII. (or X.) IMP. VII. COS. IIII. P. P. S. C.
Victory seated r., about to inscribe shield. *R.I.C. 440, 452*   90   240

649

649   **Septimius Severus,** 193-211. *N aureus,* commemorating the success of
the punitive Roman campaigns in Scotland during 209 and 210 culminating
in the illness and death of Severus at York in Feb. 211. VICTORIAE BRIT.
Victory advancing l. *R.I.C. 334*   1200   3000

650   — VICTORIAE BRIT. Victory advancing r., leading child by hand.
R.I.C. 302.   1400   3500

651   Æ *denarius.* VICTORIAE BRIT. Victory advancing r. *R.I.C. 332*   35   75

651A   — VICTORIAE BRIT. Victory stg. facing beside palm-tree with shield
attached. *R.I.C. 336.*   40   85

651B   — VICTORIAE BRIT. Victory stg. l. *R.I.C. 333.*   40   85

651C   — VICTORIAE BRIT. Victory seated l., holding shield. *R.I.C. 335.*   40   80

652

		F	VF
		£	£
652	Æ *sestertius*. VICTORIAE BRITTANNICAE S. C. Two Victories placing shield on palm-tree with captives at base. *R.I.C. 818*.	300	750
653	— P. M. TR. P. XVIII. COS. III. P. P. S. C. Similar. *R.I.C. 796*.	150	375
654	Æ *dupondius*. VICT. BRIT. P. M. TR. P. XIX. COS. III. P. P. S. C. Victory stg. r. between two captives, holding vexillum. *R.I.C. 809*	100	275
655	Æ *as*. VICTORIAE BRITTANNICAE S. C. Similar. *R.I.C. 837a*.	100	275
656	Billon *tetradrachm* of Alexandria in Egypt. NEIKH KATA BRET. Nike flying l. *Milne 2726*	*Extremely rare*	
657	**Caracalla,** 198-217. *N aureus*, commemorating the victories achieved by the Romans in Scotland during the campaigns led jointly by Severus and Caracalla in 209, and by Caracalla alone the following year during his father's illness. VICTORIAE BRIT. Victory seated l., holding shield. *R.I.C. 174*.	1200	3000

658   659A

658	Æ *denarius*. VICTORIAE BRIT. Victory advancing l. *R.I.C. 231*	40	80
658A	— VICTORIAE BRIT. Victory advancing r., holding trophy. *R.I.C. 231A*.	40	80
659	Æ *sestertius*. VICTORIAE BRITTANNICAE S. C. Victory stg. r., erecting trophy to r. of which Britannia stands facing, captive at feet. *R.I.C. 464*.	250	650
659A	— VICT. BRIT. TR. P. XIIII. COS. III. S.C. Similar. *Cf. R.I.C. 483c*	225	550
660	Æ *dupondius*. VICTORIAE BRITTANNICAE S. C. Victory stg. r., inscribing shield set on palm-tree. *R.I.C. 467*.	100	275
661	Æ *as*. VICT. BRIT. TR. P. XIIII. COS. III. S. C. Similar. *R.I.C. 490*.	100	250
662	**Geta,** 209-212. Æ *denarius*, commemorating the victories achieved by his father and brother in Scotland in 209-10 while he and his mother were resident in London. VICTORIAE BRIT. Victory stg. l. *R.I.C. 92*.	40	85
662A	— VICTORIAE BRIT. Victory advancing r. *R.I.C. 91*	40	85

663

	F £	VF £

663 Æ *sestertius*. VICTORIAE BRITTANNICAE S. C. Victory seated r.,
inscribing shield set on knee. *R.I.C. 166*.. 250 650
663A — VICT. BRIT. TR. P. III. COS. II. S. C. Similar. *R.I.C. 172b*................ 225 550
664 Æ *as*. VICTORIAE BRITTANNICAE S. C. Victory seated l., balancing
shield on knee. *R.I.C. 191a*. 100 275
665 Billon *tetradrachm* of Alexandria in Egypt. NEIKH KATA BRETAN.
Nike advancing l. *B.M.C. (Alexandria) 1481*. .... *Extremely rare*

3. OFFICIAL ROMAN COINAGE STRUCK IN BRITAIN

The London mint, and the associated 'C' mint (possibly Colchester), were created by the usurper Carausius soon after his seizure of Britain in 287. Prior to this, in the mid-2nd century, there may have been minting of 'Britannia' asses of Antoninus Pius in the province using dies brought from Rome, though this has not been firmly established. After the downfall of the rebel British regime in 296 the minting establishment in London (though not the subsidiary mint) was retained by the tetrarchal government and the succeeding Constantinian administration. Early in 325, however, Constantine the Great closed the London mint after almost four decades of operation. A possible brief revival under the usurper Magnus Maximus has been postulated for gold and silver coins marked 'AVG', 'AVGOB' and 'AVGPS', though the attribution has not received universal acceptance.

	F £	VF £

666 **Antoninus Pius,** 138-161. Æ *as*, struck in northern Britain (?) in 155.
BRITANNIA COS. IIII. S. C. Britannia seated l. on rock, shield and
vexillum in background. *R.I.C. 930*. 50 125
*Many poorly struck examples of this type have been found on Romano-
British sites, notably at Brocolitia (Carrawburgh) fort on Hadrian's Wall
in Northumberland, where no fewer than 327 specimens were discovered
in the great votive deposit in the well which formed part of the shrine of the
water-nymph Coventina. There appears to be a very real possibility that
many of these 'Britannia' asses had been issued from a temporary mint in
Britain, most likely situated in the north. The dies, however, are quite regular,
and would thus have been brought from Rome to the island province for the
express purpose of supplementing the money supply at a time of crisis.*
667 **Carausius,** usurper in Britain and northwestern Gaul, A.D. 287-293. *N*
aureus, London. CONSERVAT. AVG. Jupiter stg. l., eagle at feet, ML in
ex. *R.I.C. 1*. 5000 12500
668 *R denarius*, London. EXPECTATE VENI. Britannia stg. r. and emperor l.,
clasping hands, RSR in ex. *R.I.C. 555*. 450 1200

669   672A

		F	VF
		£	£
669	— RENOVAT. ROMANO. She-wolf r., suckling twins, RSR in ex. *R.I.C. 571.*	400	1000
670	Billon *antoninianus*, London. COMES AVG. Victory stg. l., S—P in field, ML in ex. *R.I.C. 14.*	40	100
670A	— HILARITAS AVG. Hilaritas stg. l., B—E in field, MLXXI in ex. *R.I.C. 41.*	25	60
671	— LAETITIA AVG. Laetitia stg. l., F—O in field, ML in ex. *R.I.C. 50.*	25	60
671A	— LEG. II. AVG. Capricorn l., ML in ex. *R.I.C. 58.*	70	175
	Legio II Augusta was stationed at Isca (Caerleon in South Wales).		
672	— LEG. II. XX. V. V. Boar stg. r. *R.I.C. 82.*	70	175
	Legio XX Valeria Victrix was stationed at Deva (Chester in the northwest Midlands).		
672A	— PAX AVG. Pax stg. l., F—O in field, ML in ex. *R.I.C. 101*	22	55
673	— Similar, but without mint mark. *R.I.C. 880.*	20	50
673A	— PROVIDENT. AVG. Providentia stg. l., B—E in field, MLXXI in ex. *R.I.C. 149.*	25	60
674	— SALVS AVGGG. Salus stg. r., feeding snake held in her arms, S—P in field, ML in ex. *R.I.C. 164.*	25	65
	The reverse legends with triple-ending (AVGGG.) presumably are subsequent to Carausius' recognition by Diocletian and Maximian in 289 following the failure of the latter's attempt to dislodge the usurper from his island stronghold.		
674A	— TEMPORVM FELICITAS. Felicitas stg. l., B—E in field, ML in ex. *R.I.C. 172.*	20	60
675	— VIRTVS AVGGG. Mars (or Virtus) stg. r., holding spear and shield, S—P in field, MLXXI in ex. *R.I.C. 183.*	25	65
676	Billon *antoninianus*, Colchester (?). CONCORDIA MILIT. Emperor stg. r. and Concordia l., clasping hands, C in ex. *R.I.C. 205.*	50	120
676A	— EXPECTATE VENI. Britannia stg. r. and emperor l., clasping hands, MSC in ex. *R.I.C. 216.*	100	250
677	— FELICITAS AVG. Galley with mast and rowers, CXXI in ex. *R.I.C. 221.*	80	200
677A	— FORTVNA RAEDVX. Fortuna seated l., SPC in ex. *R.I.C. 237*	40	100
678	— LAETITIA AVG. Laetitia stg. l., globe at feet, S—P in field, C in ex. *R.I.C. 255.*	25	60
678A	— MONETA AVG. Moneta stg. l., CXXI in ex. *R.I.C. 287.*	25	60
679	— ORIENS AVG. Sol stg. l., C in ex. *R.I.C. 293.*	30	75
679A	— PAX AVGGG. Pax stg. l., S—P in field, MC in ex. *R.I.C. 335.*	25	60

680

		F	VF
		£	£
680	— PROVID. AVG. Providentia stg. l., S—P in field, C in ex. *R.I.C. 353*.	25	60
680A	— SALVS AVG. Salus stg. l. at altar, feeding snake, S—C in field, C in ex. *R.I.C. 396*.	25	60
681	— SPES PVBLICA. Spes walking l., holding flower, S—P in field, C in ex. *R.I.C. 413*	25	60
681A	— VICTORIA AVG. Victory advancing l., captive at feet, MC in ex. *R.I.C. 429.*	30	75
682	**Carausius, Diocletian and Maximian,** after 289. Billon *antoninianus,* Colchester (?). Obv. CARAVSIVS ET FRATRES SVI. Conjoined busts of the three emperors l. Rev. PAX AVGGG. Pax stg. l., S—P in field, C in ex. *R.I.C. 1*	800	2000

682A 684A

682A	— MONETA AVGGG. Moneta stg. l., S—P in field, C in ex. *R.I.C. —.*. *See also nos. 693-4 and 698-700 as well as regular Carausian types with the triple-ending 'AVGGG.' on reverse.*	1000	2500
683	**Allectus,** usurper in Britain, 293-296. *N aureus,* London. ORIENS AVG. Sol stg. l. between two captives, ML in ex. *R.I.C. 4.*	7000	17500
684	Æ *antoninianus,* London. LAETITIA AVG. Laetitia stg. l., S—A in field, MSL in ex. *R.I.C. 22.*	25	65
684A	— PAX AVG. Pax stg. l., S—A in field, ML in ex. *R.I.C. 28.*	30	70
685	— PROVID. AVG. Providentia stg. l., holding globe and cornucopiae, S—P in field, ML in ex. *R.I.C. 36*	30	75
685A	— SALVS AVG. Salus stg. r., feeding snake held in her arms, S—A in field, MSL in ex. *R.I.C. 42.*	25	65
686	— TEMPOR. FELICITAS. Felicitas stg. l., S—A in field, ML in ex. *R.I.C. 47.*	25	60
686A	— VICTORIA AVG. Victory advancing l., S—P in field, ML in ex. *R.I.C. 48.*	25	60
687	Æ *antoninianus,* Colchester (?). AEQVITAS AVG. Aequitas stg. l., S—P in field, C in ex. *R.I.C. 63.*	25	65
687A	— FIDES MILITVM. Fides stg. l., holding two standards, S—P in field, C in ex. *R.I.C. 69*	25	65

688A

		F £	VF £

688 — LAETITIA AVG. Laetitia stg. l., S—P in field, CL in ex. *R.I.C. 79.*... 40 100
This form of mint mark has given rise to the alternative identification of this mint as Clausentum (Bitterne, Hants.)
688A — MONETA AVG. Moneta stg. l., S—P in field, C in ex. *R.I.C. 82.* 35 85
689 — PAX AVG. Pax stg. l., S—P in field, C in ex. *R.I.C. 86*....................... 30 70
689A — PROVIDENTIA AVG. Providentia stg. l., globe at feet, S—P in field, C in ex. *R.I.C. 111.* 25 65
690 — TEMPORVM FELIC. Felicitas stg. l., S—P in field, CL in ex. *R.I.C. 117.* 40 100
690A — VIRTVS AVG. Mars stg. r., holding spear and shield, S—P in field, C in ex. *R.I.C. 121*............. 25 65
691 Æ *'quinarius'*, London. VIRTVS AVG. Galley l., QL in ex. *R.I.C. 55.* ... 25 65
An experimental denomination issued only during this reign, the types of the so-called 'quinarius' would seem to indicate that it was in some way associated with the operations of the fleet upon which the survival of the rebel regime in Britain was totally dependent.

692   693

692 Æ *'quinarius'*, Colchester (?). LAETITIA AVG. Galley r., QC in ex. *R.I.C. 124.* 25 65
692A — VIRTVS AVG. Galley l., QC in ex. *R.I.C. 128.*.................. 30 70
693 **Diocletian,** 284-305. Billon *antoninianus* of London, struck by Carausius between 289 and 293. PAX AVGGG. Pax stg. l., S—P in field, MLXXI in ex. *R.I.C. 9.* 35 85
694 Billon *antoninianus* of Colchester (?), same date. PROVID AVGGG. Providentia stg. l., globe at feet, S—P in field, C in ex. *R.I.C. 22*............ 35 85

695

	F	VF
	£	£

695   Æ *follis*, London. GENIO POPVLI ROMANI. Genius stg. l., LON in ex.
R.I.C. 1a.   100   250
*By the time the central government had recovered control of Britain in 296
the antoninianus had been replaced by the larger follis under Diocletian's
sweeping currency reform. London was retained as an official imperial
mint, but the secondary British establishment (at Colchester?) was now
abandoned. Except for its initial issue in 297 (marked 'LON') the London
mint under the tetrarchic government produced only unsigned folles
throughout its first decade of operation. Perhaps Constantius did not
wish to draw attention to his employment of a mint which had been the
creation of a rebel regime.*

696

696   — Similar, but without mint mark. *R.I.C. 6a*..   10   25
697   — (post-abdication coinage, after 305). PROVIDENTIA DEORVM
QVIES AVGG. Quies and Providentia stg. facing each other (no mint mark).
R.I.C. 77a.   25   55
697A — QVIES AVGG. Quies stg. l., holding branch and sceptre, PLN in ex.
R.I.C. 98.   18   45
698   **Maximian,** 286-305 and 306-308. *N aureus* of London, struck by
Carausius between 289 and 293. SALVS AVGGG. Salus stg. r., feeding
snake held in her arms, ML in ex. *R.I.C. 32.* ....   *Extremely rare*
699   Billon *antoninianus* of London, same date. PROVIDENTIA AVGGG.
Providentia stg. l., S—P in field, MLXXI in ex. *R.I.C. 37.*   35   85
700   Billon *antoninianus* of Colchester (?), same date. PAX AVGGG. Pax stg.
l., S—P in field, C in ex. *R.I.C. 42*..   35   85
701   Æ *follis*, London. GENIO POPVLI ROMANI. Genius stg. l., LON in ex.
R.I.C. 2.   100   250
702   — Similar, but without mint mark. *R.I.C. 23b*..   10   25
703   — (post-abdication coinage, after 305). PROVIDENTIA DEORVM
QVIES AVGG. Quies and Providentia stg. facing each other (no mint mark).
R.I.C. 77b.   25   55

704

		F	*VF*
		£	£
704	— (second reign). GENIO POP. ROM. Genius stg. l., PLN in ex. *R.I.C. 90.*	15	35
704A	— HERCVLI CONSERVATORI. Hercules stg. l., resting on club, PLN in ex. *R.I.C. 91.*	25	65
705	**Constantius I,** 305-306 (Caesar 293-305). Æ *follis,* London (as Caesar). GENIO POPVLI ROMANI. Genius stg. l., LON in ex. *R.I.C. 4a.*	110	275

706

706	— Similar, but without mint mark. *R.I.C. 30.*	12	30
707	— (as Augustus). Similar. *R.I.C. 52a.*	15	40
708	**Divus Constantius I,** deified 306. Æ *follis,* London. MEMORIA FELIX. Altar flanked by eagles, PLN in ex. *R.I.C. 110.*	18	45
709	**Galerius,** 305-311 (Caesar 293-305). Æ *follis,* London (as Caesar). GENIO POPVLI ROMANI. Genius stg. l., LON in ex. *R.I.C. 4b.*	110	275
710	— Similar, but without mint mark. *R.I.C. 15.*	10	25
711	— (as Augustus). Similar. *R.I.C. 42.*	12	30
711A	— GENIO POP. ROM. Genius stg. l., PLN in ex. *R.I.C. 86.*	18	45
712	**Severus II,** 306-307 (Caesar 305-306). Æ *follis,* London (as Caesar). GENIO POPVLI ROMANI. Genius stg. l. (no mint mark). *R.I.C. 58a*	35	85
713	— (as Augustus). Similar. *R.I.C. 52c.*	35	85
714	**Maximinus II,** 310-313 (Caesar 305-310). Æ *follis,* London (as Caesar). GENIO POPVLI ROMANI. Genius stg. l. (no mint mark). *R.I.C. 57.*	15	40
715	— GENIO POP. ROM. Genius stg. l., PLN in ex. *R.I.C. 89a.*	15	40
716	— (as Augustus). Similar, but with star in r. field. *R.I.C. 209b.*	12	30
717	**Licinius,** 308-324. Æ *follis,* London. GENIO POP. ROM. Genius stg. l., star in r. field, PLN in ex. *R.I.C. 209c.*	12	30
717A	— Similar, but with S—F in field. *R.I.C. 3.*	8	20
718	— SOLI INVICTO COMITI. Sol stg. l., holding globe, S—P in field, MSL in ex. *R.I.C. 79.*	10	25
719	**Constantine I, the Great,** 307-337 (Caesar 306-307). Æ *follis,* London (as Caesar). GENIO POPVLI ROMANI. Genius stg. l. (no mint mark). *R.I.C. 72.*	25	65
719A	— GENIO POP. ROM. Genius stg. l., PLN in ex. *R.I.C. 88b*	15	35

	F	*VF*
	£	£

720 — PRINCIPI IVVENTVTIS. Prince stg. l., holding standards, PLN in ex.
      R.I.C. 97.   25   60
721 — (as Augustus). ADVENTVS AVG. Emperor on horseback l., captive
      on ground before, star in r. field, PLN in ex. *R.I.C. 133.*   22   55

722

722   — COMITI AVGG. NN. Sol stg. l., holding globe and whip, same mint
       mark. *R.I.C. 155.*   18   45
723   — CONCORD. MILIT. Concordia stg. l., holding standards, same mint
       mark. *R.I.C. 195.*   15   40
724   — MARTI CONSERVATORI. Mars. stg. r., holding spear and shield,
       star in l. field, PLN in ex. *R.I.C. 254.*   15   35
724A — SOLI INVICTO COMITI. Sol stg. l., holding globe, S—F in field,
       MLL in ex. *R.I.C. 27.*   8   20
725   Æ 3, London. VICTORIAE LAETAE PRINC. PERP. Two Victories
       supporting shield, inscribed VOT. / P. R., over altar, PLN in ex. *R.I.C. 159.* 10   25
726   — VIRTVS EXERCIT. Vexillum, inscribed VOT. / XX., between two
       captives, PLN in ex. R.I.C. 191.   10   25
727   — BEAT. TRANQLITAS. Altar, inscribed VOT / IS / XX., surmounted
       by globe and three stars, PLON in ex. *R.I.C. 267.*   8   20
727A — SARMATIA DEVICTA. Victory advancing r., trampling captive,
       PLON and crescent in ex. *R.I.C. 289.*   18   45
728   — PROVIDENTIAE AVGG. Gateway of military camp, PLON in ex.
       R.I.C. 293.   8   20
729   **Fausta,** wife of Constantine I. Æ 3, London. SALVS REIPVBLICAE.
       Empress stg. l., holding two children, PLON in ex. *R.I.C. 300.*   60   150
730   **Helena,** mother of Constantine I. Æ 3, London. SECVRITAS REIPVBLICE.
       Empress stg. l., holding branch, PLON in ex. *R.I.C. 299.*   60   150
731   **Crispus,** eldest son of Constantine I, Caesar 317-326. Æ 3, London.
       SOLI INVICTO COMITI. Sol stg. l., holding globe, crescent in l. field,
       PLN in ex. *R.I.C. 144.*   12   30
731A — VIRTVS EXERCIT. Vexillum, inscribed VOT. / XX., between two
       captives, PLN in ex. *R.I.C. 194.*   12   30
732   — BEATA TRANQVILLITAS. Altar, inscribed VOT / IS / XX.,
       surmounted by globe and three stars, P—A in field, PLON in ex. *R.I.C. 211.* 10   25
733   — CAESARVM NOSTRORVM around wreath containing VOT. / X.,
       PLON and crescent in ex. *R.I.C. 291.*   10   25

734 737A

	F £	VF £

734 — PROVIDENTIAE CAESS. Gateway of military camp, PLON in ex.
R.I.C. 295. .... 10 25

735 **Constantine II,** 337-340 (Caesar 317-337). Æ 3, London (as Caesar).
CLARITAS REIPVBLICAE. Sol stg. l., holding globe, crescent in l. field,
PLN in ex. *R.I.C. 131* 12 30

736 — VICTORIAE LAETAE PRINC. PERP. Two Victories supporting shield,
inscribed VOT. / P. R., over altar ornamented with wreath, PLN in ex.
R.I.C. 182. .... 12 30

737 — VIRTVS EXERCIT. Vexillum, inscribed VOT. / XX., between two
captives, PLON in ex. *R.I.C. 190.* 12 30

737A — BEATA TRANQVILLITAS. Altar, inscribed VOT / IS / XX.,
surmounted by globe and three stars, PLON in ex. *R.I.C. 236.* 10 25

738 — CAESARVM NOSTRORVM around wreath containing VOT. / X.,
PLON and crescent in ex. *R.I.C. 292.* 10 25

738A — PROVIDENTIAE CAESS. Gateway of military camp, PLON in ex.
R.I.C. 296. .... 10 25

739 **Constantius II,** 337-361 (Caesar 324-337). Æ 3, London (as Caesar).
PROVIDENTIAE CAESS. Gateway of military camp, PLON in ex.
R.I.C. 298. .... 25 60

740 **Magnus Maximus,** usurper in the West, 383-388. *N solidus,* London (?).
RESTITVTOR REIPVBLICAE. Emperor stg. r., holding labarum and
Victory, AVG in ex. *R.I.C. 1* .... *Unique*
*The attribution to London of this rare series has not been firmly established,
though Maximus was certainly proclaimed emperor in Britain and it is
well attested that the principal city of the British provinces bore the name
'Augusta' in the late Roman period (Ammianus Marcellinus XXVII, 8, 7;
XXVIII, 3, 7).*

741

741 — VICTORIA AVGG. Two emperors enthroned facing, Victory hovering
in background between them, AVGOB in ex. *R.I.C. 2b* 5000 10000
*Maximus appears to have struck a similar type in the name of the eastern
emperor Theodosius I (cf. R.I.C. 2a), though it is presently known only
from a silver-gilt specimen preserved in the British Museum.*

| | F | VF |
| | £ | £ |

742   Æ *siliqua*, London (?). VOT. / V. / MVLT. / X. within wreath, AVG below.
      R.I.C. 4.   850   2000
742A — VICTORIA AVGG. Victory advancing l., AVGPS in ex. *R.I.C. 3.*   750   1750

4. IMITATIONS OF ROMAN COINS PRODUCED IN BRITAIN

At certain periods during the three and a half centuries of its occupation Roman Britain seems to have been the source of much local imitation of the official imported coinage. This began soon after the Claudian invasion in A.D. 43 when significant quantities of sestertii, dupondii and asses (especially the last) were produced in the newly conquered territory, as evidenced by the frequency of their occurrence in archaeological finds. The technical excellence of many of these 'copies', together with the surprising extent of their minting, would seem to indicate that some, at least, of these coins were produced with official sanction in order to make good an unexpected deficiency in the currency supply. Others are much poorer and well below weight, representing the 'unofficial' branch of this operation, some of it probably emanating from territory as yet unconquered. As conditions in the new province settled down rapid Romanization and urbanization of British society brought a general increase in wealth, and with it a much greater volume of currency flowing into the country. Local imitation now virtually ceased, except for the occasional activities of criminal counterfeiters, and this state of affairs lasted down to the great political crisis and financial collapse of the second half of the 3rd century. At this point large scale minting of imitations of the debased antoniniani of the late 260s and early 270s began in Britain and in the other northwestern provinces, all of which had been serioulsy affected by the political dislocation of this turbulent era. This class of imitations is usually referred to as 'barbarous radiates', the emperor's spiky crown being a constant and conspicuous feature of the obverses. Most frequently copied were the antoniniani of the Gallic rulers Tetricus Senior and Tetricus Junior (ca. 270-273) and the posthumous issues of Claudius Gothicus (died 270). The quality of the 'barbarous radiates' is variable in the extreme, some exhibiting what appears to be a revival of Celtic art forms, others so tiny that it is virtually impossible to see anything of the design. Their production appears to have ended abruptly with Aurelian's reconquest of the western provinces in 273. A similar phenomenon, though on a lesser scale, occurred in the middle decades of the following century when normal life in Britain was again disrupted, not only by usurpation but additionally by foreign invasion. With supplies of currency from the Continent temporarily disrupted local imitation, particularly of the 'Æ 2' and 'Æ 3' issues of Constantius II and the usurper Magnentius, began in earnest. How long this continued is difficult to determine as life in the island province was now subject to increasingly frequent episodes of dislocation. By now urban life in Britain was in serious decline and when Roman rule ended early in the 5th century, bringing a total cessation of currency supplies, the catastrophic decline in monetary commerce in the former provinces rendered it no longer necessary for the deficiency to be made good.

| | F | VF |
| | £ | £ |

743   **Agrippa,** died 12 B.C. Æ as, of irregular British mintage, imitating the
      Roman issue made under Agrippa's grandson Caligula, A.D. 37-41.
      S. C. Neptune stg. l., holding dolphin and trident.   40   100
      The large official issue of Agrippa asses was made shortly before the
      Claudian invasion of Britain in A.D. 43 and would thus have comprised
      a significant proportion of the 'aes' in circulation at this time. In
      consequence, it would soon have become familiar to the new provincials
      providing an ideal prototype for imitation.
744   **Claudius,** 41-54. Æ *sestertius*, of irregular British mintage. SPES
      AVGVSTA S. C. Spes walking l., holding flower.   75   250
745   Æ *dupondius*, of irregular British mintage. CERES AVGVSTA S. C.
      Ceres enthroned l., holding corn- ears and torch.   35   100

746

	F £	VF £

746 Æ *as,* of irregular British mintage. S. C. Minerva advancing r., brandishing
spear and holding shield.. 30   85
*This is by far the commonest of the Claudian imitations and the prototypes
must have represented the bulk of the aes coinage carried by the legions at
the time of the invasion. The martial type may well have been specially
selected as a suitable theme for the initial import of coinage into the newly
conquered territory.*

747 **Nero Claudius Drusus,** father of Claudius, died 9 B.C. Æ *sestertius,* of
irregular British mintage. TI. CLAVDIVS CAESAR AVG. P. M. TR .P.
IMP. S. C. Claudius seated l. on curule chair amidst arms 85 300
*This type was issued by Claudius half a century after his father's death and
would thus have been prominently represented in the initial wave of coinage
imported into the new province.*

748 **Antonia,** mother of Claudius, died A.D. 37. Æ *dupondius,* of irregular British
mintage. TI. CLAVDIVS CAESAR AVG P.M. TR. P. IMP. P. P. S. C. Claudius
stg. l., holding simpulum.. 60 175
*Another Claudian issue for a deceased parent, this represents one of only
two dupondius types struck during this reign and would have entered
Britain in significant quantities at the time of the invasion in A.D. 43.*

749A   749B

749C

749 **'Barbarous radiates',** ca. 270-273. British and Continental imitations of
billon *antoniniani,* principally of Divus Claudius II (A), Tetricus Senior
(B) and Tetricus Junior (C). The inscriptions are usually blundered and
the types sometimes unrecognizable. British mintage can only be
established by provenance. 5   10

	F	VF
	£	£

750   **Barbarous 4th century,** mostly of the second half of the century, and
      principally imitated from 'Æ 2' and 'Æ 3' issues of the later Constantinian
      period, notably those of Constantius II ('soldier spearing fallen horseman'
      type), and the usurpers Magnentius and Decentius ('two Victories' type).
      The copies, especially those of Magnentius and Decentius, are often of
      excellent style and execution, though the legends frequently contain small
      errors. Those of Constantius II are sometimes very barbarous and poorly
      struck, occasionallyover regular issues of the earlier Constantinian period.
      Again, the likelihood of British mintage can only be established by
      provenance.   5-8   10-15

ENGLISH HAMMERED COINAGE *c*.600-1662

Grading of Hammered Coins

As the name suggests, hammered coins were struck by hand with a hammer. This can lead to the coin being struck off centre, double struck, weak in the design, suffer cracks or flan defects. It is important to take these factors into account when assessing the grade of this series. Value is considerably reduced if the coin is holed, pierced, plugged or mounted.

Extremely Fine
Design and legends
sharp and clear.

Very Fine
Design and legends
still clear but with
slight evidence of wear
and/or minor damage.

Fine
Showing quite a lot of
wear but still with
design and legends
distinguishable.

Anglo-Saxon 'Porcupine' Sceat

Gold Noble

Silver Crown

EARLY & MIDDLE ANGLO-SAXON KINGDOMS & MINTS (C.650-973)

EARLY ANGLO-SAXON PERIOD, *c.* 600-*c.* 775

The withdrawal of Roman forces from Britain early in the 5th century A.D. and the gradual decline of central administration resulted in a rapid deterioration of the money supply. The arrival of Teutonic raiders and settlers hastened the decay of urban commercial life and it was probably not until late in the 6th century that renewed political, cultural and commercial links with the kingdom of the Merovingian Franks led to the appearance of small quantities of Merovingian gold *tremisses* (one-third solidus) in England. A purse containing such pieces was found in the Sutton Hoo ship-burial. Native Anglo-Saxon gold *thrymsas* were minted from about the 630s, initially in the style of their continental prototypes or copied from obsolete Roman coinage and later being made in pure Anglo-Saxon style. By the middle of the 7th century the gold coinage was being increasingly debased with silver, and gold had been superseded entirely by about 675.

These silver coins, contemporary with the *deniers or denarii* of the Merovingian Franks, are the first English pennies, though they are commonly known today as *sceattas* (a term more correctly translated as 'treasure' or 'wealth'). They provide important material for the student of Anglo-Saxon art.

Though the earliest sceattas are a transition from the gold thrymsa coinage, coins of new style were soon developed which were also copied by the Frisians of the Low Countries. Early coins appear to have a standard weight of 20 grains (1.29 gms) and are of good silver content, though the quality deteriorates early in the 8th century. These coins exist in a large number of varied types, and as well as the official issues there are mules and other varieties which are probably contemporary imitations. Many of the sceattas were issued during the reign of Aethelbald of Mercia, but as few bear inscriptions it is only in recent years that research has permitted their correct dating and the attribution of certain types to specific areas. Some silver sceats of groups II and III and most types of groups IV to X were issued during the period (A.D. 716-757) when Aethelbald, King of Mercia, was overlord of the southern English. In Northumbria very debased sceattas or *stycas* continued to be issued until the middle of the ninth century. Though a definitive classification has not yet been developed, the arrangement given below follows the latest work on the series: this list is not exhaustive.

This section has been catalogued in line with research published by Dr D. M. Metcalf. Wherever possible the Seaby number previously in use has been retained. Where it has been necessary to allocate a new and different number, the 'old' S. number is listed, in brackets, at the end of the entry. New entries are given a new number. The primary sceattas are followed by the secondary sceattas and, finally, the continental sceattas. This is not chronologically correct but has been adopted for ease of reference and identification. The reference 'B.M.C.' is to the type given in *British Museum Catalogue: Anglo-Saxon Coins.* Other works of reference include:

North, J. J. *English Hammered Coinage*, Vol. 1, *c.* 650-1272 (1994).

Metcalf, D.M. *Thrymsas and Sceattas in the Ashmolean Museum,* Vols I-III.

Rigold, S. E. 'The two primary series of sceattas', *B.N.J.,* xxx (1960).

Sutherland, C. H. V. *Anglo-Saxon Gold Coinage in the light of the Crondall Hoard* (1948).

ᚠ ᚪ ᚦ ᚠ ᚱ ᚪ · ᚷ ᚹ ᚻ ᚾ ᛁ ᛁ ᚩ ᛋ ᛣ ᛦ ᛝ ᛏ ᛒ ᛗ ᛘ ᛚ ᛤ ᚻ ᚯ ᚠ ᚠ ᛠ ᚪ

f   u   th o r k . z w h n i j ih p x s t b e m l ng d oe a Æ ea y

Early Anglo-Saxon Runes

GOLD

		F	VF
		£	£
A.	**Early pieces, of uncertain monetary status**		
751	Thrymsa. Name and portrait of Bishop Leudard (chaplain to Queen Bertha of Kent). R. Cross. *(S.751)*		*Extremely rare*
752	Solidus. Imitating solidi of Roman rulers. Blundered legends, some with runes. *(S.757)*		*Extremely rare*

753   754   755

		F	VF
		£	£

B.   Crondall types, *c.*620 – *c.*645

Twelve different types, which are almost certainly English, were found in the Crondall hoard of 1828. All are thrysmas, containing 70-40% gold.

753   'Witmen' type. Bust r. with trident. R. Cross. Legend normally blundered.
        M. 1-21 (S.767) 750   1650
754   London-derived type. Head r. with pseudo-legend. R. Cross. Pseudo-legend.
        M. 22-32 (S.765) 950   2100
755   'Licius' type. Elegant imitation of Roman triens. Bust l. R. VOT XX.
        M. 33-41 (S.762) 1100   2750

756   757   758

756   'LEMC' type. Head l. R. Maltese cross with letters L, E, M, C in angles,
        or cross on steps. *M. 42-9 (S.753)*.. 1000   2650
757   'LONDINIV' type. Facing bust, crosslets l. and r. R. Tall cross,
        LONDVNIV and pseudo-legend around. *M. 51-7 (S.764)*........................ 1350   3000
758   — similar, but bust r. AVDVARLD REGES. R. Tall cross, LONDENV.
        Usually garbled. *M. 50 (S.771)* 1100   2650

759   762

759   Other crude types, usually with head or bust, R. Cross. *M. 58-72 (S.775)*   750   1650

C.   Ultra-Crondall types, *c.*620 – 655?

Thrymsas not represented in the Crondall hoard, but probably of the same date range.

760   'Benutigo' type. Bust r., blundered legend. R. Cross on steps, runic
        legend (Benutigoii?) *(S.756)*... 975   2450
761   'Wuneetton' type. Bust r., cross before. R. Cross. Blundered legend
        (WVNEETON or similar). *M. 77 (S.768)*.. 1000   2750
762   'York' type. Kite-shaped shield enclosing cross, crosslets to l. and r.,
        squared pattern beneath. R. Cross. Blundered (runic?) legend. *M. 76 (S.769)* 1450   3500

D.   Post-Crondall types, *c.*655 – *c.*675

Pale gold types, visibly debased and sometimes almost silvery, containing 35-10% gold.

764   'Crispus' type. Helmeted bust, r. CRISPUS NOB CAES. R. Cross and XX
        in wreath, runic legend De Lundonia (?). *N.7 (S.761)* 1350   3000
765   'Concordia' type. Radiate bust r. R. Clasped hands. *N.5 (S.759)*.............. 1350   3250
766   'Oath-taking' type. Bust r. or l. with hand placed against cross. R.
        Lyre-shaped object, or eight-rayed symbol. *N.6 (S.760)* 1100   2750

767   770/3   771/4

		F £	VF £
767	'Two emperors' type. Helmeted bust r. R. Bust of angel with wings above two facing heads. *M. 79-80 (S.763)*	725	1450
768	'Pada', Type Ia Helmeted bust r. R. Runic Pada on panel. *M.p.73. (S.777)*	750	1600
768A	— Type Ib. Similar. R. Standard TTXX, Pada in runes in legend. *M. 81.*	550	1350
769	— Type IIa. Diademed bust r. R. Pada in runes in field, blundered legend around, *M.p.73. (S.773)*	650	1250
770	— Type III. Diademed bust r. R. Cross with annulet in angles. R. Runic Pada in legend. *M.p.73. (S.773)*	600	1200
771	'Varimundus', Type A. Diademed bust r. holding sceptre. R. Cross, with CA in lower angles. VARIMVNDVS MONE. *M.p.82 (S.780)*	750	1650
772	— Type B. Similar. R. Small cross in double circle of dots. *M. 84*	650	1500

SILVER

A.   Early transitional types by thrymsa moneyers, *c.*675-685

773	'Pada', Type III. As 770, but silver. *M. 82. (S.779)*	450	950
774	'Varimundus', Type B. As 772, but silver. *M. 85-7. (S.780)*	525	1100

B.   Primary Sceattas, *c.*680 – *c.*710

Minted in various regions of England.

775   776   777

775	Series A, Radiate bust r., TIC. R. Standard, TOTII. *B.M.C.2a M. 89-94. (S.781)*	65	175
776	Series BX. Diad. bust r., VANTAVMA or similar. R. Bird r. above cross on steps. *B.M.C. 26. M. 97-9. (S.782)*	90	200
777	— BI. Similar but diad. head r. within serpent circle. R. Bird r. on cross. *B.M.C. 27a.. M. 100-106. (S.783)*	60	125
777A	— BII. Similar but simplified legend VAVAVA. R. Crosslet beside bird. *M. 113-6. (S.784)*	65	145

778   779

778	— BZ. Crude facing head. R. Crude bird on cross (imitation of 776). *M. 138-9. (S.784A)*	95	200
779	Series C. Radiate bust r., similar to 775 but runic aepa replaces TIC. R. Standard, TOTII. *B.M.C. 2b. M. 117-125. (S.785)*	45	90

780   782

		F	VF
		£	£
780	King Aethelred of Mercia? (674-704). 'Porcupine'. R. Aethiliraed on runes in two lines. *M. 134-5. (S.837)*	235	400
781	Series F. Bust r., with broad-rimmed hat, blundered legend. R. Small cross on steps, annulets around. *M. 136-7. (S.839A)*	70	160
782	Series Z. Facing head with moustaches. R. Long-legged dog r. with head lowered. *M. 140-2. (S.817)*	265	525
782A	Series Z-related. Crude animal r., perhaps copy of 782. R. Crude cross-crosslet design *M. 143-4.*	150	350

782A   784   791

783	'Vernus' type. Porcupine-related head r., VER before. R. Standard. *M. 146-8.*	110	250
784	'Saroaldo' type. Unusual bust r. R. Saltire and pellets in square, SAROALDO legend around. *M. 151-3.*	175	375
785	Series W. Half or full-length facing figure holding two crosses. R. Cross crosslet on saltire. *M. 155. (S.807A)*	275	525

C. Secondary Sceattas, c.710-760

Minted in all the main regions of southern and eastern England, but especially in the south-east and the Thames basin.

| 791 | Series J, Type 85. Large head r. R. Bird on cross. *M. 293-5.* | 70 | 150 |
| 791A | — Type 36. Bust r., cross in front. R. One large and one small bird r. *M. 301-2. (S.801)* | 135 | 325 |

792   793   797

792	— Type 37. Two heads face-to-face. R. Four birds clockwise round cross. *M. 296-300.*	85	210
792A	— Type 72. Similar. R. Bird r., looking back. *M. 303.*	160	375
793	Series U, Type 23b. Standing figure r. holds two crosses. R. Pecking bird. *M. 445-51.*	125	265
794	Series K, Type 42. Bust r. with bird, cross or flower. R. Hound 1., plant behind. *M. 311-3*	140	375
795	— Type 20. Bust r. with chalice. R. Standing figure holds cross and hawk. *M. 314-18.*	100	235
796	— Type 32a. Bust r. with cross. R. Wolf curled head to tail. *M. 309*	140	350
797	— — Similar. R. Wolf-headed serpent. *M. 310*	110	250
798	— Type 32b. Similar. but R. Wolf-serpent within torque. *M. 307-8.*	120	275

	F £	VF £
799	— Type 33. Bust r., cross in front. R. Wolf's head with long tongue, l. or r. *M. 306.*	150	350

800   801   802   803

800	'Archer' type. Kneeling archer r. R. Bird on branch r., head turned back. *M. 349. (S.800A)*	450	950
801	'Carip' group. Bust r., CARIP. R. Pecking bird, wolf-serpent, or standing figure. *M. 336-40.*	185	450
802	Series O, Type 38. Bust r. in cable border. R. Bird r. in torque. *M. 373-5.*	140	325
803	— Type 21. Similar, but bust l. R. Standing figure with two crosses. *M. 376*	175	425

804   805   806

804	'Triquetras' eclectic group. Facing bust, man and crosses, winged figure, or bird and branch. R. Interlace pattern. *M.p.425.*	200	525
805	Series H, Type 39. Pecking bird. R. Round shield with bosses. *M. 283-4.*	100	225
806	— Type 49. 'Wodan' head, annulets around. R. Pecking bird. *M. 285-8..*	110	250
807	— Type 48. Whorl of 3 wolf heads. R. Round shield with bosses. *M. 289-92.*	120	265

808   809A   810

808	Series G. Bust r., cross before. R. Standard with 3 or 4 X's. *(Minted in Northern France?) M. 267-70.*	75	165
809	— crude copies, some with bird or bird on cross. *M. 271-4.*	45	110
809A	Series M. Prancing dog l. or r. R. Spiral branch. *M. 363-6. (S.836c.)*	120	275
810	Series N. Two standing figures. R. Monster looking back r. or l. *M. 368-72.*	80	185

811   813   815

811	Series O, Type 40. Standing figure holds two crosses. R. As last. *M. 379-81.*	90	225
812	— Type 43. Interlace shield. R. As last. *M.p.482.*	145	350
813	— Type 57. Bust r. in cable border. R. Monster looking back l. *M. 377.* .	150	375
814	'Animal mask' group. Facing animal (lion?) mask. R. Bird, figure, monster or cross. *M. 354-6. (S.814v).*	300	700
815	Series V. Wolf and twins. R. Bird in vine. *M. 453.*	175	475

816   818   822

		F £	VF £
816	Series T. Diad. bust r., +LEL. R. 'Porcupine' l. *M. 442-4.*	160	375
818	Series L, Type 12. Bust r., LVNDONIA. R. Standing figure holds two crosses. *M. 319-22.*	185	475
820	— Type 13. Similar. R. Seated figure holds hawk and cross. *M.p.409.*	275	675
821	— Type 14. Similar, but bust l. R. Celtic cross. *M.p.427.*	175	450
822	— Type 15. Bust r. with cross, no legend. R. Standing figure holds two crosses. *M. 323-6.*	100	275
825	— Type 16. Bust r. with floral scroll. R. Standing figure holds branch and cross, or two branches. *M. 329-30.*	125	300
827	— Type 18. Bust r. with cross. R. Standing figure holds cross and bird. *M. 331-3.*	100	275
828	— Type 19. Similar, but bust l. *M. 335.*	125	350
828A	— Type 34. Bust r. with cross or sceptre. R. Celtic cross. *M. 345-6.* *(S.800)*	130	350
828B	Series L-related. Bust r. rosettes in field. R. Standing figure holds two crosses. *M. 347.*	210	525

829   831   832

		F	VF
829	Type 22. Victory standing with wreath. R. Winged figure, or standing figure holding two crosses. *M. 350-1.*	275	650
830	Type 23e. Standing figure holds two crosses. R. Whorl of 3 wolf heads. *M. 359-62.*	110	250
831	Series S. Female centaur. R. Whorl of 4 wolf heads. *M. 438-41.*	115	275
832	Series R. Bust r. or l. Epa, Wigraed, Spi, etc in runes. R. Standard. *M. 391-428.*	45	95

833   834A   836

		F	VF
832B	Series Q(R), Type 73. Crude radiate bust r. or l. R. Quadruped r. *M. 388.*	165	350
833	'Saltire Standard' types. Bust l. or r. with cross, two standing figures, or double croix ancree. R. Saltire and pellets in square. *M. 432-5.*	100	235
834	'Monita Scorum' type. Small bird looking back, MONITA SCORUM. R. Standard with saltire of annulets. *M.p.436.*	375	750
834A	— Bust r., MONITA SCORUM. R. 'porcupine' l., figure with two crosses, or triquetra. *M. 348.*	400	900
835	Type 70. Saltire-standard. R. Standard. *M. 436-7.*	50	110
836	Series Q, Types QII-IVd Bird l. or r. R. Quadruped l. or r. *M. 386-7.*	125	290
836A	— Type QIVe Quadruped both sides. *M.p.501*	135	325
836B	— Type QIe Bust r. with cross. R. Walking bird l. *M. 383.*	165	425

		F £	VF £
836C	— Type QIf Standing figure with two crosses. R. Walking bird l. *M. 384.*	275	625
836D	— Type QIg Facing head. R. Long-legged quadruped looking back. *M.p.492.*	250	575

844   844A

844	Type 30. Facing 'Wodan' head. R. Two standing figures, or standard. *M. 429-31.*	165	375
844A	— Type 53. 'Porcupine', similar to 787. R. Stepped cross, annulet at centre. *Mint? M. 258-62.*	100	210

C.   Continental Sceattas, *c.*695-*c.*740
Most are from the Rhine area, or Frisia

786

786	Series E. Porcupine-like figure, body with annulet at one end, triangle at other. R. 'Standard' with four pellets around central annulet. *Dorestad. M. 209-11.*	40	95

187   789   790

787	— Similar, with triangular fore-leg. R. 'Standard' with four lines and central annulet. *M. 200-5.*	35	75
788	— Similar, with parallel lines in curve of body. R. 'Standard' with VICO. *M. 194-8.*	40	85
789	— Figure developed into plumed bird. R. Standard. *M. 190-3.*	60	125
790	Later issues. R. 'Standard' 'Porcupine'. Innumerable varieties. *M. 214-53.*	30	65
832A	Type 10. Bust r., AEPA or APA. R. Porcupine modified into profile face. *Mint? M.p.248.*	175	350
838	'Porcupine' R. Small cross, S E D E in angles. *Mint? M. 263.*	300	675

839   840   843

839	Series D, Type 2c. Bust r., pseudo-runes. R. Plain cross with pellets in angles. *Domburg? M. 158-80.*	40	85
840	— Type 8. Standard. R. As 839. *M. 183-6.*	35	70
841	'Maastricht' Type. Crude head l. R. Quatrefoil interlace. *M. 265-6*	175	375
843	Series X. Facing 'Wodan' head. R. Monster l. *Ribe, Jutland, M. 275-81.*	110	260
843A	— cruder copies. *English, M. 282.*	140	350

In the North a series of silver sceats was struck with the king's name on the obverse and a fantastic animal on the reverse. Towards the end of the eighth century the coinage degenerated to one of base silver and finally to copper or brass; from the second reign of Aethelred I the design becomes standardised with the king's name retained on the obverse but with the moneyer's name on the reverse and in the centre of both sides a cross, pellet or rosette., etc. A parallel series of ecclesiastical coins was struck by the Archbishops of York.

The coinage continued until the conquest of Northumbria by the Danes and the defeat of Osbert in 867, almost a century after introduction of the broad silver penny in Southern England.

		F £	VF £
846	**Aldfrith** (685-705). Æ *sceat*. Pellet in annulet. R. Fantastic animal l. with trifid tail..	350	800
852	**Eadberht** (737-758). Æ *sceat*. Small cross. R. Fantastic quadruped to l. or r.	120	325
	Aethelwald Moll (759-765). See Archbishop Ecgberht of York		

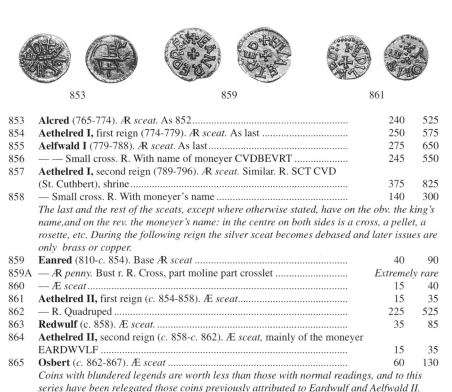

853   859   861

853	**Alcred** (765-774). Æ *sceat*. As 852...	240	525
854	**Aethelred I,** first reign (774-779). Æ *sceat*. As last	250	575
855	**Aelfwald I** (779-788). Æ *sceat*. As last..	275	650
856	— — Small cross. R. With name of moneyer CVDBEVRT	245	550
857	**Aethelred I,** second reign (789-796). Æ *sceat*. Similar. R. SCT CVD (St. Cuthbert), shrine...	375	825
858	— Small cross. R. With moneyer's name	140	300
	The last and the rest of the sceats, except where otherwise stated, have on the obv. the king's name, and on the rev. the moneyer's name: in the centre on both sides is a cross, a pellet, a rosette, etc. During the following reign the silver sceat becomes debased and later issues are only brass or copper.		
859	**Eanred** (810-*c.* 854). Base Æ *sceat*	40	90
859A	— Æ *penny*. Bust r. R. Cross, part moline part crosslet	*Extremely rare*	
860	— Æ *sceat*..	15	40
861	**Aethelred II,** first reign (*c.* 854-858). Æ *sceat*..................................	15	35
862	— R. Quadruped	225	525
863	**Redwulf** (*c.* 858). Æ *sceat*.	35	85
864	**Aethelred II,** second reign (*c.* 858-*c.* 862). Æ *sceat*, mainly of the moneyer EARDWVLF	15	35
865	**Osbert** (*c.* 862-867). Æ *sceat*	60	130
	Coins with blundered legends are worth less than those with normal readings, and to this series have been relegated those coins previously attributed to Eardwulf and Aelfwald II.		

866

		F £	VF £
866	**Ecgberht** (732 or 734-766). Æ *sceat,* with king Eadberht. As illustration, or holds cross and crozier	225	525
866A	— — with Aethelwald Moll. Cross each side	375	775
867	— — with Alchred. Cross each side.	365	725

868   870   871

868	**Eanbald II** (796-*c.* 830). Æ *sceat.* R. With name of moneyer	75	185
869	— Æ *sceat,* as last	60	135
870	**Wigmund** (837-854). Gold *solidus.* Facing bust. R. Cross in wreath	*Extremely rare*	
871	— Æ *sceat,* various	25	55
872	**Wulfhere** (854-900). Æ *sceat*	75	160

ANGLO-SAXON MIDDLE PERIOD, *c*.780-973

In the kingdom of the Franks a reformed coinage of good quality *deniers* struck on broad flans had been introduced by Pepin in 755 and continued by his son Charlemagne and his descendants. A new coinage of *pennies* of similar size and weighing about 20 grains (1.3 gms) was introduced into England, probably by Offa, the powerful king of Mercia, about 755/780, though early pennies also exist of two little known kings of Kent, Heaberht and Ecgberht, of about the same period.

The silver penny (*Lat.* 'denarius', hence the *d.* of our *£ s. d.*) remained virtually the sole denomination of English coinage for almost five centuries, with the rare exception of occasional gold coins and somewhat less rare silver halfpence. The penny reached a weight of 24 grains, i.e., a 'pennyweight' during the reign of Alfred the Great. Silver pennies of this period normally bear the ruler's name, though not always his portrait, and the name of the moneyer responsible for their manufacture.

Pennies were issued by various rulers of the Heptarchy for the kingdoms of Kent, Mercia, East Anglia and Wessex (and possibly Anglian Northumbria), by the Danish settlers in the Danelaw and the Hiberno-Norse kings of York, and also by the Archbishops of Canterbury and a Bishop of London. Under Eadgar, who became the sole ruler of England, a uniform coinage was instituted throughout the country, and it was he who set the pattern for the 'reformed' coinage of the later Anglo-Saxon and Norman period.

Halfpence were issued by most rulers from Alfred to Eadgar between 871-973 for S. England, and although all are rare today, it is probable that reasonable quantities were made.

Nos. 873-1387 are all silver pennies except where stated.

NB. Many pennies of the early part of this period have chipped flans and prices should be reduced accordingly.

KINGS OF KENT

		F	VF
		£	£
873	**Heaberht** (*c*. 765). Monogram for REX. R. Five annulets, each containing a pellet, joined to form a cross	*Extremely rare*	
874	**Ecgberht** (*c*. 780). Similar. R. Varied	850	2000

	875		877		
875	**Eadberht Praen.** Type 1. (796-798). As illustration. R. Varied			1050	2650
875A	— Type 2. (*c*. 798). His name around Ⓜ, in centre, R. Moneyer's name in angles of a tribrach			1250	3000
876	**Cuthred** (798-807). *Canterbury.* Various types without portrait			375	825
877	— As illustration			425	1000

	878		879		
878	**Anonymous** (*c*. 822-823). *Canterbury.* As illustration			600	1450
879	**Baldred** (*c*. 823-825). *Canterbury.* Head or bust r. R. Varied			750	2000

		F	*VF*
		£	£
880	— Cross each side	575	1750
881	*Rochester.* Diademed bust r. R. Varied	725	1900

ARCHBISHOPS OF CANTERBURY

882

881A	**Jaenberht** (765-792). New type (early). Under Ecgberht II of Kent (?). (before *c.* 780 ?) His name around small cross of pellets in centre. R. PONTIFEX in three lines	1250	2750
882	Under offa of Mercia (*c.* 780-792) His name around central ornament or cross and wedges. R. OFFA REX in two lines	1050	2350
883	— His name in three lines. R. OFFA or OFFA REX between the limbs of Celtic cross	1100	2450
884	**Aethelheard** (el. 792, cons. 793, d. 805). With Offa as overlord. First issue (792-?), with title *Pontifex*	1250	3000

885   887

885	— Second issue (?-796), with title *Archiepiscopus*	1200	2750
885A	— Third issue (*c.* 796-798), with title *Archiepiscopus*. His name and AR around EP in centre. R. Moneyer's name, EADGAR or CIOLHARD	1250	3000
886	— With Coenwulf as overlord. (798-800 ?) Fourth Issue. As last. R. King's name in the angles of a tribrach	900	2200
886A	— Fifth issue (*c.* 798-805?). As last R. Coenwulf's name around ᛘ in centre	950	2250
887	**Wulfred** (805-832). group I (805-*c.* 810). As illustration. R. Crosslet, alpha-omega	700	2000
888	— Group II (*c.* 810). As last. R. DOROVERNIA C monogram	575	1400
889	— Group III (pre- 823). Bust extends to edge of coin. R. As last	525	1250
890	— Groups IV and V (*c.* 822-823). Anonymous under Ecgberht. Moneyer's name in place of the Archbishop's. R. DOROBERNIA CIVITAS in three or five lines	600	1400
891	— Group VI (*c.* 823-825). Baldred type. Crude portrait. R. DRVR CITS in two lines	750	2350
892	— Group VII (*c.* 832). Second monogram (Ecgberht) type. Crude portrait r., PLFRED. R. DORIB C. Monogram as 1035	650	2200

893   894

		F £	VF £
893	**Ceolnoth** (833-870). Group I with name CIALNOD. Tonsured bust facing. R. Varied..	400	950
894	— Group II. Similar but CEOLNOD. R. Types of Aethelwulf of Wessex	375	900
895	— Group III. Diad. bust r. R. Moneyer's name in and between lunettes..	525	1350

896   898

896	**Aethelred** (870-889). Bust r. R. As illustration or with long cross with lozenge panel...	1250	3000
897	— Cross pattée. R. ELF / STAN	1350	3500
898	**Plegmund** (890-914). DORO in circle. R. As illustration above, various moneyers	425	1050
899	— Similar, but title EPISC, and XDF in centre	575	1250
900	— Small cross pattée. R. Somewhat as last	325	750
901	— Crosses moline and pommee on *obv.*	600	1350
901A	— Halfpenny. As 900...	2250	4250

KINGS OF MERCIA

Until 825 Canterbury was the principal mint of the Kings of Mercia and some moneyers also struck coins for the Kings of Kent and Archbishops of Canterbury.

GOLD

902   903

902	**Offa** (757-796). Gold *dinar*. Copy of Arabic dinar of Caliph Al Mansur, dated 157 A.H. (A.D. 774), with OFFA REX added on *rev.*	*Extremely rare*
903	Gold *penny*. Bust r., moneyer's name. R. Standing figure, moneyer's name	*Extremely rare*

SILVER

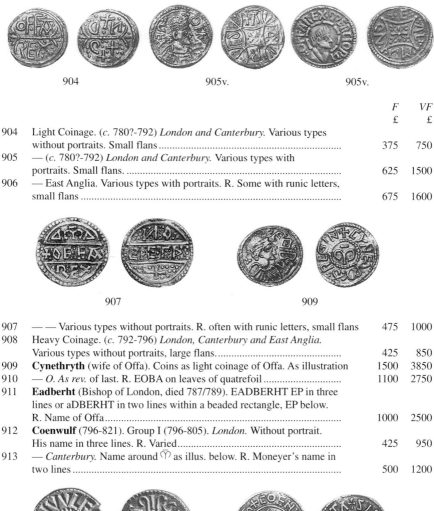

904 905v. 905v.

		F £	*VF* £
904	Light Coinage. (*c.* 780?-792) *London and Canterbury.* Various types without portraits. Small flans	375	750
905	— (*c.* 780?-792) *London and Canterbury.* Various types with portraits. Small flans.	625	1500
906	— East Anglia. Various types with portraits. R. Some with runic letters, small flans	675	1600

907 909

907	— — Various types without portraits. R. often with runic letters, small flans	475	1000
908	Heavy Coinage. (*c.* 792-796) *London, Canterbury and East Anglia.* Various types without portraits, large flans.	425	850
909	**Cynethryth** (wife of Offa). Coins as light coinage of Offa. As illustration	1500	3850
910	— *O. As rev.* of last. R. EOBA on leaves of quatrefoil	1100	2750
911	**Eadberht** (Bishop of London, died 787/789). EADBERHT EP in three lines or aDBERHT in two lines within a beaded rectangle, EP below. R. Name of Offa	1000	2500
912	**Coenwulf** (796-821). Group I (796-805). *London.* Without portrait. His name in three lines. R. Varied	425	950
913	— *Canterbury.* Name around ᛦ as illus. below. R. Moneyer's name in two lines	500	1200

914 915

914	— *Both mints.* Tribrach type as illustration	275	525
915	— Group II (*c.* 805-810). *Canterbury.* With portrait. Small flans. R. Varied but usually cross and wedges	400	825

			F £	*VF* £

916   — Groups III and IV (*c.* 810-820). *Canterbury.* Similar but larger flans.
R. Varied..   350   750

917   — *Rochester.* Large diad. bust of coarse style. R. Varied. (Moneyers:
Dun, Ealhstan)..   425   975

918   — *London.* With portrait generally of Roman style. R. Crosslet.............   450 1000

919   — *E. Anglia.* Crude diad. bust r. R. Moneyer's name LVL on leaves in
arms of cross   350   725

920   — — *O.* as last. R. Various types..   400   825

921   929

921   **Ceolwulf I** (821-823). Canterbury. Group I. Bust r. R. Varied.
(Moneyers: Oba, Sigestef) 675 1600

922   — — Group II. Crosslet. R. Varied...   625 1450

923   — — Group III. Tall cross with MERCIORŪ. R. Crosslet. SIGESTEF
DOROBERNIA 900 2000

924   — *Rochester.* Group I. Bust r. R. Varied.....................................   600 1400

925   — — Group IIA. As last but head r. 650 1500

926   — — Group IIB. Ecclesiastical issue by Bp. of Rochester. With mint
name, DOROBREBIA, but no moneyer......................................   1050 2250

927   — *East Anglia.* Crude style and lettering with barbarous portrait. R. Varied   525 1150

928   **Beornwulf** (823-825). Bust r. R. Moneyer's name in three lines 775 2100

929   — R. Cross crosslet in centre..   750 2000

930   Crude copy of 928 but moneyer's name in two lines with crosses between   1100 2750

931   **Ludica** (825-827). Bust r. R. Moneyer's name in three lines as 928........   2450 6250

932   933

932   — Similar. R. Moneyer's name around cross crosslet in centre, as 929...   2750 6750

933   **Wiglaf,** first reign (827-829). Crude head r. R. Crosslet 1600 3750

934   935

		F £	VF £
934	Second reign (830-840). Cross and pellets, or ⚹ R. Moneyer's name in and between lunettes of pellets	1350	3250
935	**Berhtwulf** (840-852). Various types with bust	650	1500
936	— Cross potent over saltire. R. Cross potent	725	1650
937	Berhtwulf with Aethelwulf of Wessex. As before. R. IAETHELWLF REX. cross pommee over cross pattee	1500	3750

938   939   940   941

938	**Burgred** (852-874). *B.M.C. type A.* Bust r. R. Moneyer's name in and between lunettes	95	175
939	— — B. Similar but lunettes broken in centre of curve	125	275
940	— — C. Similar but lunettes broken in angles	110	210
941	— — D. Similar but legend divided by two lines with a crook at each end	100	200
942	— — E. As last, but m above and below	450	950
943	**Ceolwulf II** (874-*c.* 880). Bust r. R. Two emperors seated. Victory above.	*Extremely rare*	

944   945

| 944 | — R. Moneyer's name in angles of long cross with lozenge centre | 1450 | 3750 |

KINGS OF EAST ANGLIA

945	**Beonna,** King of East Anglia, *c.* 758. Æ sceat. Pellet in centre, Runic inscription. R. EFE in Roman characters around saltire cross	325	675
945A	— Similar. R. Name in Runic	450	925
945B	— Similar. R. Interlace pattern (large flans)	900	1850
945C	**Alberht** (749-?). Pellet in centre, AETHELBERT (runic) around R. Rosette in circle, TIAELRED (runic) around.	*Extremely rare*	

946

	F	VF
	£	£

946   **Aethelberht** (d. 794). As illustration ....   *Extremely rare*
947   **Eadwald** (*c*. 798). King's name in three lines. R. Moneyer's name in
        quatrefoil or around cross   675   1500
947A   — King's name around cross or ꟽ in centre. R. Moneyer's name in
        quatrefoil   750   1600

948   951

948   **Aethelstan I** (*c*. 825-840). Bust r. or l. R. Crosslet or star   675   1750
949   Bust r. R. Moneyer's name in three or four lines   675   1750
950   Alpha or A. R. Varied...   275   600
951   *O.* and *rev.* Cross with or without wedges or pellets in angles   300   650
952   — Similar, with king's name both sides   425   900
952A   Name around ship in centre. R. Moneyer Eadgar, pellets in centre.
        (Possibly the earliest of his coins.)...   1500   3500

953   954

953   **Aethelweard** (*c*. 840-*c*. 855), A. Omega or cross and crescents. R. Cross
        with pellets or wedges..   475   975
954   **Edmund** (855-870). Alpha or A. R. Cross with pellets or wedges...........   180   375
955   — *O.* Varied. R. Similar...   180   375
*For the St. Edmund coins and the Danish issues struck in East Anglia bearing the name of Aethelred
I, see Danish East Anglia.*

Danish East Anglia, *c.* **885-915**

957

		F £	VF £
956	**Aethelstan II** (878-890), originally named Guthrum? Cross pattee. R. Moneyer's name in two lines	950	2250
957	**Oswald** (unknown except from his coins). Alpha or A. R. Cross pattee ..	1500	3750
958	— Copy of Carolinigian 'temple' type. R Cross and pellets	1750	4250
959	**Aethelred I.** (*c.*870) As last, with name of Aethelred I. R. As last, or cross-crosslet	1450	3250
959A	— As 954	1250	2500
960	**St. Edmund,** memorial coinage, Æ *penny,* type as illus. below, various legends of good style	80	150

961   962

961	— Similar, but barbarous or semi-barbarous legends	75	135
962	*Halfpenny.* Similar	375	850

963   966

963	**St. Martin of Lincoln.** As illustration	1650	3750
964	**Alfred.** (Viking imitations, usually of very barbarous workmanship.) Bust r. R. *Londonia* monogram	450	1250
965	— Similar, but *Lincolla* monogram	950	2250
966	— Small cross, as Alfred group II (*Br. 6*), various legends, some read REX DORO	190	400
967	— Similar. R. 'St. Edmund type' A in centre	475	1150
968	— Two emperors seated. R. As 964. (Previously attributed to Halfdene.)	*Extremely rare*	
969	*Halfpenny.* As 964 and 965	425	875

970

		F	VF
		£	£
970	— As 966	375	800

DANELAW, c. 898-915

971   975

971	**Alfred** (Imitations). ELFRED between ORSNA and FORDA. R. Moneyer's name in two lines (occasionally divided by horizontal long cross)	275	675
972	— *Halfpenny.* Similar, of very crude appearance	600	1250
973	**Alfred/Plegmund.** *Obv.* ELFRED REX PLEGN	650	1350
974	**Plegmund.** Danish copy of 900...	325	750
975	**Earl Sihtric.** Type as 971. SCELDFOR between GVNDI BERTVS. R SITRIC COMES in two lines..	1750	4500

Viking Coinage of York?

References are to 'The Classification of Northumbrian Viking Coins in the Cuerdale hoard', by C. S. S. Lyon and B. H. I. H. Stewart, in Numismatic Chronicle, 1964, p. 281 ff.

976	**Siefred.** C. SIEFRE DIIS REX in two lines. R. EBRAICE CIVITAS (or contractions), small cross. *L. & S. Ia, Ie, Ii*..............................	190	450
977	— Cross on steps between. R. As last. *L. & S. If, Ij*................................	300	675
978	— Long cross. R. As last. *L. & S. Ik*	325	750
979	SIEFREDVS REX, cross crosslet within legend. R. As last. *L. & S. Ih* ...	140	300

980   984

980	SIEVERT REX, cross crosslet to edge of coin. R. As last. *L. & S. Ic, Ig, Im*	150	325
981	— Cross on steps between. R. As last. *L. & S. Il*	250	575
982	— Patriarchal cross. R. DNS DS REX, small cross. *L. & S. Va*	200	475
983	— — R. MIRABILIA FECIT, small cross. *L. & S. VIb*	225	525
984	REX, at ends of cross crosslet. R. SIEFREDVS, small cross. *L. & S. IIIa, b*	185	425

		F	VF
		£	£
985	— Long cross. R. As last. *L. & S. IIIc*	175	375
986	*Halfpenny.* Types as 977, *L. & S. Ib; 980, Ic; and 983, VIb*	600	1250
987	**Cnut.** CNVT REX, cross crosslet to edge of coin. R. EBRAICE CIVITAS, small cross. *L. & S. Io, Iq*..	140	290
988	— — R. CVNNETTI, small cross. *L. & S. IIc*	130	265
989	— Long cross. R. EBRAICE CIVITAS, small cross. *L. & S. Id, In, Ir*	90	175
990	— — R. CVNNETTI, small cross. *L. & S. IIa, IId*	85	165
991	— Patriarchal cross. R. EBRAICE CIVITAS, small cross. *L. & S. Ip, Is*	80	150
992	— — R.— *Karolus* monogram in centre. *L. & S . It*	550	1250

993   995

993	— — R. CVNNETTI, small cross. *L. & S. IIb, IIe*..............................	75	140
994	*Halfpenny.* Types as 987, *L. & S. Iq; 989, Id; 991, Is; 992, Iu; 993, IIb and e*	375	725
995	As 992, but CVNNETTI around *Karolus* monogram. *L. & S. IIf*.............	400	750
996	**Cnut and/or Siefred.** CNVT REX, patriarchal cross. R. SIEFREDVS, small cross. *L. & S. IIId*	125	250
997	— — R. DNS DS REX, small cross. *L. & S. Vc.*	190	450

998

998	— — R. MIRABILIA FECIT. *L. & S. VId*	125	250
999	EBRAICE C, patriarchal cross. R. DNS DS REX, small cross. *L. & S. Vb*	175	350

1000   1002

1000	— — R. MIRABILIA FECIT. *L. & S. VIc*	125	250
1001	DNS DS REX in two lines. R. ALVALDVS, small cross. *L. & S. IVa*	675	1550
1002	DNS DS O REX, similar. R. MIRABILIA FECIT. *L. & S. VIa*	240	475
1003	*Halfpenny.* As last. *L. & S. VIa*	600	1250
1004	**'Cnut'.** Name blundered around cross pattée with extended limbs. R. QVENTOVICI around small cross. *L. & S. VII*......................................	300	650

	F £	VF £

1005 *Halfpenny.* Similar. *L. & S. VII* 475 1050
      Possibly not Northumbrian; the reverse copied from the Carolingian coins
      of Quentovic, N. France.

York, early tenth century issues

1006   1009

1006 **St. Peter coinage.** Early issues. SCI PETRI MO in two lines. R. Cross
      pattee 185 425
1007 — similar. R. 'Karolus' monogram.. 950 2250
1008 *Halfpenny.* Similar. R. Cross pattee 650 1500
1009 **Regnald** (blundered types). RAIENALT, head to l. or r. R. EARICE CT,
      'Karolus' monogram 1450 3500

1010

1010 — Open hand. R. Similar... 1050 2500
1011 — Hammer. R. Bow and arrow... 1350 3500
1012 — Similar. R. Sword 1250 3250

ENGLISH COINS OF THE HIBERNO-NORSE VIKINGS

Early period, *c.* 919-925
1013 **Sihtric** (921-927). SITRIC REX, sword. R. Cross or T 1500 3500
1014 **St. Peter coinage.** Late issues SCI PETRI MO, sword and hammer. R.
      EBORACEI, cross and pellets 550 1250

1015   1016

1015 — Similar. R. Voided hammer 500 1050
1016 — Similar. R. Solid hammer.. 675 1450
      St. Peter coins with blundered legends are rather cheaper.

Later period, 939-954 (after the battle of Brunanburh). Mostly struck at York.

			F	VF
1017	**Anlaf Guthfrithsson,** 939-941. Flower type. Small cross, ANLAF REX TO D. R. Flower above moneyer's name		2250	5250
1018	**Olaf Guthfrithsson.** Circumscription type, with small cross each side, ANLAF CVNVNC, M in field on reverse *(Derby)*		2100	5000
1018A	— Two line type. ONLAF REX. Large letter both sides *(Lincoln?)*		2000	4750

1019

1020

			F	VF
			£	£
1019	— Raven type. As illustration, ANLAF CVNVNC		1250	3250
1020	**Olaf Sihtricsson,** first reign, 941-944. Triquetra type. As illus., CVNVNC. R. Danish standard		1450	3750
1021	— Circumscription type (a). Small cross each side, CVNVNC		1450	3750
1022	— Cross moline type, CVNVN C. R. Small cross		1600	4250
1023	— Two line type. Small cross. R. ONLAF REX. R. Name in two lines		1400	3750
1024	**Regnald Guthfrithsson,** 943-944. Triquetra type. As 1020. REGNALD CVNVNC		2100	5250

1025

1030

			F	VF
1025	— Cross moline type. As 1022, but REGNALD CVNVNC		2000	4750
1026	**Sihtric Sihtricsson,** *c.* 942. Triquetra type. As 1020, SITRIC CVNVNC		2100	5000
1027	— Circumscription type. Small cross each side		2000	4750
1028	**Eric Blood-axe,** first reign, 948. Two line type. Small cross, ERICVC REX A; ERIC REX AL; or ERIC REX EFOR. R. Name in two lines		2250	4750
1029	**Olaf Sihtricsson,** second reign, 948-952. Circumscription type (b). Small cross each side. ONLAF REX		1650	4250
1029A	— Flower type. small cross ANLAF REX R. Flower above moneyer's name		2100	5250
1029B	— Two line type. Small cross, ONLAF REX. R. Moneyer's name in two lines		1550	4000
1030	**Eric Blood-axe,** second reign, 952-954. Sword type. ERIC REX in two lines, sword between. R. Small cross		2500	5500

KINGS OF WESSEX, 786-959

Later, KINGS OF ALL ENGLAND
All are silver pennies unless otherwise stated

BEORHTRIC, 786-802
Beorhtric was dependent on Offa of Mercia and married a daughter of Offa.

1031

		F £	VF £
1031	As illustration	*Extremely rare*	
1032	Alpha and omega in centre. R. Omega in centre	*Extremely rare*	

ECGBERHT, 802-839
King of Wessex only, 802-825; then also of Kent, Sussex, Surrey, Essex and East Anglia, 825-839, and of Mercia also, 829-830.

1033	*Canterbury.* Group I. Diad. hd. r. within inner circle. R. Various	950	2650
1034	— II. Non-portrait types. R. Various	675	1700

1035

1035	— III. Bust r. breaking inner circle. R. DORIB C	650	1650
1036	*London.* Cross potent. R. LVN / DONIA / CIVIT	1200	3250
1037	— — R. REDMVND MONE around TA	1000	2750
1038	*Rochester,* royal mint. Non-portrait types with king's name ECGBEO RHT	675	1700
1039	— — Portrait types, ECGBEORHT	750	1750
1040	*Rochester,* bishop's mint. Bust r. R. SCS ANDREAS (APOSTOLVS)	1000	2750
1041	*Winchester.* SAXON monogram or SAXONIORVM in three lines. R. Cross	850	1850

Son of Ecgberht; sub-King of Essex, Kent, Surrey and Sussex, 825-839; King of all southern
England, 839-855; King of Essex, Kent and Sussex only, 855-858. No coins are known of his son
Aethelbald who ruled over Wessex proper, 855-860.

1043   1045

		F	VF
		£	£
1042	*Canterbury.* Phase I (839-c. 843). Head within inner circle. R. Various. *Br. 3*	300	675
1043	— — Larger bust breaking inner circle. R. A. *Br. 1 and 2*	325	700
1044	— — Cross and wedges. R. SAXONIORVM in three lines in centre. *Br. 10*	275	625
1045	— — Similar, but OCCINDENTALIVM in place of moneyer. *Br. 11*	325	700
1046	— Phase II (*c.* 843-848?). Cross and wedges. R. Various, but chiefly a form of cross or a large A. *Br. 4*	300	625
1047	— — New portrait, somewhat as 1043. R. As last. *Br. 7*	275	625
1048	— — Smaller portrait. R. As last, with *Chi/Rho* monogram. *Br. 7*	350	750

1049   1051

1049	— Phase III (*c.* 848/851-c. 855). DORIB in centre. R. CANT mon. *Br. 5*	265	575
1050	— — CANT mon. R. CAN M in angles of cross. *Br. 6*	325	675
1051	— Phase IV (*c.* 855-859). Type as Aethelberht. New neat style bust R. Large voided long cross. *Br. 8*	250	525
1052	*Winchester.* SAXON mon. R. Cross and wedges. *Br. 9*	425	950

Son of Aethelwulf; sub-King of Kent, Essex and Sussex, 858-860; King of all southern England, 860-865/6.

1053

		F	VF
		£	£
1053	As illustration above	250	525
1054	*O.* Similar, R. Cross fleury over quatrefoil	550	1350

AETHELRED I, 865/866-871

Son of Aethelwulf; succeeded his brother Aethelberht.

1055

1055	As illustration	275	650
1056	Similar, but moneyer's name in four lines	600	1400

For another coin with the name Aethelred see 959 under Viking coinages.

Brother and successor to Aethelred, Alfred had to contend with invading Danish armies for much of his reign. In 878 he and Guthrum the Dane divided the country, with Alfred holding all England south and west of Watling Street. Alfred occupied London in 886.

Types with portraits

| | 1057 | | 1061 | | 1062 |

1057	Bust r. R. As Aethelred I. *Br. 1* (*name often* AELBRED)	265	575
1058	— R. Long cross with lozenge centre, as 944, *Br. 5*	1350	3750
1059	— R. Two seated figures, as 943. *Br. 2*	*Extremely rare*
1060	— R. As Archbp. Aethered; cross within large quatrefoil. *Br. 3*	*Extremely rare*
1061	*London.* Bust. r. R. LONDONIA monogram	575	1300
	Copies made of tin at the Wembley Exhibition are common		
1062	— R. Similar, but with moneyer's name added	650	1450
1063	— *Halfpenny.* Bust r. or rarely l. R. LONDONIA monogram as 1061.....	375	925
1064	*Gloucester.* R. Æ GLEAPA in angles of three limbed cross	*Extremely rare*

Types without portraits

1065	King's name on limbs of cross, trefoils in angles. R. Moneyer's name in quatrefoil. *Br. 4.*..	*Extremely rare*

| | 1066 | | 1069 |

1066	Cross pattée. R. Moneyer's name in two lines. *Br. 6*	250	450
1067	— As last, but neater style, as Edw, the Elder	265	500
1068	— *Halfpenny.* As 1066	375	825
1069	*Canterbury.* As last but DORO added on *obv. Br. 6a*	275	550
1070	*Exeter?* King name in four lines. R. EXA vertical...................................	2250	5250
1071	*Winchester?* Similar to last, but PIN..	2500	6500
1072	'Offering penny'. Very large and heavy. AELFRED REX SAXORVM in four lines. R. ELIMO in two lines i.e. (*Elimosina,* alms)	*Extremely rare*

For other pieces bearing the name of Alfred see under the Viking coinages.

Edward, the son of Alfred, aided by his sister Aethelflaed 'Lady of the Mercians', annexed all England south of the Humber and built many new fortified boroughs to protect the kingdom.

1074　　　　　　　　　　　　　　1078

	F	VF
	£	£

Rare types

			F	VF
1073	*Br. 1. Bath?* R. BA		1500	3250
1074	— *2. Canterbury.* Cross moline in pommee. R. Moneyer's name		900	2000
1075	— *3. Chester?* Small cross. R. Minster		1100	2750
1076	— *4.* — Small cross. R. Moneyer's name in single line		750	1750
1077	— *5.* — R. Two stars		900	2250

1081　　　　　　　　　　　　　　1082

		F	VF
1078	— *6.* — R. Flower above central line, name below	1000	2650
1079	— *7.* — R. Floral design with name across field	1000	2650
1080	— *8.* — R. Bird holding twig	1850	4750
1081	— *9.* — R. Hand of Providence	1450	3250
1082	— *10.* — R. City gate of Roman style	1350	3000
1083	— *11.* — R. Anglo-Saxon burg	850	2250

Ordinary types

1084　　　　　　　　　　　　　　1087

		F	VF
1084	*Br. 12.* Bust l. R. Moneyer's name in two lines	400	950
1085	— — As last, but in *gold*	*Extremely rare*	
1086	— *12a.* Similar, but bust r. of crude style	525	1250
1087	— *13.* Small cross. R. Similar (to 1084)	125	285
1088	*Halfpenny.* Similar to last	750	1750
1088A	— — R. Hand of Providence	1250	3000

Aethelstan, the eldest son of Eadward, decreed that money should be coined only in a borough, that every borough should have one moneyer and that some of the more important boroughs should have more than one moneyer.

1089

		F	VF
		£	£
1089	**Main issues.** Small cross. R. Moneyer's name in two lines	165	350
1090	Diad. bust r. R. As last	575	1300
1091	— R. Small cross	525	1250
1092	Small cross both sides	250	475

1093 1094

1093	— Similar, but mint name added	235	450
1094	Crowned bust r. As illustration. R. Small cross	400	950
1095	— Similar, but mint name added	375	900
1096	**Local Issues.** *N. Mercian mints.* Star between two pellets. R. As 1089	650	1450
1097	— Small cross. R. Floral ornaments above and below moneyer's name..	750	1650
1098	— Rosette of pellets each side	250	550
1099	— Small cross one side, rosette on the other side	300	625

1100 1104

1100	*N.E. mints.* Small cross. R. Tower over moneyer's name	950	2650
1101	Similar, but mint name added	1000	2750
1102	— Bust in high relief r. or l. R. Small cross	550	1250
1103	— Bust r. in high relief. R. Cross-crosslet	550	1250
1104	'Helmeted' bust r. R. As last	600	1500
1104A	Halfpenny, small cross. R. Moneyer's name in two lines	850	1850

Eadmund, the brother of Aethelstan, extended his realm over the Norse kingdom of York.

　　　　　　1105　　　　　　　　　　　　　　　　　1107

		F	VF
		£	£
1105	Small cross or rosette. R. Moneyer's name in two lines with crosses or rosettes between	145	325
1106	Crowned bust r. R. Small cross	450	975
1107	Similar, but with mint name	475	1000
1108	Small cross either side, or rosette on one side	240	475
1109	Cross of five pellets. R. Moneyer's name in two lines	240	475
1110	Small cross. R. Flower above name	900	2450
1111	'Helmeted' bust r. R. Cross-crosslet	700	1750

　　　　　　1111　　　　　　　　　　　　　　　1112

1112	*Halfpenny.* As 1105	700	1600

EADRED, 946-955

Eadred was another of the sons of Eadward. He lost the kingdom of York to Eric Bloodaxe.

　　　　　　1113　　　　　　　　　　　　　　　1115

1113	As illustration. R. Moneyer's name in two lines	135	265
1114	— Similar, but mint name after REX	300	750
1115	Crowned bust r. As illustration	350	750
1116	— R. Similar, with mint name added	400	900

		F	VF
		£	£
1117	Rosette. R. As 1113	215	425
1118	Small cross. R. Rosette	225	450
1119	— R. Flower enclosing moneyer's name. *B.M.C. II*...........	1100	2750
1120	*Halfpenny.* Similar to 1113....................................	525	1100

HOWEL DDA, d. 949/950

Grandson of Rhodri Mawr, Howel succeeded to the kingdom of Dyfed *c.* 904, to Seisyllog *c.* 920 and became King of Gwynedd and all Wales, 942.

1121

1121 HOPÆL REX, small cross or rosette. R. Moneyer's name in two lines...   *Extremely rare*

EADWIG, 955-959

Elder son of Eadmund, Eadwig lost Mercia and Northumbria to his brother Eadgar in 957.

1122   1123

1122	*Br. 1.* Type as illustration..	215	425
1123	— — Similar, but mint name in place of crosses	450	925
1123A	— Similar to 1122, but star in place of cross on *obv.*	525	1250
1124	— *2.* As 1122, but moneyer's name in one line	750	2000
1125	— *3.* Similar. R. Floral design	1250	2750
1126	— *4.* Similar. R. Rosette or small cross	300	650
1127	— *5.* Bust r. R. Small cross	2000	4750

1128

1128	*Halfpenny.* Small cross. R. Flower above moneyer's name.....................	1250	3000
1128A	— Similar. R. PIN (Winchester) across field.............................	1400	3500

King in Mercia and Northumbria from 957; King of all England 959-975.

It is now possible on the basis of the lettering to divide up the majority of Eadgar's coins into issues from the following regions: N.E. England, N.W. England, York, East Anglia, Midlands, S.E. England, Southern England, and S.W. England. (*See* 'Anglo-Saxon Coins', ed. R. H. M. Dolley.)

1129   1135

		F	VF
		£	£
1129	*Br I.* Small cross. R. Moneyer's name in two lines, crosses between, trefoils top and bottom	85	185
1130	— — R. Similar, but rosettes top and bottom (a N.W. variety)	120	240
1131	— — R. Similar, but annulets between	140	300
1132	— — R. Similar, but mint name between (a late N.W. type)	175	375
1133	— *2.* — R. Floral design	950	2400
1134	— *4.* Small cross either side	100	210
1135	— — Similar, with mint name	190	425
1136	— — Rosette either side	130	275
1137	— — Similar, with mint name	240	525
1138	— *5.* Large bust to r. R. Small cross	525	1200
1139	— — Similar, with mint name	625	1350
1140	*Halfpenny.* (8.5 grains.) *Br. 3.* Small cross. R. Flower above name	1350	3000
1140A	— — R. Mint name around cross (Chichester)	1500	3500
1140B	— Bust r. R. 'Londonia' monogram	650	140

For Eadgar 'reform' issues see overleaf

In 973 Eadgar introduced a new coinage. A royal portrait now became a regular feature and the reverses normally have a cruciform pattern with the name of the mint in addition to that of the moneyer. Most fortified towns of burghal status were allowed a mint, the number of moneyers varying according to their size and importance: some royal manors also had a mint and some moneyers were allowed to certain ecclesiastical authorities. In all some seventy mints were active about the middle of the 11th century (see list of mints pp. 77-8).

The control of the currency was retained firmly in the hands of the central government, unlike the situation in France and the Empire where feudal barons and bishops controlled their own coinage. Coinage types were changed at intervals to enable the Exchequer to raise revenue from new dies and periodic demonetization of old coin types helped to maintain the currency in a good state. No half-pence were minted during this period. During the latter part of this era, full pennies were sheared into 'halfpennies' and 'farthings'. They are far rarer than later 'cut' coins.

Eadgar, 959-975 *continued*

1141

		F	VF
		£	£
1141	**Penny.** Type 6. Small bust l. R. Small cross, name of moneyer and mint.	475	975

EDWARD THE MARTYR, 975-978

Son of Eadgar and Aethelflaed, Eadward was murdered at Corfe castle, reputedly on the orders of his stepmother Aelfthryth.

1142

| 1142 | Type as illustration above .... | 675 | 1425 |

120

LATE ANGLO-SAXON MINTS (973-1066)

1. Castle Gotha*	16. Cadbury	31. Cricklade	46. Canterbury	61. Ipswich	76. Tamworth
2. Launceston	17. Bruton	32. Oxford	47. Rochester	62. Norwich	77. Derby
3. Lydford	18. Dorchester	33. Wallingford	48. Horndon	63. Thetford	78. Leicester
4. Barnstaple	19. Wareham	34. Reading	49. Southwark	64. Huntingdon	79. Nottingham
5. Totnes	29. Shaftesbury	35. Guildford	50. London	65. Northampton	80. Peterborough
6. Exeter	21. Warminster	36. Chichester	51. Hertford	66. Warwick	81. Stamford
7. Watchet	22. Bath	37. Cissbury	52. Aylesbury	67. Worcester	82. Newark
8. Taunton	23. Bristol	38. Steyning	53. Buckingham	68. Pershore	83. Torksey
9. Langport	24. Berkeley	39. Lewes	54. Newport Pagnell*	69. Winchcombe	84. Lincoln
10. Petherton	25. Malmesbury	40. Hastings	55. Bedford	70. Gloucester	85. Horncastle
11. Crewkerne	26. Wilton	41. Romney	56. Cambridge	71. Hereford	86. Caistor
12. Bridport*	27. Salisbury	42. Lympne	57. Bury St Edmunds	72. Grantham*	87. York
13. Axbridge	28. Southampton	43. Hythe	58. Sudbury	73. Shrewsbury	88. Wilton. Norfolk*
14. Ilchester	29. Winchester	44. Dover	59. Maldon	74. Chester	89. Frome*
15. Miborne Port	30. Bedwyn	45. Sandwich	60. Colchester	75. Stafford	90. Droitwich

* Possible location of uncertain mint

He was the son of Eadgar and Aelfthryth. His reign was greatly disturbed by incursions of Danish fleets and armies which massive payments of money failed to curb. He was known as 'The Unready', from UNREDE, meaning 'without counsel', ie. he was without good advice.

1143

1144

		F £	VF £
1143	First small cross type. Style of 1142, usually backless dress, 3 pellets in front, *Br. 1; B.M.C. I*	325	750
1144	First Hand type. Bust r., no sceptre. R. Hand of Providence. *Br. 2; B.M.C. IIa*	85	150
1145	— Similar, but bust to l. *B.M.C. IIb*	375	850

1146

1147

1146	Second Hand type, with sceptre. *B.M.C. IId*	85	160
1147	Benediction type. *O.* As last. R. Hand giving Benediction. *B.M.C. IIf*	550	1250

1148

1151

1148	CRVX type. *Br. 3; B.M.C. IIIa*	70	130
1149	— Lightweight issue. Small flan, sceptre slants into drapery	80	160
1150	Intermediate small cross type. Somewhat as 1143, no pellets, similar bust to CRVX type (1148) but no sceptre	500	1200
1151	Long cross type. *Br. 5; B.M.C. IVa*	70	125

1152

	F	*VF*
	£	£
1152 Helmet type. *Br. 4; B.M.C. VIII*	85	160
1153 — — Similar, but struck in **gold**...............................	*Extremely rare*	

1154   1156

1154 Last small cross type. As 1143, but different style.....................................	65	125
1154A Similar, but bust r.	175	425
1155 — Similar, but bust to edge of coin. *B.M.C. Id*.......................................	275	625
1156 Agnus Dei type. *c.* 1009. *Br. 6; B.M.C. X*	3250	7250

Son of Swegn Forkbeard, King of Denmark, Cnut was acclaimed King by the Danish fleet in England in 1014 but was forced to leave. He returned in 1015 and in 1016 agreed on a division of the country with Eadmund Ironsides, the son of Aethelred. No coins of Eadmund are known and on his death in November 1016 Cnut secured all England, marrying Emma of Normandy, widow of Aethelred.

Main types

| 1157 | 1158 | 1159 | 1160 |

		F	VF
		£	£
1157	Quatrefoil type. *Br. 2; B.M.C. VIII*...	75	145
1158	Helmet type. *Br. 3; B.M.C. XIV*	65	125
1159	Short cross type. *Br. 4; B.M.C. XVI*	60	110
1159A	— Similar, but with banner in place of sceptre..	375	950
1160	Jewel cross type. *Br. 6; B.M.C. XX*. Type as 1163	450	1000

This type is now considered to be a posthumous issue struck under the auspices of his widow, Aelgifu Emma.

HAROLD I, 1035-1040

Harold, the son of Cnut and Aelgifu of Northampton, initially acted as regent for his half-brother Harthacnut on Cnut's death, was then recognised as King in Mercia and the north, and King through-out England in 1037.

| 1163 | 1165 |

1163	Jewel cross type, as illustration. *Br. 1; B.M.C. 1*	160	375
1164	Long cross and trefoils type. *Br. 2; B.M.C. V*	170	400
1165	— Similar, but fleur de lis in place of trefoils. *B.M.C. Vc*	150	350

He was heir to Cnut but lost the throne to his half-brother Harold owing to his absence in Denmark. On Harold's death he recovered his English realm.

	F	VF
	£	£
1166 **Early period, 1036.** Jewel cross type, as 1163; bust l. *Br. 1; B.M.C. I*	850	2000

1167   1168

1167 — Similar, but bust r. *B.M.C. Ia*	750	1800
1168 **Restoration, 1040-1042.** Arm and sceptre type, with name Harthacnut. *Br. 2; B.M.C. II*	675	1650

1169   1170

1169 — Similar, but with name 'Cnut'	335	725
1170 **Danish types,** of various designs, some of English type mostly struck at Lund, Denmark (now Sweden)	180	425

EDWARD THE CONFESSOR, 1042-1066

Edward was the son of Aethelred II and Emma of Normandy. A number of new mints were opened during his reign.

1171   1173

1171 PACX type, cross extends to edge of coin. *Br. 4; B.M.C. IVa*	135	275
1172 — Similar, but cross ends at legend. *B.M.C. IV*	150	325
1173 Radiate type. *Br. 2; B.M.C. I*	75	135

1174

1175

		F	VF
		£	£
1174	Trefoil quadrilateral type. *Br. 1; B.M.C. III*	80	145
1175	Short cross type, small flans. *Br. 3; B.M.C. II*	70	120

1176

1179

1176	Expanding cross type; light issue (18 grs.). *Br. 5; B.M.C. V*	90	165
1177	— — Heavy issue (27 grs.)	90	160
1178	— — Similar, but struck in **gold**	*Extremely rare*	
1179	Helmet type. *Br. 6; B.M.C. VII*	80	140
1180	— — Similar but bust l.	425	900

1181

1182

1181	Sovereign type. *Br. 7; B.M.C. IX*	95	180
1182	Hammer cross type. *Br. 8; B.M.C. XI*	80	140

1183

1184

1183	Facing bust type. Br. 9; B.M.C. XIII	75	135
1184	Pyramids type. Br. 10; B.M.C. XV	95	160

1185

	F	*VF*
	£	£
1185 Large facing bust with sceptre. R. Similar..	900	2250

Most York coins of this reign have an annulet in one quarter of the reverse.

HAROLD II, 1066

Harold was the son of Godwin Earl of Wessex. He was the brother-in-law of Edward the Confessor and was recognised as King on Edward's death. He defeated and killed Harald of Norway who invaded the north, but was himself defeated and killed at the Battle of Hastings by William of Normandy.

1186   1187

1186 Bust l. with sceptre. R. PAX across centre of *rev. B.M.C. I*......................	375	700
1187 Similar, but without sceptre. *B.M.C. Ia*...	425	850
1188 Bust r. with sceptre...	600	1350

In Anglo-Saxon times coins were struck at a large number of towns. The place of mintage is normally given on all coins from the last quarter of the 10th century onwards, and generally the name of the person responsible (e.g. BRVNIC ON LVND). Below we give a list of the mints, showing the reigns (Baronial of Stephen's reign omitted), of which coins have been found. After the town names we give one or two of the spellings as found on the coins, although often they appear in an abbreviated or extended form. On the coins the Anglo-Saxon and Norman *w* is like a Р or Г and the *th* is Ð. We have abbreviated the kings' names, etc.:

Alf	—	Alfred the Great	Wi	—	William I
EE	—	Edward the Elder	Wii	—	William II
A'stan	—	Aethelstan	He	—	Henry I
EM	—	Edward the Martyr	St	—	Stephen (regular issues)
Ae	—	Aethelred II	M	—	Matilda
Cn	—	Cnut	HA	—	Henry of Anjou
Hi	—	Harold I	WG	—	William of Gloucester
Ht	—	Harthacnut	T	—	'Tealby' coinage
ECfr	—	Edward the Confessor	SC	—	Short cross coinage
Hii	—	Harold II	LC	—	Long cross coinage

Abergavenny (FANI), Wi.

Axbridge (ACXEPO, AGEPOR) Ae, Cn, Ht.

Aylesbury (AEGEL) Ae, Cn, ECfr.

Barnstaple (BEARDA, BARDI), Edwig, Ae-Hi, ECfr, Wi, He.

Bath (BADAN) EE-Edmund, Edwig-ECfr, Wi, He, St.

Bedford (BEDANF, BEDEF) Edwig-T.

Bedwyn (BEDE CIN) ECfr, Wi.

Berkeley (BEORC) ECfr, Wi.

Bramber ? (BRAN) St.

Bridport (BRIPVNT, BRIDI) A'stan, Ae, Cn, Ht, ECfr, Wi.

Bristol (BRICSTO) Ae-T, M. HA, LC.

Bruton (BRIVT) Ae-Cn, ECfr

Buckingham (BVCIN) EM-Hi, ECfr.

Bury St. Edmunds (EDMVN, SEDM, SANTEA) A'stan?, ECfr, Wi, He-LC.

Cadbury CADANB) Ae, Cn

Caistor (CASTR) EM, Ae, Cn.

Cambridge (GRANTE) Edgar-He.

Canterbury (DORO, CAENT, CANTOR, CANT CAR) Alf, A'stan, Edgar-LC.

Cardiff (CAIRDI, CARDI, CARITI) Wi, He, St, M.

Carlisle (CAR, CARDI, EDEN) He-LC.

Castle Gotha ? (GEOÐA, IOÐA) Ae-Ht.

Castle Rising (RISINGE) St.

Chester (LEIGECES, LEGECE, CESTRE) A'stan, Edgar-T.

Chichester (CISSAN CIV, CICES, CICST) A'stan, Edgar-St, SC

Chippenham ? (CIPEN) St.

Christchurch, see Twynham.

Cissbury (SIÐEST) Ae, Cn.

Colchester (COLEAC, COLECES) Ae-Hi, ECfr-T.

Crewkerne (CRVCERN) Ae, Cn.

Cricklade (CROCGL, CRIC, CREC) Ae-Wii.

Derby (DEOR, DIORBI, DERBI) A'stan, Edgar-ECfr, Wi-St.

Dorchester (DORCE, DORECES) Ae-ECfr, Wi-He, WG.

Dover (DOFER) A'stan, Edgar-St.

Droitwich (PICC, PICNEH) ECfr. Hii.

Dunwich (DVNE) St.

Durham (DVRE, DVRHAN) Wi, St-LC.

Exeter (EAXANC, EXEC, XECST) Alf, A'stan, Edwig-LC.

Eye (EI, EIE) St.

Frome ? (FRO) Cn-ECfr.

Gloucester (GLEA C EC, GLE C , G C) Alf, A'stan, Edgar-St, HA, T, LC.

Guildford (GILDEF) EM-Cn, Ht-Wii.

Hastings (HAESTIN) Ae-St.

Hedon, near Hull (HEDVN) St.

Hereford (HEREFOR) A'stan, Ae-St, HA, T, LC.

Hertford (HEORTF) A'stan, Edwig-Hi, ECfr, Wi, Wii.

Horncastle ? (HORN) EM, Ae.

Horndon ? (HORNIDVNE) ECfr.

Huntingdon (HVNTEN) Edwig-St.

Hythe (HIÐEN) ECfr, Wi, Wii.

Ilchester (IVELCE, GIFELCST, GIVELC) Edgar, E M-He, T, LC.

Ipswich (GIPES C IC) Edgar-SC.

Kings Lynn (LENN, LENE) SC.

Langport (LANCPOR) A'stan, Cn, Hi, ECfr.

Launceston (LANSTF, SANCTI STEFANI) Ae, Wi, Wii, St. T.

Leicester (LIGER, LIHER, LEHRE) A'stan, Edgar-T.

Lewes (LAEPES) A'stan, Edgar-T.

Lichfield (LIHFL) SC.

Lincoln (LINCOLNE, NICOLE) Edgar-LC.

London (LVNDENE) Alf-LC.

Louth ? (LVD) Ae.

Lydford (LYDAN) EM-Hi, ECfr.

Lympne (LIMEN) A'stan, Edgar-Cn.

Maldon (MAELDVN, MAELI) A'stan, Ae-Hi, ECfr, Wii.

Malmesbury (MALD, MEALDMES) Ae-Wii, HA.

Marlborough (MAERLEB) Wi, Wii.

Milbourne Port (MYLE) Ae, Cn.

Newark (NEPIR, NIPOR) Edwig, Eadgar, Ae, Cn.

Newcastle (NEWEC, NIVCA) St, T, LC.

Newport (NIPAN, NIPEP) Edgar, ECfr.

Northampton (HAMTVN, NORHANT) Edwig, Edgar-Wi, He-LC.

Norwich (NORPIC) A'stan-LC.

Nottingham (SNOTINC) A'stan, Ae-St.

Oxford (OXNAFOR, OXENEF) A'stan, Edmund, Edred, Edgar-St, M, T-LC.

Pembroke (PAN, PAIN) He-T.

Pershore (PERESC) ECfr.

Peterborough (MEDE, BVR) Ae, Cn, Wi.

Petherton (PEDÐR) ECfr.
Pevensey (PEFNESE, PEVEN) Wi, Wii, St.
Reading (READIN) ECfr.
Rhuddlan (RVDILI, RVLA) Wi, SC.
Rochester (ROFEC) A'stan, Edgar-He, SC.
Romney (RVME, RVMNE) Ae-Hi, ECfr-He.
Rye (RIE) St.
Salisbury (SAEREB, SALEB) Ae-ECfr, Wi- T.
Sandwich (SANPIC) ECfr, Wi-St.
Shaftesbury (SCEFTESB, SCEFITI) A'stan, Ae-St.
Shrewsbury (SCROBES, SALOP) A'stan, Edgar-LC.
Southampton (HAMWIC, HAMTVN) A'stan, Edwig-Cn.
Southwark (SVDGE, SVD C EEORC) Ae-St.
Stafford (STAFF, STAEF) A'stan, Ae-Hi, ECfr, Wi, Wii, St, T.
Stamford (STANFOR) Edgar-St.
Steyning (STAENIG) Cn-Wii.
Sudbury (SVDBI, SVB) Ae, Cn, ECfr, Wi- St.
Swansea (SWENSEI) HA?

Tamworth (TOMPEARÐGE, TAMPRÐ) A'stan, Edwig-Hi, ECfr, Wi-St.
Taunton (TANTVNE) Ae, Cn, Ht-St.
Thetford (ÐEOTFOR,, TETFOR) Edgar-T.
Torksey (TORC, TVRC) EM-Cn.
Totnes (DARENT VRB, TOTANES, TOTNESE) A'stan, Edwig-Cn, Wii.
Twynham, now Christchurch (TPIN, TVEHAM) Wi, He.
Wallingford (PELING, PALLIG) A'stan, Edgar-He, T, LC.
Wareham (PERHAM) A'stan, Ae, Cn, Ht-St, M, WG.
Warminster (PORIME) Ae-Hi, ECfr.
Warwick (PAERING, PERPIC) A'stan, Edgar-St.
Watchet (PECEDPORT, PICEDI) Ae-ECfr, Wi-St.
Wilton (PILTVNE) Edgar-LC.
Winchcombe (PINCELE, PINCL) Edgar-Cn, Ht-Wi.
Winchester (PINTONIA, PINCEST) Alf-A'stan, Edwig -LC.
Worcester (PIHRAC, PIHREC) Ae-Hi, ECfr-Sc.
York (EBORACI, EOFERPIC) A'stan, Edmund, Edgar-LC

The location of the following is uncertain.
AESTHE *(? Hastings)* Ae.
DERNE, DYR *(E. Anglian mint East Dereham?)* ECfr.
DEVITVN *(? Welsh Marches* or *St. Davids)* Wi.
MAINT, Wi.
WEARDBYRIG *(? Warborough)* A'stan, Edgar.

BRYGIN *(? Bridgnorth,* but die-links with NIPAN and with *Shaftesbury)* Ae.
EANBYRIG, Cn.
ORSNAFORDA *(? Horsforth* or *Orford)* Alf.

EDWARDIAN AND LATER MINTS

London, Tower: Edw. I-Geo. III.
London, Durham House: Hen. VIII (posth.)-Edw. VI.
Aberystwyth: Chas. I.
Bridgnorth: Chas. I.
Birmingham, Heaton: Vic., Geo. V.
Birmingham, Soho: Geo. III.
Bristol: Edw. I, Edw. IV, Hen. VI rest., Hen. VIII-Edw. VI, Chas. I, Wm. III.
Canterbury: Edw. I-Edw. III, Edw. IV, Hen. VII-Edw. VI.
Chester: Edw. I, Chas. I, Wm. III.
Coventry: Edw. IV.
Exeter: Edw. I, Chas. I, Wm. III.
Hereford: Chas. I.
Lincoln: Edw. I.
Melbourne, Australia (branch mint): Vic.-Geo. V.
Newcastle-upon-Tyne: Edw. I.
Ottowa, Canada (branch mint): Edw. VII-Geo. V.
Perth, Australia (branch mint): Vic.-Geo. V.
Pretoria, South Africa (branch mint): Geo. V.
Scarborough: Chas. I.
Southwark: Hen. VIII-Edw. VI.
Tournai, Belgium: Hen. VIII.
Welsh Marches: Chas I
York: Edw. I, Edw. III-Edw. IV, Rich. III-Edw. VI, Chas. I, Wm. III.

London, Tower Hill: Geo. III-Eliz. II.
Ashby de la Zouche: Chas. I.
Aberystwyth: -Furnace: Chas. I.
Berwick-on-Tweed: Edw. I-Edw. III.
Birmingham, King's Norton: Geo. V.
Bombay, India (branch mint): Geo. V.
Bury St. Edmunds: Edw. I-Edw. III.
Calais: Edw. III-Hen. IV, Hen. VI.
Carlisle: Chas. I.
Colchester: Chas. I.
Durham: Edw. I-Edw. IV, Rich. III-Hen. VIII.
Hartlebury Castle, Worcs.: Chas. I.
Kingston-upon-Hull: Edw. I.
Llantrisant: Eliz. II (decimal coinage).
Newark: Chas. I.
Norwich: Edw. IV, Wm. III.
Oxford: Chas I
Pontefract: Chas. I.
Reading: Edw. III.
Shrewsbury: Chas. I.
Sydney, Australia (branch mint): Vic.-Geo. V.
Truro: Chas. I.
Worcester: Chas I.

129

NORMAN MINTS (WILLIAM I TO HENRY I)

1. Launceston	13. Bath	25. Chichester	37. London	49. Huntingdon	61. Rhuddlan
2. Barnstaple	14. Marlborough	26. Steyning	38. Hertford	50. Bedford	62. Chester
3. Totnes	15. Wilton	27. Lewes	39. Maldon	51. Northampton	63. Shrewsbury
4. Exeter	16. Salisbury	28. Pevensey	40. Colchester	52. Warwick	64. Stafford
5. Watchet	17. Chirstchurch	29. Hastings	41. Ipswich	53. Worcester	65. Tamworth
6. Taunton	18. Abergavenny*	30. Romney	42. Sudbury	54. Winchcombe	66. Leicester
7. Bridport	19. Winchester	31. Hythe	43. Cambridge	55. Oxford	67. Derby
8. Dorchester	20. Bedwyn	32. Dover	44. Bury	56. Gloucester	68. Nottingham
9. Wareham	21. Malmesbury	33. Sandwich	45. Thetford	57. Hereford	69. Lincoln
10. Shaftesbury	22. Cricklade	34. Canterbury	46. Norwich	58. Cardiff	70. York
11. Ilchester	23. Wallingford	35. Rochester	47. Stamford	59. Pembroke	71. Durham
12. Bristol	24. Guildford	36. Southwark	48. Peterborough	60. St Davids*	72. Carlisle

Possible location of uncertain mint

NORMAN KINGS, 1066-1154

There were no major changes in the coinages following the Norman conquest. The controls and periodic changes of the type made in the previous reigns were continued. Nearly seventy mints were
operating during the reign of William I; these had been reduced to about fifty-five by the middle of
the 12th century and, under Henry II, first to thirty and later to eleven. By the second half of the 13th
century the issue of coinage had been centralized at London and Canterbury, with the exception of
two ecclesiastical mints. Of the thirteen types with the name PILLEMVS, PILLELM, etc. (William),
the first eight have been attributed to the Conqueror and the remaining five to his son William Rufus.
Cut 'halfpennies' and 'farthings' were still made in this period and are scarce until the later issues of
Henry I and Stephen.

From William I to Edward II inclusive all are silver pennies unless otherwise stated.

WILLIAM I, 1066-1087

William Duke of Normandy was the cousin of Edward the Confessor. After securing the throne of
England he had to suppress several rebellions.

1250   1251

		F	VF
		£	£
1250	*Penny.* Profile left type. *Br. I*	165	375

1252   1253

1251	Bonnet type. *Br. II*	125	240
1252	Canopy type. *Br. III*	200	475

1254   1255

1253	Two sceptres type. *Br. IV*	150	325
1254	Two stars type. *Br. V*	120	225
1255	Sword type. *Br. VI*	175	375

1256   1257

		F	VF
		£	£
1256	Profile right type. *Br VII*	245	550
1257	PAXS type. *Br. VIII*	100	165

WILLIAM II, 1087-1100

William Rufus was the second son of William I, his elder brother Robert succeeded to the Dukedom of Normandy. He was killed while hunting in the New Forest.

1258   1259

1258	Penny. Profile type. *Br. 1*	300	650
1259	Cross in quatrefoil type. *Br. 2*	260	510

1260   1261

1260	Cross voided type. *Br. 3*	250	510
1261	Cross pattée and fleury type. *Br. 4*	300	625

1262

1262	Cross fleury and piles type. *Br. 5*	350	675

Fifteen types were minted during this reign. In 1106-7 provision was made for minting round half-pence again, none having been struck since the time of Eadgar, but relatively few can have been made. The standard of coinage manufacture was now beginning to deteriorate badly. Many genuine coins were being cut to see if they were plated counterfeits and there was a reluctance by the public to accept such damaged pieces. About 1107-8 an extraordinary decision was taken to order the official mutilation of all new coins by snicking the edges, thus ensuring that cut coins had to be accepted. Pennies of types VII to XII (Nos. 1268-1273) usually have a cut in the flan that sometimes penetrated over a third of the way across the coin.

At Christmas 1124 the famous 'Assize of the Moneyers' was held at Winchester when all the moneyers in England were called to account for their activities and a number are said to have been mutilated for issuing coins of inferior quality.

The dates and the order of Henry's issues have been modified several times since Brooke. The main changes are as follows: BMC 11 preceded 10 and bmc 9 follows 6. The order of BMC 7 and 8 remains uncertain. The issues were not made for equal periods of time, as BMC 15 began in early 1125. The contemporary chronicles mention the round halfpenny (and farthings) and the order to snick whole coins under 1107 or 1108. The halfpennies are now dated to agree with these references when BMC 6 and 9 pennies were current. A few pennies of BMC 6 are snicked as are most of the half-pennies. Snicks continue to be used on coins of BMC 13 and 14, thought the cut is smaller and only a quarter to a half of the coins are snicked. [Brooke 1916; Archibald and Conté SNC 1990; Blackburn RNS 1990.]

1263   1263A

	F	VF
	£	£
1263 **Penny.** *Br.* I. Annulets type	300	650
1263A — II. Profile l. R. Cross fleury	235	475

1264   1265

1264 — III. PAX type	225	450
1265 — IV. Facing bust. R. Five annulets and four piles	275	550

1266   1267

1266 — V. — R. Voided cross with fleur in each angle	450	950
1267 — VI. Pointing bust and stars type	625	1250

1268

		F	*VF*
		£	£
1268	*Br.* VII. Facing bust. R. Quatrefoil with piles	245	475

1269   1270

| 1269 | — VIII. Large bust l. R. Cross with annulet in each angle .... | 750 | 1750 |
| 1270 | — IX. Facing bust. R. Cross in quatrefoil .... | 475 | 950 |

1271   1272

| 1271 | — X. Small facing bust in circle. R. Cross fleury .... | 150 | 325 |
| 1272 | — XI. Very large bust l. R. 'Double inscription' around small cross pattee | 325 | 725 |

1273   1274

| 1273 | — XII. Small bust l. R. Cross with annulet in each angle .... | 250 | 550 |
| 1274 | — XIII. Star in lozenge fleury type .... | 250 | 525 |

MINTS OF STEPHEN AND THE ANARCHY

● = Regular mints of Stephen.

⊕ = Mints striking irregular coins including Angevin.

+ = Mints striking regular and irregular coins.

N.B. Attribution to some of the towns shown is uncertain.

Roxburgh⊕ Bamborough
Corbridge⊕ + Newcastle
+ Carlisle
+ Durham

York +
Hedon ●

Lincoln +
Chester ● ⊕ Newark
Derby + Nottingham
Stafford ● ⊕ Tutbury
Shrewsbury ● Leicester Stamford
Tamworth ● ⊕ Eye Castle Rising ●
Peterborough ● + Thetford Norwich +
Northampton + Huntingdon + Bury Dunwich +
Worcester ● Warwick ● ⊕ Cambridge Ipswich
Hereford + Bedford Sudbury +
+ Gloucester Colchester ●
Cirencester⊕ + Oxford
Swansea ⊕ Cricklade London
Pembroke ● Cardiff + ⊕ Malmesbury ⊕ Wallingford Canterbury + Sandwich +
Bristol ● Bath Southwark Dover
⊕ Trowbridge
Watchet ● + Ilchester + Wilton Rye
Wivelscombe⊕ Shaftesbury ● Wilton + Winchester Bramber Lewes Hastings
Taunton ● Salisbury Bramber + Pevensey
Sherborne Southampton⊕ Chichester Steyning
Exeter ● Dorchester Wareham
+ Launceston Wight

1275   1276

		F	*VF*
		£	£
1275	Br. XIV. Pellets in quatrefoil type	135	295
1276	— XV. Quadrilateral on cross fleury type	100	225

1277

		F	*VF*
1277*	*Halfpenny.* Facing head. R. Cross potent with pellets in angles	1100	2500
1277A	— As above R. Similar to penny die of type IX	1850	4250

STEPHEN, 1135-1154
and the Civil War and Anarchy, 1138-1153

Stephen of Blois, Count of Boulogne and a nephew of Henry I, hastily crossed the Channel on his uncle's death and secured the throne for himself, despite Henry's wishes that his daughter Matilda should succeed him. She was the widow of the German emperor Henry V, and was then married to Geoffrey, Count of Anjou. Two years later Matilda arrived in England to claim the throne, supported by her half-brother Robert of Gloucester.

During the protracted civil war that ensued Matilda and later her son, Henry of Anjou, set up an alternative court at Bristol and held much of the west of England, striking coins at mints under their control. Many irregular coins were struck during this troubled period, some by barons in their own name. Particularly curious are the coins from the Midlands and E. Anglia which have Stephen's head defaced, now believed to have been issued during the Interdict of 1148. In 1153, following the death of Stephen's son, Eustace, a treaty between the two factions allowed for the succession of Matilda's son Henry and a uniform coinage was once more established throughout the kingdom.

B.M.C. Norman Kings, 2 vols. (1916). *M.—* Mack, R. P., 'Stephen and the Anarchy 1135-54', *BNJ, XXXV* (1966), pp. 38-112.

Regular regal issuess

1278   1280

1281   1282

		F £	VF £
1278	**Penny.** Cross moline (Watford) type. Bust r., with sceptre. R. Cross moline with lis in angles. *B.M.C. I; M. 3-42*	100	240
1279	— Similar, but obv. reads PERERIC or PERERICM. *M. 43-50*	350	750
1280	Voided cross type. Facing bust with sceptre. R. Voided cross pattée with mullets in angles. *East and South-east mints only. B.M.C. II; M. 53-66*	135	325
1281	Cross fleury type. Bust l. with sceptre. R. Cross fleury with trefoils in angles. *East and South-east mints only. B.M.C. VI; M. 77-99*	300	675
1282	Cross pommee (Awbridge) type. Bust half-left with sceptre. R. Voided cross pommee with lis in angles. *B.M.C. VII; M. 99z-135b*	160	375

For B.M.C. types III, IV & V, see 1300-1302.

LOCAL AND IRREGULAR ISSUES OF THE CIVIL WAR

A. Coins struck from erased or defaced dies (interdict of 1148)

1283

		F £	VF £
1283	As 1278, with king's bust defaced with long cross. *East Anglian Mints.* M. *137-147*	450	950
1284	— Similar, but king's bust defaced with small cross. *Nottingham. M. 149*	400	850
1285	— Similar, but sceptre defaced with bar or cross. *Nottingham, Lincoln and Stamford. M. 148 and 150-154*	400	825
1286	— Similar, but king's name erased. *Nottingham. M. 157*	325	700
1286A	— Other defacements	400	850

B. South-Eastern variant

1287	As 1278, but king holds mace instead of sceptre. *Canterbury. M. 158*	1000	2500

C. Eastern variants

1288

1288	As 1278, but roundels in centre or on limbs of cross or in angles. *Suffolk mints. M. 159-168*	625	1350
1288A	As 1278, but star before sceptre and annulets at tips of *fleurs on reverse. Suffolk mints. M. 188*	750	1750
1289	As 1278, but thick plain cross with pellet at end of limbs, lis in angles. *Lincoln. M. 169-173*	650	1450
1290	— Similar, but thick plain cross superimposed on cross moline. *M. 174.*	750	1650
1290A	As 1278. R. Quadrilateral over voided cross. *M. 176*	1000	2350
1290B	As 1278. R. Long cross to edge of coin, fleurs outwards in angles. *Lincoln. M. 186-187*	900	2000

	F £	*VF* £

D. Southern variants

1291   As 1278, but with large rosette of pellets at end of obverse legend.
M. *184-185* 750 1650

1292   — Similar, but star at end of obverse legend. *M. 187y* 750 1650

1293   Crowned bust r. or l. with rosette of pellets before face in place of sceptre.
R. As 1280, but plain instead of voided cross. *M. 181-183* 800 1750

1291   1295

1295   As 1278, but usually collar of annulets. R. Voided cross moline with
annulet at centre. *Southampton. M. 207-212* 250 575

E. Midland variants

1296

1296   As 1278, but cross moline on reverse has fleured extensions into legend.
Leicester. M. 177-178 .... 900 2250

1297   As 1278 but crude work. R. Voided cross with lis outwards in angles.
Tutbury. M. 179 .... 900 2250

1298   1300

1298   Somewhat similar. R. Voided cross with martlets in angles. *Derby. M. 175*   1350 3250

1299   As 1278. R. Plain cross with T-cross in each angle. *M. 180* 1100 2500

1300   Facing bust with three annulets on crown. R. Cross pattée, fleurs inwards
in angles. *Northampton or Huntingdon (?). B.M.C. III; M. 67-71* 1250 2600

1301   1302

		F	VF
		£	£
1301	Facing bust with three fleurs on crown. R. Lozenge fleury, annulets in angles. *Lincoln or Nottingham. B.M.C. IV; M. 72-75*	1250	2750
1302	Bust half-right with sceptre. R. Lozenge with pellet centre, fleurs inwards in angles. *Leicester. B.M.C. V; M. 76*	1350	3250
1303	**Robert,** Earl of Leicester(?). As 1280, but reading ROBERTVS. *M. 269*	2500	5250

F. North-east and Scottish border variants

1304	As 1278, but star before sceptre and annulets at tips of fleurs on reverse. *M. 188*	750	1750
1305	As 1278, but a voided cross extending to outer circle of reverse. *M. 189-192*	900	2250
1306	As 1278, but crude style, with Stephen's name. *M. 276-279 and 281-282*	500	1250
1307	— Similar. R. Cross crosslet with cross-pattée and crescent in angles. *M. 288*	1350	2750
1308	David I (K. of Scotland). As 1305, but with name DAVID REX. *M. 280*	1500	3000
1309	**Henry** (Earl of Northumberland, son of K. David). hENRIC ERL. As 1278. *M. 283-285*	1450	3000
1310	— Similar. R. Cross fleury. *M. 286-287*	1000	2250
1311	— As 1307, but with name NENCI : COM on obverse. *M. 289*	1350	2750

G. 'Ornamented' series. *So-called 'York Group' but probably minted in Northern France*

1312	As 1278, with obverse inscription NSEPEFETI, STEFINEI or RODBDS. R. WISÐ. GNETA, etc., with ornament(s) in legend (sometimes retrograde). *M. 215-216 and 227*	1500	3500

1313   1315

1313	Flag type. As 1278, but king holds lance with pennant, star to r. R. As 1278, mostly with four ornaments in legend. *M. 217*	975	2350
1313A	— Similar, but with eight ornaments in reverse inscription. *M. 217*	975	2350
1314	As 1278, but STIEN and ornaments, sceptre is topped by pellet in lozenge. R. Cross fleury over plain cross, ornaments in place of inscription. *M. 218*	1500	3500
1314A	King stg. facing, holding sceptre and long standard with triple-tailed pennon. R. Cross pattee, crescents and quatrefoils in angles, pellets around, ornaments in legend	2500	5750
1315	**Stephen and Queen Matilda.** Two standing figures holding sceptre, as illustration. R. Ornaments in place of inscription. *M. 220*	1850	4250

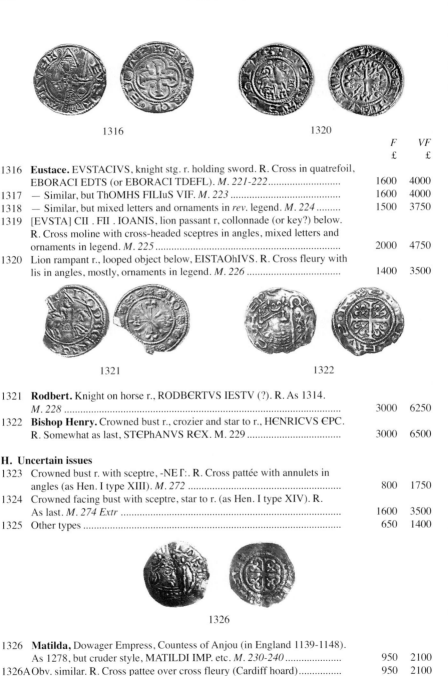

1316   1320

	F £	VF £
1316 **Eustace.** EVSTACIVS, knight stg. r. holding sword. R. Cross in quatrefoil, EBORACI EDTS (or EBORACI TDEFL). *M. 221-222*	1600	4000
1317 — Similar, but ThOMHS FILIuS VIF. *M. 223*	1600	4000
1318 — Similar, but mixed letters and ornaments in *rev.* legend. *M. 224*	1500	3750
1319 [EVSTA] CII . FII . IOANIS, lion passant r, collonnade (or key?) below. R. Cross moline with cross-headed sceptres in angles, mixed letters and ornaments in legend. *M. 225*	2000	4750
1320 Lion rampant r., looped object below, EISTAOhIVS. R. Cross fleury with lis in angles, mostly, ornaments in legend. *M. 226*	1400	3500

1321   1322

1321 **Rodbert.** Knight on horse r., RODBERTVS IESTV (?). R. As 1314. *M. 228*	3000	6250
1322 **Bishop Henry.** Crowned bust r., crozier and star to r., HENRICVS €PC. R. Somewhat as last, STEPhANVS REX. M. 229	3000	6500

H. Uncertain issues

1323 Crowned bust r. with sceptre, -NE Γ:. R. Cross pattée with annulets in angles (as Hen. I type XIII). *M. 272*	800	1750
1324 Crowned facing bust with sceptre, star to r. (as Hen. I type XIV). R. As last. *M. 274 Extr*	1600	3500
1325 Other types	650	1400

1326

1326 **Matilda,** Dowager Empress, Countess of Anjou (in England 1139-1148). As 1278, but cruder style, MATILDI IMP. etc. *M. 230-240*	950	2100
1326A Obv. similar. R. Cross pattee over cross fleury (Cardiff hoard)	950	2100
1326B Similar, but triple pellets or plumes at end of cross (Cardiff hoard)	1100	2500
1326C **Henry of Neubourg,** Bust r., R. As 1276A or 1278	2250	5000

	F	VF
	£	£
1327 **Duke Henry,** son of Matilda and Geoffrey of Anjou, Duke of Normandy from 1150 (in England 1147-1149-1150 and 1153-1154). As 1278 but hENRICVS, etc. *M. 241-245*	2000	4250
1327A As 1295 but hENRIC. *M. 246*	2000	4250
1327B As 1326B, but hENNENNVS R, etc	2100	4500
1328 Obverse as 1278. R. Cross crosslet in quatrefoil. *M. 254*	2200	4500
1329 Crowned bust r. with sceptre. R. Cross fleury over quadrilateral fleury. *M. 248-253*	2200	4500

1330   1331

1330 Crowned facing bust, star each side. R. Cross botonnée over a quadri- lateral pommée. *M. 255-258*	2400	5000
1331 Obverse as 1330. R. Voided cross botonnée over a quadrilateral pommée. *M. 259-261*	2400	5000
1331A **Robert, Earl of Gloucester,** 1143-7, Lion. r. R. Cross fleury..............	1650	3750
1332 **William,** Earl of Gloucester (succeeded his father, Earl Robert, in 1147). Type as Henry of Anjou, no. 1329. *M. 262*	2650	5250
1333 Type as Henry of Anjou, no. 1330. *M. 263*	2750	5500
1334 Type as Henry of Anjou, no. 1331. *M. 264-268*	2500	5250
1334A — Lion. R. Cross fleury....................	1600	3500
1335 **Brian Fitzcount,** Lord of Wallingford (?). Type as Henry of Anjou, no. 1330. *M. 270*	3500	7500
1336 **Patrick,** Earl of Salisbury (?). Helmeted bust r. holding sword, star behind. R. As Henry of Anjou, no. 1329. *M. 271*	3250	7000

MINTS HENRY II – EDWARD II (1158-1327)

HENRY II, 1154-1189

Cross-and-crosslets ('Tealby') Coinage, 1158-1180

Coins of Stephen's last type continued to be minted until 1158. Then a new coinage bearing Henry's name replaced the currency of the previous reign which contained a high proportion of irregular and sub-standard pennies. The new Cross and Crosslets issue is more commonly referred to as the 'Tealby' coinage, as over 5000 of these pennies were discovered at Tealby, Lincolnshire, in 1807. Thirty mints were employed in this re-coinage, but once the re-minting had been completed not more than a dozen mints were kept open. The issue remained virtually unchanged for twenty-two years apart from minor variations in the king's portrait. The coins tend to be poorly struck on irregular plans.

Cut coins occur with varying degrees of frequency during this issue, according to the type and local area.

The price quoted for coins in this section allows for the usual poor quality strike.

1337A   B   C

Penny

		F £	VF £
1337	Class A. No hair	50	120
1338	— B. Similar but mantle varies	55	145
1339	— C. Decorated collar, curl of hair	50	125

D   E   F

1340	— D. Decoration continues along shoulder	55	140
1341	— E. Similar bust, but shoulder not decorated	60	155
1342	— F. Hair in long ringlet to r. of bust	60	160

Mints and classes of the Cross-and-Crosslets coinage

Approximate dates for the various classes are as follows:

A 1158-1161, B and C 1161-1165, D 1165-1168, E 1168-1170 and F 1170-1180.

Bedford	A - - - - -	Ilchester	A B C D - F	Pembroke	A - - - - -
Bristol	A B C D E F	Ipswich	- B C D E F	Salisbury	A - - - - -
Bury St. Edmunds	A B C D E F	Launceston	A - - - - -	Shrewsbury	A - - - - -
Canterbury	A B C D E F	Leicester	A - - - - -	Stafford	A - C - - -
Carlisle	A - C D E F	Lewes	- - - - ? F	Thetford	A - C D - F
Chester	A - - D - -	Lincoln	A B C D E F	Wallingford	A - - - - -
Colchester	A - C - E -	London	A B C D E F	Wilton	A - - - - -
Durham	A B C - - -	Newcastle	A - C D E F	Winchester	A - C D ? -
Exeter	A B C D - -	Northampton	A - C ? - -	York	A - C D - -
Gloucester	A - - - - -	Norwich	A B C D - F		
Hereford	A - C - - -	Oxford	A - - D E -		

The publishers would like to thank Prof. Jeffrey Mass for re-organising and updating the short cross series. All illustrations have kindly been supplied by Prof. Mass.

'Short Cross' coinage of Henry II (1180-1189)

In 1180 a coinage of new type, known as the Short Cross coinage, replaced the Tealby issue. The new coinage is remarkable in that it covers not only the latter part of the reign of Henry II, but also the reigns of his sons Richard and John and his grandson Henry III, and the entire issue bears the name 'hENRICVS'. There are no English coins with the names of Richard or John. The Short Cross coins can be divided chronologically into various classes: ten mints were operating under Henry II and tables of mints, moneyers and classes are given for each reign.

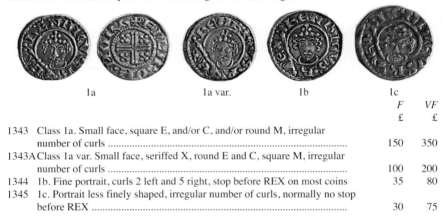

1a	1a var.	1b	1c

		F	VF
		£	£
1343	Class 1a. Small face, square E, and/or C, and/or round M, irregular number of curls	150	350
1343A	Class 1a var. Small face, seriffed X, round E and C, square M, irregular number of curls	100	200
1344	1b. Fine portrait, curls 2 left and 5 right, stop before REX on most coins	35	80
1345	1c. Portrait less finely shaped, irregular number of curls, normally no stop before REX	30	75

RICHARD I, 1189-1199

Pennies of Short Cross type continued to be issued throughout the reign, all bearing the name hENRICVS. The coins of class 4, which have very crude portraits, continued to be issued in the early years of the next reign. The only coins bearing Richard's name are from his territories of Aquitaine and Poitou in western France.

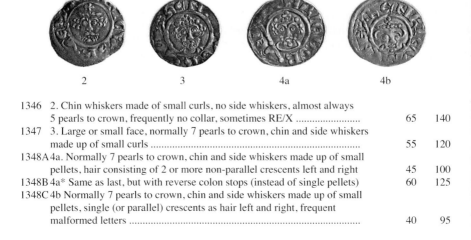

2	3	4a	4b

1346	2. Chin whiskers made of small curls, no side whiskers, almost always 5 pearls to crown, frequently no collar, sometimes RE/X	65	140
1347	3. Large or small face, normally 7 pearls to crown, chin and side whiskers made up of small curls	55	120
1348A	4a. Normally 7 pearls to crown, chin and side whiskers made up of small pellets, hair consisting of 2 or more non-parallel crescents left and right	45	100
1348B	4a* Same as last, but with reverse colon stops (instead of single pellets)	60	125
1348C	4b Normally 7 pearls to crown, chin and side whiskers made up of small pellets, single (or parallel) crescents as hair left and right, frequent malformed letters	40	95

'Short Cross' coinage *continued*. All with name hENRICVS

The Short Cross coins of class 4 continued during the early years of John's reign, but in 1205 a re-coinage was initiated and new Short Cross coins of better style replaced the older issues. Coins of classes 5a and 5b were issued in the re-coinage in which sixteen mints were employed. Only ten of these mints were still working by the end of class 5. The only coins to bear John's name are the pennies, halfpence and farthings issues for Ireland.

4c   5a1   5a2

5b   5c   6a

		F	VF
		£	£
1349	4c. Reversed S, square face at bottom, 5 pearls to crown, normally single crescents as hair left and right	60	125
1350A	5a1 Reversed or regular S, irregular curved lines as hair (or circular curls containing no pellets), cross pattee as initial mark on reverse, *London and Canterbury* only	65	135
1350B	5a2 Reversed S, circular curls left and right (2 or 3 each side) containing single pellets, cross pomme as initial mark on reverse	50	100
1350C	5a/5b or 5b/5a..	50	100
1351	5b. Regular S, circular pelleted curls, cross pattee as initial mark on reverse	35	70
1352	5c. Slightly rounder portrait, letter X in the form of a St. Andrew's cross	35	70
1353	6a. Smaller portrait, with smaller letter X composed of thin strokes or, later, short wedges	35	70

'Short Cross' coinage *continued* (1216-47)

The Short Cross coinage continued for a further thirty years during which time the style of portraiture and workmanship deteriorated. By the 1220s minting had been concentrated at London and Canterbury, one exception being the mint of the Abbot of Bury St. Edmunds.

Halfpenny and farthing dies are recorded early in this issue; a few halfpennies and now farthings have been discovered. See nos 1357 D-E.

6b   6c   6c orn.   6x   6d

		F £	VF £
1354	6b. Very tall lettering and long rectangular face	30	55
1355	6c. Lettering now shorter, face narrow and triangular	30	55
1355A	6c. orn. Various letters now ornamental in design, curls 3/3 left and right	60	125
1355B	6x. Canterbury mint only, RE/X, curls 2/2, nostril pellets outside nose ...	100	225
1355C	6d. Face less distinct in shape, N's containing a pellet along the crossbar	35	650

7a   7b   7c

1356A	7a. Small compact face, letter A with top coming to a point under crossbar	25	45
1356B	7b. Letter A with square top	20	40
1356C	7c. Portrait becoming degraded, letter A with square top	20	40

8a   8b   8c

1357A	8a. New portrait; letter X in shape of curule; cross pattee as initial mark on reverse (early style), or cross pommee (late style)	55	120
1357B	8b. Degraded portrait, wedge-shaped X, cross pomme as initial mark	35	80
1357C	8c. Degraded portrait, cross pomme X, cross pomme as initial mark	35	80
1357D	Round halfpenny in style of class 7, initial mark in shape of up-turned crescent, London mint only	800	2000
1357E	Round farthing in style of class 7, initial mark in shape of up-turned crescent, London mint only	850	2250

1357D   1357E

Moneyer tables for the short cross coinage

		Fine

Henry II:

London: Aimer (1a-b), Alain (1a-b), Alain V (1a-b), Alward (1b), Davi (1b-c),
Fil Aimer (1a-b), Gefrei (1c), Gilebert (1c), Godard (1b), Henri (1a-b),
Henri Pi (1a), Iefrei (1a-b), Iohan (1a-b), Osber (1b), Pieres (1a-c),

Pieres M (1a-b), Randvl (1a-b), Ravl (1b-c), Reinald (1a-b), Willelm (1a-b)	*From*	30
Carlisle: Alain (1b-c)	*From*	70
Exeter: Asketil (1a-b), Iordan (1a-b), Osber (1a-b), Ravl (1b), Ricard (1b-c),		
Roger (1a-c)	*From*	60
Lincoln: Edmvnd (1b-c), Girard (1b), Hvgo (1b), Lefwine (1b-c), Rodbert (1b),		
Walter (1b), Will. D.F. (1b), Willelm (1b-c)	*From*	45
Northampton: Filip (1a-b), Hvgo (1a-b), Ravl (1a-c), Reinald (1a-c), Simvn (1b),		
Walter (1a-c), Willelm (1a-b)	*From*	40
Oxford: Asketil (1b), Iefrei (1b), Owein (1b-c), Ricard (1b-c), Rodbert (1b),		
Rodbt. F. B. (1b), Sagar (1b)	*From*	60
Wilton: Osber (1a-b), Rodbert (1a-b)	*From*	60
Winchester: Adam (1a-c), Clement (1a-b), Gocelm (1a-c), Henri (1a),		
Osber (1a-b), Reinier (1b), Rodbert (1a-b)	*From*	35
Worcester: Edrich (1b), Godwine (1b-c), Osber (1b-c), Oslac (1b)	*From*	60
York: Alain (1a-b), Efrard (1a-c), Gerard (1a-b), Hvgo (1a-c), Hunfrei (1a-b),		
Isac (1a-b), Tvrkil (1a-c), Willelm (1a-b)	*From*	35

Richard I

London: Aimer (2-4a), Fvlke (4a-b), Henri (4a-b), Ravl (2), Ricard (2-4b),		
Stivene (2-4b), Willelm (2-4b)	*From*	40
Canterbury: Goldwine (3-4b), Hernavd (4b), Hve (4b), Ioan (4b), Meinir (2-4b),		
Reinald/Reinavd (2-4b), Roberd (2-4b), Samvel (4b), Simon (4b), Vlard (2-4b)	*From*	40
Carlisle: Alein (3-4b)	*From*	90
Durham: Adam (4a), Alein (4a-b), Pires (4b)	*From*	100
Exeter: Ricard (3)	*From*	85
Lichfield: Ioan (2)	*Extremely rare*	
Lincoln: Edmvnd (2), Lefwine (2), Willelm (2)	*From*	70
Northampton: Giferei (4a), Roberd (3), Waltir (3)	*From*	75
Northampton or Norwich: Randvl (4a-b), Willelm (4a-b)	*From*	75
Shrewsbury: Ive (4a-b), Reinald/Reinavd (4a-b), Willem (4a)	*From*	150
Winchester: Adam (3), Gocelm (3), Osbern (3-4a), Pires (4a), Willelm (3-4a)	*From*	55
Worcester: Osbern (2)	*From*	180
York: Davi (4a-b), Efrard/Everard (2-4b), Hvgo/Hve (2-4a), Nicole (4a-b),		
Tvrkil (2-4a)	*From*	50

John

London: Abel (5c-6a), Adam (5b-c), Beneit (5b-c), Fvlke (4c-5b), Henri (4c-5b/5a),
Ilger (5b-6a), Ravf (5c-6a), Rener (5a/b-5c), Ricard (4c-5b), Ricard B (5b-c),
Ricard T (5a/b-5b), Walter (5c-6a), Willelm (4c-5b), Willelm B (5a/b-5c),

Willelm L (5b-c), Willelm T (5b-c)	*From*	35
Canterbury: Goldwine (4c-5c), Hernavd/Arnavd (4c-5c), Hve (4c-5c), Iohan (4c-5c),		
Iohan B (5b-c), Iohan M (5b-c), Roberd (4c-5c), Samvel (4c-5c), Simon (4c-5c)	*From*	35
Bury St Edmunds: Fvlke (5b-c)	*From*	50
Carlisle: Tomas (5b)	*From*	80
Chichester: Pieres (5b/a-5b), Ravf (5b/a-5b), Simon (5b/a-5b), Willelm (5b)	*From*	50
Durham: Pieres (5a-6a)	*From*	60
Exeter: Gileberd (5a-b), Iohan (5a-b), Ricard (5a-b)	*From*	50

Ipswich: Alisandre (5b-c), Iohan (5b-c)	*From*	40
Kings Lynn: Iohan (5b), Nicole (5b), Willelm (5b)	*From*	100
Lincoln: Alain (5a), Andrev (5a-5c), Hve (5a/b-5c), Iohan (5a), Ravf (5a/b-5b),		
Ricard (5a-5b/a), Tomas (5a/b-5b)	*From*	35
Northampton: Adam (5b-c), Roberd (5b), Roberd T (5b)	*From*	40
Northampton or Norwich: Randvl (4c)	*From*	80
Norwich: Gifrei (5a/b-5c), Iohan (5a-c), Renald/Renavd (5a-c)	*From*	40
Oxford: Ailwine (5b), Henri (5b), Miles (5b)	*From*	50
Rochester: Alisandre (5b), Hvnfrei (5b)	*From*	80
Winchester: Adam (5a-c), Andrev (5b-c), Bartelme (5b-c), Henri (5a), Iohan (5a-c),		
Lvkas (5b-c), Miles (5a-c), Ravf (5b-c), Ricard (5a-b)	*From*	35
York: Davi (4c-5b), Nicole (4c-5c), Renavd (5b), Tomas (5a/b-5b)	*From*	35

Henry III

London: Abel (6b-7a), Adam (7b-c), Elis (7a-b), Giffrei (7b-c), Ilger (6b-7b),		
Ledvlf (7b-c), Nichole (7c-8c), Ravf (6b-7b), Ricard (7b), Terri (7a-b),		
Walter (6b-c)	*From*	20
Canterbury: Arnold (6c/6x, 6x), Henri (6b-6c/d, 7a-c), Hivn/Ivn (6b-7b),		
Iohan (6b-7c, 8b-c), Ioan Chic (7b-c), Ioan F. R. (7b-c), Nichole (7c, 8b-c),		
Osmvnd (7b-c), Robert (6b, 7b-c), Robert Vi (7c), Roger (6b-7b),		
Roger of R (7a-b), Salemvn (6x, 7a-b), Samvel (6b-d, 7a), Simon (6b-d, 7a-b),		
Tomas (6d, 7a-b), Walter (6b-7a), Willem (7b-c, 8b-c), Willem Ta (7b-c)	*From*	20
Bury St Edmunds: Iohan (7c-8c), Norman (7a-b), Ravf (6c-d, 7a), Simvnd (7b-c),		
Willelm (7a)	*From*	30
Durham: Pieres (7a)	*From*	75
Winchester: Henri (6c)	*From*	75
York: Iohan (6c), Peres (6c), Tomas (6c), Wilam (6c)	*From*	75

Irregular Local Issue

Rhuddlan (in chronological order): Halli, Tomas, Simond, Henricvs	*From*	75

Rhuddlan

'Long Cross' coinage (1247-72)

By the middle of Henry's reign the coinage in circulation was in a poor state, being worn and clipped. In 1247 a fresh coinage was ordered, the new pennies having the reverse cross extended to the edge of the coin to help safeguard the coins against clipping. The earliest of these coins have no mint or moneyers' names. A number of provincial mints were opened for producing sufficient of the Long Cross coins, but these were closed again in 1250, only the royal mints of London and Canterbury and the ecclesiastical mints of Durham and Bury St. Edmunds remained open.

In 1257, following the introduction of new gold coinages by the Italian cities of Brindisi (1232), Florence (1252) and Genoa (1253), Henry III issued a gold coinage in England. This was a gold 'Penny' valued at 20 silver pence and twice the weight of the silver penny. The coinage was not a success, being undervalued, and it ceased to be minted after a few years; few coins have survived.

Cut halfpennies and farthings are common for this period, with a greater concentration in the early part. They are up to 100 times commoner than in late Anglo-Saxon times.

Without sceptre

Ia	Ib

		F	*VF*
		£	£
1358	Class Ia. hENRICVS: REX. R. ANGLIE TERCI	275	650
1359	Ib. hENRICVS REX. ANG. R. LIE TERCI LON *(London)*, CAN		
	(Canterbury) or AED *(Bury St. Edmunds)*..*from*	40	85
1360	— — I/II mule..	45	90

II	IIIb	IIIc

1361	Class II. hENRICVS REX TERCI. R. Moneyer and mint	30	55
1362	— IIIa. hENRICVS REX ·. III, thin face as class II................................	20	35
1363	— IIIb. Smaller, rounder face	20	30
1364	— IIIc. Face with pointed chin, neck indicated by two lines, usually		
	REX: III	20	35

With sceptre

| | IVa | IVb | Va | Vb |

<table>
<thead>
<tr><th></th><th></th><th>F
£</th><th>VF
£</th></tr>
</thead>
<tbody>
<tr><td>1365</td><td>Class IVa. Similar to last, but with sceptre ....</td><td>75</td><td>150</td></tr>
<tr><td>1366</td><td>— IVb. Similar, but new crown with half-fleurs and large central fleur ..</td><td>100</td><td>225</td></tr>
<tr><td>1367</td><td>— Va. With class IV bust, crown as IVa or IVb, round eyes, from now on
legend begins at 10 o'clock..</td><td>25</td><td>40</td></tr>
<tr><td>1368</td><td>— Vb. Narrower face, wedge-tailed R, round eyes ....</td><td>20</td><td>35</td></tr>
<tr><td>1369</td><td>— Vc. As last, but almond-shaped eyes...</td><td>25</td><td>40</td></tr>
</tbody>
</table>

| Vd | Ve | Vf | Vg | Vh |

<table>
<tbody>
<tr><td>1370</td><td>— Vd. Portrait of quite different style; new crown with true-shaped fleur</td><td>55</td><td>135</td></tr>
<tr><td>1371</td><td>— Ve. Similar, with jewelled or beaded crown...</td><td>150</td><td>350</td></tr>
<tr><td>1372</td><td>— Vf. New style larger face, double-banded crown..................................</td><td>30</td><td>50</td></tr>
<tr><td>1373</td><td>— Vg. Single band to crown, low central fleur, curule chair shaped X ...</td><td>25</td><td>45</td></tr>
<tr><td>1374</td><td>— Vh. Crude copy of Vg, with pellets in lieu of fleur.............................</td><td>45</td><td>90</td></tr>
<tr><td>1375</td><td>— Vi. Similar to last, but triple line of pellets for beard.........................</td><td>250</td><td>525</td></tr>
</tbody>
</table>

| Vi | | 1376 |

<table>
<tbody>
<tr><td>1376</td><td>Gold penny of 20d. As illustration ....</td><td>20000</td><td>65000</td></tr>
</tbody>
</table>

Mints, Moneyers, and classes for Henry III 'Long Cross' coinage

London: Davi or David (IIIc-Vf), Henri (IIIa-Vd, f, g), Ion, Ioh, Iohs or Iohan
(Vc-g), Nicole (Ib/II mule, II-Vc), Renaud (Vg-i), Ricard (IIIc-Vg), Robert (Vg),
Thomas (Vg), Walter (Vc-g), Willem (Vc-g and gold penny) ....

Bristol: Elis (IIIa, b, c), Henri (IIIb) , Iacob (IIIa, b, c), Roger (IIIa, b, c), Walter
(IIIb, c) ....

Bury St. Edmunds: Ion or Iohs (II-Va, Vg, h, i), Randulf (Va-f), Renaud (Vg),
Stephane (Vg)...

	Fine
from	18
from	22
from	20

Fine

Canterbury: Alein (Vg, h), Ambroci (Vg), Gilbert (II-Vd/c mule, Vf, g), Ion, Ioh,
Iohs, or Iohanes (IIIe-Vd, f, g), Nicole or Nichole (Ib/II mule, II-Vh), Ricard
(Vg, h), Robert (Vc-h), Walter (Vc-h), Willem or Willeme (Ib/II mule, II-Vd, f, g)   *from*   18
Carlisle: Adam (IIIa, b), Ion (IIIa, b), Robert (IIIa, b), Willem (IIIa, b) ....   *from*   45
Durham: Philip (IIIb), Ricard (V, b, c), Roger (Vg), Willem (Vg) ....   *from*   55
Exeter: Ion (II-IIIc), Philip (II-IIIc), Robert (II-IIIc), Walter (II-IIIb) ....   *from*   30
Gloucester: Ion (II-IIIc), Lucas (II-IIIc), Ricard (II-IIIc), Roger (II-IIIc) ....   *from*   25
Hereford: Henri (IIIa, b), Ricard (IIIa, b, c), Roger (IIIa, b, c), Walter (IIIa, b, c)   *from*   40
Ilchester: Huge (IIIa, b, c), Ierveis (IIIa, b, c), Randulf (IIIa, b, c), Stephe
(IIIa, b, c)...   *from*   65
Lincoln: Ion (II-IIIc), Ricard (II-IIIc), Walter (II-IIIc), Willem (II-IIIc) ....   *from*   25
Newcastle: Adam (IIIa, b), Henri (IIIa, b, c), Ion (IIIa, b, c), Roger (IIIa, b, c) ..   *from*   22
Northampton: Lucas (II-IIIb), Philip (II-IIIc), Tomas (II-IIIc), Willem (II-IIIc).   *from*   25
Norwich: Huge (II-IIIc), Iacob (II-II Ic), Ion (II-IIIc), Willem (II-IIIc) ....   *from*   35
Oxford: Adam (II-IIIc), Gefrei (II-IIIc), Henri (II-IIIc), Willem (II-IIIc) ....   *from*   35
Shrewsbury: Lorens (IIIa, b, c), Nicole (IIIa, b, c), Peris (IIIa, b, c), Ricard (IIIa,
b, c) ....   *from*   45
Wallingford: Alisandre (IIIa, b), Clement (IIIa, b), Ricard (IIIa, b), Robert (IIIa,
b) ....   *from*   30
Wilton: Huge (IIIb, c), Ion (IIIa, b, c), Willem (IIIa, b, c) ....   *from*   40
Winchester: Huge (II-IIIc), Iordan (II-IIIc), Nicole (II-IIIc), Willem (II-IIIc).....   *from*   22
York: Alain (II-IIIb), Ieremie (II-IIIb), Ion (II-IIIc), Rener (II-IIIc), Tomas (IIIb, c)   *from*   25

EDWARD I, 1272-1307

'Long Cross' coinage (1272-79). With name hЄNRICVS

The earliest group of Edward's Long Cross coins are of very crude style and known only of Durham
and Bury St. Edmunds. Then, for the last class of the type, pennies of much improved style were
issued at London, Durham and Bury, but in 1279 the Long Cross coinage was abandoned and a completely new coinage substituted.

Cut halfpennies and farthings also occur for this issue, and within this context are not especially rare.

                                    VI   VII

		F	VF
		£	£
1377	Class VI. Crude face with new realistic curls, Є and N ligate	25	50
1378	— VII. Similar, but of improved style, usually with Lombardic U	50	110

Mints, moneyers, and classes for Edward I 'Long Cross' coinage
London: Phelip (VII), Renaud (VII) ....*from*   55
Bury St. Edmunds: Ioce (VII), Ion or Ioh (VI, VII) ....*from*   25
Durham: Roberd (VI), Robert (VII)...*from*   175

New Coinage (from 1279).

A major re-coinage was embarked upon in 1279 which introduced new denominations. In addition to the penny, halfpence and farthings were also minted and, for the first time, a fourpenny piece called a 'Groat' (from the French *Gros*).

As mint administration was now very much centralized, the practice of including the moneyer's name in the coinage was abandoned (except for a few years at Bury St. Edmunds). Several provincial mints assisted with the re-coinage during 1279-81, then minting was again restricted to London, Canterbury, Durham and Bury.

The provincial mints were again employed for a subsidiary re-coinage in 1299-1302 in order to remint lightweight coins and the many illegal *esterlings* (foreign copies of the English pennies, mainly from the Low Countries), which were usually a poorer quality than the English coins.

1379

		F £	VF £
1379	**Groat.** (=4d.; wt. 89 grs.). Type as illustration but several minor varieties	975	3000
	Extant specimens often show traces of having been mounted on the obverse		
	and gilded on the reverse; such coins are worth less.		

1a	1b	1c

1380	**Penny.** *London.* Class 1a. Crown with plain band, ЄDW RЄX; Lombardic		
	Ⲛ on *obv;* pellet 'barred' S on rev.	250	575
1381	— 1b. — ЄD RЄX; no drapery on bust, Roman N	425	950
1382	— Ic. — ЄDW RЄX; Roman N, normal or reversed; small lettering	20	45
1383	— Id. — ЄDW R;—; large lettering and face	15	40

1d(1384)	2a	2b

1384	— — — Annulet below bust (for the Abbot of Reading)	145	350
1385	— 2a. Crown with band shaped to ornaments; large face and short neck		
	similar to 1d; usually broken left petal to central fleur of crown	20	45
1386	— 2b. — tall bust; long neck; N reversed..	15	40

3a   3b   3c

F	*VF*
£	£

1387 — 3a. Crescent-shaped contraction marks; pearls in crown, drapery is
foreshortened circle 35 70

1388 — 3b. — — drapery is segment of a circle 20 45

1389 — 3c. — normal crown; drapery in one piece, hollowed in centre 15 35

3e   3f   3g

1390 — 3d. — — drapery in two pieces, broad face 15 35

1391 — 3e. — long narrow face (mostly Northern mints) 15 40

1392 — 3f. — broad face, large nose, rougher work, late S first used 30 60

1393 — 3g. — small neat bust, narrow face 12 30

4a   4b   4c   4d   4e

1394 — 4a. Comma-shaped contraction mark, late S always used, C and Є open 15 40

1395 — 4b. Similar, but face and hair shorter 12 30

1396 — 4c. Larger face with more copious hair; unbarred A first used 15 40

1397 — 4d. Pellet at beginning of *obv.* and/or *rev.* inscription 15 35

1398 — 4e. Three pellets on breast; pellet in *rev.* legend 20 40

5a   5b

1399 — 5a. Well spread coins, pellet on breast, A normally unbarred 35 75

1400 — 5b. Coins more spread, tall lettering, long narrow face, pellet on breast 35 75

6a   6b   7a   7b

		F	*VF*
		£	£
1401	— 6a. Smaller coins, initial cross almost plain, crown with wide fleurs ..	85	185
1402	— 6b. Initial cross well pattee; lettering of good style; closed Є (from now on)	50	100
1403	— 7a. Rose on breast; almond-shaped eyes, double barred N	55	120

8a   8b

1404	— 7b. — — longer hair, new crown	65	130
1404A	— Type as 7, but no rose	85	175
1405	— 8a. Smaller crown; top-tilted S; longer neck	25	55
1406	— 8b. Not unlike 9a, but top-tilted S	30	60
1406A	— 8c — — Crown with very arched band	30	60

9a   9b

1407	— 9a. Narrow face, flatter crown, star on breast	20	40
1408	— 9b. Small coins; Roman N, normal, un-barred, or usually of pot-hook form; often star or pellet on breast	12	30

10ab   10cf   10cf

1409	— 10ab. Read ЄDWARR, ЄDWARD, ЄDWR'R'. Ornate Rs	12	30
1410	Usually bi-foliate crown from now on. Also very rarely with annulet on breast.	—	—

		F	VF
		£	£
1411			
1412			
1413	— 10cf. Read CDWA. Plain Rs	12	25
1414			

For a more detailed classification of Class 10, see 'Sylloge of British Coins, 39, The J. J. North Collection, Edwardian English Silver Coins 1279-1351', The Classification of Class 10, c. 1301-10, by C. Wood.

Prices are for full flan, well struck coins.
The prices for the above types are for London. For coins of the other mints see following pages; types are in brackets, prices are for the commonest type of each mint.

| Berwick Type 1 | Type II | Type III | Type IV |

1415	*Berwick-on-Tweed.* (Blunt types I-IV) ....*from*	20	50
1416	*Bristol.* (2; 3b; c, d; 3f, g; 9b) ....*from*	15	40
1417	*Bury St. Edmunds.* Robert de Hadelie (3c, d, g; 4a, b, c) ....*from*	55	110
1418	— Villa Sci Edmundi (4e; 5b; 6b; 7a; 8a-10f) ....*from*	20	45
1419	*Canterbury.* (2; 3b-g; 4; 5; 7a; 9;10) ....*from*	12	25
1420	*Chester.* (3g; 9b) ....*from*	35	70
1421	*Durham.* King's Receiver (9b; 10a, b, e, f) ....*from*	15	35
1422	— Bishop de Insula (2; 3b, c, e, g; 4a) ....*from*	20	40
1423	— Bishop Bec (4b, c, d; 5b; 6b; 7a; 8b; 9; 10b-f) mostly with *mm.* cross moline ....*from*	20	40
1424	— — (4b) cross moline in one angle of *rev.*	125	275
1425	*Exeter.* (9b)	65	140
1426	*Kingston-upon-Hull.* (9b)	50	100
1427	*Lincoln.* (3c, d, f, g) ....*from*	20	40
1428	*Newcastle-upon-Tyne.* (3e; 9b; 10) ....*from*	25	50
1429	*York.* Royal mint (2; 3b, c, d, f; 9b) ....*from*	20	40
1430	— Archbishop's mint (3e, f; 9b). R. Quatrefoil in centre ....*from*	25	50

| 1431 | 1433 |

1431	**Halfpenny,** *London.* Class IIIb. Drapery as segment of circle	30	80
1432	— IIIc. Normal drapery as two wedges	20	50
1433	— IIIg. Similar, larger letters, wider crown	20	55
1433A	— — IV c. Comma abbreviation mark, thick waisted s.	25	70

	F	VF
	£	£
1433B — — Pellet before LON	35	85
1434 — IVe. Usually three pellets on breast, one on *rev.*	40	95
1434A — VI. Double barred N, small lettering	35	90
1435 — VII. Double barred N, large lettering	30	80
1436 — IX. Pot-hook N, usually no star on breast, crown band curved at fleurs	25	65
1437 — X. ЄDWAR R ANGL DNS hYB, thick waisted letters	25	65

The above prices are for London; halfpence of the mints given below were also struck.

1438	*Berwick-on-Tweed.* (Blunt types II and III) ....*from*	70	175
1439	*Bristol.* (IIIc; IIIg) ....*from*	30	70
1440	*Lincoln.* (IIIc)	40	100
1441	*Newcastle.* (IIIe). With single pellet in each angle of *rev.*	75	175
1442	*York.* (IIIb)	50	110

1436   1443A   1445

1443	**Farthing,** *London.* Class I. Heavy weight (6.65 grains), ЄDWARDVS REX: R. LONDONIЄNSIS, bifoliate crown	30	100
1443A	— — trifoliate crown	30	90
1444	— II. Similar, but reversed N's (6.62 grs.)	25	65
1445	— IIIc. As class I, but different bust	20	60
1446	— IIIg. Lighter weight (5.5 grs.) Є R ANGLIЄ, no inner circle on *obv...*	15	35
1446A	— IV Reads CIVITAS LONDON, narrow crown	35	100
1446B	— V — Wider crown	35	100
1447	— VI+VII. Similar, double barred N, pellet eyes	45	110
1448	— VIII. ЄR ANGL DN, closed Є	30	85
1449	— IX. Unbarred Ns	35	90
1450	— X or XI. (Edward II) ЄDWARDVS REX A or AN inner circle both sides	15	30
	Types 1449 and 1450 often appear on oval flans.		

The above prices are for London; farthings of the mints given below were also struck.

1446   1452

1451	*Berwick-on-Tweed.* (Blunt type II, III)	125	250
1452	*Bristol.* (II, IIIc (heavy), III (light))	45	100
1453	*Lincoln.* (III)	50	110

	F	VF
	£	£
1453A *Newcastle*. (IIIe), triple pellet in *rev.* quarters	200	475
1454 *York*. (II; III)	75	175

For further information see J. J. North 'Sylloge of British Coins, 39, The J. J. North Collection, Edwardian English Silver Coins 1279-1351'.

The coinage of this reign differs only in minor details from that of Edward I. No groats were issued in the years *c*. 1282-1351.

11a   12   13   14

15a   15b   15c

		F £	VF £
1455	**Penny,** *London*. Class 11a. Broken spear-head or pearl on l. side of crown; long narrow face, straight-sided N	20	45
1456	— 11b. — Є with angular back (till 15b), N with well-marked serifs	20	45
1457	— 11c. — — A of special form	45	100
1458	— 12. Central fleur of crown formed of three wedges	30	65
1459	— 13. Central fleur of crown as Greek double axe	20	50
1460	— 14. Crown with tall central fleur; large smiling face with leering eyes	20	45
1461	— 15a. Small flat crown with both spear-heads usually bent to l.; face of 14	25	50
1462	— 15b. — very similar, but smaller face	20	45
1463	— 15c. — large face, large Є	25	50

Berwick Type V   Type VI   Type VII

1464	*Berwick-on-Tweed*. (Blunt types V, VI and VII)	40	85
1465	*Bury St. Edmunds*. (11; 12; 13; 14; 15)	20	40
1466	*Canterbury*. (11; 12; 13; 14; 15)	20	40
1467	*Durham*. King's Receiver (11a), *mm*. plain cross	25	50
1468	— Bishop Bec. (11a), *mm*. cross moline	25	60
1469	— Bishop Kellawe (11; 12; 13), crozier on *rev*.	25	55
1470	— Bishop Beaumont (13; 14; 15), *mm*. lion with lis	30	75
1471	Sede Vacante (15c); *mm*. plain cross	45	110
1472	**Halfpenny** of *London*. ЄDWARDVS REX A(NG)	65	165
1473	— — *Berwick-on-Tweed*. (Blunt type V)	100	225
1474	**Farthing** of *London*. ЄDWARDVS REX (ANG)	40	90
1475	— *Berwick-on-Tweed*. (Blunt type IV, V)	125	275

During Edward's early years small quantities of silver coin were minted following the standard of the previous two reigns, but in 1335 halfpence and farthings were produced which were well below the .925 Sterling silver standard. In 1344 an impressive gold coinage was introduced comprising the Florin or Double Leopard valued at six shillings, and its half and quarter, the Leopard and the Helm. The design of the Florin was based on the contemporary gold of Philip de Valois of France.

The first gold coinage was not successful and it was replaced later the same year by a heavier coinage, the Noble, valued at 6s. 8d, i.e., 80 pence, half a mark or one third of a pound, together with its fractions. The Noble was lowered in weight in two stages over the next few years, being stabilized at 120 grains in 1351. With the signing of the Treaty of Bretigni in 1360 Edward's title to the Kingdom of France was omitted from the coinage, but it was resumed again in 1369.

In 1344 the silver coinage had been re-established at the old sterling standard, but the penny was reduced in weight to just over 20 grains and in 1351 to 18 grains. Groats were minted again in 1351 and were issued regularly henceforth until the reign of Elizabeth.

Subsequent to the treaty with France which gave England a cross-channel trading base at Calais, a mint was opened there in 1363 for minting gold and silver coins of English type. In addition to coins of the regular English mints, the Abbot of Reading also minted silver pence, halfpence and farthings with a scallop shell in one quarter of the reverse while coins from Berwick display one or two boars' or bears' heads.

There is evidence of re-use of dies at later periods, e.g. 3rd coinage halfpennies.

For further study of the English Hammered Gold Coinage see: Sylloge of Coins of the British Isles, 47. The Herbert Schneider Collection Volume One, by Peter Woodhead. 1996.

Mintmarks

| 6 | 1 | 2 | 3 | 74 | 4 | 5 | 7a |

1334-51	Cross pattée (6)	1356	Crown (74)
1351-2	Cross 1 (1)	1356-61	Cross 3 (4)
1351-7	Crozier on cross end (76a, *Durham*)	1361-9	Cross potent (5)
1352-3	Cross 1 broken (2)	1369-77	Cross pattée (6)
1354-5	Cross 2 (3)		Plain cross (7a)

The figures in brackets refer to the plate of mintmarks in Appendix III.

GOLD

Third coinage, 1344-51
First period, 1344

1476	1477	1478

	F	VF
	£	£

1476 **Florin** or **Double Leopard.** (=6s.; wt. 108 grs.). King enthroned beneath
canopy; crowned leopard's head each side. R. Cross in quatrefoil .... *Extremely rare*

1477 **Half-florin** or **Leopard.** Leopard sejant with banner l. R. Somewhat as last *Extremely rare*

1478 **Quarter-florin** or **Helm.** Helmet on fleured field. R. Floriate cross........ *Extremely rare*

Second period, 1344-46

1479

1479 **Noble** (=6s. 8d., wt. 138.46 grs.). King stg. facing in ship with sword and
shield. R. L in centre of royal cross in tressure .... *Extremely rare*

1480 **Quarter-noble.** Shield in tressure. R. As last 1250 3000

Third period, 1346-51

1481 **Noble** (wt. 128.59 grs.). As 1479, but Є in centre; large letters 750 16750

1482 **Half-noble.** Similar... 1500 3500

1483 **Quarter-noble.** As 1480, but Є in centre 275   550

Fourth coinage, 1351-77
Reference: L. A. Lawrence, *The Coinage of Edward III from 1351.*
Pre-treaty period, 1351-61. With French title.

1484 **Noble** (wt. 120 grs.), series B (1351). Open Є and C, Roman M; *mm.*
cross 1 (1).. 375   750

1485 — — *rev.* of series A (1351). Round lettering, Lombardic M and N; closed
inverted Є in centre 425   875

		F	VF
		£	£
1486	C (1351-1352). Closed Є and C, Lombardic M; *mm*. cross 1 (1)	325	650
1487	D (1352-1353). *O*. of series C. R. *Mm*. cross 1 broken (2)	475	975

1488   1498

1488	E (1354-1355). Broken letters, V often has a nick in r. limb; *mm*. cross 2 (3)	325	650
1489	F (1356). *Mm*. crown (74). Many varieties	450	875
1490	G (1356-1361). *Mm*. cross 3 (4). Many varieties	325	625
1491	**Half-noble,** B. As noble with *rev*. of series A, but closed Є in centre not inverted...	275	575
1492	C. *O*. as noble. *Rev*. as last	350	700
1493	E. As noble	475	1050
1494	G. As noble. Many varieties	245	500
1495	**Quarter-noble,** B. Pellet below shield. R. Closed Є in centre	165	325
1496	C. *O*. of series B. *Rev*. details as noble....................................	200	425
1497	E. *O*. as last. *Rev*. details as noble, pellet in centre	180	365
1498	G. *Mm*. cross 3 (4). Many varieties	150	290

Transitional treaty period, 1361. French title omitted, replaced by that of Aquitaine on the noble and (rarely) on the half-noble, but not on the quarter-noble; irregular sized letters; *mm*. cross potent (5).

1499

1499	**Noble.** R. Pellets or annulets at corners of central panel	385	775

1500   1503

		F £	*VF* £
1500	**Half-noble.** Similar	225	465
1501	**Quarter-noble.** Similar. Many varieties. Pellet and rarely Є in centre....	150	290

Treaty period, 1361-69. Omits FRANC, new letters, usually curule-shaped X; *mm*. cross potent(5).

1502	**Noble.** *London*. Saltire or nothing before ЄDWARD	350	675
1503	— Annulet before ЄDWARD (with, rarely, crescent on forecastle)	325	625
1504	*Calais*. C in centre of *rev.*, flag at stern of ship	375	750
1505	— — without flag	375	750

1506   1508

1506	**Half-noble.** *London*. Saltire before ЄDWARD	225	450
1507	— Annulet before ЄDWARD	235	475
1508	*Calais*. C in centre of *rev.*, flag at stern of ship	325	750
1509	— — without flag	375	825
1510	**Quarter-noble.** *London*. As 1498. R. Lis in centre	135	265
1511	— — annulet before ЄDWARD	140	275
1512	*Calais*. R. Annulet in centre	150	325
1513	— — cross in circle over shield	175	365
1514	— R. Quatrefoil in centre; cross over shield	225	450
1515	— — crescent over shield	300	625

Post-treaty period, 1369-1377. French title resumed.

1516	**Noble.** *London*. Annulet before ЄD. R. Treaty period die	475	950
1517	— — — crescent on forecastle	425	850
1518	— — post-treaty letters. R. Є and pellet in centre	375	725
1519	— — — R. Є and saltire in centre	425	825
1520	*Calais*. Flag at stern. R. Є in centre	400	800

1521

	F	VF
	£	£
1521 — — *Rev.* as 1518, with Є and pellet in centre	375	725
1522 — As 1520, but without flag. R. Є in centre	425	825
1523 **Half-noble.** *London. O.* Treaty die. *Rev.* as 1518	850	1750
1524 *Calais.* Without AQT, flag at stern. R. Є in centre	550	1100
1525 — — R. Treaty die with C in centre	625	1250

SILVER

First coinage, 1327-35 (.925 fineness)

1526   1530

1526 **Penny.** *London.* As Edw. II; class XVd with Lombardic n's	375	800
1527 *Bury St. Edmunds.* Similar	450	950
1528 *Canterbury; mm.* cross pattée with pellet centre	300	600
1529 — — three extra pellets in one quarter	300	600
1530 *Durham.* R. Small crown in centre	400	850
1531 *York.* As 1526, but quatrefoil in centre of *rev.*	275	550
1532 — — — pellet in each quarter of *mm.*	275	550
1533 — — — three extra pellets in one quarter	275	550
1534 — — — Roman N on *obv.*	275	550
1535 *Berwick* (1333-1342, Blunt type VIII). Bear's head in one quarter of *rev.*	400	900
1536 **Halfpenny.** *London.* If struck then indistinguishable from EDWARD II (cf. 1472)	65	165
1537 *Berwick* (Bl. VIII). Bear's head in one or two quarters	50	135
1538 **Farthing.** *London.* As Edw. II but with curl tailed R.	50	140
1539 *Berwick* (Bl. VIII). As 1537	45	125

1535   1537   1540

	F £	VF £

Second coinage, 1335-43 (.833 fineness)

1540	**Halfpenny.** *London.* ЄDWARDVS RЄX A(NG)*, rough work, tall crown	15	40
1541	*Reading.* Escallop in one quarter	275	575
1542	**Farthing.** *London.* A (N), six-pointed star after A (rarely omitted) and before LON, flat crown	35	95
1542A	— ANG, star after ANG and before LON or after DON, tall crown	40	100

Third or florin coinage, 1344-51. Bust with bushy hair. (.925 fine, 20 grs.)

1543   1555

1543	**Penny.** *London.* Class 1. ЄDW, Lombardic n's	15	45
1544	— 2, ЄDWA, n's, but sometimes N's on *rev.*	15	40
1545	— 3, ЄDW, N's, sometimes reversed or n's on *rev.*	15	40
1546	— 4, ЄDW, no stops, reversed N's, but on *rev.* sometimes n's, N's or double-barred N's	15	40
1547	*Canterbury.* ЄDWA, n's	40	110
1548	— ЄDW, reversed N's	40	100
1549	*Durham,* Sede Vacante (1345). A, ЄDW R. R. No marks	35	85
1550	— — B, similar, ЄDWAR R	65	150
1551	— Bp. Hatfield. C, similar, but pellet in centre of *rev.*	50	115
1552	— — — Crozier on *rev.*	60	135
1553	— — — — with pellet in centre of *rev.*	60	135
1554	— — D, ЄDWARDVS RЄX Aln, crozier on *rev.*	95	245
1555	*Reading. obv.* as 1546. R. Escallop in one quarter	200	425
1556	*York. obv.* as 1546. R. Quatrefoil in centre	20	50
1557	**Halfpenny.** *London.* ЄDWARDVS RЄX(An)	15	35
1558	— — pellet either side of crown	25	65
1559	— — saltire either side of crown and in one quarter of *rev.*, or pellet in each quarter	30	75
1560	*Reading. O.* Similar. R. Escallop in one quarter	225	475
1562	**Farthing.** *London.* ЄDWARDVS RЄX	30	65
1562A	*Reading.* As last. R. As halfpenny	375	750

Fourth coinage, 1351-77
Reference: L. A. Lawrence, *The Coinage of Edward III from 1351*.
Pre-treaty period, 1351-61. With French title.

1565   1567

		F £	VF £
1563	**Groat** (=4d., 72 grs.). *London,* series B (1351). Roman M, open C and Є; *mm.* cross 1	95	250
1564	— — — crown in each quarter	*Extremely rare*	
1565	— C (1351-2). Lombardic m, closed C and Є, R with wedge-shaped tail; *mm.* cross 1	35	85
1566	— D (1352-3). R with normal tail; *mm.* cross 1 or cross 1 broken (2)	40	100
1567	— E (1354-5). Broken letters, V often with nick in r. limb; *mm.* cross 2 (3)	35	85
1568	— — — lis on breast	45	110
1569	— F (1356). *Mm.* crown (74)	50	120

1570   1572

1570	— G (1356-61). Usually with annulet in one quarter and sometimes under bust, *mm.* cross 3 (4). Many varieties	35	80
1571	*York,* series D. As London	90	200
1572	— E. As London	40	110

1573   1574

1573	**Halfgroat.** *London,* series B. As groat	75	175
1574	— C. As groat	20	55

		F £	VF £
1575	— D. As groat	25	65
1576	— E. As groat	25	65
1577	— F. As groat	35	80
1578	— G. As groat	25	65
1579	— — — annulet below bust	30	75
1580	*York,* series D. As groat	60	125
1581	— E. As groat	35	80
1582	— — — lis on breast	50	115
1583	**Penny.** *London.* Series A (1351). Round letters, Lombardic m and n, annulet in each quarter; *mm.* cross pattee	55	135

1584   1587   1591

		F £	VF £
1584	— C. Details as groat, but annulet in each quarter	15	35
1585	— D. Details as groat, but annulet in each quarter	15	40
1586	— E. Sometimes annulet in each quarter	15	35
1587	— F. Details as groat	20	40
1588	— G. Details as groat	15	35
1589	— — — annulet below bust	20	45
1590	— — — saltire in one quarter..	25	60
1591	*Durham,* Bp. Hatfield. Series A. As 1583, but extra pellet in each quarter, VIL LA crozier DVRR€M..	100	250
1592	— C. Details as groat. R. Crozier, CIVITAS DVN€LMI€.....................	20	55
1593	— D — — —	30	65
1594	— E — — —	25	60
1595	— F — R. Crozier, CIVITAS DVR€M€	30	65
1596	— G — — —	25	60
1597	— — — — — annulet below bust	25	65
1598	— — — — — saltire in one quarter...	35	75
1599	— — — — — annulet on each shoulder..	35	75
1600	— — — — — trefoil of pellets on breast......................................	35	75
1601	— — — R. Crozier, CIVITAS DVR€LMI€...................................	40	85
1602	*York,* Royal Mint. Series D	25	60
1603	— — E	20	45
1604	— Archb. Thoresby. Series D. R. Quatrefoil in centre	30	60
1605	— — G —	20	45
1606	— — — annulet or saltire on breast	30	60
1607	**Halfpenny.** *London.* Series E. €DWARDVS R€X An	100	225
1608	— G, but with *obv.* of F (*mm.* crown). Annulet in one quarter	145	350
1609	**Farthing.** *London.* Series E. €DWARDVS R€X	125	250
1609A	— — Series G. Annulet in one quarter	135	300

Transitional treaty period, 1361. French title omitted, irregular sized letters; *mm.* cross potent (5).

| 1610 | **Groat.** *London.* Annulet each side of crown.. | 165 | 450 |

1611   1612

		F	VF
		£	£
1611	**Halfgroat.** Similar, but only seven arches to tressure	90	225
1612	**Penny,** *London.* Omits REX, annulet in two upper qtrs. of *mm*	75	175
1613	*York,* Archb. Thoresby. Similar, but quatrefoil enclosing pellet in centre of *rev.*..	65	135
1614	*Durham.* Bp. Hatfield. Similar. R. Crozier, CIVITAS DORELME	70	150
1615	**Halfpenny.** Two pellets over *mm.,* EDWARDVS REX An	90	200

Treaty period, 1361-69. French title omitted, new letters, usually 'Treaty' X, rarely curule chair X *mm.* cross potent (5).

		F	VF
1616	**Groat,** *London.* Many varieties	60	150
1617	— Annulet before EDWARD	65	165
1618	— Annulet on breast	75	180

1617   1619

| 1619 | *Calais.* As last .... | 135 | 325 |

1620	**Halfgroat,** *London.* As groat	30	75
1621	— — Annulet before EDWARDVS	30	75
1622	— — Annulet on breast	50	105
1623	*Calais.* As last	125	250
1624	**Penny,** *London.* EDWARD ANGL R, etc...........................	20	60
1625	— — — pellet before EDWARD	25	65
1626	*Calais.* R. VILLA CALESIE	100	225
1627	*Durham.* R. CIVITAS DVnELMIS	60	125
1628	— R. Crozier, CIVITAS DVREME	50	110

1621   1635

	F £	VF £
1629 *York,* Archb. Thoresby. Quatrefoil in centre of *rev.,* ЄDWARDVS DЄI G RЄX An	40	95
1630 — — — ЄDWARDVS RЄX AnGLI	20	55
1631 — — — — quatrefoil before ЄD and on breast	25	65
1632 — — — — annulet before ЄD	25	65
1633 — — — ЄDWARD AnGL R DnS HYB	35	75
1634 **Halfpenny.** ЄDWARDVS RЄX An, pellet stops	30	65
1635 — Pellet before ЄD, annulet stops	30	70
1636 **Farthing.** ЄDWARDVS RЄX, pellet stops	95	250

Post-treaty period, 1369-77. French title resumed, X like St. Andrew's cross; *mm.* 5, 6, 7a.

1637   1639

1637 **Groat.** Various readings, *mm.* cross pattee	75	200
1638 — — row of pellets across breast (chain mail)	165	475
1639 — row of annulets below bust (chain mail); *mm.* cross potent with four pellets	175	500
1640 **Halfgroat.** Various readings	95	250

1640A

1640A — Thin portrait of Richard II	135	325
1641 — row of pellets one side of breast (chain mail)	150	375
1642 **Penny,** *London.* No marks on breast	40	100
1643 — Pellet or annulet on breast	50	125
1644 — Cross or quatrefoil on breast	45	110
1645 *Durham,* Bp. Hatfield. *Mm.* 7a, CIVITAS DVnOLM, crozier	45	110
1646 — — — — annulet on breast	55	125
1647 — — — — lis on breast	45	110
1648 *York.* Archb. Thoresby or Neville. R. Quatrefoil in centre	35	80
1649 — — — lis on breast	40	95
1650 — — — annulet on breast	40	90
1651 — — — cross on breast	40	95

1652

		F	*VF*
		£	£
1652	**Farthing.** ЄDWARD RЄX ANGL, large head without neck	150	325

There was no significant change in the coinage during this reign. Noteworthy is the first appearance of symbols on the ship's rudder on some of the gold coins. The earlier silver coins have a portrait like that on the coins of Edward III, but the king's head and the style of lettering were altered on the later issues.

Reference: *Silver coinages of Richard II, Henry IV and V.* (B.N.J. 1959-60 and 1963).

Mintmark: cross pattée (6)

	1655		1657

		F	VF
		£	£

GOLD

		F	VF
1653	**Noble,** *London.* With altered *obv.* and/or *rev.* die of Edw. III	825	1750
1654	— Lettering as Edw. III, lis over sail	625	1350
1655	— Straight-sided letters, annulet over sail	550	1100
1656	— Late issue, fish-tail lettering; no marks, or trefoil by shield	575	1150
1657	— — — lis on rudder	750	1500
1658	— — small dumpy lettering; escallop or crescent on rudder and/or trefoil over sail or by shield	675	1300

	1658		1662

		F	VF
1659	*Calais.* Flag at stern, otherwise as 1653	725	1500
1660	— — as 1655; but quatrefoil over sail	675	1350
1661	— — as 1656; no marks	575	1150
1662	— — — lion on rudder	775	1600
1663	— — as 1658	675	1300

	1664	1672/3	1673	1677

<table>
<tr><td></td><td></td><td>F
£</td><td>VF
£</td></tr>
<tr><td>1664</td><td>Half-noble, London. As 1653</td><td>750</td><td>1500</td></tr>
<tr><td>1665</td><td>— as 1655</td><td>625</td><td>1250</td></tr>
<tr><td>1666</td><td>— as 1656; lion on rudder</td><td>700</td><td>1400</td></tr>
<tr><td>1667</td><td>— as 1658; crescent on rudder</td><td>750</td><td>1500</td></tr>
<tr><td>1668</td><td>Calais. Flag at stern, otherwise as 1653</td><td>1000</td><td>2500</td></tr>
<tr><td>1669</td><td>— — as 1655; quatrefoil over sail</td><td>950</td><td>2250</td></tr>
<tr><td>1671</td><td>— — as 1658, but one var. has saltire behind rudder</td><td>950</td><td>2250</td></tr>
<tr><td>1672</td><td>Quarter-noble, London. R in centre of rev.</td><td>315</td><td>625</td></tr>
<tr><td>1673</td><td>— Lis or pellet in centre of rev.</td><td>250</td><td>475</td></tr>
<tr><td>1674</td><td>— — obv. die of Edw. III altered</td><td>325</td><td>675</td></tr>
<tr><td>1675</td><td>— — escallop over shield</td><td>325</td><td>675</td></tr>
<tr><td>1676</td><td>— — trefoil of annulets over shield</td><td>350</td><td>725</td></tr>
<tr><td>1677</td><td>— — quatrefoil, cross or slipped trefoil over shield</td><td>300</td><td>625</td></tr>
</table>

SILVER

1679	1682

<table>
<tr><td>1678</td><td>Groat. I. Style of Edw. III, F (i.e. et) before FRANC, etc.</td><td>300</td><td>700</td></tr>
<tr><td>1679</td><td>II. New lettering, retrograde Z before FRANC, etc.</td><td>225</td><td>500</td></tr>
<tr><td>1680</td><td>III. Bust with bushy hair, 'fishtail' serifs to letters</td><td>300</td><td>750</td></tr>
<tr><td>1681</td><td>IV. New style bust and crown, crescent on breast</td><td>1000</td><td>2750</td></tr>
<tr><td>1682</td><td>Halfgroat. II. New lettering</td><td>175</td><td>425</td></tr>
<tr><td>1683</td><td>III. As 1680</td><td>275</td><td>625</td></tr>
<tr><td>1684</td><td>— — with obv. die of Edw. III (1640A)</td><td>300</td><td>650</td></tr>
<tr><td>1685</td><td>IV. As 1681, but no crescent</td><td>700</td><td>1450</td></tr>
<tr><td>1686</td><td>Penny, London. I Lettering as 1678, RICARDVS REX ANGLIE</td><td>225</td><td>550</td></tr>
<tr><td>1688</td><td>— II. As 1679, Z FRANC lis on breast</td><td>250</td><td>575</td></tr>
</table>

1689   1692

		F £	*VF* £
1689	— III. As 1680, RICARD REX AnGLIE, fish-tail letters	275	625
1690	*York*. I. Early style, usually with cross or lis on breast, quatrefoil in centre of *rev*	50	140
1691	— II. New bust and letters, no marks on breast	60	150
1692	— Local dies. Pellet above each shoulder, cross on breast, REX ANGLIE or ANGILIE	55	125
1693	— — — REX DNS EB	75	175
1694	— — — REX ANG FRANC	70	175
1695	— III. As 1680, REX ANGL Z FRANC (scallop after TAS)	60	135
1696	— IV. Very bushy hair, new letters, no crescent. R. R in centre of quatrefoil	250	550
1697	*Durham*. Cross or lis on breast, DVNOLM	150	425

1698   1699   1701   1704

1698	**Halfpenny.** Early style. LONDON, saltire or annulet on breast	60	150
1699	Intermediate style. LONDON, no marks on breast	30	70
1700	Type III. Late style. Similar, but fishtail letters	35	80
1700A	Type IV. Short, stubby lettering	35	90
1701	**Farthing.** Small bust and letters	125	275
1703	Similar but no neck	110	250
1704	Rose in each angle of *rev.* instead of pellets	165	425
1704A	Large head with broad face as Henry IV	200	450

HENRY IV, 1399-1413

In 1412 the standard weights of the coinage were reduced, the noble by 12 grains and the penny by 3 grains, partly because there was a scarcity of bullion and partly to provide revenue for the king, as Parliament had not renewed the royal subsidies. As in France, the royal arms were altered, three fleur-de-lis taking the place of the four or more lis previously displayed.

Mintmark: cross pattée (6)

GOLD

Heavy coinage, 1399-1412

1707   1705

		F	VF
		£	£
1705	**Noble** (120 grs.), *London*. Old arms with four lis in French quarters; crescent or annulet on rudder	3650	8500
1706	— New arms with three lis; crescent, pellet or no marks on rudder	3650	8500
1707	*Calais*. Flag at stern, old arms; crown on or to l. of rudder	4750	10500

1708   1710

1708	— — new arms; crown or saltire on rudder	4500	10000
1709	**Half-noble,** *London*. Old arms	3250	6500
1710	— new arms	3000	6000
1711	*Calais*. New arms	3250	6750
1712	**Quarter-noble,** *London*. Crescent over old arms	800	1750
1713	— — — new arms	750	1650
1714	*Calais*. New arms. R. *Mm*. crown	950	2250

1715

		F £	VF £

Light coinage, 1412-13

1715 **Noble** (108 grs.). Trefoil, or trefoil and annulet, on side of ship. R. Trefoil
in one quarter 850   1850

1716 **Half-noble.** Similar, but always with annulet.. 2500   5250

1717

1717 **Quarter-noble.** Trefoils, or trefoils and annulets beside shield, lis above. R.
Lis in centre... 375   750

SILVER

Heavy coinage, 1399-1412

1718   1722   1723

1718 **Halfgroat** (36 grs.). Star on breast... 1250   2500
1718A — Muled with Edw. III (1640A) *obv*. 750   1750
1719 **Penny,** *London*. Similar, early bust with long neck 600   1250
1720 — later bust with shorter neck, no star 600   1250
1721 *York*. Bust with long neck 275   600
1722 — Bust with broad face, round chin 250   550
1723 **Halfpenny.** Early small bust 135   300
1724 — later large bust, with rounded shoulders, ... 150   325
1725 **Farthing.** Face without neck 500   975

Light coinage, 1412-13

	1728	1731	1737		

			F	VF
			£	£
1726	**Groat** (60 grs.). I. Pellet to l., annulet to r. of crown; altered die of Richard II		1450	3750
1727	New dies; II. Annulet to l., pellet to r. of crown, 8 or 10 arches to tressure		1350	3250
1728	— III. Similar but 9 arches to tressure		1300	3200
1729	**Halfgroat.** Pellet to l., annulet to r. of crown		650	1400
1730	Annulet to l., pellet to r. of crown		475	950
1731	**Penny,** *London.* Annulet and pellet by crown; trefoil on breast and before CIVI		450	900
1732	— — annulet or slipped trefoil before LON		450	900
1733	— Pellet and annulet by crown		650	1350
1734	*York.* Annulet on breast. R. Quatrefoil in centre		175	475
1735	*Durham.* Trefoil on breast, DVꞂOLM		175	475
1736	**Halfpenny.** Struck from heavy dies		135	300
1737	New dies; annulets by crown or neck, or no marks		165	375
1738	**Farthing.** Face, no bust; ?trefoil after REX		500	975

There was no change of importance in the coinage of this reign. There was, however, a considerable development in the use of privy marks which distinguished various issues, except for the last issue of the reign when most marks were removed. The Calais mint, which had closed in 1411, did not re-open until early in the next reign.

Mintmarks

Cross pattee (4)   Pierced cross with   Pierced cross (18).
                   pellet centre (20)

GOLD

		F	VF
		£	£
1739	**Noble.** A. Quatrefoil over sail and in second quarter of *rev.* Short broad letters, no other marks	850	1750
1740	— B. Ordinary letters; similar, or with annulet on rudder	475	925
1741	— C. Mullet by sword arm, annulet on rudder	425	850

1742

1742	— — — broken annulet on side of ship	350	700
1743	—D. Mullet and annulet by sword arm, trefoil by shield, broken annulet on ship	400	800

1744

1744	— E. Mullet, or mullet and annulet by sword arm, trefoil by shield, pellet by sword point and in one quarter, annulet on side of ship	425	825
1745	— — Similar, but trefoil on ship instead of by shield	450	875
1746	— F. Similar, but no pellet at sword point, trefoil in one quarter	475	1000
1747	— G. No marks; annulet stops, except for mullet after first word	650	1350
1748	**Half-noble.** B. As noble; Hen. IV *rev.* die	1250	2350
1749	— C. Broken annulet on ship, quatrefoil below sail	450	900

1750

		F	VF
		£	£
1750	— — Mullet over shield, broken annulet on *rev.*	400	800
1751	— F. Similar, but no annulet on ship, usually trefoil by shield	575	1250
1752	— F/E. As last, but pellet in 1st and annulet in 2nd quarter	625	1350
1753	— G. As noble, but quatrefoil over sail, mullet sometimes omitted after first word of *rev.*	475	950
1754	**Quarter-noble.** A. Lis over shield and in centre of *rev.* Short broad letters; quatrefoil and annulet beside shield, stars at corners of centre on *rev.*	375	750
1755	— C. Ordinary letters; quatrefoil to l., quat. and mullet to r. of shield	275	525

1756   1759

1756	— — — annulet to l., mullet to r. of shield	210	400
1757	— F. Ordinary letters; trefoil to l., mullet to r. of shield	235	450
1758	— G. — no marks, except mullet after first word	235	450

SILVER

1759	**Groat.** A. Short broad letters; 'emaciated' bust	550	1350
1760	— — muled with Hen. IV *obv.* or *rev*	650	1400
1761	— — muled with later *rev.* of Hen. V	500	1100

1762   1765

1762	B. Ordinary letters; 'scowling' bust	240	525
1762A	— — mullet in centre of breast	275	550
1762B	— — mullet to r. of breast	300	625
1763	— — muled with Hen. IV or later Hen. V	325	675
1764	C. Normal bust	125	275
1765	— — mullet on r. shoulder	80	190

		F	*VF*
		£	£
1767	G. Normal bust; no marks	160	350
1766	— — R muled with Hen. IV	350	800
1768	**Halfgroat.** A. As groat, but usually with annulet and pellet by crown	525	1250
1769	B. Ordinary letters; no marks	250	575
1770	— — muled with Hen. IV or class C (HV) *obv.*	225	475
1771	C. Tall neck, broken annulet to l. of crown	65	175
1772	— — — mullet on r. shoulder...	80	200

1773   1774

1773	— — — mullet in centre of breast..	70	190
1774	F. Annulet and trefoil by crown, mullet on breast	80	200
1775	G. New neat bust: no marks.	90	225
1776	**Penny.** *London.* A. Letters, bust and marks as 1768....................	325	650
1777	— Altered Hen. IV *obv.* with mullet added to l. of crown	375	825

1778   1791

1778	— C. Tall neck, mullet and broken annulet by crown	25	60
1779	— D. Similar, but whole annulet	30	75
1780	— F. Mullet and trefoil by crown..	35	80
1781	— G. New neat bust, no marks, DI GRA	35	85
1782	*Durham.* C. As 1778 but quatrefoil at end of legend	45	100
1783	— D. As 1779...	40	95
1784	— G. Similar, but new bust. R. Annulet in one qtr.	50	120
1785	*York.* C. As 1778, but quatrefoil in centre of *rev.*	25	60
1786	— D. Similar, but whole annulet by crown	30	70
1787	— E. As last, but pellet above mullet	45	100
1788	— F. Mullet and trefoil by crown...	25	60
1789	— — Trefoil over mullet to l., annulet to r. of crown	45	100
1790	— G. Mullet and trefoil by crown (London dies)	30	75
1791	— — Mullet and lis by crown, annulet in one qtr. (usually local dies)	30	75
1792	**Halfpenny.** A. Emaciated bust, annulets by crown	60	135
1793	— altered dies of Hen. IV	90	250
1794	C. Ordinary bust, broken annulets by crown	20	50
1795	D. Annulets, sometimes broken, by hair	20	50

1796

1798

		F £	*VF* £
1767	G. Normal bust; no marks	160	350
1796	F. Annulet and trefoil by crown	20	50
1797	G. New bust; no marks, (usually muled with Henry VI annulet *rev.*)	50	125
1798	**Farthing.** G. Small face with neck	110	275

The supply of gold began to dwindle early in the reign, which accounts for the rarity of gold after 1426. The Calais mint was reopened in 1424 and for some years a large amount of coin was struck there. It soon stopped minting gold; the mint was finally closed in 1440. A royal mint at York was opened for a short time in 1423/4.

Marks used to denote various issues become more prominent in this reign and can be used to date coins to within a year or so.

Reference: C. A. Whitton *Heavy Coinage of Henry VI.* (B.N.J. 1938-41).

Mintmarks

136	7a	105	18	133	8	9	15

1422-7	Incurved pierced cross (136)	1422-34	Cross pommee (133)
1422-3	Lis (105, York)	1427-34	Cross patonce (8)
1422-60	Plain cross (7a, intermittently		Cross fleury (9)
	Lis (105, on gold)	1434-35	Voided cross (15)
1422-27	Pierced cross (18)	1435-60	Cross fleury (9)
1460	Lis (105, on rev. of some groats)		

For Restoration mintmarks see page 196.

GOLD

1799

		F	VF
	Annulet issue, 1422-7	£	£
1799	**Noble.** *London.* Annulet by sword arm, and in one spandrel on *rev.*; trefoil stops on *obv.* with lis after hЄnRIC, annulets on *rev.*, with mullet after IhC	350	675
1800	— Similar, but *obv.* from Henry V die	700	1350
1801	— As 1799, but Flemish imitative coinage	300	550
1802	*Calais.* As 1799, but flag at stern and C in centre of *rev*	450	900

1803

		F £	VF £
1803	— — with h in centre of *rev.*	425	825
1804	*York*. As London, but with lis over stern	450	875

1805

1805	**Half-noble.** *London*. As 1799	245	475
1806	— Similar, but *obv*. from Henry V die	625	1250
1807	*Calais*. As noble, with C in centre of *rev.*	550	1100
1808	— — with h in centre of *rev.*	475	950
1809	*York*. As noble	500	975
1810	**Quarter-noble.** *London*. Lis over shield; *mm*. large lis	150	285
1811	— — — trefoil below shield	175	350
1812	— — — pellet below shield	225	450
1813	*Calais*. Three lis over shield; *mm*. large lis	200	425

1814   1819

1814	— Similar but three lis around shield	225	450
1815	— As 1810, but much smaller *mm.*	200	400
1816	*York*. Two lis over shield	235	475

| | *F* | *VF* |
| | £ | £ |

Rosette-mascle issue, 1427-30

1817 **Noble**. *London*. Lis by sword arm and in *rev.* field; stops, rosettes, or
rosettes and mascles 700   1400
1818 *Calais*. Similar, with flag at stern.. 825   1750
1819 **Half-noble**. *London*. Lis in *rev.* field; stops, rosettes and mascles 925   2000
1820 *Calais*. Similar, flag at stern; stops, rosettes 1100 2650
1821 **Quarter-noble**. *London*. As 1810; stops, as noble 375   750
1822 — without lis over shield 435   875
1823 *Calais*. Lis over shield, rosettes r. and l., and rosette stops....................... 425   850

Pinecone-mascle issue, 1430-4

1824

1824 **Noble**. *London*. Stops, pinecones and mascles 625   1250
1825 **Half-noble**. *London*. O. Rosette-mascle die. R. As last............................ 1250 2750
1826 **Quarter-noble**. As 1810, but pinecone and mascle stops 650   1400

Leaf-mascle issue, 1434-5

1827 **Noble**. Leaf in waves; stops, saltires with two mascles and one leaf 1500 3500
1828 **Half-noble**. (Fishpool hoard and Reigate hoard)..................................... 1750 4250
1829 **Quarter-noble**. As 1810; stops, saltire and mascle; leaf on inner circle of *rev.* 800   1650

Leaf-trefoil issue, 1435-8

1830 **Noble**. Stops, leaves and trefoils... 2000 4500
1830A **Half-noble**. Mule with annulet issue reverse die..................................... 2250 4750
1831 **Quarter-noble**. Similar 900   2000

Trefoil issue, 1438-43

1832 **Noble**. Trefoil to left of shield and in *rev.* legend 1750 4000

Leaf-pellet issue, 1445-54

1833 **Noble**. Annulet, lis and leaf below shield 1750 4000

Cross-pellet issue, 1454-60

1834 **Noble**. Mascle at end of *obv.* legend 2500 6000

SILVER

Annulet issue, 1422-7

1836

		F £	VF £
1835	**Groat.** *London.* Annulet in two quarters of *rev.*	35	70
1836	*Calais.* Annulets at neck. R. Similar	30	60
1837	— — no annulets on *rev.*	65	135

1838   1840

		F	VF
1838	*York.* Lis either side of neck. R. As 1835	675	1500
1839	**Halfgroat.** *London.* As groat	35	85
1840	*Calais.* As 1836	25	50
1841	— — no annulets on *rev.*	35	75
1842	— — only one annulet on *rev.* (mule with annulet-trefoil *rev.*)	50	125

1843   1849   1852

		F	VF
1843	*York.* As groat	675	1500
1844	**Penny.** *London.* Annulets in two qtrs.	20	50
1845	*Calais.* Annulets at neck. R. As above	20	45
1846	— — only one annulet on *rev.*	25	60
1847	*York.* As London, but lis at neck	600	1250
1848	**Halfpenny.** *London.* As penny	15	35
1849	*Calais.* Similar, but annulets at neck	15	35
1850	*York.* Similar, but lis at neck	350	750
1851	**Farthing.** *London.* As penny, but *mm.* cross pommée	110	240
1852	*Calais.* Similar, but annulets at neck	200	425

	F	*VF*
	£	£

Annulet-trefoil sub-issue

1854	**Groat.** *Calais,* as 1836 but trefoil to l. of crown.	45	110
1855	**Halfgroat.** *Calais.* Similar, but usually with ann. or rosette mascle *rev*...	60	125
1856	**Penny.** *Calais.* Similar	65	145
1857	— — only one annulet on *rev*	70	150

Muling exists in Henry VI coins spanning two or three issues. Full flan coins in the smaller denominations are difficult to find.

Rosette-mascle issue, 1427-30. All with rosettes (early) or rosettes and mascles somewhere in the legends.

| 1858 | **Groat.** *London.* .... | 50 | 120 |

1859   1861

1859	*Calais*	35	70
1860	— mascle in two spandrels (as illus. 1863)	45	100
1861	**Halfgroat.** *London.*	60	125
1862	*Calais*	25	55

1863   1872

1863	— mascle in two spandrels, as illustrated	35	80
1864	**Penny.** *London.*	65	150
1865	*Calais*	30	70
1866	*York.* Archb. Kemp. Crosses by hair, no rosette	25	65
1867	— — Saltires by hair, no rosette	30	70
1868	— — Mullets by crown	25	65
1869	*Durham,* Bp. Langley. Large star to l. of crown, no rosette, DVnOLMI .	45	120
1870	**Halfpenny,** *London*	20	40
1871	*Calais*	20	40
1872	**Farthing,** *London*	135	275
1873	*Calais. Mm.* cross pommee	175	375

Pinecone-mascle issue, 1430-4. All with pinecones and mascles in legends.

	1874	1876/7	1879

		F	VF
		£	£
1874	**Groat,** London	35	80
1875	*Calais*	35	70
1876	**Halfgroat,** *London*	40	100
1877	*Calais*	25	60
1878	**Penny,** *London*	45	100
1879	*Calais*	30	70
1880	*York,* Archb. Kemp. Mullet by crown, quatrefoil in centre of *rev.*............	25	65
1881	— — rosette on breast, no quatrefoil.....................................	25	65
1882	— — mullet on breast, no quatrefoil	30	70
1883	*Durham,* Bp. Langley. DVNOLMI	40	100

	1884	1888

1884	**Halfpenny,** *London*..	20	40
1885	*Calais*	20	45
1886	**Farthing,** *London*	125	275
1887	*Calais. Mm.* cross pommée	175	375

Full flan coins are difficult to find in the smaller denominations.

Leaf-mascle issue, 1434-5. Usually with a mascle in the legend and a leaf somewhere in the design.

1888	**Groat.** *London.* Leaf below bust, all appear to read DONDON..............	95	225
1889	— — *rev.* of last or next coinage	80	200
1890	*Calais.* Leaf below bust, and usually below MEVM..............................	65	150
1891	**Halfgroat.** *London.* Leaf under bust, pellet under TAS and DON.	80	200

1892   1897

		F	VF
		£	£
1892	*Calais*. Leaf below bust, and sometimes on *rev.*	70	175
1893	**Penny.** *London*. Leaf on breast, no stops on *rev.*	55	120
1894	*Calais*. Leaf on breast and below SIЄ	60	125
1895	**Halfpenny.** *London*. Leaf on breast and on *rev.*	30	65
1896	*Calais*. Leaf on breast and below SIЄ	60	125

Leaf-trefoil issue, 1435-8. Mostly with leaves and trefoil of pellets in the legends.

		F	VF
1897	**Groat.** *London*. Leaf on breast	50	110
1898	— without leaf on breast	50	110
1899	*Calais*. Leaf on breast	375	750
1900	**Halfgroat.** *London*. Leaf on breast; *mm.* plain cross	45	110
1901	— *O. mm.* cross fleury; leaf on breast	45	110
1902	— — without leaf on breast	50	125
1903	**Penny.** *London*. Leaf on breast	60	125
1903A	*Calais*. Similar	275	550
1904	*Durham,* Bp. Neville. Leaf on breast. R. Rings in centre, no stops, DVΠOLM	100	225
1905	**Halfpenny.** *London*. Leaf on breast	25	50
1906	— without leaf on breast	25	55
1907	**Farthing.** *London*. Leaf on breast; stops, trefoil and saltire on *obv.*	150	325

Trefoil issue, 1438-43. Trefoil of pellets either side of neck and in legend, leaf on breast.

1908   1909   1911A   1911B

		F	VF
1908	**Groat.** *London*. Sometimes a leaf before LON.	55	125
1909	— Fleurs in spandrels, sometimes extra pellet in two qtrs.	70	165
1910	— Trefoils in place of fleurs at shoulders, none by neck, sometimes extra pellets	65	150
1911	*Calais*	160	375
1911A	**Halfgroat,** *London* Similar, but trefoil after DEUM and sometimes after POSUI Mule only with leaf trefoil *obv.*	150	325
1911B	— *Calais Obv.* Similar to 1911, only known muled with leaf mascle *rev.*	300	650
1912	**Halfpenny,** *London*	30	60

Trefoil pellet issue, 1443-5

1912	1913	1915	1917

		F	VF
		£	£

| 1913 | **Groat.** Trefoils by neck, pellets by crown, small leaf on breast; sometimes extra pellet in two quarters | 70 | 165 |

Leaf-pellet issue, 1445-54. Leaf on breast, pellet each side of crown, except where stated.

1914	**Groat.** ANGL; extra pellet in two quarters	50	110
1915	*Similar*, but ANGLI	45	95
1916	— — trefoil in *obv.* legend	60	125
1917	Leaf on neck, fleur on breast, often extra pellet in two quarters	50	100
1918	As last, but two extra pellets by hair	100	225
1919	**Halfgroat.** As 1914 *mm.* Cross patonce	50	125
1920	Similar, but *mm.* plain cross, some times no leaf on breast, no stops	45	110
1921	**Penny.** *London.* Usually extra pellets in two quarters	40	90
1922	— — pellets by crown omitted	45	95
1923	— — trefoil in legend	50	125
1924	*York,* Archb. Booth. R. Quatrefoil and pellet in centre	35	90
1925	— — two extra pellets by hair (local dies)	30	80
1926	*Durham,* Bp. Neville. Trefoil in *obv.* legend. R. Two rings in centre of cross	65	165

1927	1932

1927	— — Similar, but without trefoil	70	175
1928	**Halfpenny.** Usually extra pellet in two quarters	20	40
1929	— *mm.* plain cross	20	40
1930	**Farthing.** As last	150	325

Unmarked issue, 1453-4

1931	**Groat.** No marks on *obv.;* two extra pellets on *rev.*	300	650
1932	— four extra pellets on *rev.*	350	750
1933	**Halfgroat.** As 1931	200	475

		F	VF
		£	£

Cross-pellet issue, 1454-60

| 1934 | **Groat.** Saltire either side of neck, pellets by crown, leaf and fleur on breast, extra pellets on *rev*... | 200 | 475 |
| 1935 | Saltire on neck, no leaf, pellets by crown, usually mullets in legend; extra pellets on *rev*... | 65 | 140 |

1935   1940

1936	— Similar, but mascles in place of mullets on *obv*.	75	175
1937	— — pellets by hair instead of by crown	125	300
1938	**Halfgroat.** Saltire on neck, pellets by crown and on *rev.*, mullets in legend	200	450
1939	**Penny.** *London.* Saltire on neck, pellets by crown and on *rev.*, mascle(s), or mullet and mascle in legend	200	425
1940	*York,* Archb. Wm. Booth. Saltires by neck, usually leaf on breast, pellets by crown. R. Cross in quatrefoil in centre.	30	75
1941	*Durham,* Bp. Laurence Booth. Saltire and B or B only at neck, pellets by crown. R. Rings in centre	75	175
1942	**Halfpenny.** Saltires by neck, usually two extra pellets on *rev*..................	60	125
1943	Similar, but saltire on neck, sometimes mullet after hЄnRIC	30	65
1944	**Farthing.** Saltire on neck, usually pellets by crown and on *rev.*, but known without either...	150	350

Lis-pellet issue, 1456-60

1945

| 1945 | **Groat.** Lis on neck; pellets by crown. R. Extra pellets............................ | 165 | 375 |

THE HOUSE OF YORK, 1461-1485

EDWARD IV, First Reign, 1461-70

In order to increase the supply of bullion to the mint the weight of the penny was reduced to 12 grains in 1464, and the current value of the noble was raised to 8s. 4d. Later, in 1465, a new gold coin was issued, the Ryal or 'Rose Noble', weighing 120 grains and having a value of 10s. However, as 6s. 8d. had become the standard professional fee the old noble was missed, and a new coin was issued to take its place, the Angel of 80 grains.

Royal mints were opened at Canterbury and York to help with the re-coinage, and other mints were set up at Bristol, Coventry and Norwich, though they were not open for long.

Reference: C. E. Blunt and C. A Whitton, *The Coinage of Edward IV and Henry VI (Restored),* B.N.J. 1945-7.

Mintmarks

105	9	7a	33	99	28	74	11

1461-4	Lis (105)	1467-70	Lis (105, *York*)
	Cross fleury (9)	1467-8	Crown (74) } (often
	Plain cross (7a)		Sun (28) } combined)
1464-5	Rose (33 and 34)	1468-9	Crown (74) } (sometimes
1464-7	Pall (99, *Canterbury*)		Rose (33) } combined)
1465-6	Sun (28)	1469-70	Long cross
1466-7	Crown (74)		fitchee (l.c.f) (11) } (often
			Sun (28) } combined)

GOLD

Heavy coinage, 1461-4

		F	VF
		£	£
1946	**Noble** (=6s. 8d., wt. 108 grs.). Normal type, but *obv.* legend commences at top left, lis below shield; *mm*.-/lis (Spink's sale May 1993)	3000	6500
1947	— Quatrefoil below sword arm; *mm.* rose/lis	3250	7500
1948	— R. Roses in two spandrels; *mm.* rose	3500	8500
1949	**Quarter-noble**	*Extremely rare*	

1946

1950

	F	*VF*
	£	£

Light coinage, 1464-70

1950 **Ryal** or rose-noble (=10s., wt. 120 grs.), *London*. As illustration. Large
fleurs in spandrels; *mm.* 33-74 .... 350 675

1951 — — Small trefoils in spandrels; *mm.* 74-11 .... 350 675

1952

1952 — Flemish imitative coinage (mostly 16th cent. on a large flan) 300 550

1953 *Bristol*. B in waves, large fleurs; *mm.* sun, crown.................................... 425 825

1954 — — small fleurs in spandrels; *mm.* sun, crown 450 875

1955 *Coventry*. C in waves; *mm.* sun 750 1650

1956 *Norwich*. �050 in waves; *mm.* sun, rose 900 2000

1957 *York*. Є in waves, large fleurs in spandrels, *mm.* sun, lis 425 825

1958 — — small fleurs, *mm.* sun. lis... 475 925

1959 **Half-ryal.** *London*. As 1950 .... 295 575

1960 *Bristol*. B in waves; *mm.* sun, sun/crown... 475 950

1961 *Coventry*. C in waves; *mm.* sun 1850 4500

1962 *Norwich*. n in waves; *mm.* rose 1500 3500

1963   1965

1963 *York*. Є in waves; *mm.* 28, 105, 33/105... 300 625

1963 Similar but lis instead of Є in waves (probably York) 375 775

1964 **Quarter-ryal.** Shield in tressure of eight arcs, rose above. R. Somewhat
as half ryal; *mm.* sun/rose.. 600 1250

1965 Shield in quatrefoil, R. Є above, rose on l., sun on r.; *mm.* 33/28-74/33 .. 200 425

1966 — — sun on l., rose on r.; *mm.* 74-11 .... 225 450

1967

		F	VF
		£	£
1967	**Angel** (=6s. 8d., wt. 80 grs.). St. Michael spearing dragon. R. Ship, rays of sun at masthead, large rose and sun beside mast; *mm.*-/33	3000	6250
1968	— — small rose and sun at mast; *mm.*-/74	3250	7000

SILVER

Heavy coinage, 1461-4

1969	**Groat** (60 grs.). Group I, lis on neck, pellets by crown; *mm.* 9, 7a, 105, 9/105 Occasionally Є(dward) over hЄ(nric) *mm.* cross, fleury	100	250
1970	— Lis on breast, no pellets; *mm.* plain cross, 7a/105...............................	110	275
1971	— — with pellets at crown; *mm.* plain cross	115	285

1972

1972	II, quatrefoils by neck, crescent on breast; *mm.* rose	100	235
1973	III, similar but trefoil on breast; *mm.* rose.....................................	90	200
1974	— — — eye in *rev.* inner legend, *mm.* rose	85	185
1975	— Similar, but no quatrefoils by bust	145	325
1976	— — Similar, but no trefoil on breast...	140	300
1977	IV, annulets by neck, eye after TAS; *mm.* rose	150	350

1973   1978

1978	**Halfgroat.** I, lis on breast, pellets by crown and extra pellets in two qtrs.; *mm.* 9, 7a	400	850

		F £	VF £
1979	II, quatrefoils at neck, crescent on breast; *mm*. rose	300	625
1980	III, similar, but trefoil on breast, eye on rev.; *mm*. rose	250	550
1981	— Similar, but no mark on breast	250	550
1982	IV, annulets by neck, sometimes eye on *rev.; mm*. rose	300	650
1983	**Penny** (15 grs.), *London*. I, marks as 1978, but mascle after RЄX; *mm*.		
	plain cross	525	1100
1984	II, quatrefoils by neck; *mm*. rose..	450	900

1985

		F	VF
1985	III, similar, but eye after TAS; *mm*. rose	250	525
1986	IV, annulets by neck; *mm*. rose..	350	750
1987	*York,* Archb. Booth. Quatrefoils by bust, voided quatrefoil in centre of		
	rev.; mm. rose	135	300
1988	*Durham. O*. of Hen. VI. R. DVnOLIn......................................	150	325
	Some of the Durham pennies from local dies may belong to the heavy		
	coinage period, but if so they are indistinguishable from the light coins.		
1989	**Halfpenny.** I, as 1983, but no mascle	110	250
1990	II, quatrefoils by bust; *mm*. rose..	60	135
1991	— saltires by bust; *mm*. rose	50	120
1992	III, no marks by bust; *mm*. rose	55	125
1993	IV, annulets by bust; *mm*. rose	70	165
1994	**Farthing.** I, as 1989	325	675
1994A	II. saltires by bust; *mm*. rose	350	750
1994B	III, no marks by bust; mm. rose	300	600

Light coinage, 1464-70. There is a great variety of groats and we give only a selection. Some have pellets in one quarter of the reverse, or trefoils over the crown; early coins have fleurs on the cusps of the tressure, then trefoils or no marks on the cusps, while the late coins have only trefoils.

		F	VF
1995	**Groat** (48 grs.), *London*. Annulets at neck, eye after TAS; *mm*. 33 (struck		
	from heavy dies, IV)	75	165
1996	— — — Similar, but new dies, eye after TAS or DOn..........................	80	175
1997	— Quatrefoils at neck, eye; rose (heavy dies, III)	65	135
1998	— — — Similar, but new dies, eye in *rev*. legend..................................	70	150
1999	— No marks at neck, eye; rose	120	250

2000 2002

Light coinage, silver, *continued.*

		F	VF
		£	£
2000	— Quatrefoils at neck, no eye; *mm*. 33, 74, 28, 74/28, 74/33, 11/28	35	75
2001	— — — rose or quatrefoil on breast; *mm*. 33, 74/28	40	85
2002	— No marks at neck; *mm*. 28, 74, 11/28, 11	50	120
2003	— Trefoils or crosses at neck; *mm*. 11/33, 11/28, 11	45	100
2004	*Bristol.* B on breast, quatrefoils at neck; *mm*. 28/33, 28, 28/74, 74, 74/28	40	95
2005	— — trefoils at neck; *mm*. sun	60	135
2006	— — no marks at neck; *mm*. sun	75	175
2007	— Without B, quatrefoils at neck; *mm*. sun	85	200
	Bristol is variously rendered as BRESTOLL, BRISTOLL, BRESTOW, BRISTOW.		
2008	*Coventry.* C on breast, quatrefoils at neck, COVETRE; *mm*. 28/33, 28 ...	65	150
2009	— — Local dies, similar; *mm*. rose	90	200
2010	— — — as last, but no C or quatrefoils	100	225
2011	*Norwich.* ꞃ on breast, quatrefoils at neck, ꞃORWIC or ꞃORVIC, *mm*. 28/33, 28	60	135
2012	*York.* Є on breast, quatrefoils at neck, ЄBORACI; *mm*. 28, 105/74, 105, 105/28	40	100
2013	— Similar, but without Є on breast, *mm*. lis	60	135
2014	— Є on breast, trefoils at neck; *mm*. 105/28, 105	50	120
2015	**Halfgroat.** *London.* Annulets by neck (heavy dies); *mm*. 33	250	525
2016	— Quatrefoils by neck; *mm*. 33/-, 28/-, 74, 74/28	45	100
2017	— Saltires by neck; *mm*. 74, 74/28	50	120
2018	— Trefoils by neck; *mm*. 74, 74/28, 11/28	50	125
2019	— No marks by neck; *mm*. 11/28	90	185
2020	— *Bristol.* Saltires or crosses by neck; *mm*. 33/28, 28, 74, 74/-	135	285
2021	— Quatrefoils by neck; *mm*. 28/-, 74, 74/-	135	275
2022	— Trefoils by neck; *mm*. crown	150	325
2023	— No marks by neck; *mm*. 74/28	160	350
2024	*Canterbury,* Archb. Bourchier (1464-7). Knot below bust; quatrefoils by neck; *mm*. 99/-, 99, 99/33, 99/28	25	65
2025	— — — quatrefoils omitted *mm*. 99	25	65
2026	— — — saltires by neck; *mm*. 99/-, 99/28	30	70
2026A	— — — trefoils by neck; *mm*. 99	40	95

2027   2030

	F	VF
	£	£
2027 — — — wedges by hair and/or neck; *mm.* 99, 99/33, 99/28	35	80
2028 — — As 2024 or 2025, but no knot	35	85
2029 — Royal mint (1467-9). Quatrefoils by neck; *mm.* 74, 74/-	30	80
2030 — — Saltires by neck; *mm.* 74/-, 74	30	80
2031 — — Trefoils by neck; *mm.* 74, 74/-, 74/28, 33	20	60
2032 — No marks by neck; *mm.* sun	50	125
2033 *Coventry.* Crosses by neck; *mm.* sun	750	1750
2034 *Norwich.* Saltires by neck; *mm.* sun	700	1650
2035 *York.* Quatrefoils by neck; *mm.* sun, lis, lis/-	65	135
2036 — Saltires by neck; *mm.* lis	60	125
2037 — Trefoils by neck; *mm.* lis, lis/-	70	145
2038 — Є on breast, quatrefoils by neck; *mm.* lis/-	75	150
2039 **Penny** (12 grs.), *London.* Annulets by neck (heavy dies); *mm.* rose	225	450
2040 — Quatrefoils by neck; *mm.* 74, sun. crown	30	80
2041 — Trefoil and quatrefoil by neck; *mm.* crown	40	100
2042 — Saltires by neck; *mm.* crown	35	90
2043 — Trefoils by neck; *mm.* crown, ll	35	90
2044 — No marks by neck; *mm.* ll	125	275
2045 *Bristol.* Crosses, quatrefoils or saltires by neck, BRISTOW; *mm.* crown	165	375
2046 — Quatrefoils by neck; BRI(trefoil)STOLL	165	375
2047 — Trefoil to r. of neck BRISTOLL	175	400
2048 *Canterbury,* Archb. Bourchier. Quatrefoils or saltires by neck, knot on breast; *mm.* pall	75	165
2049 — — Similar, but no marks by neck	80	175
2050 — — As 2048, but no knot	80	175
2051 — — Crosses by neck, no knot	80	175
2052 — Royal mint. Quatrefoils by neck; *mm.* crown	185	450
2053 — *Durham,* King's Receiver (1462-4). Local dies, mostly with rose in centre of *rev.; mm.* 7a, 33	25	65
2054 — Bp. Lawrence Booth (1465-70). B and D by neck, B on *rev.; mm.* 33	35	90
2055 — — Quatrefoil and B by neck; *mm.* sun	30	80
2056 — — B and quatrefoil by neck; *mm.* crown	40	100
2057 — — D and quatrefoil by neck; *mm.* crown	35	90
2058 — — Quatrefoils by neck; *mm.* crown	30	85
2059 — — Trefoils by neck; *mm.* crown	30	85
2060 — Lis by neck; *mm.* crown	30	80
2061 *York,* Sede Vacante (1464-5). Quatrefoils at neck, no quatrefoil in centre of *rev.; mm.* sun, rose	50	125
2062 — Archb. Neville (1465-70). Local dies, G and key by neck, quatrefoil on *rev.; mm.* sun, plain cross	25	70

2063   2068

		F	VF
		£	£
2063	— — London-made dies, similar; *mm.* 28, 105, 11	25	70
2064	— — Similar, but no marks by neck; *mm.* large lis	45	120
2065	— — — Quatrefoils by neck; *mm.* large lis	35	85
2066	— — — Trefoils by neck; *mm.* large lis	30	80
2067	**Halfpenny,** *London.* Saltires by neck; *mm.* 34, 28, 74	25	65
2068	— Trefoils by neck; *mm.* 28, 74, 11	25	65
2069	— No marks by neck; *mm.* 11	60	145
2070	*Bristol.* Crosses by neck; *mm.* crown	110	250
2071	— Trefoils by neck; *mm.* crown	100	225
2072	*Canterbury.* Archb. Bourchier. No marks; *mm.* pall	95	200
2072A	— — — Trefoils by neck, *mm.* pall	95	200
2073	— Royal mint. Saltires by neck; *mm.* crown	85	175
2074	— — Trefoils by neck; *mm.* crown	70	150
2074A	*Norwich.* Quartrefoils by neck., *mm.* Sun	225	500
2075	*York.* Royal mint. Saltires by neck; *mm.* lis/-, sun/-	70	150
2076	— — Trefoils by neck; *mm.* lis/-	65	140
2077	**Farthing,** *London.* ЄDWARD DI GRA RЄX, no marks at neck, *mm.* rose	300	650
2077A	— Trefoils by neck, *mm.* crown	400	825

Full flan coins are difficult to find in the smaller denominations.

The coinage of this short restoration follows closely that of the previous reign. Only angel gold was issued, the ryal being discontinued. Many of the coins have the king's name reading hЄnRICV — another distinguishing feature is an R that looks like a B.

Mintmarks

Cross pattée (6)   Rose (33, Bristol)
Restoration cross (13)   Lis (105)
Trefoil (44 and 45)   Short cross fitchée (12)

GOLD

2079

		F	*VF*
		£	£
2078	**Angel**, *London*. As illus. but no B; *mm*. -/6, 13, -/105, none	650	1350
2079	*Bristol*. B in waves; *mm*. -/13, none	1000	2500
2080	**Half-angel**, *London*. As 2078; *mm*. -/6, -/13, -/105	1500	3250
2081	*Bristol*. B in waves; *mm*. -/13	2000	4500

SILVER

2082   2084

2082	**Groat**, *London*. Usual type; *mm*. 6, 6/13, 6/105, 13, 13/6, 13/105, 13 /12	120	275
2083	*Bristol*. B on breast; *mm*. 13, 13/33, 13/44, 44, 44/13, 44/33, 44/12	150	375
2084	*York*. C on breast; *mm*. lis, lis/sun	135	300
2085	**Halfgroat**, *London*. As 2082; *mm*. 13, 13/-	225	450
2086	*York*. C on breast; *mm*. lis	425	900
2087	**Penny**, *London*. Usual type; *mm*. 6, 13, 12	350	750

	F	VF
	£	£
2087A *Bristol*. Similar; *mm*. 12	600	1250
2088 *York*. G and key by neck; *mm*. lis..	250	525
2089 **Halfpenny,** *London*. As 2087; *mm*. 12, 13,..............................	95	200
2090 *Bristol*. Similar; *mm*. cross...	450	950

EDWARD IV, Second Reign, 1471-83

The Angel and its half were the only gold denominations issued during this reign. The main types and weight standards remained the same as those of the light coinage of Edward's first reign. The use of the 'initial mark' as a mintmark to denote the date of issue was now firmly established.

Mintmarks

33	105	12	55	44	55	28	56	17

30	37	6	18	19	20	31	11	38

1471-83	Rose (33, *York & Durham*)	1473-7	Cross pattée (6)
	Lis (105, *York*)		Pierced cross 1 (18)
1471	Short cross fitchee (12)	1477-80	Pierced cross and
1471-2	Annulet (large, 55)		pellet (19)
	Trefoil (44)		Pierced cross 2 (18)
	Rose (33, *Bristol*)		Pierced cross, central
1471-3	Pansy (30, *Durham*)		pellet (20)
1472-3	Annulet (small, 55)		Rose (33, *Canterbury*)
	Sun (28, *Bristol*)	1480-3	Heraldic cinquefoil (31)
1473-7	Pellet in annulet (56)		Long cross fitchee
	Cross and four pellets (17)		(11, *Canterbury*)
	Cross in circle (37)	1483	Halved sun and rose (38)
			(Listed under Ed. IV/V.)

GOLD

2091		2093

	F	VF
	£	£
2091 **Angel.** *London*. Type as illus.; *mm*. 12, 55, 56, 17, 18, 19, 31	275	550
2092 *Bristol*. B in waves; *mm*. small annulet......................................	1250	2650
2093 **Half-angel.** As illus.; *mm*. 55, cross in circle, 19, 20/19, 31	265	525

		F	VF
		£	£
2094	King's name and title on rev.; *mm*. 12/-	325	650
2095	King's name and the title both sides; *mm*. 55/-	350	700

SILVER

2096   2101

2096	**Groat,** *London*. Trefoils on cusps, no marks by bust; *mm*. 12-37	35	90
2097	— — roses by bust; *mm*. pellet in annulet	50	125
2098	— Fleurs on cusps; no marks by bust; *mm*. 18-20	40	100
2099	— — pellets by bust; *mm*. pierced cross	70	165
2100	— — rose on breast; *mm*. 31	40	95
2101	*Bristol*. B on breast no marks by bust; *mm*. 33, 33/55, 28/55, 55, 55/-, 28	70	165
2102	*York*. Є on breast no marks by bust; *mm*. lis	80	185
2103	**Halfgroat,** *London*. As 2096; *mm*. 12-31	40	90
2104	*Bristol*. B on breast; *mm*. 33/12	275	600
2105	*Canterbury* (Royal mint). As 2103; *mm*. 33, 11, 11/31, 31	35	80

2106

2106	— C on breast; *mm*. rose	30	70
2107	— — R. C in centre; *mm*. rose	30	75
2108	— — R. Rose in centre; *mm*. rose	30	75
2109	*York*. No Є on breast; *mm*. lis	100	250
2110	**Penny,** *London*. No marks by bust; *mm*. 12-31	35	90
2111	*Bristol*. Similar; *mm*. rose	250	525
2112	*Canterbury* (Royal). Similar; *mm*. 33, 11	55	140
2113	— C on breast; *mm*. rose	85	200
2114	*Durham*, Bp. Booth (1471-6). No marks by neck; *mm*. 12, 44	25	65

2115   2116

2115	— — D in centre of *rev.;* B and trefoil by neck; *mm*. 44, 33, 56	25	70
2116	— — — two lis at neck; *mm*. rose	30	75
2117	— — — crosses over crown, and on breast; *mm*. rose	25	65

		F	VF
		£	£
2118	— — — crosses over crown, V under CIVI; *mm.* rose, pansy	30	70
2119	— — — B to l. of crown, V on breast and under CIVI	25	65
2120	— — — As last but crosses at shoulders	25	65
2121	— Sede Vacante (1476). R. D in centre; *mm.* rose....................................	35	95
2122	— Bp. Dudley (1476-83). V to r. of neck; as last	30	70

| 2123 | 2125 | 2134 |

| 2123 | — — D and V by neck; as last, but *mm.* 31 .... | 30 | 75 |

Nos. 2117-2123 are from locally-made dies.

2124	*York,* Archb. Neville (1471-2). Quatrefoils by neck. R. Quatrefoil; *mm.* 12 (over lis)	75	75
2125	— — Similar, but G and key by neck; *mm.* 12 (over lis)	20	60
2126	— Neville suspended (1472-5). As last, but no quatrefoil in centre of *rev.*	30	75
2126A	— — no marks by bust, similar; *mm.* annulet	80	200
2127	— — No marks by neck, quatrefoil on *rev.; mm.* 55, cross in circle, 33 ..	20	60
2128	— — Similar but Є and rose by neck; *mm.* rose.....................................	20	60
2129	— Archb. Neville restored (1475-6). As last, but G and rose	25	65
2130	— — Similar, but G and key by bust	20	60
2131	— Sede Vacante (1476). As 2127, but rose on breast; *mm.* rose..............	25	70
2132	— Archb. Lawrence Booth (1476-80). B and key by bust, quatrefoil on *rev.; mm.* 33, 31	20	60
2133	— Sede Vacante (1480). Similar, but no quatrefoil on rev.; mm. rose......	25	70
2134	— Archb. Rotherham (1480-3). T and slanting key by neck, quatrefoil on *rev.; mm.* 33	20	60
2135	— — — Similar, but star on breast..	80	175
2136	— — — Star on breast and to r. of crown	75	165
2137	**Halfpenny,** *London.* No marks by neck; *mm.* 12-31	20	50
2138	— Pellets at neck; *mm.* pierced cross...	35	85
2139	*Canterbury* (Royal). C on breast and in centre of *rev.; mm.* rose	95	200
2140	— C on breast only; *mm.* rose...	85	175
2141	— Without C either side; *mm.* 11	70	160
2142	*Durham,* Bp. Booth. No marks by neck. R. DЄR ĀM, D in centre; *mm.* rose...	150	350
2142A	— — Lis either side of neck. R. D or no mark in centre	175	425
2142B	— — B to l. of crown, crosses at shoulders. R. D. in centre; *mm.* rose....	175	425
2143	— — — Bp. Dudley V to l. of neck; as last	165	375

Full flan coins are very difficult to find in the small denominations.

On the death of Edward IV, 9th April, 1483, the 12-year-old Prince Edward was placed under the guardianship of his uncle, Richard, Duke of Gloucester, but within eleven weeks Richard usurped the throne and Edward and his younger brother were confined to the Tower and never seen alive again. The boar's head was a personal badge of Richard, Edward's 'Protector'.

The consensus now favours the last year of Edward IV for the introduction of the halved-sun and rose mintmark, but it is suggested that all the coins of Edward V's reign were also struck from dies bearing this mint mark. The coins are very rare.

Mintmark: Halved sun and rose.

GOLD

		F	VF
		£	£
2144	**Angel.** As 2091	950	2100
2145	**Half-angel.** As 2093	1650	3500

SILVER

           2145   2146

2146	**Groat.** As 2098 with or without pellet below bust	475	1000
2147	**Penny.** As 2110	600	1250
2148	**Halfpenny.** As 2137	125	300

2149

COINS ATTRIBUTABLE TO RICHARD III, 1483

Recent research indicates that coins with the mint marks previously thought to be for Edward V are now attributable to Richard III, even though they bear Edward's name.

Mintmarks: Boar's head on *obv.,* halved sun and rose on *rev.*

GOLD

2149	**Angel.** As 2091	3000	7000
2150	**Half-angel.** Similar	*Extremely rare*	

SILVER

2151

		F	VF
		£	£
2151	**Groat.** As 2098	1750	3500
2152	**Halfgroat.** As 2103	900	2000
2153	**Penny.** As 2110 (*mm.* uncertain on only known specimen).....................	*Extremely rare*	

RICHARD III, 1483-85

Richard's brief reign was brought to an end on the field of Bosworth. His coinage follows the pattern of the previous reigns. The smaller denominations of the London mint are all rare.

Mintmarks

38	62	63	105	33

Halved sun and rose, 3 styles (38, 39 and another with the sun more solid, see *North*).
Boar's head, narrow (62) wide (63).
Lis (105, *Durham*)
Rose only (33).

GOLD

2154	**Angel.** Reading ЄDWARD but with R and rose by mast; *mm.* sun and rose	*Extremely rare*	
2155	— Similar, but boar's head *mm.* on *obv*	*Extremely rare*	

2156   2158

2156	Reading RICARD or RICAD. R. R and rose by mast; *mm.* various combinations	850	1700
2157	— Similar, but R by mast over rose	875	1750
2158	**Half-angel.** R. R and rose by mast; *mm.* boar's head	2250	4500

SILVER

2159   2160

		F	VF
		£	£
2159	**Groat,** *London. Mm.* various combinations	275	550
2160	— Pellet below bust	300	600
2161	*York. Mm.* Sun and rose (*obv.*)	450	975
2162	**Halfgroat.** *Mm.* sun and rose on *obv.* only	600	1250
2163	Pellet below bust; *mm.* sun and rose	650	1350
2164	— *mm.* boar's head (*obv.*)...	750	1500
2165	**Penny.** *London. mm.* boar's head (*obv.*)..	900	2000

2168   2169

2166	*York,* Archb. Rotherham. R. Quatrefoil in centre; *mm.* sun and rose	250	500
2167	— — T and upright key at neck; *mm.* rose	125	350
2168	— — — *mm.* boar's head	135	375
2169	*Durham,* Bp. Sherwood. S on breast. R. D in centre; *mm.* lis..................	100	275
2170	**Halfpenny,** *London. Mm.* sun and rose	120	275
2171	— *Mm.* boar's head	150	400
2171A	**Farthing,** *Mm.* boar's head, sun and rose	750	1600

Most small denomination coins are short of flan and unevenly struck.

THE HOUSE OF TUDOR, 1485-1603

HENRY VII, 1485-1509

For the first four years of his reign Henry's coins differ only in name and mintmark from those of his predecessors, but in 1489 radical changes were made in the coinage. Though the pound sterling had been a denomination of account for centuries, a pound coin had never been minted. Now a magnificent gold pound was issued, and, from the design of the king enthroned in majesty, was called a 'Sovereign'. The reverse had the royal arms set in the centre of a Tudor rose. A few years later the angel was restyled and St. Michael, who is depicted about to thrust Satan into the Pit with a cross-topped lance, is no longer a feathered figure but is clad in armour of Renaissance style. A gold ryal of ten shillings was minted again for a brief period.

The other major innovation was the introduction of the shilling in the opening years of the 16th century. It is remarkable for the very fine profile portrait of the king which replaces the representational image of a monarch that had served on the coinage for the past couple of centuries. This new portrait was also used on groats and halfgroats but not on the smaller denominations.

Mintmarks

39	41	40	42	33	11	7a	123
105	76b	31	78	30	91	43	57
	85	94	118	21	33	53	

1485-7	Halved sun and rose (39)	1495-8	Pansy (30)
	Lis upon sun and rose (41)		Tun (123, *Canterbury*)
	Lis upon half rose (40)		Lis (105, York)
	Lis-rose dimidiated (42)	1498-9	Crowned leopard's head (91)
	Rose (33, *York*)		Lis issuant from rose (43)
1487	Lis (105)		Tun (123, *Canterbury*)
	Cross fitchy (11)	1499-1502	Anchor (57)
1487-8	Rose (33)	1502-4	Greyhound's head (85)
	Plain cross (7a, *Durham*)		Lis (105, profile issue only)
1488-9	No marks		Martlet (94, *York*)
1489-93	Cinquefoil (31)	1504-5	Cross-crosslet (21)
	Crozier (76b, *Durham*)	1504-9	Martlet (94, (*York, Canterbury*)
1492	Cross fitchée (11, gold only)		Rose (33, *York* and
1493-5	Escallop (78)		*Canterbury*)
	Dragon (118, gold only)	1505-9	Pheon (53)
	Lis (105, *Canterbury and York*		
	Tun (123, *Canterbury*)		

GOLD

		F	VF
		£	£

2172 — Group II. Somewhat similar but throne has narrow back, lis in background. R. Large Tudor rose bearing small shield. *mm.* -/11 .... *Extremely rare*

2173 **Sovereign** (20s; wt. 240 gr.). Group I. Large figure of king sitting on backless throne. R. Large shield crowned on large Tudor rose. *mm.* 31 ... *Extremely rare*

2174

2174 — III. King on high-backed very ornamental throne, with greyhound and dragon on side pillars. R. Shield on Tudor rose; *mm.* dragon 7500 15500

2175 — IV. Similar but throne with high canopy breaking legend and broad seat, *mm.* 105/118, (also with no *obv.* i.c. *mm.* 105/118, very rare) 7000 14000

2176 — Narrow throne with a portcullis below the king's feet (like Henry VIII); *mm.* 105/21, 105/53 .... 7000 14250

2177 **Double-sovereign** and **Treble-sovereign** from same dies as 2176. These piedforts were probably intended as presentation pieces *mm.* 105/21, 105/53 *Extremely rare*

2178

2178 **Ryal** (10s.). As illustration: *mm.* -/11 .... 6750 16000

2179 **Angel** (6s. 8d). I. Angel of old type with one foot on dragon. R. PER CRVCEM. etc., *mm.* 39, 40, (also muled both ways) 525 1050

2179A — With Irish title, and legend over angel head. mm. 33/- 600 1250

2180 — — Name altered from RICARD? and h on *rev.* from R. mm. 41/39, 41/40, 41/-, 39/? 550 1100

		2181	2183	2187		

		F	*VF*
		£	£
2181	II. As 2179, but *mm*. none. 31/-..	375	750
2181A	II/III mule. *mm*. 31/78, **R**. PER CRUC or AVTEM TRANS	400	800
2182	As 2181. **R**. IhC AVTEM TRANSIENS etc.; *mm*. none, 31/-	425	825
2183	III. New dies, angel with both feet on dragons; (large straight lettering) *mm*. 78-85 except 91 (many mules exist)	250	525
2183A	— Angel with very small wings. *mm*. escallop......................................	450	950
2184	— — **R**. IhC AVTEM TRANSIENS, etc.; *mm*. escallop..........................	400	800
2185	IV. Small square lettering; *mm*. 85 (also muled with 2183).....................	275	550
2186	— Tall thin lettering; *mm*. 21 (also muled with 2185 obv.)	285	575
2187	V. Large crook-shaped abbreviation after hENRIC; *mm*. 21 and 53 (combinations and mules exist)...	235	475
2188	**Half-angel or angelet.** I. M*m*. 39, 41, (old dies RIII altered)	475	950
2189	III. Angel with both feet on dragon: *mm*. 30, 57/30, -/85 30/85	275	575
2190	IV. Small square lettering; *mm*. rose	350	750
2191	— *Obv*. as last. **R**. Tall thin lettering; *mm*. 33/21	335	700
2192	V. As angel; *mm*. pheon..	200	400

SILVER

Facing bust issues. Including 'Sovereign' type pennies.

2193	**Groat.** I. Open crown; *mm*. 40 (rose on bust), 39-42 and none (combinations)	75	175

	2194	2195

2194	— — crosses or saltires by neck, 41, 40, 105-33 and none (combinations)	85	190
2195	IIa. Large bust with out-turned hair, crown with two plain arches; *mm*. none, 31, 31/-, 31/78	60	135
2196	— — similar but crosses by neck; *mm*. none, -/105	70	150
2197	— — **R**. Portcullis over long cross; *mm*. -/lis	*Extremely rare*	

2198   2199   2201

| | | F | VF |
| | | £ | £ |

2198 **Groat.** IIIa. Bust as IIa. Crown with two jewelled arches, *mm*. 31, 78? .. 90 | 225

2198A IIIb. Similar, but new bust with realistic hair *mm*. 78, 30 .... 45 | 95

2199 IIIc. Bust as IIIb, but crown with one plain and one jewelled arch, *mm*.
30-21 and none .... 40 | 85

2199A IIId. As last, but plainer letters. mm 57, 85, 33 and none .... 45 | 95

2200 IVa. Wide single arch crown; arch is single or double bar with 4 crockets;
mm. 85, 85/33, 21 .... 50 | 110

2201 IVb. — Similar, but arch is double bar with 6 uprights or crockets as jewels;
mm. 85, 21/85, 21 .... 45 | 100
* *mm.s* muled.

2202 **Halfgroat,** *London.* I. Open crown, tressure unbroken; *mm*. 40/-, 40/39
(R. III mule) .... 325 | 700

2203 — IIIa. Double arched crown, rosettes on tressure; mm. escallop .... 65 | 150

2204 — IIIb. Similar, nothing on tressure. R. Lozenge panel in centre; *mm*. lis 40 | 95

2205 — — Similar, but also with lis on breast; mm. lis .... 40 | 100

2206 — IIIc. Unarched crown with tressure broken. R. Lozenge panel in centre;
mm. lis .... 30 | 70

2206A — — — Similar but smaller dies and much smaller lettering .... 30 | 75

2207   2211

2207 *Canterbury, Archb.* Morton. I. Open crown, crosses by neck. R. M in centre;
mm. tun/- .... 35 | 75

2208 — — II. Similar, but double-arched crown; no *mm*. .... 30 | 70

2209 III King and Archb. jointly. As last but without M; (a) early lettering,
trefoil stops; *mm*. lis, tun and lis/lis .... 35 | 75

2210 — — (b) ornate lettering, rosette stops; *mm*. tun, lis in combinations ..... 25 | 60

2211 — — (c) — saltire or no stops; *mm*. 123, 123 & 30/123 .... 20 | 50

2212 *York,* Royal mint. (a) Double-arched crown, lis on breast (rarely omitted).
R. Lozenge panel in centre; *mm*. lis .... 40 | 85

2213 — — (b) Similar, but unarched crown, tressure broken, *mm*. lis.............. 30 | 65

	2214	2221	2226	

		F £	VF £
2214	— Archb. Savage. (a) Double-arched crown, keys at neck, no tressure; ornate lettering; *mm.* martlet	25	60
2215	— — (b) Similar, but fleured tressure, small square lettering; *mm.* martlet	25	60
2216	— — (c) As last, but tall thin lettering; *mm.* martlet	25	60
2217	— As last but no keys; *mm.* martlet	35	75
2218	**Penny.** Old type. London; *mm.* 40/-	200	450
2219	— — — crosses by bust, mm. small cross (obv.)	250	550
2220	— *Canterbury,* Archb. Morton. Open crown, *mm.* tun/- R. M in centre	225	525
2221	— — King and Archb. jointly, arched crown; *mm.* tun, tun/-	45	120
2222	— *Durham,* Bp. Sherwood. S on breast. R. D in centre; *mm.* 7a/-	60	135
2223	— *York,* Archb. Rotherham. With or without cross on breast, *mm.* 33/-, T and cross or key at neck. R. **h** in centre	45	110
2224	— — — T and trefoil at neck. R. Quatrefoil in centre and two extra pellets; *mm.* 39/-	40	100
2225	'Sovereign' type. *London.* Early lettering, no stops, no pillars to throne; no *mm.*	75	175
2226	— — — single pillar on king's right side, trefoil stops; no *mm.* or 31/-	25	65
2227	— — Ornate letters, rosette stops, single pillar; *mm.* lis (can be muled with above)	30	70
2228	— — saltire stops or none, two pillars; *mm.* none, -/30	25	65
2229	— — Similar, but small square lettering; no *mm.*	25	65
2230	— — Similar, but lettering as profile groats two double pillars; *mm.* 21, 53, none (sometimes on one side only)	30	75

	2231	2233	2235	

2231	— *Durham,* Bp. Sherwood. Crozier to r. of king, throne with one pillar. R. D and S beside shield	30	70
2232	— — Throne with two pillars, no crozier. R. As last	30	75
2233	— — Bp. Fox. Throne with one pillar. R. Mitre above shield, RD or DR at sides, no *mm.*	25	65
2234	— — Similar, but two pillars	25	65

		F	*VF*
		£	£
2235	*York,* Archb. Rotherham. Keys below shield; early lettering, trefoil stops, no pillars to throne, no *mm*	25	60
2236	— — — single pillar...	25	60
2237	— — — — ornate lettering, rosette or no stops, ...	25	60
2238	— — — two pillars sometimes with crosses between legs of throne.......	25	60
2239	**Halfpenny,** *London.* I. Open crown; *mm.* 40, 42...............................	35	100
2240	— — — trefoils at neck; no *mm.,* rose	40	115
2241	— — — crosses at neck; *mm.* rose	40	110
2242	— II. Double arched crown; *mm.* cinquefoil, none.............................	25	60
2243	— — — saltires at neck; no *mm.*...	25	60
2244	— III. Crown with single arch, ornate lettering; no *mm.*	20	50

    2245   2248   2249

2245	— V. Much smaller portrait; *mm.* pheon, lis, none	20	55
2246	*Canterbury,* Archb. Morton. I. Open crown, crosses by neck; R. M in centre	95	200
2247	— — II. Similar, but arched crown, saltires by bust; *mm.* profile eye (82)	85	175
2247A	— — — no marks at neck	100	225
2248	— III. King and Archb. Arched crown; *mm.* lis, none	50	110
2249	*York,* Archb. Savage. Arched crown, key below bust	75	175
2250	**Farthing,** *London.* hᴇɴʀɪᴄ DI GRA RᴇX (A), arched crown	125	325

*No.s 2239-49 have *mm.* on *obv.* only.

Profile issue

2251	Testoon (ls.). Type as groat. hᴇɴʀɪᴄ (VS); *mm.* lis	4000	8000
2252	— hᴇɴʀɪᴄ VII; *mm.* lis..	4250	8500

                              2253

| 2253 | — hᴇɴʀɪᴄ SᴇPTIM; *mm.* lis.. | 4750 | 9500 |

2254

2258

	F	VF
	£	£

2254 **Groat,** *Tentative issue* (contemporary with full-face groats). Double band
to crown, hᴇɴʀɪᴄ VII; *mm.* none, 105/-, -/105: 105/85, 105, 85, 21 ..... | 145 | 325
2255 — — — tressure on *obv.; mm.* cross-crosslet .... | 2250 | 4500
2256 — — hᴇɴʀɪᴄ (VS); *mm.* 105, -/105, 105/ 85, none .... | 325 | 750
2257 — — hᴇɴʀɪᴄ sᴇᴘᴛɪᴍ; *mm.* -/105 .... | 2500 | 5250
2258 *Regular issue.* Triple band to crown; *mm.* 21, 53
(both *mm.*s may occur on some *obv.* or *rev.*) .... | 65 | 175
2259 **Halfgroat,** *London.* As last; *mm.* 105, 53/105, 105/53, 53 .... | 70 | 185
2260 — — no numeral after King's name, no *mm.,* -/lis .... | 600 | 1250

2261

2262

2261 *Canterbury,* King and Archb. As London, but *mm.* 94, 33, 94/33 .... | 35 | 100
2262 *York,* Archb. Bainbridge. As London, but two keys below shield; *mm.*
94, 33, 33/94.. | 30 | 90
2262A — Similar but no keys; *mm.* rose .... | 65 | 150

2263

2263 — — XB beside shield; *mm.* rose/martlet .... | 325 | 750
2263A — — Similar but two keys below shield *mm.* rose(?)/martlet .... | 350 | 850

Henry VIII is held in ill-regard by numismatists as being the author of the debasement of England's gold and silver coinage; but there were also other important numismatic innovations during his reign. For the first sixteen years the coinage closely followed the pattern of the previous issues, even to the extent of retaining the portrait of Henry VII on the larger silver coins.

In 1526, in an effort to prevent the drain of gold to continental Europe, the value of English gold was increased by 10%, the sovereign to 22s. 0d. and the angel to 7s. 4d., and a new coin valued at 4s. 6d.—the Crown of the Rose—was introduced as a competitor to the French *écu au soleil*. The new crown was not a success and within a few months it was replaced by the Crown of the Double Rose valued at 5s but made of gold of only 22 carat fineness, the first time gold had been minted below the standard 23c. At the same time the sovereign was again revalued to 22s. 6d. and the angel to 7s. 6d., with a new coin, the George Noble, valued at 6s. 8d. (one-third pound).

The royal cyphers on some of the gold crowns and half-crowns combine the initial of Henry with those of his queens: Katherine of Aragon, Anne Boleyn and Jane Seymour. The architect of this coinage reform was the chancellor, Cardinal Thomas Wolsey, who besides his other changes had minted at York a groat bearing his initials and cardinal's hat in addition to the other denominations normally authorized for the ecclesiastical mints.

When open debasement of the coinage began in 1544 to help finance Henry's wars, the right to coin of the archbishops of Canterbury and York and of the bishop of Durham was not confirmed. Instead, a second royal mint was opened in the Tower as in subsequent years were six others, at Southwark, York, Canterbury, Bristol, Dublin and Durham House in the Strand. Gold, which fell to 23c. in 1544, 22c. in 1545, and 20c. in 1546 was much less debased than silver which declined to 9oz 2dwt. in 1544, 6oz 2dwt. in 1545 and 4oz 2dwt. in 1546. At this last standard the blanched silver surface of the coins soon wore away to reveal the copper alloy beneath which earned for Henry the nickname 'Old Coppernose'.

Mintmarks

53	69	70	108	33	94	73	11
105	22	23	30	78	15	24	110
52	72a	44	8	65a	114	121	90
36	106	56	S	E	116	135	

1509-26	Pheon (53)	1509-14	Martlet (94, *York*)
	Castle (69)	1509-23	Radiant star (22, *Durham & York*)
	Castle with H (70, gold)	1513-18	Crowned T (135, *Tournai*)
	Portcullis crowned (108)	1514-26	Star (23, *York & Durham*)
	Rose (33, *Canterbury*)		Pansy (30, *York*)
	Martlet (94, *Canterbury*)		Escallop (78, *York*)
	Pomegranate (73, but broader, *Cant.*)		Voided cross (15, *York*)
	Cross fitchée (11, *Cant.*)	1523-26	Spur rowel (24, *Durham*)
	Lis (105, *Canterbury, Durham*)		
1526-44	Rose (33)	1526-32	Cross patonce (8, *Cant.*)
	Lis (105)		T (114, *Canterbury*)

Sunburst 110)
Arrow (52)
Pheon (53)
Lis (106)
Star (23, *Durham*)
1526-9 Crescent (72a, *Durham*)
Trefoil (44 variety,
Durham)
Flower of eight petals and
circle centre (*Durham*)
1526-30 Cross (7a, sometimes
slightly voided, *York*)
Acorn (65a, *York*)

Uncertain mark (121,
Canterbury)
1529-44 Radiant star (22, *Durham*)
1530-44 Key (90, *York*)
1533-44 Catherine wheel (36,
Canterbury)
1544-7 Lis (105 and 106)
Pellet in annulet (56)
S (Southwark)
Є or E (Southwark)
1546-7 WS monogram (116, *Bristol*)

GOLD

First coinage, 1509-26

		F	VF
		£	£
2264	**Sovereign** (20s.). Similar to last sov. of Hen. VII; *mm.* 108....................	3250	7000
2264A	**Ryal** (10s.) King in ship holding sword and shield. R. Similar to 1950, *mm.*-/108	*Extremely rare*	
2265	**Angel** (6s. 8d.). As Hen. VIII, but hЄNRIC? VIII DI GRA RЄX, etc.; *mm.* 53, 69, 70, 70/69, 108, R. May omit h and rose, or rose only; mm. 69, 108	235	475
2266	**Half-angel.** Similar (sometimes without VIII), *mm.* 69, 70, 108/33, 108	200	425

2265

Second coinage, 1526-44

2267

2267	**Sovereign** (22s. 6d.). As 2264, R. single or double tressure *mm.* 110, 105, 105/52...	2850	6000
2268	**Angel** (7s. 6d.). As 2265, hЄNRIC VIII D(I) G(RA) R(ЄX) etc.; mm. 110, 105	400	825
2269	**Half-angel.** Similar; *mm.* lis	525	1050

Second coinage

2270   2272

	F	VF
	£	£

2270 **George-noble** (6s. 8d.). As illustration; *mm.* rose .... | 3000 | 6500
2270A— Similar, but more modern ship with three masts, without initials hR. R.
St. George brandishing sword behind head. .... | 5750 | 12000
2271 **Half-George-noble.** Similar to 2270 *mm.* rose, lis .... | *Extremely rare* |
2272 **Crown of the rose** (4s. 6d., 23 c. 3 ¹/₂ gr.). As illustration; *mm.* rose,
two legend varieties .... | 6000 | 12500

2279   2285

2273 **Crown of the double-rose** (5s., 22 c). Double-rose crowned, hK (Henry and
Katherine of Aragon) both crowned in field. R. Shield crowned; *mm.* rose | 235 | 475
2274 — hK both sides; *mm.* rose/lis, lis, arrow .... | 245 | 500
2275* — hK/hA or hA/hK; *mm.* arrow... | 600 | 1250
2276* — hR/hK or hI/hR; *mm.* arrow .... | 500 | 1000
2277 — hA (Anne Boleyn); *mm.* arrow .... | 475 | 950
2278 — hA/hR; *mm.* arrow .... | 600 | 1250
2279 — hI (Jane Seymour); *mm.* arrow .... | 300 | 600
2280* — hK/hI; *mm.* arrow .... | 550 | 1100
2281 — hR/hI; *mm.* arrow .... | 475 | 975
2282 — hR (Rex); *mm.* arrow .... | 275 | 575
2283 — — but with hIBERIE REX; *mm.* pheon .... | 525 | 1050
2284 **Halfcrown.** Similar but king's name henric 8 on *rev.,* no initials; *mm.* rose | 300 | 600
2285 — hK uncrowned on *obv.; mm.* rose .... | 225 | 475
2286 — hK uncrowned both sides; *mm.* rose/lis, lis, arrow .... | 235 | 500
2287 — hI uncrowned both sides; *mm.* arrow .... | 300 | 650
2288 — hR uncrowned both sides; hIB REX; *mm.* pheon .... | 425 | 900

*The hK initials may on later coins refer to Katherine Howard (Henry's fifth wife).

Third coinage, 1544-7

2291

		F £	*VF* £
2289	**Sovereign,** I (20s., Wt. 200 gr., 23 c.). As illustration but king with larger face and larger design; *mm*. lis	4500	10000
2290	II (20s., wt. 200 or 192 grs., 23, 22 or 20 ct.). *Tower*. As illustration; *mm*. lis, pellet in annulet/lis	1600	3750
2291	— *Southwark*. Similar; *mm*. S, Є/S	1500	3500
2292	— — Similar but Є below shield; *mm*. S/Є	2000	4500
2293	— *Bristol*. As London but *mm*. WS/-	2350	5500
2294	**Half-sovereign** (wt. 100 or 96 gr.), *Tower*. As illus.; *mm*. lis, pellet in annulet	260	575
2295	— Similar, but with annulet on inner circle (either or both sides)	275	625
2296	*Southwark*. Mm. S	300	675
2297	— Є below shield; *mm*. S, Є, S/Є, Є/S, (known without sceptre; *mm*. S)	285	650
2298	*Bristol*. Lombardic lettering; *mm*. WS, WS/-	475	1000

2294

2303   2304

2299	**Angel** (8s., 23 c). Annulet by angel's head and on ship, hЄnRIC' 8; *mm*. lis	235	475
2300	— Similar, but annulet one side only or none	250	500
2301	**Half-angel.** Annulet on ship; *mm*. lis	250	500
2302	— No annulet on ship; *mm*. lis	265	575
2303	— Three annulets on ship; *mm*. lis	275	600
2304	**Quarter-angel** Angel wears armour; *mm*. lis	225	475
2304A	— Angel wears tunic; *mm*. lis	235	500

Third coinage

		F	*VF*
		£	£
2305	**Crown,** *London.* Similar to 2283, but hЄnRIC' 8 ; Lombardic lettering; mm . 56	235	500
2306	— without RVTILAnS; *mm.* 56	250	550
2307	— — — with annulet on inner circle	250	550
2307A	— King's name omitted. DEI GRA both sides, *mm.* 56	450	900
2308	— *Southwark.* As 2306; *mm.* S, Є, E/S, Є/-, E/Є	325	650
2309	*Bristol.* hЄnRIC VIII. ROSA etc. R. D G, etc.; *mm.*-/WS	245	525
2310	— Similar but hЄnRIC(VS) 8 R. DЄI) G(RA); *mm.* -/WS, WS	250	535
2311	**Halfcrown,** *London.* Similar to 2288; *mm.* 56, 56/-	200	400
2312	— — with annulet on inner circle *mm.* 56	210	425
2313	*Southwark.* As 2311; *mm.* S	275	550
2314	— *O.* hЄnRIC 8 ROSA SINЄ SPIn. R. DЄI GRA, etc.; *mm.* Є	285	575
2315	*Bristol. O.* RVTILAn S, etc. R. hЄnRIC 8; *mm.* WS/-	265	535

For other gold coins in Henry's name see page 218-19.

SILVER

First coinage, 1509-26

2316   2327

2316	**Groat.** Portrait of Hen. VII. *London mm.* 53, 69, 108, 108 over 135...	60	165
2317	— *Tournai; mm.* crowned T. R. CIVITAS TORnACЄn*	300	750
2318	**Halfgroat.** Portrait of Hen. VII. London; *mm.* 108, 108/-	65	175
2319	— *Canterbury,* Archb. Warham. POSVI *rev.; mm.* rose	65	175
2320	— — — WA above shield; *mm.* martlet	40	125
2321	— — — WA beside shield; *mm.* cross fitchee	40	125
2322	— — CIVITAS CAnTOR *rev.,* similar; *mm.* 73, 105, 11/105	35	100
2323	— *York,* POSVI *rev.,* Archb. Bainbridge (1508-14). Keys below shield; *mm.* martlet	40	110
2324	— — — XB beside shield no keys; *mm.* martlet	55	125
2325	— — — Archb. Wolsey (1514-30). Keys and cardinal's hat below shield; *mm.* 94, 22	95	225
2326	— — CIVITAS ЄBORACI *rev.* Similar; *mm.* 22, 23, 30, 78, 15, 15/78	40	100
2327	— — As last with TW beside shield; *mm.* voided cross	65	150
2327A	— *Tournai.* As 2317	1250	2500

*Other non-portrait groats and half-groats exist of this mint, captured during an invasion of France in 1513. (Restored to France in 1518.)

2332   2335   2336

		F £	VF £
2328	**Penny,** 'Sovereign' type, *London; mm.* 69, 108 /-	30	75
2329	— *Canterbury.* WA above shield; *mm.* martlet	70	150
2330	— — — WA beside shield; *mm.* 73/-..	55	120
2331	— *Durham,* Bp. Ruthall (1509-23). TD above shield; *mm.* lis.............	25	65
2332	— — — TD beside shield; *mm.* lis, radiant star................................	25	65
2333	— — Bp. Wolsey (1523-9). DW beside shield, cardinal's hat below; spur rowel	150	325
2334	**Halfpenny.** Facing bust, ͪenRIC DI GRA REX (AGL). *London; mm.* 69, 108/-	20	55
2335	— *Canterbury.* WA beside bust; *mm.* 73/-, 11	70	150
2335A	— *York.* Key below bust, *mm.* star.	125	275
2336	**Farthing.** *mm.* 108/-, ͪenRIC DI GRA REX, portcullis. R. CIVITAS LOnDON, rose in centre of long cross	275	625

Second coinage, 1526-44

2337   2337 D   2337 E

2337	**Groat.** His own young portrait. *London;* bust r., with heavy jowls; *mm.* rose, mainly Roman letters, both sides, roses in cross ends..........	250	600
2337A	— Obv. as last. R. Lombardic letters, saltires in cross ends; *mm.* rose	150	375
2337B	Bust as 2337 but Lombardic letters. R. Lombardic letters but roses in cross ends; *mm.* rose...	175	425
2337C	— *Obv.* as last. R. As 2337A; *mm.* rose	100	275
2337D	Second bust, Greek profile, longer hair, less heavy jowls; *mm.* rose ...	60	165
2337E	Third bust, stereotyped as ill. *mm.* 33-53 (muling occurs)	45	110
2338	— — with Irish title HIB; larger flan, saltires in cross ends; *mm.* 53, 105 53/105, 105/53, ...	275	600
2339	— *York,* Archb. Wolsey. TW beside shield, cardinal's hat below; *mm.* voided cross, acorn, muled (both ways)	80	185
2340	— — — omits TW; *mm.* voided cross	175	450

Second coinage silver

| | 2342 | 2343 | 2348 |

		F	VF
		£	£

2341	**Halfgroat.** *London;* type as groats, Lombardic lettering both sides.		
	mm. rose to arrow (*obv.*) or none (sometimes muled)	35	85
2341A	*Obv.* Similar to 2337, *mm.* rose, R Lombardic letters	225	475
2342	— — with Irish title HIB; *mm.* pheon	400	850
2343	— *Canterbury,* Archb. Warham (—1532). R. CIVITAS CAПTOR, WA		
	beside shield; *mm.* 121, 121/-, 121/33, 8, 8/T, T	25	60
2344	— — — nothing by shield; *mm.* 121/-	50	120
2345	— — Archb. Cranmer (1533—). TC beside shield; *mm.* 36, 36/-........	30	70
2346	— *York,* Archb. Wolsey (—1530). R. CIVITAS ЄBORACI, TW		
	beside shield, hat below; *mm.* 15/-, 15	40	90
2347	— — Sede Vacante (1530/1). No marks; *mm.* key	45	110
2348	— — Archb. Lee (1531-44). EL or LE beside shield; *mm.* key	30	75

| | 2350 | 2354 | 2359 |

2349	**Penny.** 'Sovereign' type h . D . G . ROSA SIПЄ SPIПA, *London;*		
	mm. rose to arrow (*obv.* only)	30	75
2350	— *Canterbury.* WA beside shield; *mm.* 121/-, 8/-, T/-	70	165
2351	— — TC beside shield; *mm.* 36/-	75	185
2352	— *Durham,* Bp. Wolsey (—1529). TW beside shield, hat below; *mm.* 23,		
	23/44, 23/-, 72a/-, 44, 44/-, 72a/44 (muled with 2333 *obv.*, *mm.* 24/44)	25	60
2353	— — Sede Vacante (1529-30). No marks; *mm.* 23/-, 22/-	35	85
2354	— — Bp. Tunstall (1530—). CD beside shield; *mm.* 23, 23/-, 22/-, 22	25	60
2355	— *York.* EL beside shield; *mm.* key/-	95	200
2356	**Halfpenny.** Facing bust, h D G ROSA SIЄ SPIA. *London; mm.* rose to		
	arrow (*obv.* only)..	20	50
2357	— *Canterbury.* WA beside bust; *mm.* 121/-, 8/-, T/-	75	165
2358	— — TC beside bust; *mm.* 36/-	30	75
2359	— *York.* TW beside bust; *mm.* 15/-, acorn/-	65	135
2359A	— — —; key below bust	125	250
2360	— — Sede Vacante. Key below bust; *mm.* 15/-	120	250
2361	— — EL or LE beside bust; *mm.* key/-	70	145
2362	**Farthing.** *O.* RVTILANS ROSA, portcullis; *mm.* 33/-, 105/-, 110/-. R.		
	DEO GRACIAS...., long cross with pellet in each angle	300	650
2363	— — *mm.* arrow/- R. DEO GRACIAS, rose on long cross	400	850
2363A	— *Canterbury.* O. Similar. R. Similar. *mm.* 36/-..........................	550	1200

2364   2368

Third coinage, 1544-7 (Silver progressively debased. 9oz (2dwt), 6oz (2dwt) 4oz (2dwt)).

		Fair	Fine	VF
2364	**Testoon.** *Tower.* hЄnRIC'. VIII, etc. R. Crowned rose between h and R.POSVI, etc.; *mm.* lis, lis and 56, lis/two lis		475	1450
2365	— hЄnRIC 8, *mm.* 105 and 56, 105/56, 105 and 56/56, 56		425	1300
2366	— — annulet on inner circle of rev. or both sides; *mm.* pellet in annulet		450	1350
2367	*Southwark.* As 2365. R. CIVITAS LOnDOn; *mm.* S, Є, S/Є, Є/S		475	1350
2368	*Bristol. Mm.*-/WS monogram. (Tower or local dies.)		600	1500

2384   Bust 1   Bust 2   Bust 3

2369	**Groat.** *Tower.* As ill. above, busts 1, 2, 3; *mm.* lis/-, lis	50	160
2369A	Bust 1, R. As second coinage; i.e. saltires in forks; *mm.* lis	70	200
2370	Bust 2 or 3 annulet on inner circle, both sides or rev. only	65	175
2371	*Southwark.* As 2367, busts 1, 2, 3, 4; no *mm.* or lis/-; S or S and Є or Є in forks	55	170
2372	*Bristol. Mm.*-/WS monogram, Bristol bust and Tower bust 2 or 3	50	160
2373	*Canterbury.* Busts 1, 2, (2 var); no *mm.* or lis/–	60	175
2374	*York.* Busts 1 var. 2, 3, no *mm.*	50	160
2375	**Halfgroat.** *Tower.* As 2365, bust 1; *mm.* lis, none	50	150
2376	*Southwark.* As 2367, bust 1; no *mm.*; S or Є and S in forks	125	275
2377	*Bristol. Mm.*-/WS monogram	45	140
2378	*Canterbury.* Bust 1; no *mm.*	35	110
2379	*York.* Bust 1; no *mm.*	40	135
2380	**Penny.** *Tower.* Facing bust; no *mm.* or lis/-	35	110
2381	*Southwark.* Facing bust; *mm.* S/-, Є/-, -/Є	110	250
2382	*Bristol.* Facing bust; no *mm.* (Tower dies or local but truncated at neck)	40	120
2383	*Canterbury.* Facing bust; no *mm.*	35	110
2384	*York.* Facing bust; no *mm.*	35	110
2385	**Halfpenny.** *Tower.* Facing bust; no *mm.* or lis/-, pellet in annulet in *rev.* centre	45	135
2386	*Bristol.* Facing bust; no *mm.*	65	175
2387	*Canterbury.* Facing bust; no *mm.*, (some read H 8)	40	125
2388	*York.* Facing bust; no *mm.*	30	100
2388A	**Farthing** *obv.* Rose. R. Cross and pellets	550	1200

These coins were struck during the reign of Edward VI but bear the name and portrait of Henry VIII, except in the case of the half-sovereigns which bear the youthful head of Edward.

Mintmarks

56	105	52	K	E	116
66	115	33	122	t	94

1547	Annulet and pellet (56)	1549	TC monogram (115, *Bristol*)
1547-8	Lis (105)		Lis (105, *Canterbury*)
1547-9	Arrow (52)		Rose (33, *Canterbury*)
	K		Grapple (122)
	Roman E (*Southwark*)	1549/50	t (*Canterbury*)
	WS monogram (116, *Bristol*)	1550/1	Martlet (94)
1548-9	Bow (66, *Durham House*)		

GOLD

		F	VF
		£	£
2389	**Sovereign** (20 c), *London*. As no. 2290, but Roman lettering; *mm*. lis	2150	4750
2390	— *Bristol*. Similar but *mm*. WS	2750	6250

2391	2391A

2395

		F	VF
		£	£
2391	**Half-sovereign.** As 2294, but with youthful portrait with sceptre. *Tower*; *mm.* 52, 105, 94 (various combinations)	250	575
2391A	— Similar but no sceptre; *mm.* 52, 52/56	275	650
2392	— — — K below shield; *mm.*-/K, none,. E/-	275	650
2393	— — — grapple below shield; *mm.* 122, none, 122/-, -/122	325	700
2394	— *Southwark. Mm.* E, E/-, -/E, Є /E. Usually Є or E (sometimes retrograde) below shield (sceptre omitted; *mm.* -/E)	275	600
2394A	— — — R. As 2296; *mm.*-/S	350	750
2395	**Crown.** Similar to 2305. *London; mm.* 52, 52/-, -/K, 122, 94,	300	650
2396	— Similar but transposed legends without numeral; *mm.* -/arrow	350	750
2396A	— As 2395, but omitting RVTILANS; *mm.* arrow	375	825
2396B	Similar, but RVTILANS both sides; *mm.* arrow	375	825
2397	— *Southwark.* Similar to 2396; *mm.* E	400	850
2398	— — King's name on *obv.*; *mm.* E/-, -/E	385	825
2399	**Halfcrown.** Similar to 2311. *London; mm.* 52, K/-, 122/-, 94, -/52	300	650
2399A	As last but E over h on *rev.*, *mm.* 56/52	450	950
2399B	As 2399 but RVTILANS etc. on both sides, *mm.* arrow	375	800
2400	— *Southwark. Mm.* E, E/-, -/E	300	650

SILVER

AR (4oz .333)		F	VF
2401	**Testoon.** *Tower.* As 2365 with lozenge stops one side; -/56, 56	650	1800
2402	*Southwark.* As 2367; *mm.* S/E	700	1850

Bust 4   Bust 5   Bust 6

Some of the Bristol testoons, groats and halfgroats with WS monogram were struck after the death of Henry VIII but cannot easily be distinguished from those struck during his reign.

2403	**Groat.** *Tower.* Busts 4, 5, 6 (and, rarely, 2). R. POSVI, etc.; *mm.* 105-94 and none (frequently muled)	55	170
2404	*Southwark.* Busts 4, 5, 6. R. CIVITAS LONDON; no *mm.* -/E; lis/-, -/lis, K/E; roses or crescents or S and Є in forks, or rarely annulets	55	170
2405	*Durham House.* Bust 6. R. REDDE CVIQUE QVOD SVVM EST; *mm.* bow	125	375
2406	*Bristol. Mm.* WS on *rev.* Bristol busts A and B, Tower bust 2 and 3	60	175
2407	— — *Mm.* TC on *rev.* Similar, Bristol bust B	85	250
2408	*Canterbury.* Busts 5, 6; no *mm.* or rose/-	60	170
2409	*York.* Busts 4, 5, 6; no *mm.* or lis/-, -/lis	55	165
2410	**Halfgroat.** Bust 1. *Tower.* POSVI, etc.; *mm.* 52, 52/-, 52/K , -/K, 52/122, 122, -/122	45	140
2411	— *Southwark.* CIVITAS LONDON; *mm.* E, -/E, none, 52/E, K/E	35	120

		F	VF
		£	£
2412	**Halfgroat.** *Durham House.* R. REDD, etc.; *mm.* bow, -/bow	300	650
2413	— *Bristol.* Mm. WS on *rev.*	45	140
2414	— — *mm.* TC on *rev.*	55	160
2415	— *Canterbury.* No *mm.* or t/-, -/t, ...	35	110
2416	— *York.* No *mm.*, bust 1 and three quarter facing	45	140

2418   2422   2427

2417	**Penny.** *Tower.* CIVI TAS LONDON. Facing bust; *mm.* 52/-, -/52, -/K,		
	122/-, -/122, none	30	95
2418	— — three-quarter bust; no *mm.*	40	110
2419	*Southwark.* As 2417; *mm.* E, -/E...	60	175
2420	*Durham House.* As groat but shorter legend; *mm.* -/bow	325	750
2421	*Bristol.* Facing busts, as 2382 but showing more body, no *mm.*	50	145
2422	*Canterbury.* Similar to 2417	30	85
2423	— three-quarters facing bust; no *mm*....................................	40	110
2424	*York.* Facing bust; no *mm.*	35	100
2425	— three-quarters facing bust; no *mm*....................................	45	125
2426	**Halfpenny.** *Tower.* 52?, none..	30	85
2427	*Canterbury.* No *mm.*, sometimes reads H8	35	120
2428	*York.* No *mm.*	30	85

Coinage in his own name

The 4 oz. 2.5dwt coins of Henry VIII and those issued under Edward in 1547 and 1548 caused much disquiet, yet at the same time government was prevented by continuing financial necessity from abandoning debasement. A stratagem was devised which entailed increasing the fineness of silver coins, thereby making them appear sound, while at the same time reducing their weight in proportion so that in practice they contained no more silver than hitherto. The first issue, ordered on 24 January 1549, at 8 oz.2 dwt. fine produced a shilling which, at 60 gr., was so light that it was rapidly discredited and had to be replaced in April by another at 6 oz. 2 dwt. Weighing 80 gr., these later shillings proved acceptable.

Between April and August 1551 the issue of silver coins was the worst ever – 3 oz. 2dwt. fine at 72s per lb. before retrenchment came in August, first by a 50% devaluation of base silver coin and then by the issue of a fine standard at 11oz. 1dwt. 'out of the fire'. This was the equivalent of 11oz.3dwt. commixture, and means that since sterling was only 11oz. 2dwt., this issue, which contained four new denominations – the crown, halfcrown, sixpence and threepence – was in effect the finest ever issued under the Tudors.

Some base 'pence' were struck in parallel with the fine silver, but at the devalued rate, they and the corresponding 'halfpence' were used as halfpence and farthings respectively.

The first dates on English coinage appear in this reign, first as Roman numerals and then on the fine issue crowns and halfcrowns of 1551-3, in Arabic numerals.

Mintmarks

| 66 | 52 | 35 | 115 | E | 53 | 122 |

| t | T | 111 | Y | 126 | 94 | 91A |

| 92 | 105 | y | 97 | 123 | 78 | 26 |

1548-9	Bow (66, *Durham House*)	1550	Martlet (94)
1549	Arrow (52)	1550	Leopard's head (91A)
	Grapple (122)	1550-1	Lion (92)
	Rose (35, *Canterbury*)		Lis (105, *Southwark*)
	TC monogram (115, *Bristol*)		Rose (33)
	Roman E (*Southwark*)	1551	Y or y (117, *Southwark*)
	Pheon (53)		Ostrich's head (97, gold only)
	t or T (*Canterbury*)	1551-3	Tun (123)
1549-50	Swan (111)		Escallop (78)
	Roman Y (*Southwark*)	1552-3	Pierced mullet (26, *York*)
1549-50	6 (126 gold only)		

First period, Apr. 1547-Jan. 1549

2429   2431

	F	VF
	£	£
2429 **Half-sovereign** (20 c). As 2391, but reading EDWARD 6. Tower; *mm.* arrow	625	1250
2430 — *Southwark* (Sometimes with E or Є below shield); *mm.* E	525	1050
2431 **Crown.** RVTILANS, etc., crowned rose between ER both crowned. R. EDWARD 6, etc., crowned shield between ER both crowned; *mm.* arrow, E over arrow/-	2250	5500
2431A — *Obv.* as last. R. As 2305, *mm.* 52/56	2500	6000
2432 **Halfcrown.** Similar to 2431, but initials not crowned; *mm.* arrow	2000	4500

Second period, Jan. 1549-Apr. 1550

2433

| 2433 **Sovereign** (22 ct). As illustration; *mm.* arrow, –/arrow, Y, ... | 1750 | 3750 |

2435   2438

		F	VF
		£	£

2434 **Half-sovereign.** Uncrowned bust. *London.* TIMOR etc., MDXLIX on
obv. mm. arrow 2250 4750

2435 — — SCVTVM, etc., as illustration; *mm.* arrow, **6, Y** 525 1100

2436 — *Durham House.* Uncrowned, 1/2 length bust with MDXLVIII at end of
obv. legend; *mm.* bow; SCVTVM etc. 3750 8500

2437 — Normal, uncrowned bust. LVCERNA, etc., on *obv.*; *mm.* bow 3000 7000

2438 — Crowned bust. *London.* EDWARD VI, etc. R. SCVTVM, etc.; *mm.* 52,
122, 111/52, 111, Y, 94 .... 425 950

2439 — *Durham House.* Crowned, half-length bust; *mm.* bow 3500 8000

2440 — — King's name on *obv.* and *rev.*; *mm.* bow (mule of 2439/37) 3250 7500

2441   2444

2441 **Crown.** Uncrowned bust, as 2435; *mm. 6,* Y, 52/-, Y/- 700 1500

2442 — Crowned bust, as 2438; *mm.* 52, 122, 111, Y (usually *obv.* only) 600 1200

2443 **Halfcrown.** Uncrowned bust; R. As 2441, *mm.* arrow, Y, Y/-, 52/- 650 1350

2444 — Crowned bust, as illus. above; *mm.* 52, 52/111, 111, 122, Y, Y/- 475 950

2445 — Similar, but king's name on *rev.*, *mm.* 52, 122 .... 625 1250

2448

Third period, 1550-3

2446 'Fine' sovereign (30s.). King on throne; *mm.* 97, 123 .... 8250 19500

2447 **Double sovereign.** From the same dies, *mm.* 97 .... *Extremely rare*

2448 **Angel** (10s.). As illustration; *mm.* 97, 123 .... 3500 7500

2449 **Half-angel.** Similar, *mm.* 97 .... *Extremely rare*

2450 **Sovereign.** (=20s.). Half-length figure of king r., crowned and holding
sword and orb. R. Crowned shield with supporters; *mm.* y, tun 950 2350

2450

2451

	F	VF
	£	£
2451 **Half-sovereign**. As illustration above; *mm*. y, tun	650	1350
2452 **Crown**. Similar, but *rev*. SCVTVM etc., *mm*. y, tun	750	1600
2453 **Halfcrown**. Similar, *mm*. tun, y	800	1700

Small denominations often occur creased or straightened.

SILVER

First period, Apr. 1547-Jan. 1549

2454

2454 **Groat**. Cr. bust r. *Tower*. R. Shield over cross, POSVI, etc.; *mm*. arrow.	475	1250
2455 — As last, but EDOARD 6, *mm*. arrow	525	1350
2456 — *Southwark*. *Obv*. as 2454. R. CIVITAS LONDON; *mm*.-/E or none, somethimes S in forks	500	1300
2457 **Halfgroat**. *Tower*. *Obv*. as 2454; *mm*. arrow	450	950
2458 *Southwark*. As 2456; *mm*. arrow, E	475	1000

2459   2460

2459 *Canterbury*. Similar. No *mm*., also reads EDOARD (as ill.)	175	450
2460 **Penny**. *Tower*. As halfgroat, but E.D.G. etc. R. CIVITAS LONDON; *mm*. arrow	250	600
2461 — *Southwark*. As last, but *mm*. -/E.	350	850
2462 *Bristol*. Similar, but reads ED6DG or E6DG no *mm*.	225	525
2463 **Halfpenny**. *Tower*. *O*. As 2460, *mm*. E (?). R. Cross and pellets	375	950
2464 — *Bristol*. Similar, no *mm*. but reads E6DG or EDG	350	900

Second period, Jan. 1549-Apr. 1550

At all mints except Bristol, the earliest shillings of 1549 were issued at only 60 grains but of 8 oz. 2 dwt standard. This weight and size were soon increased to 80 grains., (S.2466 onwards), but the fineness was reduced to 6 oz. 2 dwt so the silver content remained the same.

2465   2466

	F £	VF £

60 gr; 8oz. 2 dwt.

2465	**Shilling.** *Tower.* Broad bust with large crown. *Obv.* TIMOR etc. MDXLIX. R. Small, oval garnished shield dividing ER. EDWARD VI etc., *mm.* 52, no *mm*; slight bust var. *mm.,* –/52	135	450
2465A	*Southwark.* As last, *mm.* Y, EY/Y	150	475
2465B	*Canterbury.* As last, *mm.* -/rose	250	575
2469	*Durham House.* Bust with elaborate tunic and collar TIMOR etc. MDXLIX. R. Oval shield, very heavily garnished in different style. EDWARD VI etc., *mm.* bow...	225	650

80 gr; 6oz. 2 dwt.

2466	*Tower.* Tall, narrow bust with small crown. *Obv.* EDWARD VI etc. MDXLIX or MDL. R. As 2465 but TIMOR etc., *mm.* 52-91a (frequently muled)	80	275
2466A	— *Obv.* as last, MDXLIX. R. Heavily garnished shield, Durham House style. *mm.* grapple	165	525
2466B	*Southwark.* As 2466, *mm.* Y, Y/swan	75	265
2466C	— — — R. as 2466A. *mm.* Y	185	550

2467   2468

2467	*Bristol. Obv.* similar to 2466. R. Shield with heavy curved garniture or as 2466, *mm.* TC/rose TC, rose TC	675	1650
2468	*Canterbury.* As 2466, *mm.* T, T/t, t/T, t	100	325

2470   2472   2472C

		F	VF
		£	£
2470	— Bust as 2469. INIMICOS etc., no date. R. EDWARD etc..................	175	575
2472	— Bust similar to 2466. EDWARD VI etc. R. INIMICOS etc.	135	425
2472A	As last but legends transposed	225	675
2472B	*Tower*. Elegant bust with extremely thin neck. R. As 2466, *mm*. martlet	125	375
2472C	*Southwark*. As last, *mm*. Y	125	375

For coins of Edward VI countermarked, see p. 203

Third period, 1550-3

Very base issue (1551) 3oz. 2 dwt.

2473   2475

2473	**Shilling**, *Tower*. As 2472B. MDL or MDLI, *mm*. lion, rose, lion/rose ...	95	325
2473A	*Southwark*. As last, *mm*. lis/Y, Y/lis, lis	95	325
2474	**Base Penny**. *London. O*. Rose. R. Shield; *mm*. escallop (*obv*.)..............	50	125
2475	— — *York. Mm*. mullet (*obv*.) as illustration..	45	110
2476	**Base Halfpenny**. As penny, but single rose	165	425

* The base penny and halfpenny were used as halfpenny and farthing respectively.

Fine silver issue, (1551-3) 11oz. 3 dwt.

2478

2478	**Crown**. King on horseback with date below horse. R. Shield on cross;		
	mm. y. 1551; tun, 1551-3 (1553, wire line inner circle may be missing)	275	675

2479

		F	VF
		£	£
2479	**Halfcrown**. Walking horse with plume; *mm*. y, 1551	225	525
2480	Galloping horse without plume; *mm*. tun, 1551-3	275	650
2481	Large walking horse without plume; *mm*. tun, 1553	675	1350

2482   2483

2482	**Shilling**. Facing bust, rose l., value XII r. *mm*. y, tun (several bust varieties)	60	180
2483	**Sixpence**. *London*. Similar, as illustration; *mm*. y/-, -/y, y, tun (bust		
	varieties)	75	225
2484	*York*. As last, but CIVITAS EBORACI; *mm*. mullet	125	375

2485   2486   2487A

2485	**Threepence**. *London*. As sixpence, but III; *mm*. tun	135	425
2486	*York*. As 2484, but III by bust	250	625
2487	**Penny**. 'Sovereign' type; *mm*. tun	750	1750
2487A	**Farthing**. *O*. Portcullis, R Cross and Pellets (previously 2477)	700	1650

Mary brought English coins back to the sterling standard (11 oz. 'Out of the fire' = 11 oz. 2 dwt. at the comixture) and struck all her gold coins at the traditional fineness of 23 c. 3 ½ gr. On the latter the mintmarks appear at the end of the first or second word of the legends.

Pomegranate   Halved rose and
                                          castle

GOLD

2488

		F	VF
		£	£
2488	**'Fine' Sovereign** (30s.). Queen enthroned. R. Shield on rose, MDLIII, MDLIIII and undated, *mm.* pomegranate, half-rose (or mule)	2000	4500
2489	**Ryal** (15s.). As illus, MDLIII. R. As 1950 but A DNO etc. *mm.* pomegranate/-	7500	16000
2490	**Angel** (10s.). Usual type; *mm.* pomegranate, half-rose, none? (Known with rose and M transposed)	575	1100
2491	**Half-angel.** Similar; *mm.* pomegranate, pomegranate/-	1750	3750

2489   2492

SILVER

2492	**Groat.** Crowned bust l. R. VERITAS, etc.; *mm.* pomegranate, pomegranate/-	65	225
2493	**Halfgroat.** Similar	525	1350
2494	**Penny.** Similar, but M. D. G. ROSA, etc.	325	850
2495	— As last. R. CIVITAS LONDON; no *mm.*	325	850
2495A	— Base penny. Similar to 2474 but M.D.G. etc.................*All late 19th cent. fabrications*		

The groats and smaller silver coins of this period have Mary's portrait only, but the shillings and sixpences show the bust of the queen's husband, Philip of Spain.

Mintmarks

Lis (105)   Half-rose and castle

GOLD

2496A

		F	VF
		£	£
2496	**Angel**. As illustration; wire line inner circles, calm sea, *mm*. lis............	1650	3750
2496A	— — New-style, large wings, wire line i.c...	1750	4250
2496B	— — As above but beaded i.c..	1800	4500
2497	**Half-angel**. Similar to 2496	4750	9500

SILVER

2498   2500

2498	**Shilling**. Busts face-to-face, full titles, undated, no *mm*.	175	550
2499	— — — also without mark of value	185	600
2500	— — 1554	185	575
2501	— English titles only 1554, 1555..	200	650
2501A	— — undated	225	700
2502	— — without mark of value, 1554, 1555 (rare)...................................	225	675
2503	— — date below bust, 1554, 1555..	650	1500
2504	— — As last, but without ANG., 1555...	750	1650

2505

	F	VF
	£	£

2505 **Sixpence**. Similar. Full titles, 1554 (and undated?) .... | 165 | 525

2506

2506 — English titles only, 1555 (no *mm.*, rare), 1557 (*mm.* lis, 1557 only). | 175 | 550
2506A — As last but heavy beaded i.c. on obv. 1555. (Irish 4d. obv. mule) .... | 300 | 750
2507 — — date below bust, 1554, 1557 (very rare) .... | 475 | 950

2508

2508 **Groat**. Crowned bust of Mary 1. R. POSVIMVS etc.; *mm.* lis .... | 65 | 235
2509 **Halfgroat**. Similar, but POSVIM, *mm.* lis... | 275 | 700

2510

2510 **Penny**. Similar to 2495, but P. Z. M. etc.; *mm.* lis................................. | 250 | 650
2510A **Base penny**. Similar to 2495A, but P. Z. M . etc.; *mm.* halved rose and
castle or castle/–, (used as a halfpenny) .... | 50 | 165
Similar 'pence' of the York mint were made for currency in Ireland

Elizabeth's coinage is particularly interesting on account of the large number of different denominations issued. 'Crown' gold coins were again issued as well as the 'fine' gold denominations. In 1559 the base shillings of Edward VI's second and third coinages were called in and countermarked for recirculation at reduced values. Smaller debased coins were also devalued but not countermarked. The old debased groat became a three halfpenny and other coins in proportion. The normal silver coinage was initially struck at .916 fineness as in the previous reign but between 1560 and 1577 and after 1582 the old sterling standard of .925 was restored. Between 1578 and 1582 the standard was slightly reduced and the weights were reduced by 1/32nd in 1601. Gold was similarly reduced slightly in quality 1578-82, and there was a slight weight reduction in 1601.

To help alleviate the shortage of small change, and to avoid the expense of minting an impossibly small silver farthing, a threefarthing piece was introduced to provide change if a penny was tendered for a farthing purchase. The sixpence, threepence, threehalfpence and threefarthings were marked with a rose behind the queen's head to distinguish them from the shilling, groat, half-groat and penny.

Coins of exceedingly fine workmanship were produced in a screw press introduced by Eloye Mestrelle, a French moneyer, in 1561. With parts of the machinery powered by a horse-drawn mill, the coins produced came to be known as 'mill money'. Despite the superior quality of the coins produced, the machinery was slow and inefficient compared to striking by hand. Mestrelle's dismissal was engineered in 1572 and six years later he was hanged for counterfeiting.

Mintmarks

First Issue		Lis (105, milled)		1584-6	Escallop (79)
1558-60	Lis (106)	1569-71	Castle (71)	1587-9	Crescent (72b)
Second Issue		1572-3	Ermine (77)	1590-2	Hand (86)
1560-1	Cross crosslet (21)	1573-4	Acorn (65b)	1591-5	Tun (123)
	Martlet (94)	1573-7	Eglantine (27)	1594-6	Woolpack (124)
Third Issue		Fourth Issue		1595-8	Key (90)
1560-6	Star (23, milled)	1578-9	Greek cross (7)	1597-1600	Anchor (57)
1561-5	Pheon (53)	1580-1	Latin cross (14)	1600	0
1565	Rose (33)	1582	Sword (113)	Sixth Issue	
1566	Portcullis (107)	Fifth Issue		1601-2	1
1566-7	Lion (92)	1582-3	Bell (60)	1602	2
1567-70	Coronet (74)	1582-4	A (54)		

N.B. *The dates for* mms *sometimes overlap. This is a result of using up old dies, onto which the new mark was punched.*

GOLD

Hammered Coinage

First to Third issues, 1559-78. ('Fine' gold of .994. 'Crown' gold of .916 fineness. Sovereigns of 240 gr.). Mintmarks; lis to eglantine.

2512

		F	VF
		£	£
2511	**'Fine' Sovereign** (30 s.) Queen enthroned, tressure broken by throne, reads Z not ET, no chains to portcullis. R. Arms on rose; *mm*. lis.	2000	5250
2512	— — Similar but ET, chains on portcullis; *mm*. crosslet	1750	4250
2513	**Angel**. St. Michael. R. Ship. Wire line inner circles; *mm*. lis.	500	1100
2513A	— Similar, but beaded i.c. on *obv*., *mm*. lis	475	1000
2514	— — Similar, but beaded inner circles; ship to r.; *mm*. 106, 21, 74, 27,..	300	650
2515	— — — Similar, but ship to l.; *mm*. 77-27	325	700
2516	**Half Angel**. As 2513, wire line inner circles; *mm*. lis	950	2250
2516A	— As last, but beaded i.c.s, legend ends. Z.HIB	550	1250
2517	— As 2514, beaded inner circles; *mm*. 106, 21, 74, 77-27	300	625
2518	**Quarter Angel**. Similar; *mm*. 74, 77-27	250	550

2513   2520A

2519	**Half Pound** (10 s.) Young crowned bust l. R. Arms. Wire line inner circles; *mm*. lis...	950	2250
2520	— Similar, but beaded inner circles; *mm*. 21, 33-107..............................	400	850
2520A	— — Smaller bust; *mm*. lion	825	1850
2520B	— — Broad bust, ear visible; *mm*. 92, 74, 71	450	950
2521	**Crown**. As 2519; *mm*. lis...	1350	3250
2522	— Similar to 2520; *mm*. 21, 33-107..	375	750
2522A	— Similar to 2520B; *mm*. 74, 71, 92...	400	800
2523	**Half Crown**. As 2519; *mm*. lis...	1050	2500
2524	— Similar to 2520; *mm*. 21, 33-107 (2 busts)	375	800
2524A	— Similar to 2520B; *mm*. 107-71...	400	850

	F	VF
	£	£

Fourth Issue, 1578-82 (`Fine' gold only of .992). *Mms* Greek cross,
Latin cross and sword.

2525	**Angel**. As 2514; *mm.* 7, 14, 113	300	650
2526	**Half Angel**. As 2517; *mm.* 7, 14, 113	300	625
2527	— Similar, but without E and rose above ship; *mm.* latin cross	400	850
2528	**Quarter Angel**. As last; *mm.* 7, 14, 113	250	525

Fifth Issue, 1583-1600 (`Fine' gold of .979, `crown' gold of .916; pound of 174.5 grs. wt.).
Mintmarks: bell to **O**.

2529

| 2529 | **Sovereign** (30 s:). As 2512, but tressure not normally broken by back of throne; *mm.* 54-123 .... | 1600 | 3450 |

2530

| 2530 | **Ryal** (15 s.). Queen in ship. R. Similar to 1950; *mm.* 54-86 (*rev.* only) .. | 3000 | 7500 |

2531

2531	**Angel**. As 2514; *mm.* 60-123, 90-**O**	300	650
2532	**Half Angel**. As 2517; *mm.* 60-86, 90-57	300	600
2533	**Quarter Angel**. As 2518; *mm.* 60-123, 90-57/–	250	525
2534	**Pound** (20 s.). Old bust l., with elaborate dress and profusion of hair; *mm.*, lion and tun/tun, 123-**O**	700	1450

	F	VF
	£	£
2535 **Half Pound**. Similar; *mm*. tun	550	1100
2535A — Similar but smaller bust with less hair; *mm*. 123-**O**	525	1050
2536 **Crown**. Similar to 2534; *mm*. 123-90. **O**	400	850
2537 **Half Crown**. Similar; *mm*. -/123, 123-0, **O**..	375	800

Sixth Issue, 1601-3 ('Fine' gold of .994, 'crown' gold of .916; Pound of 172 gr.). Mintmarks: **1** and **2**

2538 **Angel**. As 2531; *mm*. **1, 2**	450	975
2539 **Pound**. As 2534; *mm*. **1, 2**	725	1550
2540 **Half Pound**. As 2535A; *mm*. **1, 2**...	650	1350

2535

2541

2541 **Crown**. As 2536; *mm*. **1, 2**	600	1250
2542 **Half Crown**. As 2537; *mm*. **1, 2**...	600	1250

Milled Coinage, 1561-70

2543 **Half Pound**. Crowned bust l.; *mm*. star, lis	900	2350
2544 **Crown**. Similar; *mm*. star, lis	850	2100
2545 **Half Crown**. Similar; *mm*. star, lis..	1200	2750

For further details on both AV and AR milled coinage, *see* D. G. Borden *'An introduction to the milled coinage of Elizabeth I'*. BNJ 1983

SILVER

2546

2547

Hammered Coinage
Countermarked Edward VI base shillings (1559)

	Fair	F
	£	£
2546 **Fourpence-halfpenny**. Edward VI 2nd period 6oz and 8oz shillings .... cmkd on obv. with a portcullis; *mm*. 66, –/33, 52, t, 111, Y and 122.......	650	1350
2547 **Twopence-farthing**. Edward VI 3rd period 3 oz. shillings .... countermarked on obverse with a seated greyhound; *mm*. 92. 105, 35 and 87	750	1600
N.B. *Occasionally the wrong countermark was used*		

First Issue, 1559-60 (.916 fine, shillings of 96 grs.)

2548   2549

	F £	VF £
2548 **Shilling**. Without rose or date. ELIZABET(H), wire line inner circles, pearls on bodice (three similar busts); *mm*. lis.	240	675
2549 — Similar, ELIZABETH, wire line and beaded inner circles, no pearls on bodice (several busts); *mm*. lis...	85	240

2551   2555

2550 **Groat**. Without rose or date, wire line or no inner circles (two busts); *mm*. lis	90	250
2551 — Similar, wire line and beaded inner circles, circles *mm*. lis	45	135
2551A— — Small bust and shield (from halfgroat punches); *mm*. lis	100	275
2552 **Halfgroat**. Without rose or date, wire line inner circles; *mm*. lis	135	350
2553 **Penny**. Without rose or date, wire line inner circles; *mm*. lis	175	475
2554 — Similar but dated 1558 on *obv*.; *mm*. lis	450	975

Second Issue, 1560-1 (.925 fineness, shilling of 96 gr.)

2555 **Shilling**. Without rose or date, beaded inner circles. ET instead of Z (several bust varieties); *mm*. 21, 94	50	175
2555A— large bust with pearls on bodice as 2548; *mm*. 21, 94	60	200
2556 **Groat**. Without rose or date, bust as 2551; *mm*. 21, 94	30	85
2557 **Halfgroat**. Without rose or date; *mm*. 21, 94	30	75
2558 **Penny**. Without rose or date (three bust varieties); *mm*. 21, 94	20	50

Third Issue, 1561-77 (Same fineness and weight as last)

		F	VF
2559	**Sixpence**. With rose and date, large flan (27 *mm*. or more), large bust with hair swept back, 1561; *mm*. pheon	125	325

2560   2561

2560	— Similar, small bust, 1561; *mm*. pheon	45	145
2561	— Smaller flan (26.5 *mm*.). Small regular bust, 1561-6; *mm*. 53-107	30	85
2561A	— Similar, without rose, 1561; *mm*. pheon	300	675
2561B	— Similar, very large bust, with rose, 1563-5; *mm*. pheon	50	165

2562   2563

2562	— Intermediate bust, ear shows, 1566-74; *mm*. 92-65b (also 1567 *mm*. 71/74)	30	80
2562A	— Similar, without date; *mm*. lion, coronet, ermine	350	825
2563	— Larger bust, 1573-7; *mm*. 77-27	30	85
2564	**Threepence**. With rose and date 1561, large flan (20.5 *mm*.); *mm*. pheon	30	95
2565	— smaller flan (19 *mm*.). Regular bust, 1561-7; *mm*. 53-92	20	65
2566	— taller bust, ear shows, 1566-77; *mm*. 92-27, 27/-, 27/65b	20	60
2566A	— Similar, without rose, 1568; *mm*. coronet	275	625

2567   2571

2567	**Halfgroat**. Without rose or date; *mm*. 107-71	40	120
2568	**Threehalfpence**. With rose and date 1561, large flan (17 *mm*.) *mm*. pheon	30	85
2569	— — Smaller flan (16 *mm*.); 1561-2, 1564-70, 1572-7; *mm*. 53-27	25	70
2570	**Penny**. Without rose or date; *mm*. 33-27, 33/107, 92/107, 74/107	20	55
2571	**Threefarthings**. With rose and date 1561-2, 1568, 1572-7; *mm*. 53, 74, 77-27	40	125

		F £	VF £

Fourth Issue, 1578-82 (.921 fineness, shilling of 95.6 gr.)

2572

2572 **Sixpence**. As 2563, 1578-82; *mm*. 7-113, 14/113, 14/7 30   80

2573   2575

2573	**Threepence**. As 2566, 1578-82; *mm*. 7-113	20	55
2574	**Threehalfpence**. As 2569, 1578-9, 1581-2; *mm*. 7-113	25	70
2575	**Penny**. As 2570; *mm*. 7-113, 7/14, 14/7	20	50
2576	**Threefarthings**. As 2571, 1578-9, 1581-2; *mm*. 7-113	45	125

Fifth Issue, 1582-1600 (.925 fineness, shilling of 96 gr.)

2577   2578A   2580   2581

2577	**Shilling**. Without rose or date, ELIZAB; ear concealed (two busts) *mm*. 60-72b, ear shows. *mm*. 79-**0** (mules occur)	50	150
2578	**Sixpence**. As 2572, ELIZABETH, 1582, 1583 *mm*. bell	40	95
2578A	— Similar, ELIZAB, 1582-1600; *mm*. 60-**0**, also 1583 *mm*. 79/54	30	85
2579	**Halfgroat**. Without rose or date, two pellets behind bust. R. CIVITAS LONDON; *mm*. 60-**0** (*mm*. bell sometimes without pellets)	15	35
2580	**Penny**. Without rose or date. R. CIVITAS LONDON; *mm*. 60-57, 90/-, 57/-, **0**/-	20	50
2581	**Halfpenny**. Portcullis. R. Cross and pellets; *mm*. none, 54-**0**	20	50

Sixth Issue, 1601-2 (.925 fineness, shilling of 92.9 gr.)

2582   2583

		F	VF
		£	£
2582	**Crown**. Similar to illustration of 2583; *mm*. **1, 2**	475	1000
2583	**Halfcrown**. As illustration, *mm*. **1, 2**	325	725

2584   2592

		F	VF
2584	**Shilling**. As 2577; *mm*. **1, 2**	60	175
2585	**Sixpence**. As 2578A, 1601-2; *mm*. **1, 2**	35	95
2586	**Halfgroat**. As 2579, *mm*. **1, 2, 2/-**	20	55
2587	**Penny**. As 2580, *mm*. **1, 2, 2/-**	20	55
2588	**Halfpenny**. As 2581, *mm*. **1, 2**	25	60

Milled coinage

		F	VF
2589	**Shilling**. Without rose or date; *mm*. star. Plain dress, large size (over 31 *mm*.)	375	950
2590	— decorated dress, large size..	150	500
2591	— — intermediate size (30-31 *mm*.).....................................	95	350
2592	— — small size (under 30 *mm*.)	75	275

2593   2594   2595

	F	VF
	£	£
2593 **Sixpence**. Small bust, large rose. R. Cross fourchee, 1561 *mm*. star.......	35	130
2594 Tall narrow bust with plain dress, large rose, 1561-2; *mm*. star	30	110
2595 — similar, but decorated dress, 1562..	35	125

2596/7   2598

2596 Large broad bust, elaborately decorated dress, small rose, 1562; *mm*. star	35	125
2597 — — cross pattée on *rev.*, 1562, 64 *mm*. star	40	145
2598 — similar, pellet border, 1563-4	50	185
2598A Bust with low ruff, raised rim, 1564, 1566 (both overdates)	60	200
2599 Small bust, 1567-8, R. As 2593; *mm*. lis...	45	150

2599   2600   2601

2600 Large crude bust breaking legend; 1570, *mm*. lis; 1571/0, *mm*. castle		
(over lis)	125	375
2601 **Groat**. As illustration..	85	300
2602 **Threepence**. With rose, small bust with plain dress, 1561	75	260
2603 Tall narrow decorated bust with medium rose, 1562............................	60	175
2604 Broad bust with very small rose, 1562......................................	65	200
2605 Cross pattee on *rev.*, 1563, 1564/3	125	375
2606 **Halfgroat**. As groat	85	275
2607 **Threefarthings**. E . D . G . ROSA, etc., with rose. R. CIVITAS LONDON,		
shield with 1563 above	1250	2750

Portcullis money

Trade coins of 8, 4, 2, and 1 Testerns were coined at the Tower Mint in 1600/1 for the first voyage of the incorporated 'Company of Merchants of London Trading into the East Indies'. The coins bear the royal arms on the obverse and a portcullis on the reverse and have the *mm.* **O**. They were struck to the weights of the equivalent Spanish silver 8, 4, 2 and 1 reales.

2607A

2607B

		F	VF
		£	£
2607A	Eight testerns	850	2000
2607B	Four testerns	450	975
2607C	Two testerns	425	925
2607D	One testern	375	800

THE HOUSE OF STUART
AND THE COMMONWEALTH, 1603-1714

JAMES I, 1603-25

With the accession of James VI of Scotland to the English throne, the royal titles and coat of arms are altered on the coinage; on the latter the Scottish rampant lion and the Irish harp now appear in the second and third quarters. In 1604 the weight of the gold pound was reduced and the new coin became known as the 'Unite'. Fine gold coins of 23 c. 3 $\frac{1}{2}$ carat and crown gold of 22 c. were both issued, and a gold four-shilling piece was struck 1604-19. In 1612 all the gold coins had their values raised by 10%; but in 1619 the Unite was replaced by a new, lighter 20s. piece, the 'Laurel', and a lighter rose-ryal, spur-ryal and angel were minted.

In 1613 the king granted Lord Harington a licence to coin farthings of copper as a result of repeated public demands for a low value coinage; this was later taken over by the Duke of Lennox. Towards the end of the reign coins made from silver sent to the mint from the Welsh mines had the Prince of Wales's plumes inserted over the royal arms.

Mintmarks

125	105	33	79	84	74	90
60	25	71	45	32	123	132
72b	7a	16	24	125	105	46

First coinage
1603-4   Thistle (125)
1604-5   Lis (105)

Second coinage
1604-5   Lis (105)
1605-6   Rose (33)
1606-7   Escallop (79)
1607   Grapes (84)
1607-9   Coronet (74)

1609-10   Key (90)
1610-11   Bell (60)
1611-12   Mullet (25)
1612-13   Tower (71)
1613   Trefoil (45)
1613-15   Cinquefoil (32)
1615-16   Tun (123)
1616-17   Book on lectern (132)
1617-18   Crescent (72b, gold)
1618-19   Plain cross (7a)

1619   Saltire cross (16, gold)

Third coinage
1619-20   Spur rowel (24)
1620-1   Rose (33)
1621-3   Thistle (125)
1623-4   Lis (105)
1624   Trefoil (46)

2610   2612

First coinage, 1603-4 (Obverse legend reads D' . G' . ANG : SCO : etc.)

		F	VF
		£	£
2608	**Sovereign** (20s.). King crowned r., half-length, first bust with plain armour. R. EXVRGAT, etc.; *mm*. thistle	700	1450
2609	— second bust with decorated armour; *mm*. thistle, lis	750	1600
2610	**Half-sovereign.** Crowned bust r. R. EXVRGAT, etc.; *mm*. thistle	1650	3750
2611	**Crown.** Similar. R. TVEATVR, etc.; *mm*. 125, 105/125	950	2450
2612	**Halfcrown.** Similar; *mm*. thistle, lis	400	825

N.B. *The Quarter-Angel of this coinage is considered to be a pattern (possibly a later strike), although coin weights are known.*

2613   2614

Second coinage, 1604-19 (Obverse legend reads D' G' MAG : BRIT : etc.)

2613	**Rose-ryal** (30s., 33s. from 1612). King enthroned. R. Shield on rose; *mm*. 33-90, 25-132	875	1850
2614	**Spur ryal** (15s., 16s. 6d. from 1612). King in ship; *mm*. 33, 79, 74, 25-32, 132	1800	4500
2615	**Angel** (10s., 11s. from 1612). Old type but larger shield; *mm*. 33-74, 60-16	475	1100
2616	— — pierced for use as touch-piece	275	525
2617	**Half-angel** (5s., 5s. 6d. from 1612). Similar; *mm*. 71-132, 7a, 16	1500	3500

Second coinage gold

2620

2622   2627

		F £	VF £
2618	**Unite** (20s., 22s. from 1612). Half-length second bust r. R. FACIAM etc.; *mm*. lis or rose	275	550
2619	— fourth bust; *mm*. rose to cinquefoil	225	450
2620	— fifth bust; *mm*. cinquefoil to saltire	235	460
2621	**Double-crown**. Third bust r. R. HENRICVS, etc.; *mm*. lis or rose	215	475
2622	Fourth bust; *mm*. rose to bell	200	450
2623	Fifth bust; *mm*. key, mullet to saltire	185	425
2624	**Britain crown**. First bust r.; *mm*. lis to coronet	150	325
2625	Third bust; *mm*. key to cinquefoil	140	300
2626	Fifth bust; *mm*. cinquefoil to saltire	140	300
2627	**Thistle crown** (4s.). As illus.; *mm*. lis to plain cross	150	325
2628	— IR on only one side or absent both sides; *mm*. 79, 74, 71-123	160	350
2629	**Halfcrown**. I' D' G' ROSA SINE SPINA. First bust; *mm*. lis to key	135	265
2630	Third bust; *mm*. key to trefoil, trefoil/tower	140	275
2631	Fifth bust; *mm*. cinquefoil to plain cross	130	250

Third coinage, 1619-25

2632	**Rose-ryal** (30s.; 196 1/2 grs.). King enthroned. R. XXX above shield; lis, lion and rose emblems around; *mm*. 24, 125, 105	1200	3000
2633	Similar but plain back to throne; *mm*. trefoil	1250	3250

2634   2635

		F	VF
		£	£
2634	**Spur-ryal** (15s.). As illus. R. Somewhat like 2614, but lis are also crowned. *mm.* 24-125, 46	1850	4650
2635	**Angel** (10s.) of new type; *mm.* 24-46	725	1600
2636	— pierced for use as touch-piece	300	625
2637	**Laurel** (20s.; 140 1/2 gr.). First (large) laur. bust l.; *mm.* 24, 24/-	300	625
2638	Second, medium, square headed bust, 'SS' tie ends; *mm.* 24, 33	265	525
2638A	Third, small rounded head, ties wider apart; *mm.* 33, 125	240	465

2638B

		F	VF
2638B	Fourth head, very small ties; *mm.* 105, 46	235	450
2638C	Fourth head variety, tie ends form a bracket to value; *mm.* lis	250	500
2639	Fifth, small rather crude bust; *mm.* trefoil	725	1650
2640	**Half-laurel**. First bust; *mm.* spur rowel	250	525
2641	— As 2638A; *mm.* rose	225	450

2640   2641A

		F	VF
2641A	— As 2638B; *mm.* 33-46, 105/-	175	385
2642	**Quarter-laurel.** Bust with two loose tie ends; *mm.* 24-105	130	235
2642A	Bust as 2638C; *mm.* 105, 46, 105/46	130	235

2642B

	F	*VF*
	£	£
2642B As last but beaded, i.c. on *rev.* or both sides; *mm.* 105, 46	140	260

Rev. mm. on $^1/_2$ *and* $^1/_4$ *laurels normally follows* REGNA.

SILVER

2643

First coinage, 1603-4

2643	**Crown**. King on horseback. R. EXVRGAT, etc., shield; *mm.* thistle, lis	475	1050
2644	**Halfcrown**. Similar..	525	1450
2645	**Shilling**. First bust, square-cut beard. R. EXVRGAT, etc.; *mm.* thistle ...	45	185

2646   2647

2646	— Second bust, beard merges with collar; *mm.* thistle, lis	35	135
2647	**Sixpence**. First bust; 1603; *mm.* thistle..	30	125

2648   2650   2651

		F	*VF*
		£	£
2648	Second bust; 1603-4; *mm*. thistle, lis	30	110
2649	**Halfgroat**. As illustration 2650 but II; *mm*. thistle, lis ...	20	55
2650	**Penny**. First bust I behind head; *mm*. thistle, lis ?	40	125
2650A	— Second bust; *mm*. thistle, lis	20	50
2651	**Halfpenny**. As illustration; *mm*. thistle, lis	15	40

Second coinage, 1604-19

2652	**Crown**. King on horseback. R. QVAE DEVS, etc. *rev*. stops; *mm*. 105-84	475	975
2653	**Halfcrown**. Similar; *mm*. 105-79	700	2000
2654	**Shilling**. Third bust, beard cut square and stands out (*cf*. illus. 2657); *mm*.		
	lis, rose	30	115
2655	— Fourth bust, armour plainer (*cf*. 2658); *mm*. 33-74, 60 over 74	30	120
2656	— Fifth bust, similar, but hair longer; *mm*. 74-7a (several bust varieties)	30	125

2657   2658

2657	**Sixpence**. Third bust; 1604-6; *mm*. lis, rose, escallop	30	95
2658	— Fourth bust; 1605-16; *mm*. rose to book, 90/60, 25/60	30	100
2658A	— Fifth bust, 1618; *mm*. plain cross	600	1250
2659	**Halfgroat**. As illus. but larger crown on *obv*.; *mm*. lis to coronet	15	40

2660   2663

2660	— — Similar, but smaller crown on *obv*.; *mm*. coronet to plain cross	15	40
2660A	As before, but TVEATVR legend both sides; *mm*. plain cross over book?	50	125
2661	**Penny**. As halfgroat but no crowns; *mm*. 105-32,7a and none, -/84, 32/-	15	35
2662	— As before but TVEATVR legend both sides; *mm*. mullet	50	125
2663	**Halfpenny**. As illus.; *mm*. 105- 25, 32; all *mms* on *rev*. only	15	35

2665

		F	VF
		£	£

Third coinage, 1619-25

2664   **Crown**. As 2652, with plain or grass ground line, colon stops on *obv.*, no stops on *rev.*; *mm.* 33-46 260   550

2665   — — plume over shield; *mm.* 125-46 300   675

2666   **Halfcrown**. As 2664 but normally plain ground line only; all have bird-headed harp; *mm.* 33-46 110   275

2666

2666A — — Similar but no ground line; *mm.* rose 325   750

2667   — — Plume over shield; groundline *mm.* 125-46 200   475

2668   **Shilling**. Sixth (large) bust, hair longer and very curly; *mm.* 24-46 40   145

2667   2668/9

2669   — — plume over shield; *mm.* 125-46 95   275

2670   2672

		F £	VF £
2670	**Sixpence**. Sixth bust; 1621-4; *mm.* 33-46; 1621/0, *mm.* rose	30	110
2671	**Halfgroat**. As 2660 but no stops on *rev.*; *mm.* 24-46 and none, 105 and 46, 46/- *mm.* 24 with *rev.* stops known	15	40
2671A	Similar but no inner circles; *mm.* lis, trefoil..	20	50
2672	**Penny**. As illus.; *mm.* 24, 105, two pellets, none, trefoil,.........................	15	30
2672A	— Similar but without inner circles on one or both sides; *mm.* lis, two pellets	15	35
2673	**Halfpenny**. As 2663, but no *mm.*	15	30

COPPER

For mintmarks see C. Wilson Peck, *English Copper, Tin and Bronze Coins in the British Museum, 1558-1958.*

2675   2676   2679

2674	**Farthing**. 'Harington', small size. 1a, letter or other mark below crown (originally tinned surface) ....*from*	??	??
2675	— — 1b, central jewel on circlet of crown with *mm.* below or crown unmodified	??	??
2676	— 2, normal size of coin; *mm.* on *rev.*	??	??
2677	'Lennox'. 3a; *mm. rev.* only	??	??
2678	— 3b; *mm.* both sides	??	??
2679	— — 3c; *mm. obv.* only	??	??
2680	— — 3d; larger crown	??	??
2681	— 4; oval type, legend starts at bottom l..	??	??

Numismatically, this reign is one of the most interesting. Some outstanding machine-made coins were produced by Nicholas Briot, a French die-sinker, but they could not be struck at sufficient speed to supplant hand-hammering methods. In 1637 a branch mint was set up at Aberystwyth to coin silver extracted from the Welsh mines. After the king's final breach with Parliament the parliamentary government continued to issue coins at London with Charles's name and portrait until the king's trial and execution. The coinage of copper farthings continued to be manufactured privately under licences held first by the Duchess of Richmond, then by Lord Maltravers and later by various other persons. The licence was finally revoked by Parliament in 1644.

During the Civil War coins were struck at a number of towns to supply coinage for those areas of the country under Royalist control. Many of these coins have an abbreviated form of the 'Declaration' made at Wellington, Shropshire, Sept., 1642, in which Charles promised to uphold the Protestant Religion, the Laws of England and the Liberty of Parliament. Amongst the more spectacular pieces are the gold triple unites and the silver pounds and half-pounds struck at Shrewsbury and Oxford, and the emergency coins, some made from odd-shaped pieces of silver plate during the sieges of Newark, Scarborough, Carlisle and Pontefract.

Mintmarks

105	10	96	71	57	88	101	35

87	107	60	75	123	57	119a	23

119b	98	112	81	120	109

Tower Mint under Charles I

1625	Lis (105)	1633-4	Portcullis (107)
1625-6	Cross Calvary (10)	1634-5	Bell (60)
1626-7	Negro's head (96)	1635-6	Crown (75)
1627-8	Castle (71)	1636-8	Tun (123)
1628-9	Anchor (57)	1638-9	Anchor (57)
1629-30	Heart (88)	1639-40	Triangle (119a)
1630-1	Plume (101)	1640-1	Star (23)
1631-2	Rose (35)	1641-3	Triangle in circle
1632-3	Harp (87)		(119b)

Tower Mint under Parliament

1643-4	P in brackets (98)
1644-5	R in brackets (112)
1645	Eye (81)
1645-6	Sun (120)
1646-8	Sceptre (109)

Mint mark no. 57 is often horizontal to left or right.

59	B	58 *var*	58

Briot's Mint

1631-2	Flower and B (59)	1638-9	Anchor (57)
1632	B		Anchor and B (58)
			Anchor and mullet (58v)

On mint mark no. 58 the 'B' below the anchor is sometimes shown as ꓭ

61   104   35   92   103   6   65b   71

89   91 *var*   131   84   94 *var*   64   93   34

102   67   127   128   129   25   83   100

134   71   A   B   75

Provincial Mints

1638-42	Book (61, *Aberystwyth*)
1642	Plume (104, *Shrewsbury*)
	Pellets or pellet (*Shrewsbury*)
1642-3	Rose (35, *Truro*)
	Bugle (134, *Truro*)
1642-4	Lion (92, *York*)
1642-6	Plume (103, *Oxford*)
	Pellet or pellets (*Oxford*)
	Lis (105, *Oxford*)
1643	Cross pattee (6, *Bristol*)
	Acorn (65b, *Bristol*)
	Castle (71, *Worcester* or *Shrewsbury*)
	Helmet (89, *Worcester* and *Shrewsbury*)
1643-4	Leopard's head (91 *var. Worcester*)
	Two lions (131, *Worcester*)
	Lis (105, *Worcs.* or *Shrews.*)
	Bunch of grapes (84, *Worcs.* or *Shrews.*)
	Bird (94 var., *Worcs.* or *Shrews.*)

1643-4	Boar's head (64 *Worcs.* or *Shrews.*)
	Lion rampant (93, *Worcs.* or *Shrews.*)
	Rosette (34, *Worcs.* or *Shrews.*)
1643-5	Plume (102, *Bristol*)
	Br. (67, *Bristol*)
	Pellets (*Bristol*)
	Rose (35, *Exeter*)
	Rosette (34, *Oxford*)
1643-6	Floriated cross (127, *Oxford*)
1644	Cross pattee (6, *Oxford*)
	Lozenge (128, *Oxford*)
	Billet (129, *Oxford*)
	Mullet (25, *Oxford*)
1644-5	Gerb (83, *Chester*)
	Pear (100, *Worcester*)
	Lis (105, *Hereford?*)
	Castle (71, *Exeter*)
1645-6	Plume (102, *Ashby, Bridgnorth*)
1645	A (*Ashby*)
1646	B (*Bridgnorth*)
1648-9	Crown (75, *Aberystwyth Furnace*)

GOLD

Tower mint, under the King, 1625-42

Tower Gold

		F	VF
		£	£
2682	**Angel**. As for James I last issue, but *rev*. reads AMOR POPVLI etc; without mark of value; *mm*. lis and cross calvary	850	2650
2683	— — pierced for use as touch-piece	375	825
2684	— X in field to r.; *mm*. 96-88, 71 and 96/71, 57 and 71/57	800	2500
2685	— — — pierced for use as touch-piece	375	825
2686	— X in field to l.; *mm*. 96, 88, 35-23	800	2500

2687

2687	— — — pierced for use as touch-piece	375	825

2688   2697

2688	**Unite** (20s.). First bust with ruff and collar of order, high double-crown. R. Square-topped shield; *mm*. lis.	265	550
2688A	— Similar, but extra garnishing to shield; *mm*. lis..................................	275	575
2689	— Similar, but flat single-arched crown; *mm*. lis, cross calvary	275	575
2689A	R. As 2688A. *mm*. lis	285	600
2690	Second bust with ruff and armour nearly concealed with scarf; R. Square-topped shield with slight garnishing *mm*. 10-88	240	500
2690A	Similar but more elongated bust, usually dividing legend. *mm*. 57-101, 88/101...	240	510
2691	— As 2690A but *mm*. anchor below bust	625	1350
2691A	*Obv*. as 2690A. R. As next: *mm*. plume	550	1200
2692	Third bust, more armour visible. R. Oval shield with CR at sides; *mm*. 101, 35.	275	575
2693	Fourth bust, small lace collar with large high crown usually breaking i.c., long hair. Garter ribbon on breast. R. Oval shield with crowned CR at sides; *mm*. harp, portcullis..	250	525

	F	VF
	£	£

2693A Similar, but unjewelled crown, within or touching i.c.; *mm*. 107-23 .... 240 500

2694 Sixth (Briot's) bust, large lace collar. R. Similar; *mm*. 119a-119b 260 550

2695 Briot's hammered issue, (square-topped shield); *mm*. anchor 2000 5000

2696 **Double-crown**. First bust. As 2688. R. Square-topped shield; *mm*. lis 240 525

2696A Similar to last but wider flatter double-arched crown; *mm*. 105, 10 .... 265 550

*2697 Second bust. R. Similar to 2690; *mm*. 10-57 .... 200 450

*2697A Similar to 2690A: *mm*. 57-101 .... 200 450

2697B *Obv*. as last. R. As next: *mm*. plume 300 625

2698 Third bust. Flat or domed crown. R. Oval shield with CR at
sides; *mm*. plume, rose 250 525

2699 Fourth bust, large head, high wide crown. R. Oval shield with crowned CR
at sides; *mm*. portcullis 225 475

2699A — Similar to last, but flat crown, jewelled outer arch: *mm*. 87-123 .... 200 435

2699B — Similar, but smaller head, unjewelled crown: *mm*. 60-57 .... 200 435

2699C — Sim. to 2699, but bust within i.c.; *mm*. bell 300 625

2700 Fifth bust (Early Aberystwyth style). R. Similar; *mm*. anchor 300 650

2700A — (Late Aberystwyth style). R. *mm*. anchor, triangle 275 600

2701 Sixth bust. R. Normal; *mm*. 119a-119b 235 500

2702 — R. Briot's square-topped shield; *mm*. anchor 950 2500

*For these coins inner circles are sometimes omitted on *obv*., *rev*., or both. *See also 2704, 2704A
and 2707.*

2703   2707

2703 **Crown**. First bust with small round crown. R. Square-topped shield; *mm*.
lis, cross calvary 140 300

2703A As 2696A. *mm*. cross calvary 150 325

2704 Second bust as 2690. R. Similar; *mm*. 10-71 .... 135 275

2704A As 2690A. *mm*. 57-101, 88/-, 57/-, 101/- 135 275

2704B As 2691. Wire line i.c.s on *rev*. 250 500

2705 *Obv*. as 2690A. R. As next; 101, 35, 101/- 145 300

2706 Third bust. R. Oval shield with CR at sides; *mm*. plume 250 575

2707 Fourth bust. R. Oval shield with crowned CR at sides; *mm*. -/87, 87-119b,
23/119a, 107/60 .... 135 275

2708 Fifth (Aberystwyth style) bust. R. Similar; *mm*. anchor 235 525

2709 Sixth (Briot's) bust. R. Similar; *mm*. anchor 700 1500

Tower mint, under Parliament, 1642-9. All Charles I types

2710 **Unite**. Fourth bust, as 2693A; *mm*. (P), (P)/- 400 825

2711 Sixth bust, as 2694 but crude style; *mm*. (P), (R), 119b 425 875

2712 Seventh bust, crude r style; *mm*. eye, sun, sceptre 525 1050

2713 **Double-crown**. Fourth bust, as 2699B; *mm*. eye 575 1200

2714

	F	VF
	£	£
2714 Fifth bust, as 2700A; *mm*. sun, sceptre	450	900
2715 Sixth bust, as 2701; *mm*. (P)	425	850
2716 Eighth, dumpy bust with single flat-arched crown; *mm*. sun	650	1250
2717 **Crown**. Fourth bust, as 2707 jewelled crown; *mm*. -/98 , 98/-, 98-120	215	425
2717A Sim. but unjewelled crown. R. Small crude shield; *mm*. 81-109	250	500

Nicholas Briot's coinage, 1631-2

2718 **Angel**. Type somewhat as Tower but smaller and neater; *mm*. -/B	3000	6750

2719

2719 **Unite**. As illustration. R. FLORENT etc.; *mm*. flower and B/B	950	2500
2720 **Double-crown**. Similar but X. R. CVLTORES, etc. *mm*. flower and B/B	750	1600
2720A Similar but King's crown unjewelled: *mm*. flower and B/B, B	750	1650
2721 **Crown**. Similar; *mm*. B	1350	3500

Briots Hammered Gold: See No. 2695, 2702 and 2709

Provincial issues, 1638-49

Chester mint, 1644

2722 **Unite**. As Tower. Somewhat like a crude Tower sixth bust. R. Crowned, oval shield, crowned CR, *mm*. plume	10000	25000

Shrewsbury mint, 1642 (See also 2749)

2723 **Triple unite**, 1642. Half-length figure l holding sword and olive-branch; *mm*.: R. EXVRGAT, etc., around RELIG PROT, etc., in two wavy lines. III and three plumes above, date below .... *Extremely rare*

Oxford mint, 1642-6

2724

		F	VF
		£	£
2724	**Triple unite.** As last, but *mm.* plume, tall narrow bust, 1642	2250	5000
2725	Similar, but 'Declaration' on continuous scroll, 1642-3	2600	6250
2725A	Large bust of fine style. King holds short olive branch; *mm.* small lis.....	7500	22500
2726	As last, but taller bust, with scarf behind shoulder, 1643, *mm.* plume	2500	5750
2727	Similar, but without scarf, longer olive branch, 1643...............................	2400	5350
2728	Similar, but OXON below 1643, rosette stops..	4000	9000
2729	Smaller size, olive branch varies, bust size varies, 1644 OXON..............	2600	6000
2730	— Obv. as 2729, 1644 / OX...	2650	6250

2731

2731	**Unite.** Tall thin bust. R. 'Declaration' in two wavy lines, 1642; *no mm.*...	700	1450
2732	— R. 'Declaration' in three lines on continuous scroll, 1642-3	725	1500
2733	Tall, well-proportioned bust. R. Similar, 1643, no *mm.*	800	1750
2734	Shorter bust, king's elbow not visible. R. Similar, 1643; *mm.* plume/-	650	1350
2735	Similar but longer olive branch curving to l. 1644 / OX; *mm.* plume	700	1450
2735A	Similar, but dumpy bust breaking lower i.c., small flan	725	1500
2736	Tall bust to edge of coin. R. Similar, 1643	875	2100
2737	As 2734. R. 'Declaration' in three straight lines, 1644 / OX	1500	3500
2738	Similar to 2734, but smaller size; small bust, low olive branch. 1645	850	1850
2739	— R. Single plume above 'Declaration', 1645-6 / OX; *mm.* plume, rosette, none	900	2000
2740	**Half-unite.** 'Declaration' in three straight lines, 1642	1200	2750
2741	'Declaration' on scroll; *mm.* plume; 1642-3	950	2250

2742

		F	VF
		£	£
2742	Bust to bottom of coin, 1643; Oxford plumes	700	1450
2743	— 1644 / OX. Three Shrewsbury plumes (neater work)	1350	3000

Bristol mint, 1645

*2744 **Unite.** Somewhat as 2734; Two busts known. *mm.* Br. or Br/ plumelet.;
1645.. 6500   15000

2745 **Half-unite.** Similar 1645 .... *Extremely rare*

Truro mint, 1642–3

2745A **Half-Unite.** Crowned bust l. (similar to Tower 4th bust). R.
CVLT, etc., crowned shield .... *Extremely rare*

Exeter mint, 1643–4

2746 **Unite.** *obv.* sim. to early Oxford bust. R. FLORENT, etc., crowned oval
shield between crowned CR, *mm.* rose 10000   27500

2747 — R. CVLTORES, etc., similar but no CR 9500   25000

Worcester mint, 1643-4

2748 **Unite.** Crude bust R. FLORENT, etc., double annulet stops, crowned oval
shield, lion's paws on either side of garniture, no *mm*............................. 7000   20000

Salopia (Shrewsbury) mint, 1644

2749 **Unite.** *Obv.* bust in armour. R. Cr. shield, crowned CR. *mm.* lis/- .... *Extremely rare*

Colchester besieged, 1648

2750 **Ten Shillings** Gateway of castle between CR; below OBS CO L 16 S/X 48.
Uniface – now considered a later concoction ....

Pontefract besieged, 1648-9. After the death of Charles I, in the name of Charles II

2751 **Unite.** DVM : SPIRO : SPERO around CR crowned. CAROLVS :
SECVИDVS : 16 48, castle, OBS on l., PC above................................. *Extremely rare*

2752 **Unite.** CAROL : II, etc., around HANC : DEVS, etc. R. POST : MORTEM, etc.,
around castle. *Octagonal*.. *Extremely rare*

SILVER

Tower mint, under the King, 1625-42

2753 **Crown.** King on horseback with raised sword. 1a. Horse caparisoned with
plume on head and crupper. R. Square-topped shield over long cross
fourchee; *mm.* lis, cross calvary.. 300   700

2754 — 1b. Similar, but plume over shield, no cross; *mm.* 105, 10, 71 650   1450

2755 — 2a. Smaller horse, plume on hd. only, cross on housings, king holds
sword on shoulder. R. Oval garnished shield over cross fourchee, CR
above; *mm.* harp 275   625

2756 — 2b¹. — — plume divides CR, no cross; *mm.* plume, rose................... 325   725

2757 — 2b². — — — with cross; *mm.* harp.. 425   900

2758 — 3a. Horse without caparisons. R. Oval shield without CR; *mm.* 60-23 275   625

2759

	F	VF
	£	£
2759 — 3b. — — plume over shield; *mm*. 107, 75, 123	300	700
2760 'Briot' horse with ground-line; *mm*. triangle in circle	2500	5000
2761 **Halfcrown**. As 2753. 1a¹. Rose on housings, ground-line; *mm*. lis	135	400
2761A — Similar, but no rose on housings; *mm*. lis	325	750

2762

	F	VF
2762 — 1a². Similar, but no rose or ground-line; *mm*. 105, 10 over 105	95	235
2763 — 1a³. As last but shield not over cross; *mm*. 10 sometimes over lis on one or both sides, 96	100	250
2763A — Similar but only slight garnishing to shield; *mm*. 10, 71	145	375
2763B — As 2763, light weight (204 grains as standard) *mm* 10, (usually over lis)	300	675
2764 — 1a⁴. — — with ground-line; *mm*. lis	450	925
2765 — 1b. Heavy garnishing, plume over shield; *mm*. 105, 10, 96	475	950
2765A — Similar but only slight garnishing; *mm*. 96-57	475	950
2766 — 2/1b. As 2755 but rose on housings. R. As last; *mm*. heart, plume......	600	1250
2767 — 2a. As 2755. R. Flattened oval garnished shield without cross; *mm*. 101/35 plume, rose, (CR above, divided by rose (rare), lis over rose (rare), lis)	65	160
2768 — 2b. Similar, but large plume between the CR; *mm*. plume, (rare) rose	110	325
2769 — 2c. As 2a, but differently garnished oval shield with CR at sides; *mm*. harp, portcullis, 107/87	50	135
2770 — 2d. Similar, but with plume over shield; *mm*. harp	600	1250

2771   2775

F	*VF*
£	£

2771 — 3a¹. No caparisons on horse, upright sword, scarf flies out from waist.
       R. Round garnished shield, no CR; *mm.* 60-119a, 60/75 .... 40 — 110

2772 — 3b. — — plume over shield; *mm.* 107-123 .... 80 — 250

2773 — 3a². — cloak flies from king's shoulder; R. Shields vary; *mm.* 123-23,
       119b, 119b over 119a/119b .... 40 — 120

2774 — — — — rough ground beneath horse; R. Shields vary; *mm.* 119a, 23, ... 45 — 135

2775 — 4. Foreshortened horse, mane before chest, tail between legs; *mm.* 23,
       119b .... 30 — 95

Most late Tower halfcrowns have irregular flans.

2776   2776A

2776 **Shilling**. l. Bust in ruff, high crown, jewelled arches. R. Square-topped
       shield over cross fourchée; *mm.* lis, (normal weight 92.9 gr.) .... 50 — 185

2776A — Similar but larger crown, plain inner arch; *mm.* 105, 10 .... 45 — 165

2777 Similar but light weight (81.75 grs.); *mm.* cross calvary .... 70 — 200

2778 — 1b¹. As 2776A, but plume over shield, no cross; *mm.* 105, 10 .... 200 — 525

2779 — 1a. Bust in ruff and armour concealed by scarf. R. As 2776; 10-71 .... 45 — 165

2780 — — — — light weight; *mm.* cross Calvary (often extremely small XII) .... 70 — 200

2781 — 1b². As 2779, but plume over shield, no cross; *mm.* 10-101
       (five bust varieties) .... 90 — 240

2781A — — light weight 1b² *mm.* 10 .... 150 — 375

2782 — 1b³. — — — cross; *mm.* negro's head .... 375 — 750

2783 — 2a. More armour visible. R. Oval shield, CR above; *mm.* 35, 101, 101
       over 88/101, (two bust varieties) .... 40 — 125

2784 — 2b. — — plume over shield; *mm.* 101, 35, 101 over 88/101,
       (three bust varieties) .... 120 — 325

2785 — 3¹. Bust with lace collar, (six bust varieties). R. Flattish oval shield, CR
       at sides; *mm.* harp, portcullis .... 35 — 105

2786 — 3². — — plume over shield; *mm.* harp (three bust varieties) .... 325 — 700

		F	VF
		£	£

2787   — 3a. — no inner circles, rounder shield without CR; *mm*. 60-123 (five
          bust varieties) 30   85

2788   — 3b. — — plume over shield; *mm*. 60-123 (Two bust varieties)........... 60   145

2789   — 4¹. Large Aberystwyth bust, medium or small XII. R. Square-topped
          shield over cross fleury; *mm*. tun, 57 over 123 (obv.) small neat cross ends 50   135

2790   — 4¹. var. Similar, but rounder shoulders, large XII; *mm*. 57, 119a, (cross
          ends vary) 35   95

2790A — O as above. R As Briot hammered issue *mm* Δ over anchor 175   375

2791   — 4². Smaller Aberystwyth bust with small double-arched crown, small
          XII; *mm*. tun, small neat cross ends, large XII, *mm*. anchor 40   120

2792   — 4³. — single-arches, large XII; *mm*. 123, 57, 119a, 119b (cross ends vary) 35   95

2793   — 4⁴. Older (Briot's style) bust, very pointed beard; *mm*. 119a-119b 30   85

2793A — *Obv*. as last. R. As 2790A (Briot hammered). *mm*. Δ/Δ over anchor...   175   375

2794   **Sixpence**. 1. As 2776, but dated 1625-6; small bust *mm*. lis, large bust
          mm. lis. 10 (*rare*).. 45   140

2794A — Lightweight, 40.85 grains; large bust *mm* 10, 1625-6 100   300

2795   — 1a¹. As 2779, but dated 1625-9; *mm*. 10-88 (busts vary).................... 65   175

2796   — 1a². — no cross, 1630; *mm*. heart, plume 135   375

2797   — 2a. As 2783, no date; *mm*. plume, rose 40   140

2798   — 2b. — plume dividing CR; *mm*. plume, rose, plume/rose................... 50   175

2799   — 3. As 2785; *mm*. harp, portcullis (busts and crowns vary)................... 35   125

2799A — 3. As above but no CR *mm*. portcullis 125   350

2800   — 3a. no inner circles; *mm*. 60-123 (busts and crowns vary)................. 30   100

2801   — 4¹. As first Aberystwyth sixpence, double-arch crown, small VI. R.
          Square-topped shield over cross; *mm*. tun 35   125

2801A — 4¹. Similar but lyre cross ends on *rev*, *mm*. tun 45   145

2802   — 4¹. var. — similar, but large VI; *mm*. tun, anchor 30   100

2803   — 4². Second Aberystwyth bust, single-arched crown; *mm*. 123, 57, 119a 30   110

2804   — 4². larger bust, *mm*. triangle 45   145

2805   — 4³. Older (Briot's style) bust; *mm*. 119a-119b (moline cross ends)..... 30   135

2806   2808   2818

		F	VF
		£	£
2806	**Halfgroat**. 1. Crowned rose type. Beaded and/or wire line inner circles on one or both sides. *mm* 105, 105/–, 10	20	45
2807	— 1a. — — similar but without inner circles, *mm* 96–101	20	50
2808	— 2a. King's 2nd bust in ruff and mantle. R. Oval shield; *mm*. plume, rose	20	50
2809	— 2b. Similar, but with plume over shield; *mm*. plume, rose, plume/-	25	70
2809A	— — 2a Var. 3rd bust, with more armour. breaks i.c. at top. R. As last; *mm*. plume, rose	20	50
2809B	— — Sim. but plume over shield; *mm*. plume	25	70
2810	— 3¹. Bust with lace collar. R. Oval shield between CR; no inner circles; *mm*. rose, harp, portcullis, crown	15	40
2811	— 3²⁻⁴. — — inner circles sometimes only on one side; *mm*. harp, portcullis	15	40
2814	— 3⁵. — — no CR, no inner circles; *mm*. portcullis	20	45
2815	— 3⁶. — — — inner circles on *obv*.; *mm*. portcullis, harp	20	45
2816	— 3a¹. — R. Rounder shield, different garniture, no i.cs.; *mm*. 60-119a.	15	35
2817	— 3a². — — inner circle on *obv*.; *mm*. triangle, anchor	15	40
2818	— 3a³. — — inner circles both sides; *mm*. 119a-119b	15	35
2819	— 3a⁴. Aberystwyth bust, no inner circles; *mm*. anchor	20	55
2820	— 3a⁵. — inner circle on *rev*.; *mm*. anchor	20	55
2821	— 3a⁶. Very small bust, no inner circles; *mm*. anchor	25	65

2822   2828   2831   2837

2822	**Penny**. 1. Rose each side; i.cs.; *mm*. 96, :/lis, lis/:, one or two pellets, lis	12	30
2823	— 1a. — no i.cs.; *mm*. lis, one or two pellets, anchor	12	30
2824	— 1b. — i.c. on *rev*.; *mm*. negro's head/two pellets	20	50
2825	— 2. Bust in ruff and mantle. R. Oval shield; i.cs.; *mm*. plume, plume/rose, rose	20	50
2826	— 2¹. — — no i.cs.; *mm*. plume, rose	20	45
2827	— 2a¹. More armour visible; no i.cs.; *mm*. plume, rose, plume/rose	15	35
2828	— 2a². — i.c. on *obv*.; *mm*. plume, rose, plume over rose	15	35
2829	— 2a³. — i.cs. both sides; *mm*. plume, rose	15	35
2830	— 2a⁴. — i.c. on *rev*.; *mm*. rose over plume	15	40
2831	— 3¹. Bust in lace collar. R. CR at sides of shield; no i.cs.; *mm*. harp, one or two pellets. ··/harp (also *obv*. i.c. *mm*. harp)	12	30
2832	— 3². — similar but no CR; *mm*. 87, 107, 107/··, pellets, none	12	30
2833	— 3³. — — i.c. on *obv*.; *mm*. harp,··	15	30
2834	— 3⁴. — — i.c. on *rev*.; *mm*. harp	15	35
2835	— 3a¹. — similar, but shield almost round and with scroll garniture; no i.cs.; *mm*. bell, triangle, one to four pellets, none, bell/··	12	30
2835A	— 3a¹ variety — i.c. on *obv*., *rev*. or both sides; *mm*. triangle/two pellets, Δ,··	15	40
2836	— 3a³. Aberystwyth bust; i.c. on *obv*. or none; *mm*. one or two pellets or triangle or none, or mule of these *mms*.	15	35
2837	**Halfpenny**. Rose each side; no legend or *mm*.	12	35

Many small denominations have uneven irregular flans.

		F £	VF £

Tower mint, under Parliament, 1642-8. All Charles I type

2838	**Crown**. 4. Foreshortened horse; *mm*. (P) to sun	300	700
2839	— 5. Tall spirited horse; *mm*. sun	425	900
2840	**Halfcrown**. 3a³. As 2773, but coarse work; *mm*. (P) to sun, 81/120	30	100
2841	— 4. Foreshortened horse; *mm*. (P)	125	325
2842	— 5. Tall horse; *mm*. sun, sceptre	50	150
2843	**Shilling**. 4⁴. Briot style bust, *mm*. (P), (R); coarse work; *mm*. eye, sun ..	30	100

2844   2845   2845A

2844	— 4⁵. Long narrow coarse bust; *mm*. sun, sceptre	40	130
2845	— 4⁶. Short bust with narrow crown; *mm*. sceptre	45	135
2845A	— — Short broad bust, as illus., broader crown; *mm*. sceptre	45	150
2846	**Sixpence**. 4³. Briot style bust; *mm*. (P) (R)	60	165

2847   2848   2855

2847	— 4⁴. Late Aberystwyth bust modified; *mm*. (R) to sceptre	45	135
2848	— 4⁵. Squat bust of crude style; *mm*. eye, sun, sun over eye	85	200
2849	**Halfgroat**. 3a³. Sim. to 2818; *mm*. (P) to eye, sceptre, 98/119b	20	50
2850	— 3a⁷. Older, shorter bust, pointed beard; *mm*. eye to sceptre	15	45
2851	**Penny**. 3a². Older bust; *mm*. pellets, i.c. on *obv*. only	20	50

Nicholas Briot's coinage, 1631-9

First milled issue, 1631-2

2852	**Crown**. King on horseback. R. Crowned shield between CR crowned; *mm*. flower and B / B	350	900
2853	**Halfcrown**. Similar	190	475
2854	**Shilling**. Briot's early bust with falling lace collar. R. Square-topped shield over long cross fourchee; R. Legend starts at top or bottom *mm*. flower and B/B, B	135	375
2855	**Sixpence**. Similar, but VI behind bust; *mm*. flower and B/B, flower and B/-	65	185

CHARLES I AND CIVIL WAR MINTS (1643-49)

2856   2857

	F £	VF £
2856 **Halfgroat**. Briot's bust, B below, II behind. R. IVSTITIA, etc., square-topped shield over long cross fourchee	30	70
2856A Pattern halfgroat. Uncrowned bust in ruff r. R. crowned, interlocked Cs. (North 2687). (Included because of its relatively regular appearance.)....	30	70
2857 **Penny**. Similar, but I behind bust, B below bust; position of legend may vary	35	75

Second milled issue, 1638-9

2858   2859

2858 **Halfcrown**. As 2853, but *mm.* anchor and B	165	375
2859 **Shilling**. Briot's late bust, the falling lace collar is plain with broad lace border, no scarf. R. As 2854 but cross only to inner circle; *mm.* anchor and B, anchor or muled	60	165
2860 **Sixpence**. Similar, but VI; *mm.* anchor, anchor and mullet/anchor	25	75

The two last often exhibit flan reduction marks.

Briot's hammered issue, 1638-9

2861 **Halfcrown**. King on Briot's style horse with ground line. R. Square-topped shield; *mm.* anchor, triangle over anchor. Also muled with Tower *rev*....	525	1250
2862 **Shilling**. Sim. to 2859; R. Square-topped shield over short cross fleury; usually *mm.* triangle over anchor. Each *mm.* alone is very rare. Often muled with Tower *obv. (*see 2790A, 2793A) *or rev*	275	650

Provincial and Civil War issues, 1638-49
York mint, 1643-4. *Mm.* lion

2863 **Halfcrown**. 1. Ground-line below horse. R. Square-topped shield between CR	275	750
2864 — 2. — R. Oval shield as Tower 3a, groundline grass or dotted	235	600
2865 — 3. No ground-line. R. Similar..	235	600
2866 *— 4. As last, but EBOR below horse with head held low. Base metal, often very base	80	250
2867 — 5. Tall horse, mane in front of chest, EBOR below. R. Crowned square-topped shield between CR, floral spray in legend	175	475

*These pieces are contemporary forgeries (Besly, English Civil War Hoards BM 51, 1987)

2868

		F	VF
		£	£
2868	— 6. As last, but shield is oval, garnished (*rev*. detail variations)	125	325
2869	— 7. Similar, but horse's tail shows between legs. R. Shield as last, but with lion's skin garniture, no CR or floral spray	110	275

2870/2

2870	**Shilling**. 1. Bust in scalloped lace collar 3[1]. R. EBOR above square-topped shield over cross fleury	85	235
2871	— 2. Similar, but bust in plain armour, mantle; coarse work	110	275
2872	— 3. *Obv*. as 2870. — R. EBOR below oval shield	120	300
2873	— 4. — Similar, but crowned oval shield (*obv*. finer style)	80	225
2874	— 5. — As last, but lion's skin garniture	80	225
2875	**Sixpence**. *Obv*. Sim. to 2870. Crowned oval shield	175	425

2876   2877

2876	— — Crowned CR at sides..	150	325
2877	**Threepence**. As type 1 shilling, but III behind bust. R. As 2870.............	35	90

	F £	VF £

Aberystwyth mint, 1638/9-42. *Mm*. book.

Plume 1=with coronet and band. Plume 2=with coronet only

2878	**Halfcrown**. Horseman similar to 2773, but plume 2 behind. R. Oval garnished shield with large plume above. *Obv.* plume 2, *rev.* plume 1. ...	400	850
2879	— Similar to 2774, plume 1 behind King, ground below horse. *Obv.* squat plume 1, *rev.* plume 1	425	950
2880	As 2773 but more spirited horse, no ground. FRAN ET HIB, plume 2/1	425	950
2881	**Shilling**. Bust with large square lace collar, plume 2 before, small XII. R. As before. No inner circles	185	500

2882   2884

2886

2882	— inner circle on *rev*.	175	450
2883	As 2881, but large plume 1 or 2, large XII, inner circles, large or .... small shield	175	450
2884	As last, but small narrow head, square lace collar, large or square plume	200	525
2885	Small Briot style face, small crown, plume 2	375	850
2885A	**Sixpence**. *Obv.* as Tower bust 3a, plume before. R. as 2889; *mm*. book (*obv*. only)	325	675
2886	Somewhat as 2881, but double-arched crown, small VI; no inner circles	150	375
2887	Similar to 2886, but single arched crown, plume 2, inner circle *obv*. Large VI	165	425
2888	Similar, but with inner circles both sides	150	400
2889	— — *Rev*. with small squat-shaped plume above, sometimes no *rev*. *mm*.	150	375
2890	Bust as the first Oxford sixpence; with crown cutting inner circle	225	525

2891   2894   2895-9

	F £	VF £
2891 **Groat**. Large bust, lace collar, no armour on shoulder. Crown breaks or touches inner circle. R. Shield, plume 1 or 2	30	75
2892 — Similar, armour on shoulder, shorter collar. R. Similar	35	80
2893 — Smaller, neater bust well within circle. R. Similar	30	70
2894 **Threepence**. Small bust, plume 2 before. R. Shield, plume 1 or 2 above, *obv*. legend variations	25	65
2895-9 — Similar, but crown cuts i.c. squat pl. on *obv*., R. Pl. 2, *Obv*. legend variations	30	70
2900 **Halfgroat**. Bust as Tower type 3. R. Large plume. No inner circles, *mm*. pellet/book,book	35	90

2900A   2905   2907

	F	VF
2900A Bust as 2886. R. As last, no inner circle	45	125
2901 Bust with round lace collar; single arch crown, inner circles, colon stops	30	80
2902 After Briot's bust, square lace collar: inner circles	35	85
2903 **Penny**. As 2901; CARO; no inner circles	60	140
2904 As 2901; CARO; inner circles	50	135
2905 As last but reads CAROLVS; inner circles	65	160
2906 *Obv*. similar to 2890, tall narrow bust, crown touches inner circle	70	175
2907 **Halfpenny**. No legend. O. Rose. R. Plume	135	350

Aberystwyth-Furnace mint, 1648/9. *Mm*. crown

2908 **Halfcrown**. King on horseback. R. Sim. to 2878	1350	2750
2909 **Shilling**. Aberystwyth type, but *mm*. crown	1500	3500
2910 **Sixpence**. Similar	950	2100

2911   2913

	Fair	F	VF
	£	£	£
2911 **Groat**. Similar		165	400
2912 **Threepence**. Similar		160	350
2913 **Halfgroat**. Similar. R. Large plume		225	525
2914 **Penny**. Similar		625	1250

Uncertain mint (? Hereford) 1644-5

2915   2930/1

2915 **Halfcrown**. As illustration, dated 1645 or undated	1250	2500
2915A — Scarf with long sash ends. CH below horse. R. Oval shield 1644	1750	4000
2915B — R. Crowned oval shield, lion paws	1750	4000

Shrewsbury mint, 1642. Plume without band used as *mm*. or in field.

2917 **Pound**. King on horseback, plume behind, similar to Tower grp. 3 crowns. R. Declaration between two straight lines, XX and three Shrewsbury plumes above, 1642 below; *mm*. pellets, pellets/-	1350	2850
2918 Similar, but Shrewsbury horse walking over pile of arms; no *mm*., pellets	1100	2500
2919 As last, but cannon amongst arms and only single plume and XX above Declaration, no *mm*.	1500	3250
2920 **Half-pound**. As 2917, but X; *mm*. pellets	600	1250
2921 Similar, but only two plumes on *rev*.; *mm*., pellets	850	2000
2922 Shrewsbury horseman with ground-line, three plumes on *rev*.; *mm*., none, pellets/-	575	1200
2923 — with cannon and arms or arms below horse; *mm*. pellets/-	600	1250
2924 — no cannon in arms, no plume in *obv*. field; *mm*. plume/pellets, plume/-	47	950
2925 **Crown**. Aberystwyth horseman, no ground line	*Extremely rare*	

2926

		F	VF
		£	£
2926	Shrewsbury horseman with ground-line; *mm*. -/pellets, pellets/-, none	450	925
2927	**Halfcrown**. *O*. From Aberystwyth die; (S2880); *mm*. book. R. Single plume above Declaration, 1642	725	1600
2928	Sim. to Aberystwyth die, fat plume behind. R. Three plumes above Declaration; *mm*. pellets, pellets/-.........	325	725
2929	Shrewsbury horseman, no ground line. R. As 2927, single plume, no *mm*.	375	800
2929A	— — R. As 2933.........	300	650
2930	— R. 2: plume; 6, above Declaration.........	650	1350
2931	— with ground-line. R. Similar	650	1350
2932	— — R. As 2927, single plume	375	800
2933	— — R. Three plumes above Declaration; *mm*. none or pellets	275	600
2933A	— — R. Aberystwyth die, plume over shield; *mm*. -/book	750	1650
2934	As 2933 but no plume behind king; *mm*. plume/pellets.........	250	550
2935	**Shilling**. *O*. From Aberystwyth die; S2885 *mm*. book. R. Declaration type	650	1350
2936	*O*. From Shrewsbury die. R. Similar.........	750	1650

Oxford mint, 1642-6. *Mm*. usually plume with band, except on the smaller denominations when it is lis or pellets. There were so many dies used at this mint that we can give only a selection of the more easily identifiable varieties.

2937

2937	**Pound**. Large horseman over arms, no exergual line, fine workmanship. R. Three Shrewsbury plumes and XX above Declaration, 1642 below; *mm*. plume/pellets	1750	4000

		F	*VF*
		£	£
2938	— Similar, but three Oxford plumes, 1643; *mm.* as last	1650	3750
2939	Shrewsbury horseman trampling on arms, exergual line. R. As last, 1642	1200	2750
2940	— — cannon amongst arms, 1642-3; *mm.* similar	1050	2400
2941	— as last but exergue is chequered, 1642; *mm.* similar	1350	3000
2942	Briot's horseman, 1643; *mm.* similar	2500	5750
2943	*O.* As 2937. R. Declaration in cartouche, single large plume above, 1644 OX below	2750	7000
2944	**Half-pound.** As next. R. Shrewsbury die, 1642; *mm.* plume/-	450	975
2945	Oxford dies both sides, 1642-3; *mm.* plume/pellets	400	900
2946	**Crown.** *O.* Shrewsbury die with ground-line. R. As last but V, 1642-3 ..	325	675
2947	Oxford horseman with grass below, 1643	600	1250
2948	By Rawlins. King riding over a view of the city. R. Floral scrolls above and below Declaration, 1644/OXON below. (Electrotypes of the B.M. coin often appear)	6250	16500
2949	**Halfcrown.** *O.* From Shrewsbury die S2931 or 2934. R. 3 Ox plumes over 'Dec' 1642	235	525
2950	Ox plume, Shrewsbury horse. R. From Shrewsbury die, 1642	185	425
2951	Both Oxford dies, but Shrewsbury type horse, ground-line, 1642	100	300

      2951   2954

2952	— — without ground-line, 1642	120	325
2953	Oxford type horse, ground-line, 1643	110	300
2954	— without ground-line, 1643	100	285
2954A	— — R. 3 Shrewsbury plumes, 1642	135	375
2955	Briot's horse, grass below, 1643, 1643 / OX below date	110	325
2956	— — large central plume, 1643, 1643 / OX, 1644 / OX	125	350
2957	— lumpy ground, 1643, 1643 / OX	120	350
2958	— — large central plume, 1643-4 / OX	110	325
2959	— plain ground, 1644- 5 / OX	110	325

      2957-8   2961

	F	VF
	£	£
2960 — — large central plume, 1644 / OX	110	325
2960A — large central plume with a small Shrewsbury one each side, 1644/OX	135	425
2961 — large central plume, large date in script, 1644/OX	135	400
2962 Rocky ground, two small plumes at date, 1644 / OX	225	525
2963 Large horse (as Briot's, but clumsier), plain ground, 1644-5 / OX	110	335
2964 — lumpy ground, 1644-5 / OX	120	350
2965 — — large central plume, 1644 / OX	120	350
2966 — pebbly ground, 1645-6 / OX	120	350
2967 — — pellets or annulets by plumes and at date, 1645-6 / OX	135	425
2968 — grass below, 1645-6 / OX	135	425
2969 — — rosettes by plumes and at date, 1645 / OX	245	550
2970 **Shilling**. *O*. From Shrewsbury die. R. Declaration type, 1642	300	675
2971 Both Oxford dies. Small bust, 1642-3	120	300
2972 Similar, but coarser work, 1643	120	300
2973 Large bust of fine work, 1643-4	120	325
2974 — 1644-6 / OX (1645 rare)	125	350

2974A

2974A — — 1644 OX. Large date in script	135	375
2975 Bust with bent crown, 1643-4	140	350
2976 — 1644 / OX	140	350
2977 Rawlins' dies. Fine bust with R on truncation, 1644	225	600
2978 — — 1644 / OX	250	650
2979 Small size, 1646, annulets or pellets at date	165	400

2980

2980 **Sixpence**. *O*. Aberystwyth die S2890. R. With three Oxford plumes, 1642-3; *mm*. book/-	135	350

2985   2991

		F	VF
		£	£
2981	— R. With three Shrewsbury plumes, 1643; *mm*. book/-	125	325
2982	— R. As *rev*. of 2985 (see ill) 1644 OX. *mm*. book/–	350	825
2983	**Groat**. *O*. Aberystwyth die S2892. R. As 2985	70	175
2984	As last but three plumes above Declaration	85	225
2985	As illustration, with lion's head on shoulder	60	150
2985A	*Obv*. as last R. 3 Shrewsbury plumes, 1644 / OX	80	200
2986	Large bust reaching to top of coin. R. As 2985	85	200
2987	Large bust to bottom of coin, lion's head on shoulder, legend starts at bottom l. R. As last	90	200
2988	Rawlins' die; similar, but no i.c., and with R on shoulder. R. As last	110	250
2989	*O*. As 2985. R. Large single plume and scroll above Declaration, 1645	100	235
2990	*O*. As 2987. R. As last	75	185
2991	*O*. As 2988. R. Large single plume above Declaration, which is in cartouche, 1645-6 (over 5)	120	285
2992	**Threepence**. *O*. Aberystwyth die; *mm*. book R. Declaration type, 1644 / OX	60	175
2993	Rawlins' die, R below shoulder; *mm*. lis. R. Aberystwyth die with oval shield; *mm*. book	55	165
2994	— R. Declaration type, three lis above, 1644 below; *mm*. lis/-	45	120

2995   2996/7   3000

2995	— Similar, without the R, 1646 (over 1644); no *mm*.	50	150
2996	**Halfgroat**. R. Aberystwyth type with large plume, *mm* cross/-, cross/lis	80	165
2997	— R. Declaration type, 1644 / OX; *mm*. cross	80	175
2998	**Penny**. *O*. Aberystwyth die S2904; *mm*. book. R. Type, small plume	100	250
2999	As 2906 R. Type, large plume	110	275
3000	— Rawlins' bust as 2995 R. Type, small plume	125	300
3001	— Wider bust similar to the halfgroat. R. Similar	110	275
3002	— — R. Declaration type, 1644	375	900

	F	VF
	£	£

Bristol mint, 1643-5. *Mm.* usually plume or Br., except on small denominations

3003	**Halfcrown**. *O.* Oxford die with or without ground-line. R. Declaration, three Bristol plumes above, 1643 below	160	425
3004	— Obv. as above. R as above, but *mm.* Br. 1643	175	450
3005	King wears unusual flat crown, *obv. mm.* acorn? between four pellets. R. As 3003, 1643	175	450
3006	— Obv. as above. R as 3004 but 1643-4	140	375
3007	Shrewsbury plume behind king. R. As last	135	325
3008	— Obv. as above. R as 3004 but Br below date instead of as *mm* . 1644	145	365

3009

3009	— Obv. as 3007 but Br below horse. R as above but 1644-5	135	325
3010	— Obv. as above. R as 3004 but Br. as *mm.* as well as 1644-5	145	365
3011	**Shilling**. *O.* Oxford die. R. Declaration, 1643, 3 crude plumes above, no *mm.*	165	425

3012	3014	3015	3017

3012	— — R Similar, but *mm.* Br., 1643-4, less crude plumes	160	400
3013	—Obv. Coarse bust. R. As 3011, no *mm.*	175	450
3014	— — Coarse bust, R. as 3012, *mm.* Br, but 1644	175	450
3015	Obv. Bust of good style, plumelet before face. R. As 3012 *mm.* Br. but 1644-5	135	350
3016	— — R.as 3012, 1644, but Br below date instead of *mm*	160	400
3016A	— — R as 3012, 1644 but plume and plumelet either side.....................	135	350
3017	—Obv. Taller bust with high crown, no plumelets before, *mm.* Br. on its side. R As 3016 Br.below 1644-5	175	450
3018	—Obv. As 3017 but no *mm.* R as above but *mm..* no Br. below 1644-5 ..	185	475
3018A	— — R as above but plume and plumelets, 1645	185	475
3019	**Sixpence**. Small bust, nothing before. R. Declaration, 1643; *mm.* ./Br....	235	525
3020	Fine style bust. Plumelet before face, 1644; *mm.* ./Br. (on its side)	135	300

		F £	VF £
3021	**Groat**. Bust l. R. Declaration, 1644	145	325
3022	— Plumelet before face, 1644	110	250
3023	— Br. below date, 1644	110	250
3023A	— Similar, but larger bust and more spread plume before. Mm. pellet/Br; nothing below 1644	120	275

3024   3027

		F	VF
3024	**Threepence**. *O*. As 2992. Aberystwyth die; *mm*. book. R. Declaration, 1644	135	325
3025	Bristol die, plume before face, no *mm*., 1644	175	450
3026	**Halfgroat**. Br. in place of date below Declaration	175	450
3027	**Penny**. Similar bust, I behind. R. Large plume with bands	275	625

Late 'Declaration' issues, 1645-6
(Previously given as Lundy Island and/or Appledore and Barnstaple/Bideford, it seems likely that coins marked A, 1645 may be Ashby de la Zouch and the coins marked B or plumes, 1646 may be Bridgnorth on Severn.)

		F	VF
3028	**Halfcrown**. A below horse and date and as *rev. mm.* 1645	1200	2500
3029	Similar but *rev.* from altered Bristol die (i.e. the A's are over Br.)	1000	2250
3030	As 3028 but without A below date 1645	950	2000
3031	A below horse and as *rev. mm*. Scroll above Declaration, B below 1646	1650	3500
3032	Plumelet below horse struck over A. R. *Mm*. Shrewsbury plumes; scroll above Declaration, 1646	525	1250

3033

		F	VF
3033	— Similar, but plumelet below date	600	1350
3034	**Shilling**. Crowned bust l., *mm*. plume. R. Declaration type; *mm*. A and A below 1645	600	1350
3035	— Similar, but plumelet before face	650	1450
3036	— — Scroll above 'Declaration', 1646; *mm* plume/plumelet	250	575
3036A	— Bristol obv. die, no plumelet, similar to 3018 *mm*. Br. R. As last but *mm*. pellet. 1646.	325	725
3037	Obv as above, but Shrewsbury plume before face. plume over Br. *mm*. R. As above	275	600
3038	**Sixpence**. *O*. Plumelet before face; *mm*. A; R. 1645, 3 plumelets over 'Dec'	425	900

3039

| | | F | VF |
| | | £ | £ |

3039   *O*. Large Shrewsbury plume before face; *mm*. B. R. Scroll above Declaration, 1646, Shrewsbury plume and two plume plumelets 100   250

3040   **Groat**. As 3038 350   750

3041   Somewhat similar, but *obv. mm.* plumelet; R *mm.* pellet or plume,1646 . 85   200

3042   **Threepence**. Somewhat as last but only single plumelet above Declaration, no line below, 1645; no *mm*. 250   525

3043   — Scroll in place of line above, 1646 below 90   215

3044   **Halfgroat**. Bust l., II behind. R. Large plume with bands dividing 1646; no *mm*. 350   750

The penny listed under Bristol may belong to this series. It has the same reverse plume punch as 3044.

Truro mint, 1642-3. *Mm*. rose except where stated

  Entries from here to 3092 have been revised to follow E. Besly (BNJ 1992). The original catalogue numbers are therefore no longer sequential.

3048   **Crown**. King on horseback, head in profile, sash flies out in two ends. R. CHRISTO, etc., round garnished shield 225   525

3048A **Halfcrown**. King on walking horse, groundline below, R. Oblong shield, CR above, *mm.* bugle/– 950   2000

3050   Galloping horse, king holds baton. R. Oblong shield, CR at sides 1100   2750

3054   Walking horse, king holds sword. R. Similar 550   1200

3055   — R. Similar, but CR above 575   1250

3051   Galloping horse, king holds sword. R. Similar, but CR at sides 850   2250

3052   — R. Similar, but CR above 825   2100

3053   3054

		F	*VF*
		£	£
3053	Trotting horse. R. Similar, but CR at sides	600	1350
3056	**Shilling**. Small bust of good style. R. Oblong shield	1500	4000

Exeter mint, 1643-6. Undated or dated 1644-6 *Mm.* rose except where stated

3045	**Half-pound**. King on horseback, face towards viewer, sash in large bow. R. CHRISTO, etc., round garnished shield. Struck from crown dies on a thick flan	*Extremely rare*	
3046	**Crown**. King on horseback, sash in large bow. R. Round garnished shield	175	450
3047	— Shield garnished with twelve even scrolls	225	550
3070	As 3046, R Date divided by *mm*. 16 rose 44...	225	525
3071	— R Date to l. of *mm*. 1644	170	425
3072	— *mm*: rose/EX, 1645..	200	475
3073	King's sash flies out in two ends; *mm*. castle/rose, 1645........................	350	725
3074	— *mm*. castle/EX, 1645	180	450
3075	— *mm*. castle, 1645..	165	400

3064   3067-9, 3079

3062	**Halfcrown**. King on horseback, sash tied in bow. R. Oblong shield CR at sides	275	725
3063	— R. Round shield with eight even scrolls...	175	400
3064	— R. Round shield with five short and two long scrolls	135	320
3066	— R. Oval shield with angular garnish of triple lines	450	975
3067	Briot's horseman with lumpy ground. R. As 3063	200	475
3069	— R. As 3064..	175	425
3068	— R. As 3066..	450	975
3079	— R. As 3064, date to l. of *mm*. 1644..	275	625

3049 3080

		F	VF
		£	£
3049	King on spirited horse galloping over arms. R. Oval garnished shield, 1642 in cartouche below	1100	2750
3076	— R. As 3079, date to 1. of *mm.* 1644-5	1650	3500
3077	— R. *mm.* castle, 1645	1750	3750
3078	Short portly king, leaning backwards on ill-proportioned horse, 1644, 16 rose 44	400	900
3065	Horse with twisted tail, sash flies out in two ends R. As 3063	250	575
3080	— R. As 3079, date divided by *mm.* 16 rose 44, or date to 1. of *mm.* 1644-5	225	525
3081	— R. *mm.* castle, 1645	325	725
3082	— R. *mm.* EX, 1645	300	700
3083	— R. Declaration type; *mm.* EX. 1644-5	1250	2500
3084	— R. Similar, EX also below declaration, 1644	1100	2250
3057	**Shilling.** Large Oxford style bust. R. Round shield with eight even scrolls	600	1350
3058	— R. Oval shield with CR at sides	550	1200
3060	Normal bust with lank hair. R. As 3057	450	950
3059	— R. As 3058	475	1000
3061	— R. Round shield with six scrolls	350	750

3085 3087A

3085	— R. Similar, date to r. of *mm.* 1644, divided 16 rose 44, or to left of *mm.* 1644-5	175	450
3086	— R. Declaration type, 1645	600	1350
3087	**Sixpence.** Similar to 3085, large bust and letters 1644 rose	185	475
3087A	— Smaller bust and letters from punches used on 3088, small or large VI, 16 rose 44	175	450
3088	**Groat.** Somewhat similar but 1644 at beginning of *obv.* legend	60	140

3089   3091

			F	VF
			£	£
3089	**Threepence**. Similar. R. Square shield, 1644 above		75	165
3090	**Halfgroat**. Similar, but II. R. Oval shield, 1644		110	275
3091	— R. Large rose, 1644		125	300
3092	**Penny**. As last but I behind head		235	525

Worcester mint 1643-4

3093	**Halfcrown**. King on horseback l., W below; *mm*. two lions. R. Declaration type 1644 altered from 1643 Bristol die; *mm*. pellets	650	1500
3094	— R. Square-topped shield; *mm*. helmet, castle	450	1100
3095	— R. Oval shield; *mm*. helmet	475	1200

3096

3096	Similar but grass indicated; *mm*. castle. R. Square-topped shield; *mm*. helmet or pellets. (Illustrated above)	400	1000
3097	— R. Oval draped shield, lis or lions in legend	450	1100
3098	— R. Oval shield CR at sides, roses in legend	475	1150
3099	— R. FLORENT etc., oval garnished shield with lion's paws each side	550	1350
3100	Tall king, no W or *mm*. R. Oval shield, lis, roses, lions or stars in legend	425	1050
3101	— R. Square-topped shield; *mm*. helmet	500	1200
3102	— R. FLORENT, etc., oval shield; no *mm*.	550	1350
3103	Briot type horse, sword slopes forward, ground-line. R. Oval shield, roses in legend; *mm*. 91v, 105, none (combinations)	525	1200
3104	— Similar, but CR at sides, 91v/-	550	1250
3105	Dumpy, portly king, crude horse. R. As 3100; *mm*. 91v, 105, none	475	1150
3106	Thin king and horse. R. Oval shield, stars in legend; *mm*. 91v, none	425	1050

3106

Worcester or Salopia (Shrewsbury) 1643-4

		F £	VF £
3107	**Shilling**. Bust of king l., adequately rendered. R. Square-topped shield; *mm*. castle	675	1700
3108	— R. CR above shield; *mm*. helmet and lion	675	1700
3109	— R. Oval shield; *mm*. lion, pear	625	1600
3110	— Bust a somewhat crude copy of last (two varieties); *mm*. bird, lis. R. Square-topped shield with lion's paws above and at sides; *mm*. boar's head, helmet	750	1800

3111

3111	— — CR above	750	1800
3112	— R. Oval shield, lis in legend; *mm*. lis	650	1600
3113	— R. Round shield; *mm*. lis, 3 lis	600	1500
3114	Bust r.; *mm*. pear/-, pear/lis. R. draped oval shield with or without CR. (Halfcrown reverse dies)	1500	3250
3115	**Sixpence**. As 3110; *mm*. castle, castle/boar's hd	650	1500

3116   3117

3116	**Groat**. As 3112; *mm*. lis/helmet, rose/helmet	425	900
3117	**Threepence**. Similar; *mm*. lis obv.	225	450
3118	**Halfgroat**. Similar; *mm*. lis (*O*.) various (*R*.)	375	825

Salopia (Shrewsbury) mint, 1644

3119	**Halfcrown**. King on horseback l. SA below; *mm*. lis. R. (*mm*. lis, helmet, lion rampant, none). Cr. oval shield; CHRISTO etc. *mm*. helmet	2400	5250
3120	— R. FLORENT, etc., crowned oval shield, no *mm*.	2400	5250
3121	— SA erased or replaced by large pellet or cannon ball; *mm*. lis in legend, helmet. R. As 3119	1250	2750
3122	Tall horse and king, nothing below; *mm*. lis. R. Large round shield with crude garniture; *mm*. helmet	600	1250
3123	— R. Uncrowned square-topped shield with lion's paw above and at sides; *mm*. helmet	700	1500
3124	— R. Small crowned oval shield; *mm*. various	550	1200
3125	— R. As 3120	675	1450
3126	Finer work with little or no mane before horse. R. Cr. round or oval shield	600	1350
3127	Grass beneath horse. R. Similar; *mm*. lis or rose	750	1650
3128	Ground below horse. R. As 3120	825	1750

Hartlebury Castle (Worcs.) mint, 1646

3129

		F	VF
		£	£
3129	**Halfcrown**. *O. Mm*. pear. R. HC (Hartlebury Castle) in garniture below shield; *mm*. three pears	975	2500

Chester mint, 1644

3130

3130	**Halfcrown**. As illus. R. Oval shield; *mm*. three gerbs and sword	450	975
3131	— Similar, but without plume or CHST; R. Cr. oval shield with lion skin; *mm*. prostrate gerb; -/cinquefoil, ⁻/∴	525	1050
3132	— R. Crowned square-topped shield with CR at sides both crowned *rev*.; *mm*. cinquefoil...	350	750
3133	As 3130, but without plume or CHST. R. Declaration type, 1644 *rev*.; *mm*. plume..	675	1450
3133A	**Shilling**. Bust l. R. Oval garnished shield; *mm*. ∴ (obv. only)	750	1650
3133B	— R. Square-topped shield; *mm*. as last	750	1650
3133C	— R . Shield over long cross	750	1650
3134	**Threepence**. R. Square-topped shield; *mm*.-/ prostrate gerb...................	700	1450

3135

<table>
<tr><td></td><td>F
£</td><td>VF
£</td></tr>
</table>

Welsh Marches mint? 1644

3135 **Halfcrown**. Crude horseman, l. R. Declaration of Bristol style divided by a
dotted line, 3 plumes above, 1644 below 625   1350

Carlisle besieged, 1644-5

3136 **Three shillings**. Large crown above C. R / .III. S. R. OBS . CARL
/ . 1645.. 2750   5750

3137   Similar but : OBS :/-: CARL :./.1645 2850   6000

3137   3146

3138 **Shilling**. Similar 1750   3750

3139   R. Legend and date in two lines 1850   4250

Note. *(3136-39) Round or Octagonal pieces exist.*

Newark besieged, several times 1645-6, surrendered May 1646

3140   3144

3140 **Halfcrown**. Large crown between CR ; below, XXX. R. OBS / NEWARK /
1645 or 1646 375   725

3141   **Shilling**. Similar but crude flat shaped crown, NEWARKE, 1645 300   575

3142   Similar but normal arched crown, 1645 275   500

3143   — NEWARK, 1645 or 1646 275   500

3144 **Ninepence**. As halfcrown but IX, 1645 or 1646 250   475

3145   — NEWARKE, 1645 275   500

3146 **Sixpence**. As halfcrown but VI, 1646 250   475

Pontefract besieged, June 1648-March 1648-9

3147 **Two shillings** (lozenge shaped). DVM : SPIRO : SPERO around CR
      crowned. R. Castle surrounded by OBS, PC, sword and 1648 ....   *Extremely rare*
3148 **Shilling** (lozenge shaped, octagonal or round). Similar   675   1350
3149 — Similar but XII on r. dividing PC   625   1250
      After the death of Charles I (30 Jan. 1648/9), in the name of Charles II

3148

3149   3150

3150 **Shilling** (octagonal). *O.* As last. R. CAROLVS : SECVИDVS : 1648, castle
      gateway with flag dividing PC, OBS on l., cannon protrudes on r...........   675   1350
3151 CAROL : II : etc., around HANC : DE / VS : DEDIT 1648. R. POST :
      MORTEM : PATRIS : PRO : FILIO around gateway etc. as last............   700   1400

Scarborough besieged, July 1644-July 1645

3156   3165   3168

£

Type I. Castle with gateway to left, value punched below or to side

3152	**Five shillings and eightpence**	*Extremely rare*
3153	**Crown**. Similar but SC also punched	*Extremely rare*
3154	**Three shillings and fourpence**. As 3152	*Extremely rare*
3155	**Three shillings**. Similar	*Extremely rare*
3156	**Two shillings and tenpence**. As illustration......................	7500
3157	**Halfcrown**. Similar	8000
3158	**Two shillings and fourpence**. Similar..............................	*Extremely rare*
3159	**Two shillings and twopence**. Similar..............................	*Extremely rare*
3160	**Two shillings**. Similar	*Extremely rare*
3161	**One shilling and ninepence**. Similar...............................	6250
3162	**One shilling and sixpence**. Similar	*Extremely rare*
3163	**One shilling and fourpence**. Similar...............................	6250
3164	**One shilling and threepence**. Similar	6250
3165	**Shilling**. As illustration...	*Extremely rare*
3166	**Sixpence**. Similar..	7250
3167	**Groat**. Similar	*Extremely rare*

Type II. Castle with two turrets, value punched below

3168	**Two shillings**. Two castles...	*Extremely rare*
3170	**One shilling and sixpence**. Single castle	*Extremely rare*
3171	**One shilling and fourpence**. Similar...............................	5250
3172	**One shilling and threepence**. Similar	*Extremely rare*
3173	**One shilling and twopence**. Similar...............................	*Extremely rare*
3174	**One shilling and one penny**. Similar	*Extremely rare*
3175	**Shilling**. Similar...	5500
3176	**Elevenpence**. Similar	*Extremely rare*
3177	**Tenpence**. Similar	*Extremely rare*
3178	**Ninepence**. Similar	*Extremely rare*
3179	**Sevenpence**. Similar	*Extremely rare*
3180	**Sixpence**. Similar	*Extremely rare*

COPPER

For mintmarks see C. Wilson Peck, *English Copper, Tin and Bronze Coins in the British Museum, 1558-1958*.

3185   3191   3194

		F	VF
		£	£
3181	**Royal farthing**. 'Richmond' round, colon stops, 1a. CARO over IACO; *mm*. on *obv*..	8	22
3182	— — 1b. CARA; *mm*. on *obv*...	75	150
3183	— — 1c. CARO; *mm*. on *obv*...	5	15

		F £	*VF* £

Royal farthing.

3184	'Richmond' round apostrophe stops. 1d. Eagle-headed harp	8	22
3185	— 1e. Beaded harp	6	17
3186	— 1f. Scroll-fronted harp, 5 jewels on circlet	12	35
3187	— 1g. — — 7 jewels on circlet	6	17
3188	Transitional issue, double-arched crowns	18	50
3189	'Maltravers' round, 3a; *mm.* on *obv. only*	9	24
3190	— 3b. *Mm.* both sides	5	15
3191	— 3c. Different *mm.* either side	6	18
3192	'Richmond' oval. 4a. CARO over IACO; *mm.* both sides	18	45
3193	— — — *mm.* on *obv.*	18	45
3194	— 4b. CARO, colon stops; *mm.* on *obv.*	15	40
3195	— — — — *mm.* on *rev.*	15	40
3196	— — — — *mm.* both sides	15	40
3197	— 4c. apostrophe stops; *mm.* rose on *obv.*	18	45
3198	— — — *mm.* rose both sides	18	45
3199	— — — *mm.* rose (*obv.*); scroll (*rev.*)	18	45
3200	'Maltravers' oval. 5. CAROLVS; *mm.* lis both sides	22	50

3201   3207

3201	**Rose farthing**. 1a. Double-arched crowns; double rose; sceptres within inner circle, BRIT; *mm.* on *obv.* or *rev.* or both sides, or different each side	9	24
3202	— 1b. — — sceptres just break circle, BRIT; *mm.* on *obv.* or both sides or no *mm.*	7	20
3203	— 1c. — — sceptres almost to outer circle, BRIT; *mm.*s as 3201	6	18
3204	— 1d. — — — BRI; *mm.* on *obv.* or both sides, or different each side	6	18
3205	Transitional mules of types 1d/2, with double and single arched crowns; *mm.* as 3204	9	24
3206	— 2. Single-arched crowns; single rose; *mm.* as 3204	4	12
3207	— 3. Sceptres below crown; *mm.* mullet	18	45

The coins struck during the Commonwealth have inscriptions in English instead of Latin which was considered to savour of too much popery. St. George's cross and the Irish harp take the place of the royal arms. The silver halfpenny was issued for the last time. Coins with *mm*. anchor were struck during the protectorship of Richard Cromwell.

Mintmarks

1649-57 Sun   1658-60 Anchor

GOLD

3208   3209

		F	*VF*
		£	£
3208	**Unite.** As illustration; *mm*. sun, 1649-57	450	925
3209	Similar, *mm*. anchor, 1658, 1660	1250	2850
3210	**Double-crown.** As illus., but X; *mm*. sun, 1649-57	375	775
3211	Similar, *mm*. anchor, 1660	1200	2750
3212	**Crown.** Similar, but V; *mm*. sun, 1649-57	300	600
3213	As illus., *mm*. anchor, 1658, 60	1200	2750

SILVER

3214	**Crown.** Same type; *mm*. sun, 1649, 51-4, 56	350	675
3215	**Halfcrown.** Similar; *mm*. sun, 1649, 1651-7	125	300

3215

3216

3216	— *mm*. anchor, 1658-1660	475	975
3217	**Shilling.** Similar; *mm*. sun, 1649, 1651-7	80	175
3218	— *mm*. anchor, 1658-60	325	650
3219	**Sixpence.** Similar; *mm*. sun, 1649, 1651-7	75	160
3220	— *mm*. anchor, 1658-60	300	600
3221	**Halfgroat.**	20	55
3222	**Penny.** Similar, but I above shields	20	45
3223	**Halfpenny.**	25	50

OLIVER CROMWELL

Although often referred to as patterns, there is in fact nothing to suggest that the portrait coins of Oliver Cromwell were not intended for circulation. Authorised in 1656, the first full production came in 1657 and was followed by a second more plentiful one before Cromwell's death. All coins were machine made, struck from dies by Thomas Simon in the presses of the Frenchman, Pierre Blondeau.

GOLD

		F £	VF £	EF £
3224	**Fifty shillings**. laur. head l. R. Crowned Shield of the Protectorate, 1656. Inscribed edge			15000

3225

3225	**Broad.** of Twenty Shillings, similar, but grained edge 1656.	1650	3500	6000

SILVER

3226

3226	**Crown.** Dr. bust l. R. Crowned shield, 1658/7. Inscribed edge	700	1250	1950
3227	**Halfcrown.** Similar, 1656 different obverse legend	1000	2000	—

3227A

3227A —	1658 Similar to 3226	375	650	1200

3228

	F	VF	EF
	£	£	£
3228 **Shilling.** Similar, but grained edge, 1658	275	500	850
3229 **Sixpence.** Similar 1658...		*Extremely rare*	

COPPER

3230

3230 **Farthing.** Dr. bust l. R. CHARITIE AND CHANGE, shield	1250	3000	—

There are also other reverse types for this coin.

For the first two years after the Restoration the same denominations, apart from the silver crown, were struck as were issued during the Commonwealth although the threepence and fourpence were soon added. Then, early in 1663, the ancient hand hammering process was finally superceded by the machinery of Blondeau.

For the emergency issues struck in the name of Charles II in 1648/9, see the siege pieces of Pontefract listed under Charles I, nos. 3150-1.

Hammered coinage, 1660-2

Mintmark: Crown.

3301   3302

GOLD

		F	VF
	First issue. Without mark of value	£	£
3301	**Unite** (20s.). Type as illustration	675	1450
3302	**Double-crown.** As illustration	600	1250
3303	**Crown.** Similar	575	1200

3304

	Second issue. With mark of value		
3304	**Unite.** Type as illustration..	600	1250
3305	**Double-crown.** As illustration	475	925
3306	**Crown.** Similar	525	1050

SILVER

			F	VF
			£	£
	First issue. Without inner circles or mark of value			
3307	**Halfcrown.** Crowned bust, as 3308		550	1350

3308   3309

3308	**Shilling**. Similar	165	525
3309	**Sixpence**. Similar	135	375
3310	**Twopence**. Similar	25	70
3311	**Penny**. Similar	25	65
3312	As last, but without mintmark	25	65

3313   3322

Second issue. Without inner circles, but with mark of value

3313	**Halfcrown.** Crowned bust	675	1500
3314	**Shilling.** Similar	375	800
3315	**Sixpence.** Similar	825	1750
3316	**Twopence.** Similar, but mm. on obv. only	95	240

3310   3317   3326

3317	Similar, but mm. both sides (machine made)	15	35
3318	Bust to edge of coin, legend starts at bottom l. (machine made, single arch crown)	15	35
3319	**Penny.** As 3317	15	40
3320	As 3318 (single arch crown)	15	35

		F £	VF £
	Third issue. With inner circles and mark of value		
3321	**Halfcrown**. Crowned bust to i.c. (and rarely to edge of coin)	110	350
3322	**Shilling**. Similar	70	185
3323	**Sixpence**. Similar	65	175
3324	**Fourpence**. Similar	20	55
3325	**Threepence**. Similar	25	55
3326	**Twopence**. Similar	15	40
3327	**Penny**. Similar	20	50

Grading of Early and Later Milled Coinage

Milled coinage refers to coins that are struck by dies worked in a mechanical coining press. The early period is defined from the time of the successful installation of Peter Blondeau's hand powered machinery at the mint, initiated to strike the first portrait coins of Oliver Cromwell in 1656. The early period continuing until the advent of Matthew Boulton's steam powered presses from 1790. The coinage of this early period is therefore cruder in it's execution than the latter. When grading coins of the early peiod, we only attribute grades as high as extremely fine, and as high as uncirculated for the latter period. Most coins that occur of the early period in superior grades than those stated will command considerably higher prices, due to their rarity. We suggest the following definitions for grades of preservation:

Milled Coinage Conditions

Proof A very carefully struck coin from speciallly prepared dies, to give a superior definition to the design, with mirror-like fields. Occurs occasionally in the Early Milled Coinage, more frequently in the latter period. Some issues struck to a matt finish for Edward VII.

FDC *Fleur-de-coin*. Absolutely flawless, untouched, without wear, scratches, marks or hairlines. Generally applied to proofs.

UNC *Uncirculated*. A coin in as new condition as issued by the Mint, retaining full lustre or brilliance but, owing to modern mass-production methods of manufacture and storage, not necessarily perfect.

EF *Extremely Fine*. A coin that exhibits very little sign of circulation, with only minimal marks or faint wear, which are only evident upon very close scrutiny.

VF *Very Fine*. A coin that exhibits some wear on the raised surfaces of the design, but really has only had limited circulation.

F *Fine*. A coin that exhibits considerable wear to the raised surfaces of the design, either through circulation, or damage perhaps due to faulty striking

Fair *Fair*. A coin that exhibits wear, with the main features still distinguishable, and the legends, date and inscriptions still readable.

Poor *Poor*. A coin that exhibits considerable wear, certainly with milled coinage of no value to a collector unless it is an extremely rare date or variety.

Examples of Condition Grading

Early Milled

Gold *AV*   Silver *AR*   Copper *Æ*

Extremely Fine

Gold A̸V   Silver Æ̸R   Copper Æ

Very Fine

Fine

James II
Two Guineas

William III
Crown

George III
Halfpenny

Later Milled

Gold A̸V   Silver Æ̸R   Copper Æ

Uncirculated

Later Milled *continued*

Gold *N* Silver *R* Copper *Æ*

Extremely Fine

Very Fine

Fine

Victoria
Sovereign

Victoria
Halfcrown

George III
Twopence

Early in 1663, the ancient hand hammering process was finally superceded by the machinery of Blondeau. The Roettiers engraved the dies as a safeguard against clipping, the larger coins were made with the edge inscribed DECVS ET TVTAMEN and the regnal year. The medium-sized coins were given a grained edge.

The new gold coins were current for 100s., 20s. and 10s., and they came to be called 'guineas' as the gold from which some of them were made was imported from Guinea by the Africa Company (whose badge was the Elephant and Castle). It was not until some years later that the guinea increased in value to 21s. and more. The Africa Co. badge is also found on some silver and so is the plume symbol indicating silver from the Welsh mines. The four smallest silver denominations, though known today as 'Maundy Money', were actually issued for general circulation: at this period the silver penny was probably the only coin distributed at the royal Maundy ceremonies. Though never part of the original agreement smaller coins were eventually also struck by machinery.

A good regal copper coinage was issued for the first time in 1672, but later in the reign, farthings were struck in tin (with a copper plug) in order to help the Cornish tin industry.

GOLD

3328

Milled coinage

	F £	VF £	EF £			F £	VF £	EF £

3328 Five guineas. First laur. bust r., pointed truncation, regral date on edge in words (e.g. 1669=VICESIMO PRIMO)

	F	VF	EF			F	VF	EF
1668 VICESIMO	950	1950	4800	1675	V. SEPTIMO	950	1950	4800
1669 – PRIMO	950	1950	4800	1676	– OCTAVO	1100	2200	5200
1670 – SECVNDO	950	1950	4800	1676	– SEPTIMO	1000	2000	5000
1671 – TERTIO	1100	2200	5200	1677	– NONO	950	1950	4800
1672 – QVARTO	950	1950	4800	1678/7	– TRICESIMO	950	1950	4800
1673 – QVINTO	950	1950	4800	1678	– TRICESIMO	1000	2000	5000
1674 – SEXTO	1100	2200	5200					

3329 — with elephant below bust

	F	VF	EF			F	VF	EF
1668 VICESIMO	950	1750	4500	1675	V. SEPTIMO	1250	2500	6000
1669 – PRIMO	1250	2500	6000	1677/5	– NONO		*Extremely rare*	

3330 — with elephant and castle below

	F	VF	EF			F	VF	EF
1675 – SEPTIMO		*Extremely rare*		1678/7	– TRICESIMO	1250	2500	5500
1676 – OCTAVO	950	1950	4800	1678	TRICESIMO	1250	2500	5500
1677 – NONO	1100	2200	5200					

3331 Second laur. bust r., rounded truncation

	F	VF	EF			F	VF	EF
1678/7 TRICESIMO	1250	2200	5200	1682	T. QVARTO	950	1950	4800
1679 – PRIMO	950	1950	4800	1683	– QVINTO	950	1950	4800
1680 – SECVNDO	950	1950	4800	1684	– SEXTO	950	1950	4800
1681 – TERTIO	950	1950	4800					

	F	VF	EF			F	VF	EF
	£	£	£			£	£	£

3332 — — with elephant and castle below

1680 T. SECVNDO........		*Extremely rare*		1683	T. QVINTO .1200	2400	5500
1681 – TERTIO......1250	2200	5200		1684	– SEXTO 950	1950	4800
1682 – QVARTO 950	1950	4800					

3333   3335

3333   Two guineas. First laur. bust r., pointed truncation

| 1664 | ....550 | 1200 | 3500 | 1669 | .... | | *Extremely rare* | |
| 1665 | .... | *Extremely rare* | | 1671 | ....550 | 1250 | 3750 |

3334   Two Guineas First laur. bust r., pointed truncation, with elephant below

| 1664 | ....475 | 1000 | 3250 |

3335   Second laur. bust r., rounded truncation

1675	575	1250	3750	1680	600	1300	4000
1676	475	1000	3250	1681	475	1000	3250
1677	475	1000	3250	1682	475	1000	3250
1678/7	475	1000	3250	1683	475	1000	3250
1679	475	1000	3250	1684	525	1100	3500

3336 — with elephant and castle below

1676	475	1000	3250	1682	475	1000	3250
1677	....	*Extremely rare*		1683	600	1300	4000
1678	475	1000	3250	1684	600	1300	4000

3337 — with elephant only below, 1678 .... *Extremely rare*

Overstruck dates are listed only if commoner than the normal date or if no normal date is known.

3338   Guinea. First laur. bust r., 1663 475   1250   3000

3339 — with elephant below, 1663 425   1200   2750

3340 Second laur. bust r., 1664 375   1000   2500

3341 — with elephant below, 1664 .... *Extremely rare*

3339   3342

3342   Third laur. bust r., normal portrait

1664	300	850	2000	1669	300	875	2250
1665	275	750	1750	1670	275	750	1750
1666	275	750	1750	1671	275	750	1750
1667	275	750	1750	1672	325	925	2400
1668	275	750	1750	1673	350	975	2600

3344   3345

	F	VF	EF		F	VF	EF
	£	£	£		£	£	£

3343 — with elephant below

	F	VF	EF		F	VF	EF
1664	400	950	2500	1668		*Extremely rare*	
1665	350	875	2400				

3344 Fourth laur. bust r., rounded truncation

1672	250	625	1650	1679	225	600	1600
1673	250	625	1650	1680	225	600	1600
1674	300	800	2250	1681	280	700	2000
1675	280	700	2000	1682	250	625	1650
1676	225	600	1600	1683	225	600	1600
1677	225	600	1600	1684	250	625	1650
1678	225	600	1600				

3345 Fourth laur. bust r., with elephant and castle below

1674		*Extremely rare*		1680	450	1150	3000
1675	350	850	2250	1681	350	800	2250
1676	275	650	1750	1682	300	750	2000
1677	300	700	1850	1683	450	1150	3000
1678	350	850	2250	1684	300	750	2000
1679	350	850	2250				

3346 — — with elephant below

1677		*Extremely rare*		1678		*Extremely rare*	

3347   3348

3347 **Half-guinea.** First laur. bust r., pointed truncation

1669	280	650	2000	1671	325	750	2200
1670	250	550	1750	1672	325	750	2200

3348 Second laur. bust r., rounded truncation

1672	260	600	1900	1679	250	550	1750
1673	375	850	2500	1680	375	850	2500
1674	395	900	2750	1681	375	850	2500
1675		*Extremely rare*		1682	375	850	2500
1676	260	550	1750	1683	260	600	1900
1677	260	600	1900	1684	250	550	1750
1678	280	650	2000				

3349 **Half guinea.** Second laur. bust r., rounded truncation, with elephant and castle below

1676	425	1000	—	1681		*Extremely rare*	
1677	380	900	2750	1682	380	900	2750
1678/7	325	750	2200	1683		*Extremely rare*	
1680		*Extremely rare*		1684	280	650	2000

3350

	F	*VF*	*EF*		*F*	*VF*	*EF*
	£	£	£		£	£	£
3350 **Crown**. First dr. bust r., rose below, edge undated, 1662	75	300	1250
3351 — — edge dated, 1662	85	350	1350
3352 — no rose, edge dated, 1662	95	375	1500
3353 — — edge not dated, 1662	85	350	1500

3354 — — new reverse, shields altered, 1663, regnal year on edge in
Roman figures ANNO REGNI XV 90   375   1500

3355 Second dr. bust r., regnal year on edge in Roman figures (e.g. 1664 = XVI)

1664 edge XVI.......... 75	350	1350	1666 XVIII 75	400	1450
1665 XVII 400	900	—	1667 XVIII 1500	*Extremely rare*	

3356

3356 — — elephant below bust, 1666 XVIII 150   550   —

3357

3357 — regnal year on edge in words (e.g. 1667= DECIMO NONO)

1667 D. NONO 75	300	1330	1670 V. SECVNDO ...95	400	1350
1668 VICESIMO 60	250	1250	1671 – TERTIO 75	350	1400
1669 – PRIMO..........180	500	—			

	3358				3359		
	F	VF	EF		F	VF	EF
	£	£	£		£	£	£

3358 Crown Third dr. bust r.

	F	VF	EF		F	VF	EF
1671 V. TERTIO	70	300	1350	1676 V. OCTAVO.....70	300	1350
1671 – QVARTO............		*Extremely rare*		1677 – NONO............90	325	1750
1672 – QVARTO......	70	300	1350	1678/7 TRICESIMO.100	400	—
1673 – QVINTO.......	70	300	1350	1679 – PRIMO 75	300	1500
1674 – SEXTO		*Extremely rare*		1680/79 – SECVNDO.90	325	1450
1675/3 – SEPTIMO ..250	750	—				

3359 Fourth dr. bust r.

	F	VF	EF		F	VF	EF
1679 T. PRIMO 70	300	1250	1682/1 T. QVARTO ...60	225	1350
1680 – SECVNDO 75	300	1350	1683 – QVINTO.......250	850	—
1681 – TERTIO 75	300	1350	1684 – SEXTO 150	500	—

3360   — elephant and castle below bust, 1681 – TERTIO 1500   3500   —

3361	3362	3364

3361 Halfcrown. First dr. bust r., regnal year on edge in Roman figures

			F	VF	EF
1663 XV 65	275	1250
3362 Second dr. bust r., 1664 XVI...80	350	1750
3363 Third dr. bust r., 1666 XVIII 550	1950	—
3364 — elephant below bust, 1666 XVIII 400	850	—

3365   — regnal date on edge in words (eg. 1667=DECIMO NONO)

	F	VF	EF		F	VF	EF
1667/4 D. NONO............		*Extremely rare*		1669/4 V. PRIMO 120	375	—
1668/4 VICESIMO ...140	400	—		1670 – SECVNDO 50	200	1350

3366 Third bust variety r.

	F	VF	EF		F	VF	EF
1671 V. TERTIO 50	185	950	1672 V. QVARTO......50	200	1350

| | 3367 | | 3369 | | 3370 | |

	F	*VF*	*EF*		*F*	*VF*	*EF*
	£	£	£		£	£	£
3367 Halfcrown Fourth dr. bust r.							
1672 V. QVARTO......50	200	1000		1679 T. PRIMO..........50	185	950	
1673 – QVINTO.........50	185	950		1680 – SECVNDO ...110	325	—	
1674 – SEXTO 85	300	1500		1681 – TERTIO..........60	220	1050	
1675 – SEPTIMO 60	225	1050		1682 – QVARTO 70	275	1350	
1676 – OCTAVO........45	175	825		1683 – QVINTO.........50	200	1000	
1677 – NONO.............50	200	1000		1684/3 – SEXTO 100	375	—	
1678 TRICESIMO....140	400	—					

3368 — plume below bust
1673 V. QVINTO ...1000   —   —   1683 T. QVINTO ....   *Extremely rare*
3369 — plume below bust and in centre of *rev*., 1673 V. QVINTO .... *Extremely rare*
3370 — elephant and castle below bust, 1681 T. TERTIO..........................1350   —   —

| | 3371 | | 3372 | | 3374 | |

	F	*VF*	*EF*
3371 Shilling. First dr. bust r., 1663 50	140	400	

3372 First bust variety r.

1663 50	140	400	1668 200	450	—
1666	*Extremely rare*		1669/6	*Extremely rare*	

3373 Shilling. First bust variety r. elephant below bust, 1666 200   600   1750
3374 Guinea head, elephant below bust, 1666...600   1500   —

3375

3376

	F £	VF £	EF £		F £	VF £	EF £

3375 Shilling Second dr. bust r.

1666		*Extremely rare*		1676	65	200	500
1668	45	125	400	1677	65	200	500
1669		*Extremely rare*		1678	80	250	700
1670	80	250	700	1679	65	200	500
1671	100	325	800	1680		*Extremely rare*	
1672	65	200	550	1681	95	325	800
1673	100	325	800	1682/1	300	650	—
1674	100	325	800	1683		*Extremely rare*	
1675	125	375	—				

3376 — plume below bust and in centre of *rev.*

1671	150	450	1200	1676	165	475	1300
1673	165	475	1300	1679	200	600	1650
1674	150	450	1200	1680	275	750	1900
1675	165	475	1300				

3377 — plume *rev.* only, 1674 ....200 600 1650

3378 — plume *obv. only*

1677	200	600	1650	1679	185	550	1500

3379 — elephant and castle below bust, 1681/0 ....900 — —

3380

3381

3382

3380 Third dr. (large) bust r.

1674	200	550	1650	1675/3	150	375	1100

3381 Fourth dr. (large) bust r., older features

1683	120	275	900	1684	100	300	800

3382 Sixpence, dr. bust r.

1674	35	85	200	1680	55	150	350
1675	35	85	200	1681	35	85	165
1676	55	150	350	1682/1	40	95	225
1677	35	85	200	1683	35	85	200
1678/7	40	95	225	1684	40	95	225
1679	40	95	225				

3383 Fourpence. Undated. Crowned dr. bust l. to edge of coin, value
behind. R. Shield 6 15 30

	3384			3386	3388		3390	
	F	*VF*	*EF*			*F*	*VF*	*EF*
	£	£	£			£	£	£

3384 Fourpence Dated. *O*. As illustration 3384. R. Four interlinked Cs

1670 10	20	45	1678 6	15	30
1671 8	18	40	1679 6	15	30
1672/1 7	16	35	1680 6	15	30
1673 7	16	35	1681 6	15	30
1674 7	16	35	1682 6	15	30
1675 7	16	35	1683 6	15	30
1676 7	16	35	1684/3 6	15	30
1677 6	15	30			

3385 Threepence. Undated. As 3383 8   18   40

3386 Threepence. Dated. As illustration

1670 6	12	28	1678 6	10	25
1671 6	10	25	1679 6	10	25
1672/1 6	10	25	1680 6	10	25
1673 6	10	25	1681 6	10	25
1674 6	10	25	1682 6	10	25
1675 6	12	28	1683 6	10	25
1676 6	10	25	1684 6	10	25
1677 6	12	28			

3387 Twopence. Undated. As 3383 (double arch crown) 6   10   25

3388 Dated. As illustration

1668 8	14	30	1677 8	14	30
1670 6	10	25	1678 6	10	25
1671 6	10	25	1679 6	10	25
1672/1 6	10	25	1680 6	10	25
1673 8	14	30	1681 6	10	25
1674 6	10	25	1682 8	14	30
1675 6	10	25	1683 6	10	25
1676 6	10	25	1684 8	14	30

3389 Penny. Undated. As 3383 (double arch crown) 6   16   40

3390 Dated. As illustration

1670 8	14	35	1678 10	18	45
1671 8	14	35	1679 10	18	45
1672/1 8	14	35	1680 8	14	35
1673 8	14	35	1681 12	20	50
1674 8	14	35	1682 10	18	40
1675 8	14	35	1683 8	14	35
1676 10	18	45	1684 10	18	45
1677 8	14	35			

3391 Maundy Set. Undated. The four coins 65   125   200

	F	VF	EF		F	VF	EF
	£	£	£		£	£	£

3392 Maundy Set Dated. The four coins. Uniform dates

	F	VF	EF		F	VF	EF
1670	60	95	200	1678	70	140	250
1671	50	85	180	1679	60	95	200
1672	60	95	200	1680	50	85	180
1673	50	85	180	1681	70	140	250
1674	50	85	180	1682	60	95	200
1675	50	85	180	1683	50	85	180
1676	50	85	180	1684	50	95	200
1677	50	85	180				

COPPER AND TIN

3393

3393 Copper halfpenny Cuir. bust l.

	F	VF	EF		F	VF	EF
1672	45	125	375	1675	40	110	350
1673	35	100	325				

3394

3395

3394 Copper farthing. As illustration

	F	VF	EF		F	VF	EF
1672	35	95	250	1675	35	95	250
1673	35	95	250	1679	45	125	300
1674	45	125	300				

	Fair	F	VF	EF
	£	£	£	£

Prices for tin coinage based on corrosion free examples, and in the top grades with some lustre

3395 Tin farthing. Somewhat similar, but with copper plug, edge inscribed NUMMORVM FAMVLVS, and date on edge only

	Fair	F	VF	EF
1684	35	95	350	950
1685			*Extremely rare*	

Tin halfpence and farthings provided the only base metal coinage during this short reign. All genuine tin coins of this period have a copper plug.

GOLD

	F £	VF £	EF £		F £	VF £	EF £
3396 **Five guineas.** First laur. bust l., sceptres misplaced date on edge in							
words (e.g. 1686 = SECVNDO), 1686 SECVNDO			1300		2500	5500	
3397 — sceptres normal.							
1687 TERTIO	1000	2000	4850	1688 QVARTO	1000	2000	4850

3397A

3397A Second laur. bust l.

1687 TERTIO	1000	2000	4850	1688 QVARTO	1000	2000	4850

3398

3398 First laur. bust l. Elephant and castle below bust

1687 TERTIO	1250	2500	5500	1688 QVARTO	1250	2500	5500

3399

3399 **Two guineas.** Similar

1687	650	1800	4500	1688/7	650	1600	4750

	F £	VF £	EF £		F £	VF £	EF £
3400 **Guinea.** First laur. bust l.							
1685	275	550	1400	1686	300	750	1950
3401 — elephant and castle below							
1685	350	800	2200	1686		*Extremely rare*	
3402 Second laur. bust l.							
1686	250	500	1300	1688	275	550	1500
1687	250	500	1300				

3403

3404

	F £	VF £	EF £		F £	VF £	EF £
3403 — elephant and castle below							
1686	425	1000	2950	1688	300	600	1750
1687	300	600	1750				
3404 **Half-guinea** laur. bust l.							
1686	225	450	1450	1688	275	500	1600
1687	325	650	1900				
3405 Elephant and castle below, 1686					375	1650	—

SILVER

3406

3406 **Crown.** First dr. bust, l. date on edge in words (e.g. 1686 = SECVNDO) 1686 SECVNDO 100   400   1500

3407

	F £	*VF* £	*EF* £		*F* £	*VF* £	*EF* £

3407 Crown Second dr. bust

1687 TERTIO 90	300	675	1688 QVARTO 95	350	850

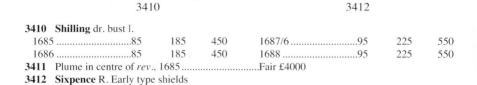

3408   1st bust   2nd bust

3408 Halfcrown. First dr. bust, l. date on edge in words (e.g. 1685 = PRIMO)

1685 PRIMO 80	195	675	1687 TERTIO 80	195	675
1686 SECVNDO 80	195	675			

3409 Second dr. bust l.

1687 TERTIO 95	250	800	1688 QVARTO 75	185	675

3410   3412

3410 Shilling dr. bust l.

1685 85	185	450	1687/6 95	225	550
1686 85	185	450	1688 95	225	550

3411 Plume in centre of *rev.*, 1685 ....Fair £4000

3412 Sixpence R. Early type shields

1686 75	175	375	1687/6 75	175	375

	3413			3414		3415	
	F £	*VF* £	*EF* £		*F* £	*VF* £	*EF* £

3413 Sixpence R. Late type shields

1687 55	160	325	1688 70	175	375

3414 Fourpence. *O.* As illus. R. IIII crowned

1686 8	15	40	1688 8	15	40
1687/6 6	12	35			

3415 Threepence. – R. III crowned

1685 5	14	35	1687/6 5	14	35
1686 5	14	35	1688 5	14	35

3416 Twopence. – R. II crowned

1686 7	14	35	1688 8	16	40
1687 7	14	35			

3416　　　　　　3417

3417 Penny. – R. I crowned

1685 8	15	40	1687 8	15	40
1686 8	15	40	1688 8	15	40

3418 Maundy Set. As last four. Uniform dates

1686 65	120	250	1688 65	120	250
1687 65	120	250			

TIN

3419

	Fair £	*F* £	*VF* £	*EF* £

Prices for tin coinage based on corrosion free examples, and in the top grades with some lustre

3419 Halfpenny. Draped bust r.; date on edge

1685 45	100	300	800
1686 55	120	350	850
1687 45	100	300	800

3420

		Fair	F	VF	EF
		£	£	£	£
3420	**Farthing.** Cuirassed bust r.; date on edge				
	1684			*Extremely rare*	
	1685 40	40	90	250	700
	1686 45	45	100	275	775
	1687			*Extremely rare*	
3421	Draped bust r.; date on edge, 1687 50	50	100	300	850

Due to the poor state of the silver coinage, much of it worn hammered coin, the guinea, which was valued at 21s. 6d. at the beginning of the reign, circulated for as much as 30s. by 1694. The tin halfpennies and farthings were replaced by copper coins in 1694. The rampant lion of Orange is now placed as an inescutcheon on the centre of the royal arms.

GOLD

3422

	F	VF	EF		F	VF	EF
	£	£	£		£	£	£

3422 Five guineas. Conjoined busts r. date on edge in words (e.g. 1691 = TERTIO)

	F	VF	EF		F	VF	EF
1691 TERTIO	950	1850	4500	1694/2 SEXTO	1000	2200	5000
1692 QVARTO	950	1850	4500	1694 SEXTO	1200	2500	5500
1693 QVINTO	950	1850	4500				

3423   3424

3423 — elephant and castle below

1691 TERTIO	1100	2250	5000	1694/2 SEXTO	1100	2500	5250
1692 QVARTO	1100	2250	5000	1694 SEXTO	1200	2750	5500
1693 QVINTO	1250	2500	5500				

3424 Two guineas. Conjoined busts r.

1693	600	1450	3250	1694/3	600	1450	3250

3425 — elephant and castle below

1691		Extremely rare		1694/3	700	1750	4000
1693	700	1750	4000				

3426 Guinea. Conjoined busts r.

1689	275	600	1750	1692	300	750	2250
1690	300	675	2000	1693	300	675	2000
1691	300	675	2000	1694	275	625	1900

3427

	F £	VF £	EF £		F £	VF £	EF £
3427 — elephant and castle below							
1689	300	675	2000	1692	300	750	2250
1690	375	850	2500	1693		*Extremely rare*	
1691	300	750	2250	1694	300	750	2250
3428 — elephant only below							
1692	375	900	2500	1693		*Extremely rare*	

Overstruck dates are listed only if commoner than the normal date or if no normal date is known.

34229   3430

3429 **Half-guinea.** First busts r. 1689		350	650	1850
3430 — Second busts r. normal portraits				
1690	250	550	1500	1693		*Extremely rare*	
1691	275	600	1750	1694	250	550	1500
1692	300	550	1600				
3431 — — elephant and castle below				
1691	225	475	1350	1692	275	600	1750
3432 — — elephant only below, 1692				*Extremely rare*

SILVER

3433

3433 **Crown.** Conjoined busts r. date on edge in words (e.g. 1691 = TERTIO)

1691 TERTIO	175	450	1250	1692/2 QVINTO	175	450	1250
1692 QVARTO	175	450	1250				

3434 3435

	F	VF	EF		F	VF	EF
	£	£	£		£	£	£

3434 Halfcrown. First busts, r. first shields, 1689 PRIMO R. Crown with caul and interior frosted with pearls 45 125 500

3435 — second shield

| 1689 PRIMO R. Caul | 55 | 160 | 550 | 1690 SECVNDO .... | 65 | 200 | 650 |
| and interior frosted with pearls | | | | 1690 TERTIO .... | 100 | 300 | 850 |

3436

3436 Second busts r. R. Crowned cruer form sheilds, WM monogram in angles

| 1691 TERTIO .... | 50 | 160 | 600 | 1692 QVINTO .... | 125 | 400 | — |
| 1692 QVARTO .... | 60 | 175 | 600 | 1693 QVINTO .... | 50 | 150 | 550 |

3437 3438

3437 Shilling. Conjoined bust r. R. Similar

| 1692 ....75 | 200 | 550 | 1693 ....70 | 200 | 500 |

3438 Sixpence. Similar

| 1693 ....70 | 150 | 300 | 1694 ....85 | 185 | 450 |

3439 Fourpence. First busts, r. no tie to wreath

| 1689 G below bust ....8 | 14 | 35 | 1691/0 ....11 | 18 | 42 |
| 1690 ....10 | 16 | 40 | 1694 ....12 | 20 | 50 |

3440 Second busts r. tie to wreath

| 1692 ....11 | 18 | 42 | 1694 ....12 | 25 | 55 |
| 1693/2 ....12 | 50 | 48 | | | |

	F £	VF £	EF £		F £	VF £	EF £
3441 Threepence. First busts, r. no tie to wreath							
1689 7		12	30	1691 30		60	100
1690 8		14	35				
3442 Second busts, r. tie to wreath							
1691 10		20	45	1693/2 9		16	40
1692 10		20	45	1694 9		16	40
3443 Twopence. Conjoined busts r.							
1689 8		14	35	1693 9		16	40
1691 8		14	35	1694 10		18	45
1692 9		16	40				
3444 Penny. Legend continuous over busts, 1689				150		275	400
3445 Legend broken by busts							
1690 14		28	65	1693 12		25	60
1691/0 12		25	60	1694 12		25	60
1692 14		28	65				

3446

3446 Maundy Set. As last pieces. Uniform dates

1689 225	425	650	1693 100	200	375
1691 85	150	300	1694 85	150	300
1692 85	150	300			

TIN AND COPPER

	Fair £	F £	VF £	EF £
Prices for tin coinage based on corrosion free examples, and in the top grades with some lustre				
3447 Tin **Halfpenny.** Small draped busts r.; date on edge 1689 ...250	500	—	—

3448

3448 Large cuirassed busts r.; date only on edge

1690 60	120	350	800
3449 — date in ex. and on edge			
1691 50	100	300	750
1692 50	100	300	750

	F £	VF £	EF £		F £	VF £	EF £

3450   Tin **Farthing.** Small draped busts r.

1689 120   300   750   —

1689, edge 1690 ....   *Extremely rare*

3451

3451   Large cuirassed busts r.

1690, edge 1689 ....   *Extremely rare*

1690 40   100   300   750

1691 40   100   300   750

1692 50   125   350   800

3452

3452   Copper **Halfpenny,** 1694   50   120   375

3453

3453   Copper **Farthing,** 1694   60   140   425

In 1696 a great re-coinage was undertaken to replace the hammered silver that made up most of the coinage in circulation, much of it being clipped and badly worn. Branch mints were set up at Bristol, Chester, Exeter, Norwich and York to help with the re-coinage. For a short time before they were finally demonetized, unclipped hammered coins were allowed to circulate freely provided they were officially pierced in the centre. Silver coins with roses between the coats of arms were made from silver obtained from the West of England mines.

GOLD

3454

	F £	VF £	EF £		F £	VF £	EF £

3454 Five guineas. First laur. bust r. date on edge in words (e.g. 1699 = UNDECIMO)

1699 UNDECIMO 975	2000	4000	1700 DVODECIMO 1100		2200	4500

3455 — elephant and castle below, 1699 UNDECIMO 1350 2950 5000

3456   3457

3456 Second laur. bust r. ('fine work'), 1701. Plain or ornamental
sceptres DECIMO TERTIO 1000 2750 4800
3457 Two guineas ('fine work'), similar 1701 ....1000 1950 3950

3458

3458 Guinea. First laur. bust r.

1695	200	500	1200	1697	225	550	1450
1696	225	550	1450				

	F	VF	EF		F	VF	EF
	£	£	£		£	£	£

3459 — elephant and castle below

| 1695 | 250 | 650 | 1750 | 1696 | | *Extremely rare* | |

3460   3463

3460 Second laur. bust, r. human-headed harp

| 1697 | 225 | 550 | 1450 | 1699 | 250 | 650 | 1750 |
| 1698 | 200 | 450 | 11000 | 1700 | 200 | 450 | 1100 |

3461 — elephant and castle below

| 1697 | 450 | 1000 | — | 1699 | | *Extremely rare* | |
| 1698 | 300 | 750 | 1850 | 1700 | 500 | 1200 | — |

3462 Second laur. bust. r. R. Human headed harp. Large lettering and

| large date, 1698 | | | | | 200 | 500 | 1100 |

3463 — R. Narrow crowns, plain or ornamented sceptres, 1701 ... 200 | 500 | 1100 |

3464 — — elephant and castle, 1701 .... | *Extremely rare* |

3465 Third laur. bust r. ('fine work'), 1701 .... 350 | 800 | 2500 |

3466   3468

3466 **Half-guinea.** R. With early harp, 1695 .... 185 | 350 | 950 |

3467 — Elephant and castle. R. With early harp

| 1695 | 275 | 650 | 1650 | 1696 | 200 | 500 | 1250 |

3468 — R. With late harp

1697	240	575	1400	1700	150	275	700
1698	150	275	700	1701	150	275	700
1699		*Extremely rare*					

3469 — elephant and castle, 1698 .... 225 | 500 | 1400 |

SILVER

3470

	F £	VF £	EF £		F £	VF £	EF £
3470 Crown. First dr. bust, r. R.First harp, date on edge in words (e.g. 1696 = OCTAVO)							
1695 SEPTIMO 60	175	500		1696 OCTAVO 50	150	450	
1695 OCTAVO 65	200	550					

3471

3471 Second dr. bust r. R. Second harp (hair across breast), 1696 (two varieties)
OCTAVO .... *Each unique*

3472

3472 Third dr. bust, r. R. First harp, 1696 OCTAVO 55   140   500
1696 TRICESIMO .... *Extremely rare*
3473 — second harp, 1697 NONO 450   1250   9500

3474

	F	VF	EF		F	VF	EF
	£	£	£		£	£	£
3474 **Crown** Third bust variety r. R. Third harp, 1700 DVODECIMO			...65			175	500
1700 D. TERTIO			...80			250	750
3475 **Halfcrown.** R. Small shields, 1696 OCTAVO			...35			90	225
3476 — B (*Bristol*) below bust, 1696 OCTAVO			...40			100	325

3477   3478

	F	VF	EF
3477 — C (*Chester*) below bust, 1696 OCTAVO ...90		250	525
3478 — E (*Exeter*) below bust, 1696 OCTAVO ...110		300	675
3479 — N (*Norwich*) below bust, 1696 OCTAVO ...55		150	325
3480 — y (*York*) below bust, 1696 OCTAVO ...90		250	525

3481

	F	VF	EF
3481 — R. Large shield, early harp, 1696 OCTAVO ...40		100	225
3482 — — B (*Bristol*) below bust, 1696 OCTAVO ...45		125	300
3483 — — C (*Chester*) below bust, 1696 OCTAVO ...55		150	325
3484 — — E (*Exeter*) below bust, 1696 OCTAVO ...65		200	425

	F	VF	EF		F	VF	EF
	£	£	£		£	£	£

3485 — — N *(Norwich)* below bust, 1696 OCTAVO ....90 | 250 | 575
3486 — — y *(York)* below bust, 1696 OCTAVO...60 | 160 | 350

3487   3488

3487 – R. Large shields, ordinary harp

1696 OCTAVO 85	250	575	1697 NONO...............40	100	225

3488 — — B *(Bristol)* below bust, 1697 NONO..40 | 110 | 300
3489 — — C *(Chester)* below bust

1696 OCTAVO 90	250	575	1697 NONO...............45	125	300

3490   3496

3490 — — E *(Exeter)* below bust

1696 OCTAVO 90	250	575	1697 NONO...............35	100	275
1696 NONO	*Extremely rare*		1697 OCTAVO	*Extremely rare*	

3491 — — N *(Norwich)* below bust

1696 OCTAVO 100	300	675	1697 OCTAVO	*Extremely rare*	
1697 NONO...............45	125	300			

3492 — — y *(York)* below bust,

1697 NONO...............35	100	275	1697 OCTAVO	*Extremely rare*	

3493 Second dr. bust r. (hair across breast), 1696 OCTAVO .... *Unique*

3494 Dr. bust R. Modified large shields

1698 DECIMO 35	90	225	1700 DVODECIMO...35	100	250
1698 OCTAVO	*Extremely rare*		1700 D. TERTIO 45	125	325
1698 UNDECIMO	*Extremely rare*		1701 D. TERTIO 45	125	325
1699 UNDECIMO 65	195	400			

3495 – Elephant and castle below bust, 1701 D. TERTIO .... *Fair* 450
3496 – R. Plumes in angles, 1701 D. TERTIO ....125 | 300 | 650

	3500			1st bust		2nd bust		
	F	*VF*	*EF*			*F*	*VF*	*EF*
	£	£	£			£	£	£

3497 Shilling. First dr. bust

1695	30	70	175	1697	18	40	95
1696	18	40	95				

3498 — B *(Bristol)* below bust

1696	30	65	150	1697	30	70	175

3499 — C *(Chester)* below bust

1696	30	70	175	1697	30	70	175

3500 — E *(Exeter)* below bust

1696	30	70	175	1697	30	70	175

3501 – N *(Norwich)* below bust

1696	30	70	175	1697	30	70	175

3502 — y *(York)* below bust

1696	30	70	175	1697	30	70	175

3503 — Y *(York)* below bust

1696	40	80	200	1697	40	80	200

3504 Second dr. bust r. (hair across breast), 1696 ....   *Unique*

	3rd bust		Chester Mint 3507		3rd bust var.		

3505 Third dr. bust r., 1697...18   40   90

3506 — B *(Bristol)* below bust, 1697 40   90   200

3507 — C *(Chester)* below bust

1696	80	200	450	1697	35	75	175

3508 — E *(Exeter)* below bust,

1696	....	*Extremely rare*		1697	40	80	200

3509 — N *(Norwich)* below bust, 1697 40   80   200

3510 — y *(York)* below bust

1696	....	*Extremely rare*		1697	40	80	200

3511 Third bust variety r.

1697	20	45	100	1698	30	70	175

3512 — B *(Bristol)* below bust, 1697 40   80   200

3513 — C *(Chester)* below bust, 1697 80   200   500

3514 — R. Plumes in angles, 1698 90   225   550

	4th bust				5th bust		
	F	*VF*	*EF*		*F*	*VF*	*EF*
	£	£	£		£	£	£

3515 Shilling Fourth dr. bust ('flaming hair') r.
1698 55   150   450   1699 55   150   450
3516 Fifth dr. bust (hair high) r.
1699 40   90   250   1701 40   90   225
1700 25   50   110
3517 — R. Plumes in angles
1699 65   150   400   1701 65   150   350

3518   3520

3518 — R. Roses in angles, 1699 80   200   450
3519 — plume below bust, 1700 850   —   —
3520 Sixpence. First dr. bust, r. early harp
1695 35   75   175   1696 12   30   65
3521 — — B below bust, 1696 15   35   75
3522 — — C below bust, 1696 30   65   135
3523 — — E below bust, 1696 35   75   175
3524 — — N below bust, 1696 30   60   120
3525 — — y below bust, 1696 20   50   100
3526 — — Y below bust, 1696 35   75   175
3527 — later harp, large crowns, 1696 45   100   225
3528 — — — B below bust
1696 40   100   225   1697 35   75   175
3529 — — — C below bust, 1697 40   100   225
3530 — — — E below bust, 1697 40   100   225
3531 — — small crowns
1696 40   80   190   1697 18   35   70

3532

3532 — — — B below bust
1696 25   65   160   1697 30   65   125

	F	VF	EF		F	VF	EF
	£	£	£		£	£	£

3533 — — — C below bust
1696 ....50 | 125 | 300 | 1697 ....25 | 55 | 120
3534 — — — E below bust, 1697 ....30 | 65 | 135
3535 — — — N below bust
1696 ....50 | 125 | 275 | 1697 ....20 | 40 | 90
3536 — — — y below bust, 1697 ....45 | 100 | 225

3537   3540

3537 Second dr. bust r.
1696 ....175 | 350 | — | 1697 ....60 | 150 | 350
3537A Third dr. bust, r. early harp, large crowns. E below bust, 1696 .... *Extremely rare*
3537B — — — Y below bust, 1696.. *Extremely rare*
3538 Third dr. bust, later harp, large crowns
1697 ....12 | 25 | 50 | 1700 ....15 | 30 | 65
1698 ....15 | 30 | 65 | 1701 ....20 | 40 | 90
1699 ....40 | 100 | 240
3539 — — B below bust, 1697..30 | 65 | 135
3540 — — C below bust, 1697..40 | 85 | 200
3541 — — E below bust, 1697 ....50 | 125 | 275
3542 Third dr. bust, r. small crowns, 1697 ....20 | 40 | 90
3543 — — C below bust, 1697..35 | 75 | 180
3544 — — E below bust, 1697 ....30 | 65 | 150
3545 — — Y below bust, 1697..45 | 100 | 250
3546 — — R. Plumes in angles
1698 ....25 | 55 | 120 | 1699 ....30 | 60 | 140
3547 — R. Roses in angles, 1699 ....45 | 100 | 225
3548 — plume below bust, 1700 ....600 | — | —
3549 **Fourpence.** R. 4 crowned
1697 .... | | *Unique* | 1700 ....11 | 18 | 45
1698 ....14 | 20 | 55 | 1701 ....14 | 20 | 55
1699 ....11 | 18 | 45 | 1702 ....10 | 18 | 40
3550 **Threepence.** R. 3 crowned
1698 ....11 | 18 | 45 | 1700 ....11 | 18 | 45
1699 ....12 | 20 | 50 | 1701 ....11 | 18 | 45
3551 **Twopence.** R. Crown to edge of coin, large figure 2
1698 ....12 | 20 | 50
3551A – R Crown within inner circle of legend, smaller figure 2
1699 ....9 | 15 | 40 | 1701 ....9 | 15 | 40
1700 ....9 | 15 | 40
3552 **Penny.** R. 1 crowned
1698 ....9 | 15 | 40 | 1700 ....10 | 16 | 45
1699 ....10 | 16 | 45 | 1701 ....9 | 15 | 40

3553

	F	VF	EF			F	VF	EF
	£	£	£			£	£	£

3553 Maundy Set. As last four. Uniform dates

1698	70	125	225		1700	85	175	300
1699	85	175	300		1701	70	125	225

COPPER

3554

3554 Halfpenny. First issue. R. Britannia with r. hand raised

1695	35	75	275		1697	25	65	225
1696	25	65	225		1698	35	85	300

3555 Second issue. R. Date in legend

1698 Stop after date	30	75	275		1699 No stop after date	25	65	225

3556 Third issue. R. Britannia with r. hand on knee

1699	25	65	225		1701	30	70	250
1700	25	65	225					

3557   3558

3557 Farthing. First issue

1695	35	95	350		1698	100	300	—
1696	30	80	325		1699	35	95	350
1697	25	70	300		1700	25	70	300

3558 Second issue. R. Date at end of legend

1698 Stop after date	40	125	450		1699 No stop after date	30	95	325

The Act of Union of 1707, which effected the unification of the ancient kingdoms of England and Scotland into a single realm, resulted in a change in the royal arms—on the after-Union coinage the English lions and Scottish lion are emblazoned per pale on the top and bottom shields. After the Union the rose in the centre of the reverse of the gold coins is replaced by the Garter star.

Following a successful Anglo-Dutch expedition against Spain, bullion seized in Vigo Bay was sent to be minted into coin, and the coins made from this metal had the word VIGO placed below the queen's bust.

GOLD

3560

Before Union with Scotland

	F	VF	EF		F	VF	EF
	£	£	£		£	£	£
3560 Five guineas Dr. bust l, date on edge in words (e.g. 1705 = QVARTO)							
1705 QVARTO	1450	2650	6500	1706 QVINTO	1250	2250	6000
3561 VIGO below bust, 1703 (Three varieties) SECVNDO	—	—	45000				

3562   3564

3562 Guinea Dr. bust l.							
1702	250	600	1750	1706	350	750	2250
1705	350	750	2250	1707	400	850	2500
3563 VIGO below bust, 1703					2500	4500	—
3564 Half-guinea Dr bust l.							
1702	250	600	1750	1705	250	600	1750
3565 VIGO below bust, 1703					1750	5000	—

3566

	F	VF	EF		F	VF	EF
	£	£	£		£	£	£

After Union with Scotland. The shields on the reverse are changed to Post-Union type

3566 Five guineas. Dr. bust, date on edge in words 1706 QVINTO 1350 2500 5500

3567   3568

3567 – R. Narrower shields, tall narrow crowns, larger rev. letters,
1709 OCTAVO 1250 2200 5200
3568 – R. Broader shields

1711 DECIMO 1250	2200	5200	1714/3 D. TERTIO .1250	2200	5200
1713 DVODECIMO 1250	2200	5200	1714 D. TERTIO 1350	2500	5500

3569

3569 Two guineas Dr. bust l.

1709 500	1000	2250	1713 500	1000	2250
1711 500	1000	2250	1714/3 600	1250	2650

3570 Guinea. First dr. bust l.

| 1707 ....250 | 500 | 1100 | 1708 .... | *Extremely rare* | |

	3571				3574		
	F	*VF*	*EF*		*F*	*VF*	*EF*
	£	£	£		£	£	£

3571 — elephant and castle below

1707	450	1000	2500

3572 Second dr. bust l.

1707		*Extremely rare*	
1708	225	450	1000

3573 — elephant and castle below

1708	450	1000	2000

3574 Third dr. bust l.

1710	220	350	950
1711	220	350	950
1712	250	500	1250

1708		*Extremely rare*	
1709	250	550	1250
1709	400	900	1750
1713	220	325	900
1714	220	325	900

3575

3575 **Half-guinea** Dr. bust l.

1707	225	500	1200	1711	225	400	950
1708	275	550	1350	1712	225	450	1200
1709	200	400	950	1713	200	400	950
1710	200	400	950	1714	200	400	950

SILVER

3576

Before Union with Scotland

3576 **Crown.** VIGO below bust, l., date on edge in words (e.g. 1703 =
TERTIO) 1703 TERTIO 175   400   1500

	3577				3578		
	F	VF	EF		F	VF	EF
	£	£	£		£	£	£

3577 – R. Plumes in angles, 1705 QVINTO 300   850   2250

3578 – R. Roses and plumes in angles

1706 QVINTO 120   300   750   1707 SEXTO 135   350   850

3579 Halfcrown. Nothing below bust or in angles on *rev*. (i.e. plain),

1703 TERTIO...350   900   —

	3580			3581		

3580 VIGO below bust, 1703 TERTIO 65   150   350

3581 – R. Plumes in angles

1704 TERTIO..............95   250   600   1705 QVINTO 75   200   500

	3582			3584		

3582 – R. Roses and plumes in angles

1706 QVINTO 50   125   300   1707 SEXTO 45   100   250

3583 Shilling. First dr. bust l. 1702 45   120   300

3584 — R. Plumes in angles, 1702 60   150   350

3585 — VIGO below bust, 1702 55   130   325

	3586			3592		

3586	**Shilling** Second dr. bust, l. VIGO below, 1703 40	100	250

3587 — plain

1704 300	600	—	1705 65	150	350

3588 — R. Plumes in angles

1704 70	175	400	1705 55	130	300

3589 — R. Roses and plumes in angles

1705 50	120	250	1707 50	120	275

3590	**Sixpence.** VIGO below dr. bust, l. 1703 25	55	100
3591	Plain, 1705...40	95	200
3592	– R. Early shields, plumes in angles, 1705...30	75	150

	3593	Early Shield	Late Shield

3593	– R. Late shields, plumes in angles, 1705 40	85	175

3594 – R. Roses and plumes in angles

1705 40	95	200	1707 30	65	125

3595 **Fourpence.** First dr. bust,l. small face, curls at back of head point downwards.
   R Small crown above the figure 4

1703 8	15	35	1704 6	12	30

3595A Second dr. bust, l. larger face, curls at back of head point upwards

1705 8	15	35	1709 6	12	30
1706 6	12	30	1710 6	12	30
1708 6	12	30			

3595B – R Large crown with pearls on arch, larger serifs on the figure 4

1710 6	12	30	1713 6	12	30

3595C Second dr. bust, but with re-engraved hair.

1710 6	12	30	1713 6	12	30

3596 **Threepence.** First dr. bust, broader, tie riband pointing outwards. R. Crowned 3

1703 10	18	40

3596A Second dr. bust, taller and narrow, tie riband pointing inwards

1704 8	15	35	1706 6	12	30
1705 8	15	35			

3596B Third dr. bust, similar to first bust but larger and hair more finely engraved

1707 6	12	30	1710 6	12	30
1708 6	12	30	1713 6	12	30
1709 6	12	30			

| | F | VF | EF | | F | VF | EF |
| | £ | £ | £ | | £ | £ | £ |

3597 Twopence. First dr. bust, as fourpence R. Crown to edge of coin, small figure 2

1703	10	15	35	1706	7	12	28
1704	6	11	26	1707	7	12	28
1705	6	11	26				

3597A Second dr. bust, as fourpence R Crown within inner circle of legend, large figure 2.

| 1708 | 6 | 11 | 26 | 1710 | 6 | 11 | 26 |
| 1709 | 8 | 14 | 30 | 1713 | 6 | 11 | 26 |

3598 Penny. R. Crowned 1

1703	10	18	40	1709	8	15	35
1705	8	15	35	1710	12	20	45
1706	8	15	35	1713	10	18	40
1708	12	20	45				

3599

3599 Maundy Set. As last four. Uniform dates

1703	65	110	200	1709	85	150	275
1705	65	110	200	1710	65	110	200
1706	55	90	175	1713	65	110	200
1708	65	110	200				

After Union with Scotland

The shields on reverse are changed to the Post-Union types. The Edinburgh coins have been included here as they are now coins of Great Britain.

3600

3600 Crown. Second dr. bust, l. E (Edinburgh) below, date on edge in wors (e.g. 1708 = SEPTIMO)

| 1707 SEXTO | 85 | 250 | 500 | 1708 SEPTIMO | 95 | 280 | 550 |

3601 — plain

| 1707 SEPTIMO | 80 | 220 | 500 | 1708 SEPTIMO | 110 | 300 | — |

3602 – R. Plumes in angles, 1708 SEPTIMO 125 325 750

3603

	F	VF	EF		F	VF	EF
	£	£	£		£	£	£

3603 **Crown** Third dr. bust. l. R. Roses and plumes, 1713 DVODECIMO ...80 · · · 300 · · · 650

3604

3604 **Halfcrown**. R. Plain, date on edge in words (e.g. 1709 = OCTAVO)

1707 SEPTIMO...........40	100	250	1709 OCTAVO 35	90	225
1708 SEPTIMO...........35	90	225	1713 DVODECIMO...40	100	250

3605 — E below bust

1707 SEXTO 35	85	225	1709 OCTAVO 175	400	—
1708 SEPTIMO...........35	85	225			

3606   3609

3606 – R. Plumes in angles, 1708 SEPTIMO ....55 · · · 140 · · · 300

3607 – R. Roses and plumes in angles

1710 NONO 50	125	350	1713 DVODECIMO...50	140	350
1712 UNDECIMO 45	110	325	1714 D. TERTIO 45	120	325

3608 **Shilling.** Second dr. bust, l. E below

1707 30	75	175	1708 60	150	325

3609 — E* below

1707 66	165	375	1708 40	95	225

	F	VF	EF		F	VF	EF
	£	£	£		£	£	£

3610 Shilling Third dr. bust. l. R. Plain.

1707	20	45	100	1709	20	45	100
1708	18	40	90	1711	80	220	475

3611 — R. Plumes in angles

1707	35	80	200	1708	30	65	150

3612 — E below

1707	30	60	140	1708	50	125	275

3613 Second dr. bust l. R. Roses and plumes, 1708 ....85 200 450

3614   3620

3614 Third dr. bust l. R. Roses and plumes

1708	40	95	225	1710	20	45	100

3615 — 'Edinburgh' bust, E* below

1707		*Extremely rare*		1709	60	140	325
1708	55	125	300				

3616 — E below, 1709 ....175 400 —

3617 Fourth dr. bust. l. R. Roses and plumes

1710	45	120	275	1713/2	25	65	175
1712	20	50	100	1714	20	50	100

3618 — plain, 1711 ....18 40 90

3619 Sixpence. Normal dr. bust. l. R. Plain

1707	18	40	85	1711	15	30	65
1708	20	45	95				

3620 — E below bust

1707	20	45	95	1708	30	60	125

3621 — E* below bust, 1708 ....30 70 165

3622 'Edinburgh' bust, l. E* below, 1708 ....35 75 175

3623

3623 Normal dr. bust. l. R. Plumes in angles

1707	18	45	100	1708	30	60	150

3624 — R. Roses and plumes in angles, 1710 ....30 70 175

COPPER

3625

3625 **Farthing,** dr. bust l. 1714 150   250   375

THE HOUSE OF HANOVER
GEORGE I, 1714-27

The coins of the first of the Hanoverian kings have the arms of the Duchy of Brunswick and Luneberg on one of the four shields, the object in the centre of the shield being the crown of Charlemagne. The King's German titles also appear, in abbreviated form, and name him 'Duke of Brunswick and Luneberg. Arch-treasurer of the Holy Roman Empire, and Elector', and on the guinea of 1714, 'Prince Elector'. A quarter-guinea was struck for the first time in 1718, but it was an inconvenient size and the issue was discontinued.

Silver coined from bullion supplied to the mint by the South Sea Company in 1723 shows the company's initials S.S.C.; similarly Welsh Copper Company bullion has the letters W.C.C. below the king's bust and plumes and an interlinked CC on the reverse. Roses and plumes together on the reverse indicate silver supplied by the Company for Smelting Pit Coale and Sea Coale.

GOLD

3626

	F	VF	EF		F	VF	EF
	£	£	£		£	£	£

3626 Five guineas laur. head r. date on edge in words (e.g. 1717 = TERTIO)

1716 SECVNDO	1400	2600	6000	1720 SEXTO	1500	2950	6500
1717 TERTIO	1500	2950	6500	1726 D. TERTIO	1400	2600	6000

3627

3627 Two guineas laur. head r.

1717	500	1100	2500	1726	400	900	2250
1720	450	1000	2500				

	3628			3630	3631	
	F	VF	EF		F	VF	EF
	£	£	£		£	£	£

3628 Guinea. First laur. head. r. R. Legend ends ET PR . EL (Prince Elector),

1714				600	1100	2300

3629 Second laur. head, r. tie with two ends, 1715 ....225 | 450 | 1000

3630 Third laur, head, r. no hair below truncation

1715	225	450	1000	1716	250	500	1150

3631 Guinea. Fourth laur. head, r. tie with loop at one end

1716	200	475	1000	1720	200	475	1000
1717	225	500	1100	1721	225	550	1250
1718		*Extremely rare*		1722	200	475	1000
1719	200	475	1000	1723	225	500	1100

3632 — elephant and castle below

1721		*Extremely rare*		1722		*Extremely rare*	

	3633				3635		

3633 Fifth (older) laur. head, r. tie with two ends

1723	225	500	1100	1726	200	450	1000
1724	225	500	1100	1727	250	600	1500
1725	225	500	1100				

3634 — elephant and castle below, 1726 ....600 | 1500 | —

3635 Half-guinea. First laur. head r.

1715	200	400	750	1721		*Extremely rare*	
1717	175	350	650	1722	175	350	650
1718	150	300	600	1723		*Extremely rare*	
1719	150	300	600	1724	200	400	750
1720	225	450	800				

3636 — elephant and castle below, 1721 .... | | *Extremely rare* | |

	3637				3638		

3637 Second (older) laur. head r.

1725	150	200	400	1727	175	300	750
1726	150	250	500				

3638 Quarter-guinea, 1718 ....60 | 100 | 200

SILVER

3639

	F £	VF £	EF £		F £	VF £	EF £

3639 Crown. R. Roses and plumes in angles, date on edge in words (e.g. 1716 = SECVNDO)

| 1716 SECVNDO | 140 | 300 | 800 | 1720/18 SEXTO | 175 | 350 | 1000 |
| 1718/6 QVINTO | 175 | 325 | 1000 | 1726 D. TERTIO | 195 | 475 | 1650 |

3640 – R. SSC (South Sea Company) in angles, 1723 DECIMO 175   375   850

3641

3641 Halfcrown. R. Angles plain (pattern only), 1715 *FDC* £4000

3642   3643

3642 – R. Roses and plumes in angles, date on edge in words (e.g. 1717 = TIRTIO)

| 1715 SECVNDO | 95 | 225 | 500 | 1720/17 SEXTO | 95 | 225 | 500 |
| 1717 TIRTIO | 120 | 275 | 600 |

3643 – R. SSC in angles, 1723 DECIMO 85   275   500

3644 R. Small roses and plumes, 1726 D. TERTIO 1250   2500   4000

	F £	VF £	EF £		F £	VF £	EF £

3645 Shilling. First dr. bust. r. R. Roses and plumes

1715	35	75	150	1720	40	85	175
1716	75	185	400	1721/0	40	95	200
1717	40	85	175	1722	40	85	175
1718	35	75	150	1723	55	125	275
1719	70	175	375				

3646 — plain (i.e. no marks either side)

| 1720 | ....35 | 75 | 150 | 1721 | ....90 | 200 | 500 |

| 3647 | | | | 3649 | | | |

3647 – R. SSC in angles, 1723 25   45   85

3648 Second dr. bust, r. bow to tie. R. Similar, 1723 30   65   150

3649 — R. Roses and plumes

1723	40	85	175	1726	380	700	—
1724	40	85	175	1727	350	650	—
1725	40	85	175				

| 3650 | | | | 3651 | | | |

3650 — W.C.C. (Welsh Copper Company) below bust

| 1723 | ....200 | 400 | 1000 | 1725 | ....200 | 400 | 1100 |
| 1724 | ....200 | 400 | 1100 | 1726 | ....200 | 400 | 1100 |

3651 Sixpence. R. Roses and plumes in angles

| 1717 | ....45 | 100 | 250 | 1720/17 | ....45 | 100 | 250 |

| 3652 | | | | 3653 | | | |

3652 – R. SSC in angles, 1723 20   40   75

3653 – R. Small roses and plumes, 1726 35   75   175

3654 Fourpence Dr. bust r. R. crowned 4

| 1717 | ....9 | 16 | 40 | 1723 | ....9 | 16 | 40 |
| 1721 | ....9 | 16 | 40 | 1727 | ....12 | 20 | 45 |

	F £	VF £	EF £		F £	VF £	EF £

3655 Threepence R. crowned 3

| 1717 | 8 | 15 | 35 | 1723 | 9 | 16 | 40 |
| 1721 | 9 | 16 | 40 | 1727 | 9 | 16 | 40 |

3656 Twopence R. crowned 2

1717	6	12	22	1726	5	10	20
1721	5	10	20	1727	8	14	25
1723	9	18	30				

3657 Penny R. crowned 1

1716	5	9	18	1725	5	9	18
1718	5	9	18	1726	8	14	25
1720	5	9	18	1727	8	14	25
1723	6	11	22				

3658

3658 Maundy Set. As last four. Uniform dates

| 1723 | 70 | 125 | 275 | 1727 | 70 | 125 | 275 |

COPPER

3659

3659 Halfpenny. 'Dump' issue

| 1717 | 25 | 70 | 275 | 1718 | 25 | 70 | 275 |

3660

3660 Second issue, second obverse, plain left shoulder strap, less hair to the right of tie knot

1719	35	85	300	1722	30	70	250
1720	25	65	225	1723	25	65	225
1721	30	70	250	1724	25	65	225

3661 3662

	F	VF	EF			F	VF	EF
	£	£	£			£	£	£
3661 Farthing. 'Dump' issue, 1717	120	300	500					
3662 Second issue								
1719	25	65	200	1722	30	75	220
1720	25	65	200	1723	30	75	220
1721	25	65	200	1724	30	75	220

Silver was coined only spasmodically by the Mint during this reign and no copper was struck after 1754. Gold coins made from bullion supplied by the East India Company bear the Company's initials. Some of the treasure seized by Admiral Anson during his circumnavigation of the globe, 1740-4, and by other privateers, was made into coin which had the word LIMA below the king's bust to celebrate the expedition's successful harassment of the Spanish colonies in the New World. Hammered gold was finally demonetized in 1733.

GOLD

3664				3663A		
F	*VF*	*EF*		*F*	*VF*	*EF*
£	£	£		£	£	£

3663 Five guineas. Young laur. head l. R. crowned shield of arms, date on edge in words (e.g. 1729 = TERTIO) 1729 TERTIO 1000   1950   4500

3663A – R. Revised shield garnish

1731 QVARTO 1000	1750	4750	1741/35 D. QVARTO 1000	2000	4750
1735 OCTAVO 1000	1750	4750	1741 D. QVARTO....950	1950	4000
1738 DVODECIMO 1000	1950	4750			

3664 — E.I.C. (East India Company) below, 1729 TERTIO 950   1950   4500

3665   3667

3665 Old laur. head, l. LIMA below, 1746 D. NONO................................1000   1950   4750

3666 — plain

1748 V. SECVNDO ..950	1850	4000	1753 V. SEXTO 950	1850	4000

3667* Two guineas. Young laur. head l. R Crown with rounded arches

1734/3 800   1750   —

3667A – R. Crown with pointed arches, new type of shield garnishing

1735 375	750	1650	1739 300	500	1100
1738 350	500	1000			

* Beware recent forgeries

3668

	F £	VF £	EF £			F £	VF £	EF £

3668* Two Guineas Intermediate laur. head l.

1739	350	500	1200		1740	375	500	1200

3669* Old laur. head l.

1748	375	700	1600		1753	475	900	2250

*Beware recent forgeries.
Overstruck dates are listed only if commoner than normal date or if no normal date is known.

3670 Guinea. First young laur. head, l. small lettering, 1727 500   1000   2500

3671   3674

3671 — larger lettering, smaller shield

1727	300	650	1800		1728	350	750	2000

3672 Second (narrower) young laur. head l.

1730	300	650	1600		1732	300	650	1600
1731	250	550	1400					

3673 — E.I.C. below

1729	450	1000	2250		1732	350	750	2000
1731	400	700	2000					

3674 — larger lettering on *obv*.

1732	275	600	1500		1736	250	550	1400
1733	200	450	1100		1737	275	600	1500
1734	200	450	1100		1738	275	600	1500
1735	225	500	1250					

3675 — — E.I.C. below, 1732..350   750   2000

3676 Intermediate laur. head l.

1739	200	450	1100		1741/39		*Extremely rare*	
1740	225	500	1250		1743		*Extremely rare*	

3677 — E.I.C. below, 1739 350   750   2000

3678 — larger lettering on *obv*., GEORGIUS

1745						275	600	1500

3678A – As last but reads GEORGIVS

1746						250	450	1100

	3679		3680			3681A		
		F	VF	EF		F	VF	EF
		£	£	£		£	£	£

3679 — LIMA below, 1745 500   1000   2750

3680 Old laur. head l.

1747	200	350	800	1753	175	275	700
1748	175	275	700	1755	200	375	850
1749	175	275	700	1756	175	250	650
1750	200	300	700	1758	150	225	600
1751	175	250	650	1759	150	225	600
1752	175	250	650	1760	175	250	650

3681 **Half-guinea**. Young laur. head. l. R First shield

1728	200	450	1250	1729	250	500	1500

3681A – R. Modified garnished shield

1730	450	1000	—	1735			?exists
1731	300	700	2000	1736	200	450	1250
1732	250	500	1500	1737		Extremely rare	
1733			?exists	1738	175	400	1000
1734	175	400	1000	1739	175	400	1000

3682 — E.I.C. below

1729	300	700	2000	1732		Extremely rare	
1730	500	1000	—	1739		Extremely rare	
1731		Extremely rare					

3683 Intermediate laur. head l.

1740	300	700	2000	1745	300	700	2000
1743		Extremely rare					

3683A As last but reads GEORGIVS, 1746 175   400   1000

	3684					3685		

3684 — LIMA below, 1745 500   1500   3000

3685 Old laur. head l.

1747	250	550	1500	1753	150	300	600
1748	150	325	700	1755	125	275	550
1749		Extremely rare		1756	125	275	550
1750	175	350	850	1758	125	275	550
1751	175	350	800	1759	120	250	500
1752	175	350	800	1760	120	250	500

SILVER

3686

	F	VF	EF		F	VF	EF
	£	£	£		£	£	£

3686 **Crown.** Young dr. bust. l. R. Roses and plumes in angles, date on edge in words (e.g. 1736 = NONO)

1732 SEXTO 100	300	650	1735 OCTAVO 100	300	650
1732 Proof, plain edge *FDC* £2500			1736 NONO...............90	300	650
1734 SEPTIMO.........120	350	800			

3687 — R. Roses in angles

1739 DVODECIMO .125	300	650	1741 D. QVARTO....100	250	600

3688

3688 Old dr. bust l. R. Roses in angles, 1743 D. SEPTIMO 100   300   600

3689 — LIMA below, 1746 D. NONO 100   300   600

3690   3691

3690 — Plain (i.e. no marks either side)

1746 Proof only, VICESIMO *FDC* £1500

1750 V. QVARTO 140	300	650	1751 V. QVARTO....160	350	700

3691 **Halfcrown.** Young dr. bust l. R. plain (pattern only), 1731 *FDC* £1950

	3692				3693	
	F	VF	EF		F	VF	EF
	£	£	£		£	£	£

3692 Halfcrown. Young dr. bust l. R. Roses and plumes, date on edge in words (e.g. 1732 = SEXTO)

1731 QVINTO 65	200	500	1735 OCTAVO 75	225	550
1732 SEXTO 65	200	500	1736 NONO...............95	250	650
1734 SEPTIMO 75	225	550			

3693 — R. Roses

1739 DVODECIMO ...50	125	350	1741 D. QVARTO.....60	150	400

3694 Old dr. bust. l. GEORGIUS R. Roses

1743 D. SEPTIMO 45	100	300	1745 D. NONO..........45	100	300

3695 — LIMA below 1745 D. NONO 35 85 175

3695A – As last but reads GEORGIVS 1746 D. NONO 35 85 175

3696

3696 — R. Plain

1746 *proof only* VICESIMO *FDC* £850

1750 V. QVARTO 65	175	450	1751 V. QVARTO......90	250	650

3697				3698		

3697 Shilling. Young dr. bust. l. R. Plumes

1727 45	125	400	1731 65	200	550

3698 — R. Roses and plumes

1727 30	75	175	1731 30	75	175
1728 40	85	200	1732 40	85	200
1729 40	85	200			

	F £	VF £	EF £		F £	VF £	EF £

3699 — larger lettering. R. Roses and plumes

1734	25	60	125	1736	25	60	125
1735	25	60	125	1737	25	60	125

3700

3701

3700 — R. plain, 1728 100   250   500

3701 — R. Roses

1739	25	55	110	1741	25	60	125

3702

3703A

3702 Old dr. bust, l. GEORGIUS R. Roses

1743	15	40	100	1747	20	60	125
1745	30	75	125				

3703 — LIMA below 1745 15   40   100

3703A – As last but reads GEORGIVS

1746	75	175	400

3704 — R. plain

1746 Proof only *FDC* £500				1751	50	125	250
1750	30	75	175	1758	15	25	40

3705

3706

3707

3705 Sixpence. Young dr. bust. l. R. Plain, 1728 60   150   300

3706 — R. Plumes, 1728 40   90   200

3707 — R. Roses and plumes

1728	20	50	100	1734	30	60	150
1731	20	50	100	1735	30	60	150
1732	20	50	100	1736	25	55	125

3708   3711

	F £	VF £	EF £		F £	VF £	EF £

3708 — R. Roses
1739 20   50   100   1741 20   50   100

3709 Old dr. bust. l. R. Roses
1743 20   50   100   1745 20   50   100

3710 — LIMA below
1745 15   35   75

3710A– As last but reads GEORGIVS
1746 10   30   70

3711 — plain
1746 *proof only FDC* £350
1750 30   65   150   1757 10   15   25
1751 35   90   200   1758 10   15   25

3712 **Fourpence.** Young dr. bust l. R. Small dome-shaped crown without pearls on arch, figure 4
1729 8   12   25   1731 8   12   25

3712A – R.Double domed crown with pearls, large figure 4
1732 8   12   25   1740 8   12   25
1735 8   12   25   1743 8   12   25
1737 8   12   25   1746 6   10   22
1739 8   12   25   1760 8   12   25

3713 **Threepence.** Young dr. bust l. R. Crowned 3, pearls on arch
1729 8   12   25

3713A – R. Ornate arch
1731 8   12   25

3713B – R. Double domed crown with pearls
1732 8   12   25   1740 6   10   22
1735 8   12   25   1743 6   10   22
1737 6   10   22   1746 6   10   22
1739 6   10   22   1760 6   10   22

3714 **Twopence.** Young dr. bust l. R. Small crown and figure 2
1729 4   9   18   1731 4   9   18

3714A Twopence. Young dr. bust l. R. Large crown and figure 2
1732 4   9   18   1743 4   9   18
1735 4   9   18   1746 4   9   18
1737 4   9   18   1756 4   9   18
1739 5   10   20   1759 4   9   18
1740 8   14   25   1760 4   9   18

3715 **Penny.** Young dr. bust l. head. R. Date over small crown and figure 1
1729 6   12   20   1731 5   10   18

3715A Penny R. Large crown dividing date

	F £	VF £	EF £		F £	VF £	EF £
1732	5	10	18	1753	4	8	16
1735	6	12	22	1754	4	8	16
1737	6	12	20	1755	4	8	16
1739	5	10	18	1756	4	8	16
1740	5	10	18	1757	4	8	16
1743	5	10	18	1758	4	8	16
1746	5	10	18	1759	4	8	16
1750	4	8	16	1760	6	12	22
1752	4	8	16				

3716

3716 Maundy Set. As last four. Uniform dates

	F £	VF £	EF £		F £	VF £	EF £
1729	45	95	175	1739	40	90	150
1731	45	95	175	1740	40	90	150
1732	40	90	150	1743	40	90	150
1735	40	90	150	1746	40	90	150
1737	40	90	150	1760	50	110	200

COPPER

3717

3717 Halfpenny. Young Cuir. bust l.

	F £	VF £	EF £		F £	VF £	EF £
1729	15	35	140	1735	12	30	120
1730	12	35	125	1736	15	40	140
1731	12	30	120	1737	15	40	140
1732	12	35	125	1738	10	25	120
1733	12	30	120	1739	12	30	120
1734	12	30	120				

3718 Old Cuir. bust l., GEORGIUS

	F £	VF £	EF £		F £	VF £	EF £
1740	10	25	100	1744	10	25	100
1742	10	25	100	1745	10	25	100
1743	10	25	100				

3719

	F £	*VF* £	*EF* £		*F* £	*VF* £	*EF* £
3719 — GEORGIVS							
1746	10	22	85	1751	10	20	85
1747	10	25	100	1752	10	20	85
1748	10	25	100	1753	10	20	85
1749	10	20	85	1754	10	25	100
1750	10	25	100				

3720   3722

	F £	*VF* £	*EF* £		*F* £	*VF* £	*EF* £
3720 **Farthing.** Young Cuir. bust l.							
1730	12	30	125	1735	10	25	100
1731	12	30	125	1736	12	30	125
1732	15	35	150	1737	10	25	100
1733	12	30	125	1739	10	25	100
1734	15	35	150				
3721 Old Cuir. bust. GEORGIUS							
1741	15	35	125	1744	10	20	95
3722 — GEORGIVS							
1746	8	20	85	1750	15	35	120
1749	15	35	120	1754	5	12	40

During the second half of the 18th century very little silver or copper was minted. In 1797 Matthew Boulton's 'cartwheels', the first copper pennies and twopences, demonstrated the improvement from the application of steam power to the coining press.

During the Napoleonic Wars bank notes came into general use when the issue of guineas was stopped between 1797 and 1813, but gold 7s. pieces were minted to relieve the shortage of smaller money. As an emergency measure Spanish 'dollars' were put into circulation for a short period after being countermarked, and in 1804 Spanish dollars were overstruck and issued as Bank of England dollars.

The transition to a 'token' silver coinage began in 1811 when the Bank of England had 3s and 1s. 6d. tokens made for general circulation. Private issues of token money in the years 1788-95 and 1811-15 helped to alleviate the shortage of regal coinage. A change over to a gold standard and a regular 'token' silver coinage came in 1816 when the Mint, which was moved from its old quarters in the Tower of London to a new site on Tower Hill, began a complete re-coinage. The guinea was replaced by a 20s. sovereign, and silver coins were made which had an intrinsic value lower than their face value. The St. George design used on the sovereign and crown was the work of Benedetto Pistrucci.

GOLD

Early coinages

3724

3723 Five guineas. Pattern only, laur. bust r.

1770 *FDC* £50,000   1777 *FDC* £50,000

1773 *FDC* £50,000

3724 Two guineas. Pattern only, laur. bust r.

1768 *FDC* £25,000   1777 *FDC* £25,000

1773 *FDC* £25,000

There are six different bust varieties for 3723 and 3724, for further details see Douglas-Morris, November 1974, lots 127-132.

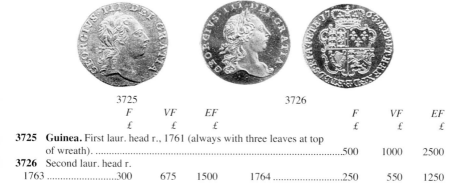

	F	VF	EF		F	VF	EF
	£	£	£		£	£	£
3725 Guinea. First laur. head r., 1761 (always with three leaves at top of wreath).	500	1000	2500				
3726 Second laur. head r.							
1763 300	675	1500		1764 250	550	1250	

3727   3728   3729

	F £	VF £	EF £		F £	VF £	EF £
3727 Guinea Third laur. head r.							
1765	130	250	475	1770	135	275	500
1766	110	200	375	1771	130	250	450
1767	150	275	600	1772	110	200	375
1768	120	220	450	1773	110	200	375
1769	120	220	450				
3728 Fourth laur. head r.							
1774	95	175	300	1781	100	200	350
1775	95	175	300	1782	100	200	350
1776	120	225	375	1783	100	200	350
1777	95	175	300	1784	100	200	350
1778	120	225	375	1785	95	175	300
1779	100	200	350	1786	95	175	300
3729 Fifth laur. head r. R. 'Spade'-shaped shield							
1787	95	175	300	1794	95	175	300
1788	95	175	300	1795	120	225	400
1789	95	175	300	1796	120	225	400
1790	95	175	300	1797	95	175	300
1791	95	175	300	1798*	95	175	300
1792	100	200	350	1799	100	180	350
1793	95	175	300	*Beware counterfeits*			

3730   3732

		F £	VF £	EF £
3730 Sixth laur. head. r. R. Shield in Garter, known as the Military guinea,				
1813		200	400	800
3731 Half-guinea. First laur. head r.				
1762	275	550	1300	1763 ....300 700 1500
3732 Second laur. head r.				
1764	100	250	550	1772 .... *Extremely rare*
1765	300	600	—	1773 ....100 250 550
1766	100	250	550	1774 ....175 400 1000
1768	100	250	550	1775 ....200 500 1200
1769	125	300	700		

3733

3734

3735

	F £	VF £	EF £		F £	VF £	EF £

3733 Half-guinea Third laur. head (less fine style) r.

1774		*Extremely rare*		1775	300	750	1750

3734 Fourth laur. head r.

1775	75	150	300	1781	80	175	400
1776	75	150	300	1783	300	800	—
1777	70	125	275	1784	75	150	300
1778	80	175	350	1785	70	125	275
1779	100	200	500	1786	70	125	275

3735 Fifth laur. head. r. R. 'Spade' shaped shield, date below

1787	70	120	250	1794	75	150	300
1788	70	120	250	1795	100	200	450
1789	85	175	350	1796	75	150	300
1790	70	120	250	1797	70	125	250
1791	75	150	300	1798	70	125	250
1792	350	850	—	1800	125	350	—
1793	70	120	250				

3736 Sixth laur. head. r. R. Shield in Garter, date below

1801	50	65	125	1803	55	75	150
1802	55	75	150				

3737 Seventh laur. head. r. with short hair. R. As last

1804	50	65	125	1809	55	75	150
1805		*Extremely rare*		1810	55	75	150
1806	55	75	150	1811	90	175	350
1808	55	75	150	1813	75	150	300

3737

3738

3739

3738 Third-guinea. First head r. R. Crown, date in legend

1797	40	55	125	1799	45	75	175
1798	40	55	125	1800	40	55	125

3739 – R. Similar but date below crown

1801	40	55	125	1803	40	55	125
1802	40	55	125				

3740   3741

	F	VF	EF		F	VF	EF
	£	£	£		£	£	£

3740 Third Guinea Second head r. with short hair, R. similar

1804	40	55	125	1810	40	55	125
1806	40	55	125	1811	150	300	700
1808	40	55	125	1813	85	175	350
1809	40	55	125				

3741 Quarter-guinea, 1762 45   75   150

For gold of the 'new coinage', 1817-20, see page 354.

SILVER

3742   3743

3742 Shilling. Young dr. bust, r. known as the 'Northumberland' shilling,
1763 125   225   400
3743 Older dr. bust, R. no semée of hearts in the Hanoverian shield, 1787 ...15   20   35
3744 — — R. no stop over head, 1787 20   25   50
3745 — — R. no stops at date, 1787 25   35   65
3745A— — R. no stops on *obv*., 1787 75   200   500

no hearts   with hearts   3747

3746 — R. with semée of hearts, 1787 15   20   35
3747 — R. no stop over head, 1798: known as the 'Dorrien and Magens' shilling *UNC* £4000
3748 Sixpence. R. Without hearts, 1787 10   14   25
3749 — R. with hearts, 1787...10   15   30

3749

3750   3751   3755

	F £	VF £	EF £		F £	VF £	EF £
3750 Fourpence. Young dr. bust r. R. Crowned 4							
1763	4	8	16	1776	4	8	16
1765	150	300	750	1780	4	8	16
1766	5	9	18	1784	5	9	18
1770	5	9	18	1786	6	10	20
1772	5	9	18				
3751 Older dr. bust. R. Thin 4 ('Wire Money'), 1792					10	20	35
3752 — R. Normal 4							
1795	5	8	16	1800	5	8	16
3753 Threepence. Young dr. bust r. R. Crowned 3							
1762	3	5	10	1772	4	7	15
1763	3	5	10	1780	4	7	15
1765	125	275	650	1784	5	9	18
1766	5	9	18	1786	4	7	15
1770	5	9	18				
3754 Older dr. bust. r. R. Thin 3 ('Wire Money'), 1792					10	20	35
3755 — R. Normal 3							
1795	5	8	15	1800	5	8	15
3756 Twopence. Young dr. bust r. R. Crowned 2							
1763	6	10	15	1776	4	8	14
1765	100	250	550	1780	4	8	14
1766	4	8	14	1784	4	8	14
1772	4	8	14	1786	3	6	12
3757 Older dr. bust. r. R. Thin 2 ('Wire Money'), 1792					10	15	30
3758 — R. Normal 2							
1795	3	6	12	1800	3	6	12
3759 Penny. Young dr. bust r. R. Crowned 1							
1763	5	9	15	1779	4	7	12
1766	4	7	12	1780	5	9	15
1770	3	5	11	1781	3	5	11
1772	4	7	12	1784	3	5	11
1776	4	7	12	1786	3	5	11
3760 Older dr. bust. r. R. Thin 1 ('Wire Money'), 1792					8	15	25
3761 — R. Normal 1							
1795	3	5	12	1800	3	5	12
3762 Maundy Set. Young dr. bust. r. Uniform dates							
1763	45	80	160	1780	45	80	160
1766	45	80	160	1784	45	80	160
1772	45	80	160	1786	45	80	160
3763 — Older dr. bust. r. R. Thin numerals ('Wire Money'), 1792					80	120	250
3764 — R. Normal numerals. Uniform dates							
1795	40	70	110	1800	35	60	95

3765A   3767   3766

Emergency issue

	F £	VF £	EF £

3765 **Dollar** Pillar type (current for 4s 9d). Spanish American 8 *reales*, oval countermark with head of George III. Mints of Mexico, Potosi & Lima..*from* 500 800 —

3765A Portrait type, oval countermark. Mints of Mexico, Potosi, Lima, Santiago, Guatemala, Madrid & Seville ....*from* 75 150 300

3766 — octagonal countermark.Mints of Mexico, Potosi, Lima, Santiago, Guatemala, Madrid & Seville ....*from* 150 350 600

3767 **Half-dollar** with similar oval countermark. Mints of Madrid, Potosi, Santiago, Madrid & Seville ....*from* 100 225 425

Also struck on Ecus of France up to Constitutional type, USA, Naples & Sicily

Bank of England issue

3768

3768 **Dollar** (current for 5s.). laur. and dr. bust of king. r. R. Britannia seated l., Several varieties occur

1804 ....65 125 300

These dollars were re-struck from Spanish-American 8 reales until at least 1811. Dollars that show dates of original coin are worth rather more.

	3769				3770	
F	*VF*	*EF*		*F*	*VF*	*EF*
£	£	£		£	£	£

3769 Three shillings. Dr and laur. bust in armour. r. R. BANK / TOKEN / 3 SHILL / date (in oak wreath)

1811	15	30	60	1812	15	30	65

3770 — Laureate head r. Top leaf between I/G R. As before but wreath of oak and laurel

1812	15	30	60	1815	15	30	60
1813	15	30	60	1816	150	300	700
1814	15	30	60				

3771   3772

3771 Eighteen pence. Dr. and laur. bust r. in armour R Bank/Token/Is. 6D./date (in oak wreath)

1811	10	20	50	1812	10	20	50

3772 — Laureate head r.

1812	10	15	40	1815	10	15	40
1813	10	15	40	1816	10	15	40
1814	10	15	40				

3773 Ninepence. Similar, 1812 (pattern only) *FDC* £800 Laureate head

COPPER

First issue — Tower Mint London

3774

3775

	F £	VF £	EF £		F £	VF £	EF £
3774 Halfpenny. Cuirassed bust r. R. Britannia							
1770	12	26	65	1773	10	26	65
1771	10	26	65	1774	14	30	80
1772	10	26	65	1775	10	26	65
3775 Farthing Similar							
1771	18	45	100	1774	12	28	70
1773	10	22	55	1775	12	28	70

3776

Second issue—Soho Mint. Birmingham 'Cartwheel' coinage

3776 Twopence. Legends incuse on raised rim, 1797	15	50	150
3777 Penny, 1797. Similar	10	30	85

Halfpence and farthings of this issue are patterns.

3777

Third issue—Soho Mint Birmingham

3778   3779

	VF £	EF £	UNC £
3778 Halfpenny. Dr. bust r., 1799 9		30	75
3779 Farthing, 1799 6		22	60

Fourth issue—Soho Mint Birmingham

3780   3782

	VF £	EF £	UNC £		VF £	EF £	UNC £
3780 Penny. Shorter haired, dr. bust r. date below							
1806 10		30	95	1807 10		35	110
3781 Halfpenny							
1806 6		25	75	1807 8		30	85
3782 Farthing							
1806 6		22	65	1807 8		28	75

Last or new coinage, 1816-20

The year 1816 is a landmark in the history of our coinage. For some years at the beginning of the 19th century Mint production was virtually confined to small gold denominations, regular full production being resumed only after the Mint had been moved from the Tower of London to a new site on Tower Hill. Steam powered minting machinery made by Boulton and Watt replaced the old hand-operated presses and these produced coins which were technically much superior to the older milled coins.

In 1816 for the first time British silver coins were produced with an intrinsic value substantially below their face value, the first official token coinage.

Our present 'silver' coins are made to the same weight standard and are still legal tender from 1816 with the exception of the halfcrown shilling and sixpence. The old guinea was replaced by a sovereign of twenty shillings in 1817, the standard of 22 carat (.916) fineness still being retained.

Engraver's and/or designer's initials:
B.P. (Benedetto Pistrucci)

GOLD

3783   3784

3783 Five pounds, 1820 (Pattern only) *FDC* £50,000

	F	VF	EF	UNC		F	VF	EF	UNC
	£	£	£	£		£	£	£	£

3784 Two pounds, 1820 (Pattern only) *FDC* £15,000

3785 Sovereign. laur. head r. coarse hair, legend type A (Descending colon after BRITANNIAR, no space between REX and F:D:). R. St. George

| 1817 | 100 | 175 | 450 | 600 | 1819 | | | | *Extremely rare* |
| 1818 | 110 | 200 | 500 | 700 | | | | | |

3785A — legend type B (Ascending colon after BRITANNIAR, space between REX and F:D:)

1818 110   200   500   700

3785B laur head r. Hair with wiry curls, legend type A. (as above)

1818 .... *Extremely rare*

3785C — legend type B. (as above)

1818 .... *Extremely rare*   1820 100   175   450   600

3785   3785A   3785C

3786

	F	VF	EF	UNC		F	VF	EF	UNC
	£	£	£	£		£	£	£	£

3786 Half-sovereign. laur head r. R. Crowned shield

1817	60	100	175	300	1820	65	110	200	350
1818	65	110	200	350					

SILVER

3787

3787 Crown. Laur. head r. R. Pistrucci's St. George and dragon within Garter

			F	VF	EF	UNC
1818, edge	LVIII		22	55	165	350
— —	LIX		22	55	165	350
1819 —	LIX		20	50	150	325
— —	LX		25	60	185	375
1820 —	LX		22	55	165	350

3788

3788 Halfcrown. Large laur. bust or 'bull' head

1816	15	35	90	200	1817	15	35	90	200

3789

	F £	VF £	EF £	UNC £			F £	VF £	EF £	UNC £
3789 Halfcrown. Small laur. head r.										
1817	15	35	90	200	1819		15	40	100	200
1818	20	40	100	225	1820		25	55	150	325

3790   3791

	F £	VF £	EF £	UNC £			F £	VF £	EF £	UNC £
3790 Shilling. laur head r. R. Shield in Garter										
1816	10	15	30	55	1819		10	18	35	80
1817	10	18	35	60	1820		10	18	35	80
1818	20	40	95	175						
3791 Sixpence. laur head r. R. Shield in Garter										
1816	6	12	22	50	1819		10	20	30	60
1817	8	15	25	55	1820		10	20	30	60
1818	10	20	30	60						

3792

	VF £	EF £	FDC £			VF £	EF £	FDC £
3792 Maundy Set (4d., 3d., 2d. and 1d.)								
1817	60	95	175	1820		60	95	175
1818	60	95	175					
3793 — fourpence, 1817, 1818, 1820				*from*			14	30
3794 — threepence, 1817, 1818, 1820				*from*			14	30
3795 — twopence, 1817, 1818, 1820				*from*			8	15
3796 — penny, 1817, 1818, 1820				*from*			8	14

The Mint resumed the coinage of copper farthings in 1821, and pennies and halfpennies in 1825. A gold two pound piece was first issued for general circulation in 1823.

Engraver's and/or designer's initials:

B. P. (Benedetto Pistrucci) W.W.P. (William Wellesley Pole)

J. B. M. (Jean Baptiste Merlen)

GOLD

3797

3797 Five pounds, 1826 Bare head l. R. Crowned Shield and mantle, inscribed edge Proof *FDC* £7500

3798

	VF £	EF £	UNC £
3798 Two pounds, 1823. Large bare head. l. R. St. George, inscribed edge .	350	550	950

3799 — 1826. Type as 3797 inscribed edge Proof *FDC* £3000

3800

	F £	VF £	EF £	UNC £		F £	VF £	EF £	UNC £
3800 Sovereign. Laur. head. l. R. St. George									
1821 95		165	425	575	1824 95		165	450	600
1822* 95		165	450	600	1825 175		400	1000	—
1823 175		400	1000	—					

Beware counterfeits.

3801   3802

| | F | VF | EF | UNC | | F | VF | EF | UNC |
| | £ | £ | £ | £ | | £ | £ | £ | £ |

3801 Sovereign. Bare head. l. R. Crowned shield

1825	95	175	350	600	1828	700	1750	4000	—
1826	95	175	350	600	1829	110	200	400	650
— Proof *FDC* £2000					1830	110	200	400	650
1827*	110	200	400	650					

Beware counterfeits

3803   3804   3804A

3802 Half-sovereign. Laur. head. l. R. Ornately garnished shield.

| 1821 | | | | 250 | 600 | 1250 | 1950 |

3803 — R. Plain shield

| 1823 | 80 | 150 | 375 | 500 | 1825 | 70 | 125 | 325 | 450 |
| 1824 | 75 | 135 | 350 | 475 | | | | | |

3804 — Bare head. l. R. Garnished shield

| 1826 | 70 | 120 | 300 | 450 | 1827 | 70 | 120 | 300 | 450 |
| — Proof *FDC* £1000 | | | | | 1828 | 65 | 110 | 275 | 425 |

3804A — with extra tuft of hair to l. ear, much heavier border

| 1826 | 70 | 120 | 300 | 450 | 1827 | 70 | 120 | 300 | 450 |
| — Proof *FDC* £1000 | | | | | 1828 | 65 | 110 | 275 | 425 |

SILVER

3805

3805 Crown. Laur. head. R. St. George

1821, edge SECUNDO	25	75	350	850
1822 — SECUNDO	30	90	400	950
— — TERTIO	27	80	350	850

3806

3806 Crown. Bare head. l. R. Shield with crest inscribed edge, 1826 Proof *FDC* £2250

3807   3808

	F	VF	EF	UNC		F	VF	EF	UNC
	£	£	£	£		£	£	£	£

3807 Halfcrown. Laur. head. l. R. Garnished shield

	F	VF	EF	UNC		F	VF	EF	UNC
1820	16	35	100	200	1823	350	950	3000	—
1821	16	35	100	200					

3808 — R. Shield in Garter and collar

	F	VF	EF	UNC		F	VF	EF	UNC
1823	20	45	125	275	1824	25	60	175	350

3809

3809 Bare head. l. R. Shield with crest

	F	VF	EF	UNC		F	VF	EF	UNC
1824	*Extremely rare*				1826 Proof *FDC* £450				
1825	20	40	90	200	1828	30	75	185	425
1826	16	35	85	200	1829	25	65	165	375

	3810				3811		3812		

	F	VF	EF	UNC		F	VF	EF	UNC
	£	£	£	£		£	£	£	£

3810 Shilling. Laur. head. l. R. Garnished shield

1821 ....10 30 70 175

3811 — R. Shield in Garter

1823 ....20 50 175 400 1825 ....18 35 85 200

1824 ....10 30 70 175

3812 Bare head l. R. Lion on crown

1825 ....10 30 60 125 1827 ....18 50 140 325

1826 ....8 20 50 100 1829 ....15 35 90 220

— Proof *FDC* £200

	3813			3814			3815	

3813 Sixpence. Laur. head. l. R. Garnished shield

1821 ....10 18 50 100

3814 — R. Shield in Garter

1824 ....10 18 50 100 1826 ....18 60 150 300

1825 ....10 18 50 100

3815 Bare head. l. R. Lion on crown

1826 ....6 15 40 85 1828 ....10 25 65 150

— Proof *FDC* £125 1829 ....10 18 50 100

1827 ....18 50 150 300

3816

	EF	FDC		EF	FDC
	£	£		£	£

3816 Maundy Set (4d., 3d., 2d. and 1d.)

1822 .... 70 130 1827 .... 60 120

1823 .... 60 120 1828 .... 60 120

1824 .... 80 140 1829 .... 60 120

1825 .... 60 120 1830 .... 60 120

1826 .... 60 120

		EF	FDC
		£	£
3817	**Maundy fourpence,** 1822-30 ....*from*	11	18
3818	**— threepence,** small head, 1822	25	40
3819	**— —** normal head, 1823-30 ....*from*	10	17
3820	**— twopence,** 1822-30 ....*from*	9	12
3821	**— penny,** 1822-30..*from*	7	10

COPPER

First issue, 1821-6

3822					3824			
	F	VF	EF	UNC		F	VF	EF	UNC
	£	£	£	£		£	£	£	£

3822 Farthing. Laur. bust, dr. l.

1821 2	8	25	60		1825 2	8	22	55
1822 2	8	22	55		1826 5	15	35	85
1823 3	10	28	65					

3823

3827

Second issue, 1825-30

3823 Penny. Laur. head. l. R. Britannia

1825 12	28	70	250		1826 Proof *FDC £225*			
1826 10	25	60	250		1827 150	300	1000	—

3824 Halfpenny. Similar

1825 120	45	100	175		1826 Proof *FDC £150*			
1826 8	20	40	85		1827 10	25	50	100

3825 Farthing. Similar

1826 2	8	20	45		1828 2	8	25	60
— Proof *FDC £125* .					1829 3	12	40	90
1827 3	8	30	70		1830 2	5	25	60

3826 Half-farthing (for use in Ceylon). Similar

1828 7	20	50	125		1830 7	20	50	125

3827 Third-farthing (for use in Malta). Similar

1827		10	25	50

Copper coins graded in this catalogue as UNC have full mint lustre.

PSI *Proof Set,* new issue, **1826.** Five pounds to farthing (11 coins) *FDC* £18000
PSIA — — Similar, including Maundy Set (15 coins) *FDC* £18500

In order to prevent confusion between the sixpence and half-sovereign the size of the latter was reduced in 1834, although the weight remained the same. The smaller gold piece was not acceptable to the public and in the following year it was made to the normal size. In 1836 the silver groat was again issued for general circulation: it is the only British silver coin which has a seated Britannia as the type. Crowns were not struck during this reign for general circulation; but proofs or patterns of this denomination were made and are greatly sought after. Silver threepences and three-halfpence were minted for use in the Colonies.

Engraver's and/or designer's initials:
W. W. (William Wyon)

GOLD

3828

3828 Two pounds, 1831 (proof only). As illus. ....*FDC* £4500

3829   3829B

	F	VF	EF	UNC		F	VF	EF	UNC
	£	£	£	£		£	£	£	£

3829 Sovereign. First bust. r. Top of ear narrow and rounded, nose to 2nd N of BRITANNIAR, fine obv. beading. R. Crowned shield.

1831 150	250	550	750	1832 125	200	525	750
— Proof *FDC* £2250							

3829A — — WW without stops

1831	*Extremely rare*

3829B Second bust. r. Top of ear broad and flat, nose to 2nd I in BRITANNIAR, coarser obv. beading.

1832* 125	195	450	675	1836 125	195	450	675
1833 125	195	450	675	1837 140	225	500	725
1835 125	195	475	700				

3830   3831

3830 Half-sovereign. Small size
1831 Proof *FDC* £1250

1834 100	185	475	750

* Beware of counterfeits

	F	VF	EF	UNC		F	VF	EF	UNC
	£	£	£	£		£	£	£	£

3831 Half-sovereign. Large size

1835	100	195	450	700	1837	100	220	500	725
1836	120	250	550	750					

3832 *Obv.* struck from 6d. die in error, 1836 ....750 1250 2750 —

SILVER

3832   3833

3833 Crown. R. Shield on mantle, 1831 (proof only) ....*FDC* £4750

ww script

3834

ww block

3834 Halfcrown. R. Shield on mantle

1831 Proof *FDC* £400					1836	20	45	110	275
1834	20	45	110	275	1837	35	100	250	600
1835	30	90	200	500					

3834A — block WW on truncation

1834	40	120	325	—

3835   3836

3835 Shilling. R. Value in wreath

1831 Proof *FDC* £250					1836	20	40	90	185
1834	15	35	80	175	1837	28	60	150	350
1835	20	40	90	185					

3836 Sixpence. R. Value in wreath

1831	10	20	50	100	1835	10	20	50	100
— Proof *FDC* £175					1836	18	40	100	175
1834	10	20	50	100	1837	15	35	95	175

3837

| | F | VF | EF | UNC | | F | VF | EF | UNC |
| | £ | £ | £ | £ | | £ | £ | £ | £ |

3837   Groat. R. Britannia seated

| 1836 | 5 | 10 | 25 | 40 | 1837 | 7 | 14 | 30 | 50 |

3838   Threepence (for use in the West Indies). As Maundy threepence but with a dull surface

| 1834 | 2 | 8 | 35 | 85 | 1836 | 2 | 8 | 35 | 85 |
| 1835 | 2 | 7 | 30 | 75 | 1837 | 7 | 15 | 50 | 100 |

3839

3839   Three-halfpence (for Colonial use). R. Value, Crowned in wreath

| 1834 | 5 | 10 | 22 | 45 | 1836 | 6 | 12 | 30 | 55 |
| 1835/4 | 6 | 12 | 30 | 55 | 1837 | 15 | 35 | 100 | 175 |

3840

| | EF | FDC | | EF | FDC |
| | £ | £ | | £ | £ |

3840   Maundy Set (4d., 3d., 2d. and 1d.).

1831	90	175	1834	85	150
— Proof *FDC* £250			1835	85	150
1832	85	150	1836	85	150
1833	85	150	1837	85	150
3841 — **fourpence,** 1831-7			*from*	11	20
3842 — **threepence,** 1831-7			*from*	20	30
3843 — **twopence,** 1831-7			*from*	8	13
3844 — **penny,** 1831-7			*from*	9	14

COPPER

3845

	F £	VF £	EF £	UNC £		F £	VF £	EF £	UNC £
3845 Penny. No initials on truncation									
1831 18	40	100	400	1834 20	50	120	425
— Proof *FDC £250*				1837 40	95	225	600
3846 W.W on truncation, 1831 25	75	175	500
3847 Halfpenny. As penny									
1831 10	20	45	100	1834 10	20	50	115
— Proof *FDC £200*				1837 8	18	40	90

3847

3848

	F	VF	EF	UNC		F	VF	EF	UNC
3848 Farthing. Similar									
1831 2	8	25	50	1835 2	8	25	50
— Proof *FDC £150*				1836 5	10	35	75
1834 2	8	25	50	1837 2	6	25	50

3849 Half-farthing (for use in Ceylon). Similar

1837 35   80   195   —

3850 Third-farthing (for use in Malta). Similar

1835 5   10   25   50

Copper coins graded in this catalogue as UNC have full mint lustre

3849

3850

PS2 *Proof* set. Coronation, **1831.** Two pounds to farthing (14 coins). *FDC £16000*

In 1849, as a first step towards decimalization, a silver florin ($^1/_{10}$ th pound) was introduced, but the coins of 1849 omitted the usual *Dei Gratia* and these so-called 'Godless' florins were replaced in 1851 by the 'Gothic' issue. The halfcrown was temporarily discontinued but was minted again from 1874 onwards. Between 1863 and 1880 reverse dies of the gold and silver coins were numbered in the course of Mint experiments into the wear of dies. The exception was the florin where the die number is on the obverse below the bust.

The gold and silver coins were redesigned for the Queen's Golden Jubilee in 1887. The double-florin which was then issued was abandoned after only four years; the Jubilee sixpence of 1887, known as the 'withdrawn' type, was changed to avoid confusion with the half-sovereign. Gold and silver were again redesigned in 1893 with an older portrait of the Queen, but the 'old head' was not used on the bronze coinage until 1895. The heavy copper penny had been replaced by the lighter bronze 'bun' penny in 1860. In 1874-6 and 1881-2 some of the bronze was made by Heaton in Birmingham, and these have a letter H below the date. From 1897 farthings were issued with a dark surface.

Early sovereigns had a shield-type reverse, but Pistrucci's St. George design was used again from 1871. In order to increase the output of gold coinage, branches of the Royal Mint were set up in Australia at Sydney and Melbourne and, later, at Perth for coining gold of imperial type.

Engraver's and/or designer's initials:

W. W. (William Wyon)	T. B. (Thomas Brock)
L. C. W. (Leonard Charles Wyon)	B. P. (Benedetto Pistrucci, d.1855)
J. E. B. (Joseph Edgar Boehm)	

GOLD

Young head coinage, 1838-87

3851

3851   Five pounds. 1839. Young filleted bust l. R. 'Una and the lion' (proof only)
varieties occur, inscribed edge   *FDC*   £18,500

3852

3852   Sovereign. Type I, first (small) young head. l. R. First shield. London mint

1838	85	225	450	750	1844	60	80	150	225
1839	125	275	900	1400	1845	60	80	150	225
— Proof *FDC* £2000					1846	60	80	150	225
1841	600	950	2750	—	1847	60	80	150	225
1842	60	80	150	225	1848	200	—	—	—
1843	60	80	150	225					

3852A	3852B	3852C
Leaves differently arranged	Narrow shield	Second large head

	F	VF	EF	UNC		F	VF	EF	UNC
	£	£	£	£		£	£	£	£

3852A — R similar but leaves of the wreath arranged differently with tops of leaves closer to crown.
1838 ....1000 — — —

3852B — narrower shield. Considerably modified floral emblems, different leaf arrangement
1843 .... *Extremely rare*

3852C Type I, second (large) head. l. W W still in relief. R. Shield with repositioned legend

	F	VF	EF	UNC		F	VF	EF	UNC
1848	55	75	120	200	1853	55	80	120	200
1849	55	75	120	200	1854	175	325	650	—
1850	55	75	125	220	1855	110	185	300	—
1851	55	75	120	200	1872	55	70	110	200
1852	55	70	110	200					

3852D	3852E	3852F/3853A
WW Incuse	Extra line in ribbon	827 on truncation

3852D — — WW incuse on truncation

	F	VF	EF	UNC		F	VF	EF	UNC
1853	90	150	275	—	1858	55	80	175	275
— Proof *FDC £5000*					1859	55	75	120	200
1854	55	75	120	200	1860	55	75	110	200
1855	55	75	110	200	1861	55	75	110	200
1856	55	75	120	200	1862	55	75	110	200
1857	55	75	110	200	1863	55	75	110	200

3852E — — As 3852D 'Ansell' ribbon. Additional raised line on the lower part of the ribbon
1859 ....125 275 950 —

3852F — — As 3852D with die number 827 on truncation
1863 ....1650 3000 — —

3853   3853B

Die number location

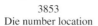

	F £	VF £	EF £	UNC £		F £	VF £	EF £	UNC £

3853 — — As 3852D R. die number in space below wreath, above floral emblem

1863	55	65	110	185	1868	55	65	110	185
1864	55	65	100	165	1869	55	65	100	165
1865	55	65	110	200	1870	55	65	125	225
1866	55	65	100	165					

3853A — — As 3853 with die number 827 on truncation R. die number is always no. 22

| 1863 | | | | | | 1500 | 2500 | — | — |

3853B — — WW in relief on truncation R. die number below wreath, above floral emblem

1870	55	65	110	185	1873	55	65	110	185
1871	55	65	100	165	1874	600	1250	3000	—
1872	55	65	100	165					

Melbourne mint mark   Sydney mint mark
3854   3855

3854 Sovereign Type I. Second (large) head. l. WW in relief R. M below wreath for Melbourne mint

1872 M	55	80	150	275	1882 M	65	90	175	275
1873 M		*Extremely rare*			1883 M	100	175	400	600
1874 M	55	80	150	300	1884 M	65	90	175	275
1879 M		*Extremely rare*			1885 M	65	90	175	275
1880 M	250	750	2500	4000	1886 M	350	1250	3000	—
1881 M	60	90	175	275	1887 M	250	600	1950	—

3855 — — As 3854 R. with S below wreath for Sydney mint

1871 S	55	65	150	300	1881 S	55	65	150	300
1872 S	55	65	150	300	1882 S	55	65	130	175
1873 S	55	65	150	300	1883 S	55	65	130	175
1875 S	55	65	150	300	1884 S	55	65	130	175
1877 S	55	65	150	300	1885 S	55	65	140	200
1878 S	55	65	150	250	1886 S	55	65	140	200
1879 S	55	65	150	250	1887 S	55	65	140	200
1880 S	55	65	150	300					

3855A Second (large) head WW incuse on truncation, R. with S below wreath for Sydney mint

| 1871 S | | | | | | 95 | 125 | 200 | 400 |

3856A
Horse with long tail

3856C
Horse with short tail

	F	VF	EF	UNC		F	VF	EF	UNC
	£	£	£	£		£	£	£	£

3856 — Type II, first young head. l. WW buried in narrow truncation. R. St. George. London mint. Horse with short tail. Large BP in ex.

1871						55	65	100	150

3856A — — As 3856 R. Horse with long tail. Small BP in ex.

1871		65	90	150	1876		65	90	225
1872		65	90	175	1878		65	90	150
1873		65	90	150	1879	110	175	600	—
1874	55	70	100	200	1880		65	90	150

3856B — — As 3856 R. Horse with short tail, small BP in ex.

1880		65	90	175	1885	55	70	100	175
1884		65	90	160					

3856C — — As 3856 R. Horse with short tail, no BP in ex.

1880						65	90	150

3856D Sovereign. Type II, second head. l. WW complete, on broad truncation. R. Horse with long tail, small BP in ex.

1880						55	65	90	150

3856E — — As 3856D R. Horse with short tail. No BP in ex.

1880						65	90	150

3856F — — As 3856E R. Horse with short tail, small BP in ex.

1880	80	100	150	185	1885	60	80	100	175
1884		70	100	150					

3857
Melbourne mint
WW buried in truncation

3857A

3857 — — First head. l. WW buried in truncation, M below head for Melbourne mint. R. Horse with long tail, small BP

1872 M	65	120	200	400	1877 M		65	135	400
1873 M	55	100	175	400	1878 M		65	135	400
1874 M	55	100	175	400	1879 M	55	65	135	300
1875 M	55	100	175	350	1880 M		65	135	400
1876 M	55	100	200	400	1881 M		65	135	400

3857A — — As 3857 R. horse with short tail, no BP in ex.

1881 M		75	150	300	1882 M		65	90	150

	VF	EF	UNC		F	VF	EF	UNC
	£	£	£		£	£	£	£

3857B— — As 3857A R. Horse with short tail, small BP in ex.

1882 M	65	90	150	1884 M		65	90	150
1883 M	65	90	150	1885 M		65	90	150

3857C— — Second head. l. WW complete on broad truncation. R. Horse with short tail, small BP in ex.

1882 M	65	90	150	1885 M		65	90	150
1883 M	65	90	180	1886 M		65	90	150
1884 M	65	90	150	1887 M		65	90	150

3858 Sovereign First head. l. WW buried in narrow truncation, S below head for Sydney mint. R. Horse   with short tail, large BP in ex.

1871 S			.75			95	150	300

3858A— — As 3858 R. Horse with long tail, small BP in ex.

1871 S	.55	95	150	300	1876 S		60	135	300
1872 S	.55	95	175	300	1877 S		*Extremely rare*		
1873 S	.55	95	175	350	1879 S	.70	100	275	750
1874 S		75	125	250	1880 S		75	150	300
1875 S		75	125	200					

3858B— — As 3858 R. Horse with long tail, no BP in ex.

1880 S	65	150	300	1881 S		65	150	300

3858C
Sydney mint
WW on broad truncation

3859
Type A1

3859A

3858C Sovereign. Second head. l. WW complete on broad truncation. R. Horse with long tail, small BP in ex.

1880 S			.55			85	150	400

3858D — — As 3858C R. Horse with short tail, no BP in ex.

1881 S	55	150	500	1882 S		55	85	125

3858E — — As 3858D R. Horse with short tail small BP in ex.

1882 S	55	85	125	1885 S		55	85	125
1883 S	55	85	125	1886 S		55	85	125
1884 S	55	85	125	1887 S		55	85	125

3859 Half-sovereign. Type A1, first (smallest) young head. l. R. First shield

1838	60	95	225	400	1850	105	225	750	—
1839 Proof only *FDC* £1100					1851		75	175	300
1841	65	100	275	450	1852	65	90	200	350
1842		75	150	275	1853		70	150	275
1843	65	100	275	450	— Proof *FDC* £3000				
1844	60	75	225	400	1854		*Extremely rare*		
1845	120	300	950	—	1855		75	160	275
1846	60	85	225	400	1856		75	160	275
1847	60	85	225	400	1857	65	90	200	350
1848	60	85	225	400	1858	65	90	200	350
1849		75	175	300					

3859A Type A2, second (larger) young head. l. R. First shield

1858		70	160	275	1861		70	160	275
1859		70	160	275	1862		750	—	—
1860		70	160	275	1863		70	160	275

| 3860 | 3860C | 3860D | 3860E |

Die number location

	F £	VF £	EF £	UNC £		F £	VF £	EF £	UNC £
3860 — As last R. die number below shield									
1863	65	90	225	400	1867		70	150	275
1864		70	150	275	1869		70	150	275
1865		70	150	275	1870	60	80	160	275
1866		70	150	275	1871		70	150	275

3860A — R. Re-engraved shield legend and rosettes closer to border, coarse boarder teeth both sides, with die number below shield

| 1870 | 85 | 200 | 550 | — | 1871 | 85 | 200 | 550 | — |

3860B — R. As last but with normal border teeth and no die number below shied

| 1871 | | | | | | | | *Extremely rare* | |

3860C — obv. with repositioned legend, nose now points to т in VICTORIA.
R Similar to last but with die number below shield

| 1871 | 105 | 225 | 650 | — | 1872 | 90 | 200 | 550 | — |

3860D Type A3, third (larger still) young head. l. R. As 3860A, with die number below shield

1872		70	150	275	1875		65	150	250
1873		70	150	275	1876		65	150	250
1874		75	150	275	1877		65	150	250

3860E Type A4, fourth young head, l. hair ribbon now narrow. R. As last with die number below shield

| 1876 | | 65 | 140 | 250 | 1878 | | 65 | 140 | 250 |
| 1877 | | 65 | 140 | 250 | 1879 | 60 | 85 | 275 | 450 |

3860F Type A5, fifth young head, l. in very low relief. R. As last with die number below shield

| 1880 | | | | | | 75 | 275 | 450 | |

| 3861 | 3862 |
| | Sydney mint |

3861 Obv. as last. R. Cross on crowned crown buried in border. Legend and rosettes very close to heavy border, no die number below shield

| 1880 | | 75 | 165 | 300 | 1884 | | 65 | 125 | 200 |
| 1883 | | 65 | 135 | 200 | 1885 | | 65 | 125 | 200 |

3862 Type A2, second (larger) young head. l. R. First shield with S below shield for Sydney mint

| 1871 S | | | | | | 70 | 175 | 600 | — |

3862A — obv. with repositioned legend, nose now points to т in VICTORIA. R Re-engraved shield, S below shield

| 1872 S | | | | | | 80 | 175 | 650 | — |

3862B Type A3, third (larger still) young head. l. R. As last

| 1875 S | | | | | | 75 | 170 | 600 | — |

	VF	EF	UNC		F	VF	EF	UNC
	£	£	£		£	£	£	£

3862C Type A4, fourth young head, l. hair ribbon now narrow. R. As last

| 1879 S | | | | | 90 | 225 | 750 | — |

3862D Type A5, fifth young head, l. in low relief. R as last.

| 1882 S | 600 | — | — | 1883 S | 85 | 170 | 675 | — |

3862E — R. Cross on crown buried in border. Legend and rosettes very close to heavy border, S below shield

1880 S	80	225	850	—	1883 S	80	115	650	—
1881 S	100	275	850	—	1886 S	70	165	650	—
1882 S	225	600	—	—	1887 S	70	175	800	—

Melbourne mint
3863

3863 Type A3, third (larger still) young head. l. R. Re-engraved shield with M below shield for Melbourne mint

| 1873 M | 90 | 140 | 650 | — | 1877 M | 75 | 200 | 850 | — |

3863A Type A4, fourth young head. l. hair ribbon now narrow. R. As last

| 1877 M | 70 | 200 | 850 | — | 1882 M | 90 | 180 | 750 | — |

3863B Type A5, fifth young head, l. in low relief. R. As last

1881 M	150	300	900	—	1885 M	150	450	1500	—
1882 M	90	150	750	—	1886 M	90	250	1000	—
1884 M	110	200	750	—	1887 M	125	500	—	—

Jubilee coinage, 1887-93

3864

3864* Five pounds. R. St. George 1887 400   500   600   750
  — Proof *FDC* £2250

3864A* R. St George, S on ground for Sydney mint 1887S .... *Extremely rare*

* Beware recent forgeries

3865   3866

	VF £	EF £	UNC £		F £	VF £	EF £	UNC £

3865* Two pounds. Similar 1887 ....150 | 200 | 275 | 350
— Proof *FDC* £800

3865A* R. St George, S on ground for Sydney mint 1887S.......... *Extremely rare*

3866* Sovereign. Normal JEB designer's initials on truncation. R. St. George. London mint

1887 .... 55 80 110   1888 .... 55 80 110

3866A with tiny designer's initials on truncation

1887 .... *Extremely rare*

3866B Repositioned legend. G: of D:G: now closer to crown. Normal JEB initials on truncation

1887 Proof *FDC* £550 .   1889 .... 55 80 110

1888 .... 55 80 110   1890 .... 55 80 110

3866C Obv. as last. R. Horse with longer tail

1891 .... 55 80 110   1892 .... 55 80 110

3867   3869
Melbourne Mint

3867 With small spread designer's initials on truncation. R. M on ground for Melbourne mint

1887M 55 120 200

3867A With normal designer's initials on truncation 1887M 55 80 110

3867B Repositioned legend. G: of D: G: now closer to crown. Normal initials on truncation

1887M .... 55 80 110   1889M 55 80 110

1888M .... 55 80 110   1890M 55 80 110

3867C Obv. as last. R. Horse with longer tail

1891M .... 55 80 110   1893M 55 80 110

1892M 55 80 110

3868 With small spread initials on truncation. R. S on ground for Sydney mint

1887S 175 400 700

3868A With normal designer's initials on truncation 1888S 60 95 125

3868B Repositioned legend. G: of D:G: now closer to crown. Normal initials on truncation

1888S .... 60 95 125   1890S 55 80 110

1889S 55 80 110

3868C Obv. as last. R. Horse with longer tail

1891S .... 55 80 110   1893S 55 80 110

1892S 55 80 110

3869 Half-sovereign. Obv. normal JEB. on truncation R. High Shield

1887 .... 60 85   1890 .... 125 250 —

— Proof *FDC* £225

* *Beware recent forgeries*

	VF	EF	UNC		F	VF	EF	UNC
	£	£	£		£	£	£	£

3869A Small close JEB. on truncation R. High shield 1887 .... 125 250 —

3869B Normal JEB. on truncation R. Lower shield, date therefore spread apart

1890 .... 125 250 — 1892 .... 125 200 —

3869C Half-sovereign. No JEB on truncation. R. High Shield

1887 .... 125 250 — 1891 .... 125 250 —

1890 .... BV 60 85 1892 .... 125 250 —

3869D As last. R. Lower Shield, date therefore spread apart

1890 .... BV 60 85 1892 .... BV 60 85

1891 .... BV 80 110 1893 .... BV 90 120

3870 Small very spread JEB on truncation. R. High shield, M below for Melbourne mint

1887M 100 150 350 750

3870A Small close JEB on truncation. R. As last

1887M 100 150 350 750

3870B Normal JEB on truncation. R. Lower shield, date therefore spread apart

1893M ....110 195 450 —

3871 Small very spread JEB on truncation. R. High shield S below for Sydney mint

1887S ....95 150 400 —

3871A Small close JEB on truncation. R As last.

1887S ....95 150 400 —

3871B Normal JEB on truncation. R. Lower shield, date therefore spread apart,
     S below for Sydney mint

1889S ....95 150 350 —

3871C Normal JEB on truncation R. High shield, S below for Sydney mint

1891S 95 150 400 750

3871D No JEB initials on truncation. R. As last

1891S 95 150 400 750

Old head coinage, 1893-1901

3872

3872* Five pounds. R. St. George

1893 ....395 675 975 1250

— Proof *FDC* £2750

* Beware recent forgeries

3873   3874

	F	VF	EF	UNC		F	VF	EF	UNC
	£	£	£	£		£	£	£	£

3873* Two pounds. Similar

1893 ....150 250 400 550

— Proof *FDC* £1000

3874 Sovereign. R. St. George, London mint

1893	85	1898	75
— Proof *FDC* £600		1899	75
1894	75	1900	75
1895	75	1901	75
1896	75		

3875 — R. St. George. M on ground for Melbourne mint

1893 M	75	1898 M	75
1894 M	75	1899 M	75
1895 M	75	1900 M	75
1896 M	75	1901 M	75
1897 M	75		

* beware recent forgeries

3876   3877
Perth mint mark   Sydney mint mark

3876 Sovereign. R. St. George, P on ground for Perth mint

1899 P 110	200	1901 P	120
1900 P	120		

3877 — — S on ground for Sydney mint

1893 S	75	1898 S	75
1894 S	75	1899 S	75
1895 S	75	1900 S	75
1896 S	95	1901 S	75
1897 S	75		

3878

	F £	VF £	EF £	UNC £		F £	VF £	EF £	UNC £

3878 Half-sovereign. R. St. George. London mint

	F	VF	EF	UNC		F	VF	EF	UNC
1893			60	85	1897			60	85
— Proof *FDC* £450					1898			60	85
1894			60	85	1899			60	85
1895			60	85	1900			60	85
1896			60	85	1901			60	85

3879 — — M on ground for Melbourne mint

1893 M	750	—	—	—	1899 M	70	125	450	—
1896 M	70	125	450	—	1900 M	70	125	450	—

3880 — — P on ground for Perth mint

1899 P		Proof only *unique*			1900 P	300	500	—	—

3881 — — S on ground for Sydney mint

1893 S	60	120	300	—	1900 S		80	350	—
1897 S	55	90	250	—					

SILVER

Young head coinage

3882

3882 Crown. Young head. l. R. Crowned shield, date on edge in Roman figures (eg 1847 = XI)

	F	VF	EF	UNC
1839 Proof only *FDC* £3000				
1844 Star stops VIII	30	95	550	1200
1844 Cinquefoil stops VIII	30	95	550	1200
1845 Star stops VIII	30	95	550	1200
1847 XI	35	120	650	1500

	3883					3885 Type 'A'		
F	VF	EF	UNC		F	VF	EF	UNC
£	£	£	£		£	£	£	£

3883*'Gothic' type, as illustration; inscribed edge,
mdcccxlvii=1847 Undecimo 200   375   550   1250
— Proof, Plain edge *FDC* £1650

*Beware of recent forgeries.

3884 — — mdcccliii=1853. SEPTIMO on edge Proof *FDC* £4500

3885 Halfcrown. Type A[1]. Young head l. with one ornate and one plain fillet binding hair. WW in relief on truncation,

1839   250   600   2000   1839 Proof plain edge.   *FDC* £600

3886 Halfcrown Type A[2] Similar, but two ornate fillets. — 1839 Proof *FDC* £1500

3886A Type A2/3 Similar, Two plain fillets, WW relief plain edge Proof *FDC* £2500

3887 — Type A[3]. Two plain fillets. WW incuse on truncation

| 1839 | ....300 | 650 | 2500 | — | 1840 | ....30 | 75 | 275 | 450 |

3888 — Type A[4]. Similar but no initials on truncation

1841	85	275	750	1250	1846	20	50	200	350
1842	25	75	250	450	1848/6	60	150	500	1000
1843	30	100	350	600	1849 large date	30	80	300	500
1844	20	50	200	350	1850	25	70	300	550
1845	20	50	200	350	1853 Proof *FDC* £1000				

3889   3890

3889 — Type A[5]. As last but design of inferior workmanship

1874	12	25	75	150	1881	12	25	75	150
1875	12	25	75	150	1882	15	30	90	175
1876	15	30	90	175	1883	12	25	75	150
1877	12	25	75	150	1884	12	25	75	150
1878	12	25	75	150	1885	12	25	75	150
1879	15	35	110	200	1886	12	25	75	150
1880	12	25	80	150	1887	15	30	90	175

3890 Florin, 'Godless' type A (i.e. without D.G.),
1848 Plain edge (Pattern) *FDC* £550

| 1849 | ....18 | 35 | 85 | 175 |

	F £	VF £	EF £	UNC £		F £	VF £	EF £	UNC £

3891 'Gothic' type B[1]. Reads brit:, WW below bust, date at end of obverse legend in gothic numerals (1851 to 1863)

	F	VF	EF	UNC		F	VF	EF	UNC
mdcccli		*Extremely rare*			mdccclvii	18	45	110	200
mdccclii	18	40	100	175	mdccclviii	18	45	110	200
mdcccliii	18	40	100	175	mdccclix	18	45	110	200
— Proof *FDC £1100*					mdccclx	20	50	135	225
mdcccliv	225	500	1750	—	mdccclxii	35	120	300	600
mdccclv	18	45	110	200	mdccclxiii	55	200	650	1000
mdccclvi	20	50	135	225					

3892

3892 — type B[2]. As last but die number below bust (1864 to 1867)

	F	VF	EF	UNC		F	VF	EF	UNC
mdccclxiv	18	45	110	200	mdccclxvi	20	50	135	225
mdccclxv	18	45	110	200	mdccclxvii	18	70	175	275

3893 Florin, 'Gothic' type B[3]. Reads britt:, die number below bust (1868 to 1879)

	F	VF	EF	UNC		F	VF	EF	UNC
mdccclxviii	20	50	135	225	mdccclxxiv	18	45	110	200
mdccclxix	18	45	110	200	mdccclxxv	18	45	110	200
mdccclxx	18	45	110	200	mdccclxxvi	18	45	110	200
mdccclxxi	18	45	110	200	mdccclxxvii	18	45	110	200
mdccclxxii	18	40	75	150	mdccclxxix		*Extremely rare*		
mdccclxxiii	18	40	75	150					

3894 — type B[4]. As last but with border of 48 arcs and no WW below bust

	F	VF	EF	UNC
1877 mdccclxxvii		*Extremely rare*		

3895 — type B[5]. Similar but 42 arcs (1867, 1877 and 1878)

	F	VF	EF	UNC		F	VF	EF	UNC
mdccclxvii		*Extremely rare*			mdccclxxviii	18	45	110	200
mdccclxxvii	18	45	110	200					

3896 — type B[5/6]. As last but no die number below bust (1877, 1879)

	F	VF	EF	UNC		F	VF	EF	UNC
mdccclxxvii		*Extremely rare*			mdccclxxix		*Extremely rare*		

3897 — type B[6]. Reads britt:, WW; 48 arcs (1879)

	F	VF	EF	UNC
mdccclxxix	15	45	110	200

3898 — type B[7]. As last but no WW, 38 arcs (1879)

	F	VF	EF	UNC
mdccclxxix	15	45	110	200

3899 — type B[3/8]. As next but younger portrait (1880)

	F	VF	EF	UNC
mdccclxxx		*Extremely rare*		

3900 — type B[8]. Similar but 34 arcs (1880 to 1887)

	F	VF	EF	UNC		F	VF	EF	UNC
mdccclxxx	18	45	110	200	mdccclxxxiv	18	40	95	175
mdccclxxxi	18	40	95	175	mdccclxxxv	18	40	95	175
mdccclxxxiii	18	40	95	175	mdccclxxxvi	18	40	95	175

3901 — type B[9]. Similar but 46 arcs

	F	VF	EF	UNC
1887 mdccclxxxvii	15	40	140	225

3902 Shilling. Type A[1]. First head l., WW on truncation

	F	VF	EF	UNC		F	VF	EF	UNC
1838	10	20	75	135	1839	10	20	75	135

F	VF	EF	UNC		F	VF	EF	UNC
£	£	£	£		£	£	£	£

3903 — Type A². Second head, l. WW (proof only), 1839 *FDC £225*

3904

3904 — Type A³. Second head, l. no initials on truncation

1839	10	20	65	125	1853	10	20	50	85
1840	15	40	110	180	— Proof *FDC £400*				
1841	15	40	110	180	1854	50	150	450	800
1842	10	20	55	100	1855	10	20	50	100
1843	15	30	85	140	1856	10	20	50	100
1844	10	20	55	100	1857	10	20	50	100
1845	10	20	65	120	1858	10	20	50	100
1846	10	20	55	100	1859	10	20	50	100
1848 over 6	35	85	400	600	1860	15	25	80	135
1849	15	25	70	120	1861	15	25	80	135
1850	120	400	950	—	1862	20	40	110	175
1851	30	85	250	400	1863	25	60	225	400
1852	10	20	55	100					

3905 — Type A⁴. As last, R. Die number above date

1864	10	20	50	100	1866	10	20	50	100
1865	10	20	50	100	1867	10	20	55	110

3906   Die number location

3906 Shilling. Type A⁶. Third head, l. R. Die number above date

1867	45	100	450	—	1874	8	18	35	75
1868	10	25	50	90	1875	8	18	35	75
1869	18	35	70	140	1876	12	30	55	110
1870	18	35	70	140	1877	8	18	35	75
1871	8	18	35	75	1878	8	18	35	75
1872	8	18	35	75	1879	25	60	175	300
1873	8	18	35	75					

3907 — Type A⁷. Fourth head, l. R. No die number above date

1879	10	20	50	85	1884	8	15	27	60
1880	8	15	27	60	1885	8	12	25	55
1881	8	15	27	60	1886	8	12	25	55
1882	15	40	80	135	1887	10	25	60	110
1883	8	15	27	60					

	F £	VF £	EF £	UNC £			F £	VF £	EF £	UNC £

3908 Sixpence. Type A[1]. First head l.

| 1838 | 8 | 15 | 40 | 65 |
| 1839 | 8 | 15 | 40 | 65 |
| — Proof *FDC* £175 |
1840	8	15	45	75
1841	8	18	50	100
1842	8	15	40	85
1843	8	15	40	85
1844 Small 44	6	14	35	75
1845	7	15	40	85
1846	6	14	35	75
1848	30	75	300	450
1850	7	15	40	85
1851	7	15	40	85

| 1852 | 4 | 12 | 40 | 70 |
| 1853 | 6 | 14 | 35 | 60 |
| — Proof *FDC* £300 |
1854	50	120	400	700
1855	6	14	35	75
1856	7	15	40	85
1857	7	15	40	85
1858	7	15	40	85
1859	6	14	35	75
1860	7	15	40	85
1862	30	70	275	400
1863	18	40	175	300
1866		*Extremely rare*

3909
Die number location

3912

3909 — Type A[2]. First head; R. die number above date

| 1864 | 7 | 15 | 40 | 85 |
| 1865 | 8 | 18 | 50 | 100 |

| 1866 | 7 | 15 | 40 | 85 |

3910 — Type A[3]. Second head; l. R. die number above date

1867	10	18	55	110
1868	10	18	55	110
1869	10	20	80	150
1870	10	20	80	150
1871	7	15	40	85
1872	7	15	40	85
1873	5	12	35	75

1874	5	12	35	75
1875	5	12	35	75
1876	10	18	60	125
1877	5	12	35	75
1878	5	12	35	75
1879	10	18	60	125

3911 Sixpence. Type A[4]. Second head; l. No die number

| 1871 | 8 | 16 | 50 | 90 |
| 1877 | 7 | 15 | 40 | 75 |

| 1879 | 7 | 15 | 40 | 75 |
| 1880 | 8 | 16 | 50 | 90 |

3912 — Type A[5]. Third head l.

1880	5	10	22	40
1881	5	10	20	35
1882	10	25	60	110
1883	5	10	20	35

1884	5	10	20	35
1885	5	10	20	35
1886	5	10	20	35
1887	4	8	18	30

3913

	F £	VF £	EF £	UNC £		F £	VF £	EF £	UNC £

3913 Groat (4d.). R. Britannia seated

1838	2	8	22	40	1847/6 (or 8)	25	75	225	—
1839	3	9	28	45	1848	3	9	25	45
1839 die axis ↑↑ Proof *FDC* £125					1849	3	9	25	45
1840	3	9	25	45	1851	20	65	175	300
1841	4	10	35	55	1852	35	90	250	400
1842	4	10	32	55	1853	40	100	300	450
1843	4	10	32	55	— Proof *FDC* £300 milled edge				
1844	4	10	32	55	1854	3	9	25	45
1845	4	10	32	55	1855	3	9	25	45
1846	4	10	32	55					

Threepence. R. Crowned 3; as Maundy threepence but with a less prooflike surface

3914 Type A¹. First bust, young head, high relief, ear fully visible.

R Tie ribbon closer to tooth border, cross on crown further from tooth border, figure 3

1838*	5	10	40	75	1850	3	5	35	55
1839*	5	15	60	120	1851	5	9	45	80
— Proof (see Maundy)					1852*		—	375	—
1840*	5	14	55	100	1853	10	20	75	150
1841*	5	14	55	100	1854	4	9	45	80
1842*	5	14	55	100	1855	5	15	60	120
1843*	5	10	40	75	1856	5	10	40	75
1844*	5	14	55	100	1857	5	14	55	100
1845	3	5	30	60	1858	5	10	40	75
1846	10	20	75	150	1859	5	10	40	75
1847*		—	400	700	1860	5	14	55	100
1848*		—	375	—	1861	5	10	40	75
1849	5	15	60	120					

*Issued for Colonial use only.

3914	3914A	3914C	3914D

3914A — Type A². First bust variety, slightly older portrait with aquiline nose

1859	5	10	40	75	1864	5	10	40	75
1860	5	10	40	75	1865	5	14	55	100
1861	5	10	40	75	1866	5	10	40	75
1862	5	10	40	75	1867	5	10	40	75
1863	5	14	55	100	1868	5	10	40	75

3914B — Type A³. Second Bust, slightly larger, lower relief, mouth fuller, nose more pronounced, rounded truncation

| 1867 | | | | | | 5 | 15 | 60 | 120 |

	F	VF	EF	UNC			F	VF	EF	UNC
	£	£	£	£			£	£	£	£

3914C Threepence Type A⁴. Obv. as last. R. Tie ribbon further from tooth border, cross on crown nearer to tooth border

1867	5	14	55	100	1874	3	8	25	45
1868	5	15	60	120	1875	3	8	25	45
1869	10	20	70	125	1876	3	8	25	45
1870	4	12	45	75	1877	4	10	35	55
1871	5	14	50	90	1878	4	10	35	55
1872	5	14	50	90	1879	4	10	35	55
1873	3	8	25	45	1884	3	6	20	40

3914D — Type A⁵. Third bust, older features, mouth closed, hair strands leading from 'bun' vary

1880	4	10	35	55	1885	3	6	20	40
1881	3	6	20	40	1886	3	6	20	40
1882	5	10	45	85	1887	4	10	35	55
1883	3	6	20	40					

3914E Twopence Young head. R Date divided by a crowned 2 within a wreath

1838	3	7	12	20	1848	5	10	18	35

3915 Three-halfpence (for Colonial use). R. Value, etc.

1838	5	12	25	45	1842	5	14	30	60
1839	4	10	20	40	1843	3	6	15	35
1840	8	22	65	100	1860	6	18	50	85
1841	5	14	30	60	1862	6	18	50	85

3916

	EF	FDC			EF	FDC
	£	£			£	£

3916 Maundy Set (4d., 3d., 2d. and 1.)

1838	50	85	1858	45	85
1839	50	85	1859	45	85
— Proof *FDC* £250			1860	45	75
1840	50	85	1861	45	75
1841	60	100	1862	45	75
1842	50	85	1863	45	75
1843	50	85	1864	45	75
1844	50	85	1865	45	75
1845	50	85	1866	45	75
1846	50	85	1867	45	75
1847	50	85	1868	45	75
1848	50	85	1869	45	75
1849	60	100	1870	40	65
1850	50	85	1871	40	65
1851	50	85	1872	40	65
1852	50	85	1873	40	65
1853	50	85	1874	40	65
— Proof *FDC* £350			1875	40	65
1854	45	85	1876	40	65
1855	60	100	1877	40	65
1856	45	85	1878	40	65
1857	45	85	1879	40	65

	EF	FDC		EF	FDC
	£	£		£	£

3916 Maundy Set (4d., 3d., 2d. and 1.)

1880	40	65	1884	40	65
1881	40	65	1885	40	65
1882	40	65	1886	40	65
1883	40	65	1887	45	85

3917 — **fourpence**, 1838-87 ......*from*	6	10
3918 — **threepence**, 1838-87 ......*from*	12	22
3919 — **twopence**, 1838-87 ......*from*	6	10
3920 — **penny**, 1838-87 ......*from*	5	8

Maundy Sets in the original dated cases are worth approximately £10, and £5 for undated cases more than the prices quoted.

Jubilee Coinage 1887-93

3921

	F	VF	EF	UNC		F	VF	EF	UNC
	£	£	£	£		£	£	£	£

3921 Crown. R. St. George

1887	15	25	40	75	1890	15	30	60	95
— Proof *FDC* £375					1891	15	30	65	120
1888 narrow date	15	30	60	95	1892	20	40	80	150
1889	15	25	40	75					

3922

3922 Double-florin (4s.). R. Cruciform shields. Roman I in date

1887	12	20	30	50

3923 — R. Similar but Arabic 1 in date

1887	12	20	30	50	1889	12	20	30	55
— Proof *FDC* £175					1890	12	20	35	60
1888	12	20	35	60					

3924   3925

	F	VF	EF	UNC		F	VF	EF	UNC
	£	£	£	£		£	£	£	£

3924 Halfcrown. R. Shield in garter and collar

1887	7	12	20	40	1890	10	18	45	70
— Proof *FDC* £100					1891	10	18	45	70
1888	10	15	35	60	1892	10	18	45	70
1889	10	15	35	60					

3925 Florin. R. Cruciform shields, sceptres in angles

1887	5	8	15	25	1890	10	25	60	120
— Proof *FDC* £75					1891	20	50	125	250
1888	6	12	22	35	1892	20	45	110	220
1889	6	12	24	40					

3926   3927

3926 Shilling. Small head. R. Shield in Garter

1887	3	5	10	18	1888	5	9	18	30
— Proof *FDC* £55					1889	35	90	300	450

3927 Large head. R. As before

1889	5	9	25	40	1891	5	10	35	50
1890	5	10	30	45	1892	5	10	35	50

3928   3929   3930

3928 Sixpence. JEB below truncation, R. Shield in Garter (withdrawn type)

1887	2	5	10	15
—Proof *FDC* £40				

3929 — R. Value in wreath

1887	2	5	10	15	1891	5	10	18	35
1888	4	8	15	25	1892	5	10	18	35
1889	4	8	15	25	1893	100	350	1000	1500
1890	4	8	16	30					

	F £	VF £	EF £	UNC £		F £	VF £	EF £	UNC £
3930 Groat (for use in British Guiana). R. Britannia seated									
1888				...8		20	35	60	
3931 Threepence. As Maunday but less prooflike surface									
1887	—	1	3	7	1890	1	3	7	12
— Proof *FDC* £30					1891	1	3	7	12
1888	2	5	12	20	1892	2	5	12	20
1889	1	3	7	12	1893	15	40	95	175

3932

	EF £	FDC £		EF £	FDC £
3932 Maundy Set (4d., 3d., 2d. and 1d.)					
1888	45	70	1891	45	70
1889	45	70	1892	45	70
1890	45	70			
3933 — fourpence, 1888-92 ....*from*			9	13	
3934 — threepence, 1888-92 ....*from*			10	20	
3935 — twopence, 1888-92 ....*from*			5	10	
3936 — penny, 1888-92 ....*from*			5	10	

Maundy Sets in the original dated cases are worth approximately £10 and £5 for undated cases more than the prices quoted.

Old head coinage 1893-1901

3937

	F	VF	EF	UNC
	£	£	£	£

3937 Crown. R. St. George. Regnal date on edge

1893 edge LVI	15	30	90	150
— — Proof *FDC* £400				
— — LVII	25	60	150	300
1894 — LVII	15	40	120	225
— — LVIII	15	40	120	225
1895 — LVIII	15	35	100	200
— — LIX	15	35	100	200
1896 — LIX	18	50	135	250
— — LX	15	35	100	200
1897 — LX	15	35	100	200
— — LXI	15	35	100	200
1898 — LXI	25	60	150	300
— — LXII	15	40	115	225
1899 — LXII	15	40	115	225
— — LXIII	15	40	115	225
1900 — LXIII	15	35	100	200
— — LXIV	15	35	100	200

3938

3938 Halfcrown. R. Shield in collar

	F	VF	EF	UNC		F	VF	EF	UNC
	£	£	£	£		£	£	£	£
1893	8	15	25	50	1897	8	15	25	50
— Proof *FDC* £120					1898	9	16	30	60
1894	10	18	45	85	1899	9	16	30	60
1895	9	16	30	60	1900	8	15	25	50
1896	9	16	30	60	1901	8	15	25	50

3939

	F £	VF £	EF £	UNC £		F £	VF £	EF £	UNC £

3939 Florin. R. Three shields within Garter

	F	VF	EF	UNC		F	VF	EF	UNC
1893	5	10	25	45	1897	6	12	25	50
— Proof *FDC* £95					1898	6	12	30	60
1894	8	16	45	80	1899	6	12	25	50
1895	7	15	35	60	1900	6	12	25	50
1896	6	12	25	50	1901	5	10	25	45

3940A   3941

3940 Shilling. R. Three shields within Garter, small rose

	F	VF	EF	UNC		F	VF	EF	UNC
1893	4	8	15	30	1894	5	10	20	45
— Proof *FDC* £65									

3940A Second reverse, large rose

	F	VF	EF	UNC		F	VF	EF	UNC
1895	4	9	18	40	1899	4	9	20	40
1896	4	9	18	35	1900	4	9	18	35
1897	4	9	18	35	1901	4	9	15	30
1898	4	9	18	35					

3941 Sixpence. R. Value in wreath

	F	VF	EF	UNC		F	VF	EF	UNC
1893	3	6	12	25	1897	4	8	12	25
— Proof *FDC* £45					1898	4	8	12	25
1894	5	10	16	30	1899	4	8	14	25
1895	4	8	12	25	1900	4	8	12	20
1896	4	8	12	25	1901	4	8	12	20

3942 Threepence. R. Crowned 3. As Maundy but less prooflike surface

	F	VF	EF	UNC		F	VF	EF	UNC
1893	1	2	4	8	1897	1	2	5	10
— Proof *FDC* £35					1898	1	2	5	10
1894	1	3	7	15	1899	1	2	4	8
1895	1	3	7	15	1900	1	2	4	8
1896	1	2	5	10	1901	1	2	4	8

3943

	EF	FDC			EF	FDC
	£	£			£	£
3943 Maundy Set (4d., 3d., 2d. and 1d.)						
1893	35	55		1898	35	55
1894	35	55		1899	45	60
1895	35	55		1900	35	55
1896	35	55		1901	35	55
1897	35	55				

			EF	FDC
3944 — fourpence, 1893-1901		*from*	5	9
3945 — threepence, 1893-1901		*from*	10	17
3946 — twopence, 1893-1901		*from*	5	8
3947 — penny, 1893-1901		*from*	5	8

Maundy Sets in the original dated cases are worth approximately £5 more than the prices quoted.

3948

Young head copper coinage, 1838-60

3948 Penny. R. Britannia

	F	VF	EF	UNC		F	VF	EF	UNC
	£	£	£	£		£	£	£	£
1839 Bronzed proof *FDC* £275					1853	5	12	30	60
1841	5	10	25	60	— Proof *FDC* £275				
1843	35	100	400	—	1854	5	12	30	60
1844	10	15	40	80	1855	5	12	30	60
1845	15	25	75	150	1856	25	50	125	350
1846	10	20	55	120	1857	5	10	30	60
1847	8	15	40	80	1858	5	10	30	60
1848/7	5	15	35	75	1859	5	10	30	60
1849	50	150	450	—	1860/59*	175	450	950	—
1851	10	20	55	120					

These 1860 large copper pieces not to be confused with the smaller and commoner bronze issue with date on reverse (nos. 3954, 3956 and 3958).

3949

	F £	VF £	EF £	UNC £		F £	VF £	EF £	UNC £
3949 Halfpenny. R. Britannia									
1838	5	10	20	50	1852	8	15	30	75
1839 Bronzed proof *FDC* £150					1853	3	6	12	30
1841	4	8	14	45	— Proof *FDC* £150				
1843	20	40	70	200	1854	3	6	12	30
1844	6	12	25	60	1855	3	6	12	30
1845	50	95	300	—	1856	5	10	25	65
1846	8	15	30	75	1857	4	8	15	40
1847	8	15	30	75	1858	5	10	18	55
1848/7	8	15	30	75	1859	5	10	18	55
1851	5	10	25	65	1860*		—	2750	—

Overstruck dates are listed only if commoner than normal date, or if no normal date is known.

3950

	F £	VF £	EF £	UNC £		F £	VF £	EF £	UNC £
3950 Farthing. R. Britannia									
1838	5	10	20	45	1850	5	10	25	50
1839	4	8	20	40	1851	10	20	45	95
— Bronzed proof *FDC* £120					1852	10	20	45	95
1840	4	8	20	40	1853	5	10	25	50
1841	4	8	20	40	— Proof *FDC* £275				
1842	15	35	85	150	1854	5	10	25	50
1843	4	8	20	40	1855	5	10	25	55
1844	45	100	250	—	1856	8	20	40	85
1845	5	10	25	50	1857	5	10	25	50
1846	8	15	40	80	1858	5	10	25	50
1847	5	10	25	50	1859	10	20	45	95
1848	5	10	25	50	1860*	—	—	3000	—
1849	30	60	150	—					

These 1860 large copper pieces not to be confused with the smaller and commoner bronze issue with date on reverse (nos. 3954, 3956 and 3958).

| | 3951 | | | | | 3952 | | | | 3953 |

	F £	VF £	EF £	UNC £			F £	VF £	EF £	UNC £
3951 Half-farthing. R. Value										
1839	.5	10	25	45		1852	.4	10	30	45
1842	.5	10	25	45		1853	.5	15	40	75
1843		5	10	20		— Proof *FDC* £250				
1844		3	8	18		1854	.8	25	65	100
1847	.4	8	20	35		1856	.8	25	65	100
1851	.5	10	30	45						

3952 Third-farthing (for use in Malta). R. Britannia

| 1844 | | | | | | | 20 | 35 | 75 | 120 |

3953 Quarter-farthing (for use in Ceylon). R. Value

1839	10	18	35	55		1853	10	20	40	65
1851	10	20	40	65		— Proof *FDC* £700				
1852	10	18	35	55						

Copper coins graded in this catalogue as UNC have full mint lustre.

Bronze coinage, 'bun head' issue, 1860-95

3954

3954 Penny. R. Britannia

		F	VF	EF	UNC			F	VF	EF	UNC
1860	.2	10	35	75		1878	.3	15	50	140
1861	.2	10	35	75		1879	.2	7	25	65
1862	.2	10	35	75		1880	.3	15	65	120
1863	.2	10	35	75		1881	.4	15	50	140
1864	20	75	250	500		1882*		*Extremely rare*		
1865	.8	20	65	150		1883	.3	10	35	75
1866	.5	15	45	95		1884	.2	8	25	50
1867	.8	25	65	150		1885	.2	8	25	50
1868	15	35	100	275		1886	.2	10	25	60
1869	50	175	400	950		1887	.2	8	25	50
1870	.8	25	75	175		1888	.2	10	25	60
1871	25	75	250	400		1889	.2	8	20	50
1872	.5	15	40	95		1890	.2	8	20	50
1873	.5	15	40	95		1891	.2	7	18	45
1874	.5	15	55	140		1892	.2	8	20	50
1875	.2	10	35	85		1893	.2	8	20	50
1877	.2	10	35	85		1894	.3	15	40	80

* not to be confused with Heaton mint (see over page)

H mint mark location
3955

3956

	F	VF	EF	UNC		F	VF	EF	UNC
	£	£	£	£		£	£	£	£

3955 Penny. R. Britannia, H mint mark below date – (struck by Ralph Heaton & Sons, Birmingham)

1874 H	5	20	50	100	1881 H	3	15	35	80
1875 H	35	95	300	—	1882 H	2	10	25	60
1876 H	2	15	35	75					

3956 Halfpenny. R. Britannia

1860	1	5	20	45	1878	3	15	50	150
1861	1	5	20	45	1879	1	5	20	50
1862	1	4	15	40	1880	2	7	30	75
1863	2	6	35	80	1881	2	7	30	75
1864	2	10	40	90	1883	1	7	30	75
1865	3	15	50	150	1884	1	4	15	40
1866	2	10	40	90	1885	1	4	15	40
1867	3	15	50	150	1886	1	4	15	40
1868	2	10	45	100	1887	1	4	12	35
1869	10	40	150	275	1888	1	4	15	40
1870	2	8	35	80	1889	1	4	15	40
1871	15	50	175	300	1890	1	4	12	35
1872	2	7	30	75	1891	1	4	12	35
1873	2	10	40	90	1892	1	6	30	70
1874	5	25	85	225	1893	1	4	15	40
1875	1	6	30	70	1894	1	7	30	70
1877	1	6	30	70					

3957 — R. Britannia, H below date

1874 H	1	5	30	60	1881 H	1	5	30	60
1875 H	2	6	35	80	1882 H	1	5	30	60
1876 H	1	5	30	60					

3958   3960

	F £	VF £	EF £	UNC £		F £	VF £	EF £	UNC £
3958 Farthing. R. Britannia									
1860		3	15	30	1879			10	20
1861		3	18	35	1880		3	20	40
1862		3	18	35	1881		2	10	25
1863	20	45	125	300	1883	2	10	30	60
1864		5	25	50	1884			8	18
1865		3	18	35	1885			8	18
1866		3	15	30	1886			8	18
1867		4	20	45	1887		2	12	25
1868		4	20	45	1888			10	20
1869		10	30	70	1890			10	20
1872		3	18	35	1891			8	18
1873		2	12	35	1892	2	10	30	60
1875	10	20	50	100	1893			8	18
1877 Proof only £2000					1894			10	20
1878			10	20	1895	10	20	50	100

Bronze coins graded in this catalogue as UNC have full mint lustre

3959 — R. Britannia. H below date									
1874 H	2	5	15	35	1881 H	2	5	12	30
1875 H		2	8	15	1882 H	2	5	12	30
1876 H	5	10	30	60					
3960 Third-farthing (for use in Malta). R. Value									
1866	1	3	10	25	1881	2	4	12	30
1868	1	3	10	25	1884	1	3	10	25
1876	2	4	12	30	1885	1	3	10	25
1878	1	3	10	25					

Old head issue, 1885-1901

3961

3961 Penny. R. Britannia									
1895		2	6	30	1899		2	5	25
1896		2	5	25	1900			3	10
1897		2	5	25	1901			2	8
1898		3	10	35					

3961 'High Tide'
Horizon is level with folds in robe

3961A 'Low Tide'
Horizon is level with hem line of robe

	VF £	EF £	UNC £		VF £	EF £	UNC £
3961A Penny. As last but 'Low tide', 1895					35	125	250
3962 Halfpenny. Type as Penny. R. Britannia							
1895	2	6	15	1899		5	12
1896	2	5	12	1900		3	6
1897	2	5	12	1901		2	5
1898	2	5	12				
3963 Farthing. R. Britannia. Bright finish							
1895	2	5	10	1897	2	5	12
1896	2	5	10				

3962   3964

3964 — Dark finish							
1897	2	5	10	1900	1	4	9
1898	2	5	9	1901		2	5
1899	2	5	9				

Proof Sets

PS3	Young head, **1839.** 'Una and the Lion' Five Pounds, and Sovereign to Farthing (15 coins)	*FDC*	£27,500
PS4	— **1853.** Sovereign to Quarter-Farthing, including Gothic type Crown (16 coins)	*FDC*	£22,500
PS5	Jubilee head. Golden Jubilee, **1887.** Five pounds to Threepence (11 coins)	*FDC*	£5,500
PS6	— — **1887.** Crown to Threepence (7 coins)	*FDC*	£950
PS7	Old head, **1893.** Five Pounds to Threepence (10 coins)	*FDC*	£6,500
PS8	— — **1893.** Crown to Threepence (6 coins)	*FDC*	£1000

EDWARD VII, 1901-10

Five pound pieces, two pound pieces and crowns were only issued in 1902. A branch of the Royal Mint was opened at Ottawa and coined sovereigns of imperial type from 1908.

Unlike the coins in most other proof sets, the proofs issued for the Coronation in 1902 have a matt surface in place of the more usual brilliant finish.

Designer's initials: De S. (G. W. De Saulles)
              B. P. (Benedetto Pistrucci, d. 1855)

GOLD

3965

	VF	EF	UNC
	£	£	£

3965	**Five pounds.** 1902. R. St. George	450	550	750
3966	— Proof. 1902. *Matt surface FDC* £750			
3966A	— Proof 1902S. S on ground for Sydney mint		*Extremely rare*	

3967   3969

	EF	UNC
	£	£

3967	**Two pounds.** 1902. Similar	175	250	300
3968	— Proof. 1902. *Matt surface FDC* £300			
3968A	— Proof 1902S. S on ground for Sydney mint		*Extremely rare*	

3969 Sovereign. R . St. George. London mint

1902 Matt proof *FDC* £120		1906		75
1902	75	1907		75
1903	75	1908		75
1904	75	1909		75
1905	75	1910		75

3970 — C on ground for Ottawa mint

1908 C (Satin proof only) *FDC* £2750			1910 C	100	200
1909 C	100	200			

	UNC £			UNC £

3971 Sovereign. R. St. George M on ground for Melbourne mint

1902 M	75	1907 M		75
1903 M	75	1908 M		75
1904 M	75	1909 M		75
1905 M	75	1910 M		75
1906 M	75			

3972 — P on ground for Perth mint

1902 P	75	1907 P		75
1903 P	75	1908 P		75
1904 P	75	1909 P		75
1905 P	75	1910 P		75
1906 P	75			

3973 — S on ground for Sydney mint

1902 S	75	1906 S		75
— Proof	*Extremely rare*	1907 S		75
1903 S	75	1908 S		75
1904 S	75	1909 S		75
1905 S	75	1910 S		75

3974

	VF £	EF £	UNC £		VF £	EF £	UNC £

3974 Half-sovereign. R. St. George. London mint

1902 Matt proof *FDC £80*				1906		45	55
1902		45	55	1907		45	55
1903		45	55	1908		45	55
1904		45	55	1909		45	55
1905		45	55	1910		45	55

3975 — M on ground for Melbourne mint

1906 M	55	80	175	1908 M	55	80	200
1907 M	55	80	175	1909 M	55	80	175

3976 — P on ground for Perth mint

1904 P	175	550	—	1909 P	140	400	—
1908 P	175	600	—				

3977 — S on ground for Sydney mint

1902 S	60	125	250	1906 S	55	110	175
— Proof		*Extremely rare*		1908 S	55	110	175
1903 S	55	110	175	1910 S	55	110	175

SILVER

3978

	F £	VF £	EF £	UNC £
3978 Crown. R. St. George				
1902 25		50	75	100

3979 — *matt proof FDC £100*

3980

	F £	VF £	EF £	UNC £

3980 Halfcrown. R. Shield in Garter

	F	VF	EF	UNC			F	VF	EF	UNC
1902	8	15	35	60		1906	15	35	90	200
— Matt proof *FDC* £60						1907	15	35	90	200
1903	60	140	400	800		1908	20	45	150	275
1904	40	100	300	600		1909	15	35	100	225
1905*	150	350	750	1250		1910	10	25	75	150

3981 Florin. R. Britannia standing

	F	VF	EF	UNC			F	VF	EF	UNC
1902	5	10	35	55		1906	10	25	75	150
— Matt proof *FDC* £50						1907	10	30	85	200
1903	10	25	75	150		1908	15	40	125	250
1904	12	30	85	200		1909	15	40	100	225
1905	40	95	300	500		1910	10	20	60	100

*Beware of recent forgeries.

| | 3981 | | | 3982 | | | | 3983 |

	F £	VF £	EF £	UNC £		F £	VF £	EF £	UNC £

3982 Shilling. R. Lion on crown

1902	3	8	25	40	1906	5	10	30	65
— Matt proof *FDC* £35					1907	5	10	35	75
1903	8	20	65	150	1908	10	20	65	175
1904	8	15	55	100	1909	10	20	65	175
1905	50	150	375	750	1910	3	10	25	45

3983 Sixpence. R. Value in wreath

1902	3	5	20	30	1906	4	10	25	50
— Matt proof *FDC* £30					1907	5	10	30	55
1903	4	10	25	50	1908	5	12	35	65
1904	6	15	40	80	1909	4	10	30	55
1905	5	12	30	65	1910	3	5	20	30

3984 Threepence. As Maundy but dull finish

1902	2	5	10		1907	1	7	25	45
1903	1	7	25	45	1908	1	2	10	25
1904	3	7	35	60	1909	1	7	25	45
1905	2	7	25	45	1910		1	10	30
1906	2	7	25	45					

3985

	EF £	FDC £		EF £	FDC £

3985 Maundy Set (4d., 3d., 2d. and 1d.)

1902	35	50	1906	35	50
— Matt proof *FDC* £60			1907	35	50
1903	35	50	1908	35	50
1904	35	50	1909	45	65
1905	35	50	1910	40	60

| | EF | FDC |
	£	£
3986 — **fourpence,** 1902-10 ....*from*	5	9
3987 — **threepence**, 1902-10 ....*from*	5	11
3988 — **twopence**, 1902-10 ....*from*	5	8
3989 — **penny,** 1902-10 ....*from*	6	9

Maundy sets in the original dated cases are worth approximately £5 more than the prices quoted.

BRONZE

3990A

3990 'High Tide'   3990A 'Low Tide'

| | VF | EF | UNC | | F | VF | EF | UNC |
	£	£	£		£	£	£	£
3990 Penny. R. Britannia								
1902 1	4	10		1907 2		8	25
1903 2	8	25		1908 2		8	25
1904 3	12	30		1909 2		8	25
1905 2	10	27		1910 1		7	20
1906 2	8	25					

| **3990A** — R. As last but 'Low tide', 1902 ....5 | 10 | 30 | 50 |

3991

	VF	EF	UNC		F	VF	EF	UNC
	£	£	£		£	£	£	£

3991 Halfpenny. R. Britannia

	VF	EF	UNC		F	VF	EF	UNC
1902	1	4	10	1907	1		5	15
1903	2	8	20	1908	1		5	15
1904	2	8	25	1909	2		8	25
1905	2	8	25	1910	2		7	20
1906	2	8	20					

3991A — R. As last but 'Low tide', 1902 .... 10 25 40 65

3992   3993

3992 Farthing. Britannia. Dark finish

	VF	EF	UNC		F	VF	EF	UNC
1902		3	8	1907	1		5	12
1903	1	5	12	1908	1		5	12
1904	2	7	15	1909	1		5	12
1905	1	5	12	1910	2		7	15
1906	1	5	12					

3993 Third-farthing (for use in Malta).

1902 R. Value 5 10

No proofs of the bronze coins were issued in 1902

Proof Sets

PS9 Coronation, **1902.** Five Pounds to Maundy Penny, matt surface, (13 coins) *FDC* £1,450
PS10 — **1902.** Sovereign to Maundy Penny, matt surface, (11 coins) ....*FDC* £475

THE HOUSE OF WINDSOR, 1910-
GEORGE V, 1910-36

Paper money issued by the Treasury during the First World War replaced gold for internal use after 1915 but the branch mints in Australia and South Africa (the main Commonwealth gold producing countries) continued striking sovereigns until 1930-2. Owing to the steep rise in the price of silver in 1919/20 the issue of standard (.925) silver was discontinued and coins of .500 silver were minted.

In 1912, 1918 and 1919 some pennies were made under contract by private mints in Birmingham. In 1918, as half-sovereigns were no longer being minted, farthings were again issued with the ordinary bright bronze finish. Crown pieces had not been issued for general circulation but they were struck in small numbers about Christmas time for people to give as presents in the years 1927-36, and in 1935 a special commemorative crown was issued in celebration of the Silver Jubilee.

As George V died in January, it is likely that all coins dated 1936 were struck during the reign of Edward VIII.

Designer's initials:
B. M. (Bertram Mackennal)   P. M. (Percy Metcalfe)
K. G. (Kruger Gray)   B. P. (Benedetto Pistrucci; d. 1855)

GOLD

3994

	FDC
	£
3994 Five pounds.* R. St. George, 1911 (Proof only)	1200
3995 Two pounds.* R. St. George, 1911 (Proof only)	600

3996

3996 Sovereign. R. St. George. London mint

	VF	EF	UNC
	£	£	£
1911 75	1915		75
— Proof *FDC* £225	1916		85
1912 75	1917* 1500	2750	—
1913 75	1925		70
1914 75			

Forgeries exist of these and of most other dates and mints.

	VF	EF	UNC		VF	EF	UNC
	£	£	£		£	£	£

3997 Sovereign. R. St George, C on ground for the Ottawa mint

	VF	EF	UNC		VF	EF	UNC
1911 C		95	125	1917 C		95	125
1913 C	100	450	—	1918 C		95	125
1914 C	175	300	—	1919 C		95	125
1916 C*	3500	7000	—				

* *Beware of recent forgeries*

3997
Canada mint mark

3998
India mint mark

4004
South Africa mint mark

3998 — I on ground for India (Bombay) mint, 1918 80

3999 — M on ground for Melbourne mint

	VF	EF	UNC		VF	EF	UNC
1911 M			75	1920 M	1250	2500	—
1912 M			75	1921 M	1500	4000	—
1913 M			75	1922 M	1450	3750	—
1914 M			75	1923 M			75
1915 M			75	1924 M			75
1916 M			75	1925 M			75
1917 M			75	1926 M			75
1918 M			75	1928 M	650	1950	—
1919 M			90				

4000 — small head

	VF	EF	UNC		VF	EF	UNC
1929 M	325	1100	—	1931 M	200	325	—
1930 M	175	275	—				

4001

4001 — P on ground for Perth mint

	VF	EF	UNC		VF	EF	UNC
1911 P			75	1920 P			75
1912 P			75	1921 P			75
1913 P			75	1922 P			75
1914 P			75	1923 P			75
1915 P			75	1924 P	70	95	115
1916 P			75	1925 P	100	125	160
1917 P			75	1926 P	350	700	1000
1918 P			75	1927 P	100	150	250
1919 P			75	1928 P	80	100	125

	VF £	EF £	UNC £		VF £	EF £	UNC £
4002 Sovereign. — — small head							
1929 P			75	1931 P			75
1930 P			75				
4003 — S on ground for Sydney mint							
1911 S			75	1919 S			75
1912 S			75	1920 S			*Extremely rare*
1913 S			75	1921 S	650	1500	—
1914 S			75	1922 S	4000	12000	—
1915 S			75	1923 S	2500	5000	—
1916 S			75	1924 S	500	950	1500
1917 S			75	1925 S			75
1918 S			75	1926 S	6000	16000	—
4004 — SA on ground for Pretoria mint							
1923 SA		1250	2250	1926 SA			75
1923 SA Proof *FDC* £600				1927 SA			75
1924 SA		1950	—	1928 SA			75
1925 SA			75				
4005 — — small head							
1929 SA			75	1931 SA			75
1930 SA			75	1932 SA			100

4002

4006

4006 Half-sovereign. R. St. George. London mint

	VF	EF	UNC		VF	EF	UNC
1911		45	50	1913		45	50
— Proof *FDC* £175				1914		45	50
1912		45	50	1915		45	50
4007 — M on ground for Melbourne mint							
1915 M					55	80	125
4008 — P on ground for Perth mint							
1911 P	55	80	100	1918 P	200	450	600
1915 P	55	80	100				
4009 — S on ground for Sydney mint							
1911 S	50	70	90	1915 S	45	50	60
1912 S	50	70	90	1916 S	45	50	60
1914 S	50	60	75				
4010 — SA on ground for Pretoria mint							
1923 SA Proof *FDC* £475				1926 SA		45	50
1925 SA		45	50				

First coinage. Sterling silver (.925 fine)

4011

	F	VF	EF	UNC		F	VF	EF	UNC
	£	£	£	£		£	£	£	£

4011 Halfcrown. R. Crowned shield in Garter

1911	5	12	25	70	1915	4	8	14	40
— Proof *FDC* £70					1916	4	18	14	40
1912	6	14	30	85	1917	5	10	20	55
1913	8	16	35	80	1918	4	8	14	40
1914	4	8	14	40	1919	5	10	20	55

4012

4012 Florin. R. Cruciform shields

1911	5	10	25	60	1915	4	8	15	40
— Proof *FDC* £60					1916	4	8	15	40
1912	5	12	30	70	1917	5	10	20	55
1913	8	20	40	100	1918	4	8	15	40
1914	4	8	15	40	1919	5	10	20	50

4013 Shilling. R. Lion on crown, within circle

1911	2	5	10	20	1915		3	10	25
— Proof *FDC* £40					1916		3	10	25
1912	3	8	20	40	1917		3	12	28
1913	5	10	30	55	1918		3	10	25
1914		3	10	25	1919	2	5	15	35

4013

4014

	F	VF	EF	UNC			F	VF	EF	UNC
	£	£	£	£			£	£	£	£

4014 Sixpence. R. Similar

1911	2	5	10	20	1916	2	5	10	20
— Proof *FDC* £30					1917	2	6	15	45
1912	2	5	15	30	1918	2	5	10	20
1913	3	8	18	35	1919		3	22	25
1914	2	5	10	20	1920	2	5	15	30
1915	2	5	10	20					

4015 Threepence. As Maundy but dull finish

1911	....	4	14	1916	....	3	10
1912	....	4	14	1917	....	3	10
1913	....	4	14	1918	....	3	10
1914	....	4	14	1919	....	3	10
1915	....	4	14	1920	....	4	12

4016

	EF	FDC			EF	FDC
	£	£			£	£

4016 Maundy Set (4d., 3d., 2d. and 1d.)

1911	....	40	65	1916	....	40	65
— Proof *FDC* £70				1917	....	40	65
1912	....	40	65	1918	....	40	65
1913	....	40	65	1919	....	45	70
1914	....	40	65	1920	....	40	65
1915	....	40	65				

4017 — fourpence, 1911-20 ....*from*	7	11
4018 — threepence, 1911-20 ....*from*	8	12
4019 — twopence, 1911-20 ....*from*	6	10
4020 — penny, 1911-20 ....*from*	7	11

Second coinage. Debased silver (.500 fine). Types as before.

	F	VF	EF	UNC		F	VF	EF	UNC
	£	£	£	£		£	£	£	£

4021 Halfcrown

	F	VF	EF	UNC		F	VF	EF	UNC
1920	4	8	20	50	1924	5	10	30	60
1921	5	10	25	60	1925	20	50	150	250
1922	4	8	20	50	1926	5	10	30	65
1923	3	5	12	30					

4022 Florin

	F	VF	EF	UNC		F	VF	EF	UNC
1920	3	8	25	45	1924	4	10	32	60
1921	3	8	25	45	1925	25	45	100	175
1922	3	6	20	40	1926	3	10	32	60
1923	2	5	16	35					

4023 Shilling

	F	VF	EF	UNC		F	VF	EF	UNC
1920	3	6	18	35	1924	3	8	22	40
1921	4	10	22	55	1925	5	10	40	70
1922	3	6	18	35	1926	3	6	14	35
1923	2	5	16	30					

4024 Sixpence

	F	VF	EF	UNC		F	VF	EF	UNC
1920	2	4	10	20	1923	3	6	16	35
1921	2	4	10	20	1924	2	4	10	20
1922	2	5	12	25	1925	2	4	12	25

4025   4026

4025 — new beading and broader rim

	F	VF	EF	UNC		F	VF	EF	UNC
1925	2	4	10	20	1926	2	4	12	20

4026 Threepence

	F	VF	EF	UNC		F	VF	EF	UNC
1920		1	3	10	1925	—	2	14	20
1921		1	3	10	1926	1	3	15	25
1922		1	10	16					

	EF	FDC		EF	FDC
	£	£		£	£

4027 Maundy Set (4d., 3d., 2d. and 1d.)

	EF	FDC		EF	FDC
1921	40	65	1925	40	65
1922	40	65	1926	40	65
1923	40	65	1927	40	65
1924	40	65			

		EF	FDC
4028 — **fourpence,** 1921-7	*from*	8	11
4029 — **threepence,** 1921-7	*from*	8	12
4030 — **twopence,** 1921-7	*from*	6	10
4031 — **penny,** 1921-7	*from*	7	11

2nd coinage   3rd coinage

Third coinage. As before but modified effigy, with details of head more clearly defined. The BM on truncation is nearer to the back of the neck and without stops; beading is more pronounced.

	F £	VF £	EF £	UNC £		F £	VF £	EF £	UNC £
4032 Halfcrown									
1926	5	10	30	50	1927	4	7	18	30
4033 Shilling									
1926	2	4	14	20	1927	2	6	20	30
4034 Sixpence									
1926		3	8	14	1927	2	4	10	18
4035 Threepence									
1926							1	5	20

Fourth coinage. New types, 1927-36

4036

4036 Crown. R. Crown in wreath

1927 Proof only *FDC £125*

1928	35	75	110	185
1929	35	75	110	185
1930	35	75	110	185
1931	35	85	130	200

1932	85	120	200	300
1933	35	75	110	185
1934	200	450	600	950
1936	65	100	175	275

4037   4038

	F £	VF £	EF £	UNC £		F £	VF £	EF £	UNC £

4037 Halfcrown. R. Shield

1927 Proof only *FDC* £35					1932	4	8	15	30
1928	2	5	10	15	1933	2	5	10	16
1929	2	5	10	15	1934	4	10	25	45
1930	10	25	85	175	1935		5	10	15
1931	2	5	10	18	1936		3	8	12

4038 Florin. R. Cruciform sceptres, shield in each angle

1927 Proof only *FDC* £40					1932	20	40	95	225
1928		3	10	16	1933		3	10	20
1929		3	10	16	1935		3	10	15
1930	2	5	10	20	1936		2	8	14
1931	2	5	10	20					

4039   4040

4039 Shilling. R. Lion on crown, no inner circles

1927	2	4	15	25	1932	2	4	10	16
— Proof *FDC* £25					1933		3	10	15
1928		3	10	15	1934	2	5	16	25
1929		3	10	15	1935		3	10	15
1930	3	6	20	35	1936		3	8	14
1931	2	4	10	15					

4040 Sixpence. R. Three oak sprigs with six acorns

| 1927 Proof only *FDC* £18 | | | | | 1929 | | 2 | 4 | 8 |
| 1928 | | 2 | 4 | 8 | 1930 | | 2 | 4 | 8 |

4041 — closer milling

1931	2	3	8	16	1934	2	3	10	18
1932	2	4	14	22	1935		2	6	12
1933	2	3	8	14	1936		2	4	8

4042   4043

	F £	VF £	EF £	UNC £		F £	VF £	EF £	UNC £

4042 Threepence. R. Three oak sprigs with three acorns

	F	VF	EF	UNC		F	VF	EF	UNC
1927 Proof only *FDC £35*									
1928	1	3	14	30	1933			1	5
1930	1	3	14	30	1934			1	5
1931			1	5	1935			1	5
1932			1	5	1936			1	5

	EF £	FDC £		EF £	FDC £

4043 Maundy Set. As earlier sets

	EF	FDC		EF	FDC
1928	40	65	1933	40	65
1929	45	70	1934	40	65
1930	40	65	1935	45	70
1931	40	65	1936	45	70
1932	40	65			

The 1936 Maundy was distributed by King Edward VIII

		EF	FDC
4044 — fourpence, 1928-36	*from*	8	12
4045 — threepence, 1928-36	*from*	9	12
4046 — twopence, 1928-36	*from*	7	11
4047 — penny, 1928-36	*from*	8	13

Silver Jubilee Commemorative issue

4048

	VF £	EF £	UNC £
4048 Crown, 1935. R. St. George, incuse lettering on edge	10	15	20
4049 — Specimen striking issued in box			35
4050 — raised lettering on edge .Proof (.925 Æ) *FDC £225*			

BRONZE

4052

H mint mark location – 4052

KN mint mark location – 4053

	F £	VF £	EF £	UNC £		F £	VF £	EF £	UNC £
4051 Penny. R. Britannia									
1911			5	15	1918			5	15
1912			5	15	1919			5	15
1913			8	20	1920			5	15
1914			5	15	1921			5	15
1915			5	15	1922			15	25
1916			5	15	1926			20	35
1917			5	15					

4052 — R. Britannia, H (Heaton Mint, Birmingham, Ltd.) to l. of date

	F £	VF £	EF £	UNC £		F £	VF £	EF £	UNC £
1912 H		2	35	75	1919 H		8	85	175
1918 H		10	100	175					

4053 — R. Britannia KN (King's Norton Metal Co.) to l. of date

	F £	VF £	EF £	UNC £		F £	VF £	EF £	UNC £
1918 KN	3	15	125	250	1919 KN	3	18	150	300

4054 — modified effigy

	F £	VF £	EF £	UNC £		F £	VF £	EF £	UNC £
1926	10	45	350	650	1927			3	8

4055 — small head

	EF £	UNC £		EF £	UNC £
1928	3	8	1933	*Extremely rare*	
1929	3	8	1934	10	22
1930	5	10	1935	2	8
1931	5	14	1936	1	5
1932	12	25			

4056 Halfpenny. R. Britannia

	EF £	UNC £		EF £	UNC £
1911	5	15	1919	5	15
1912	5	15	1920	5	15
1913	5	15	1921	5	15
1914	5	15	1922	7	20
1915	5	15	1923	5	15
1916	5	15	1924	5	15
1917	5	15	1925	5	15
1918	5	15			

4057 — modified effigy

	EF £	UNC £		EF £	UNC £
1925	8	22	1927	5	15
1926	6	20			

4056   4058

	EF	UNC			EF	UNC
	£	£			£	£

4058 Halfpenny. Small head

1928	2	8		1933	2	8
1929	2	8		1934	4	14
1930	2	8		1935	2	8
1931	2	8		1936	1	5
1932	2	8				

4059   4062

4059 Farthing. R. Britannia. Dark finish

1911	3	7		1915	4	9
1912	2	5		1916	2	5
1913	2	5		1917	1	3
1914	2	5		1918	9	18

4060 — Bright finish, 1918-25 1   3

4061 — Modified effigy

1926	1	3		1932	0.50	2
1927	1	3		1933	1	3
1928	1	3		1934	2	5
1929	1	3		1935	2	5
1930	1	3		1936	0.75	3
1931	1	3				

4062 Third-farthing (for use in Malta). **R.** Value

1913 5   10

Proof Sets

PS11 Coronation, **1911.** Five pounds to Maundy Penny (12 coins) .... *FDC*   £2,500

PS12 — **1911.** Sovereign to Maundy Penny (10 coins) .... *FDC*   £600

PS13 — **1911.** Half crown to Maundy Penny (8 coins) .... *FDC*   £300

PS14 New type, **1927.** Wreath type Crown to Threepence (6 coins) .... *FDC*   £225

Abdicated 10 December. Created Duke of Windsor (1936-72)

No coins of Edward VIII were issued for currency within the United Kingdom bearing his name and portrait. The mint had commenced work on a new coinage prior to the Abdication, and various patterns were made. No proof sets were issued for sale and only a small number of sets were struck.

Coins bearing Edward's name, but not his portrait, were issued for the colonial territories of British East Africa, British West Africa, Fiji and New Guinea. The projected U.K. coins were to include a shilling of essentially `Scottish' type and a nickel brass threepence with twelve sides which might supplement and possibly supersede the inconveniently small silver threepence.

Designer's initials:

H. P. (T. Humphrey Paget)	B.P. (Benedetto Pistrucci, d. 1855)
K. G. (Kruger Gray)	M. K. (Madge Kitchener)
W. P. (Wilson Parker)	

4063

4063 Proof Set

Gold, £5, £2 and £1, 1937 .... *not issued*

Silver Crown, Halfcrown, Florin, Scottish shilling, sixpence and threepence, 1937   *not issued*

£

Sovereign,..	*Extremely rare*
Crown,...	*Extremely rare*
Halfcrown,..	*Extremely rare*
Florin,..	*Extremely rare*
Shilling,...	*Extremely rare*
Sixpence,...	*Extremely rare*
Threepence,..	*Extremely rare*

Nickel brass. Threepence, 1937	*not issued*
Bronze. Penny. Halfpenny and Farthing, 1937	*not issued*

Pattern

4064   Nickel brass dodecagonal threepence, 1937. R. Thrift plant of more
naturalistic style than the modified proof coin. A small number of these
coins were produced for experimental purposes and a few did get into
circulation   *Extremely rare*

GEORGE VI, 1936-52

Though they were at first issued concurrently, the twelve-sided nickel-brass threepence superseded the small silver threepence in 1942. Those dated 1943-4 were not issued for circulation in the U.K. In addition to the usual English 'lion' shilling, a shilling, of Scottish type was issued concurrently. This depicts the Scottish lion and crown flanked by the shield of St. Andrew and a thistle. In 1947, as silver was needed to repay the bullion lent by the U.S.A. during the war, silver coins were replaced by coins of the same type and weight made of cupro-nickel. In 1949, after India had attained independence, the title *Indiae Imperator* was dropped from the coinage. Commemorative crown pieces were issued for the Coronation and the 1951 Festival of Britain.

Designer's initials:
  K. G. (Kruger Gray)   B. P. (Benedetto Pistrucci, d. 1855)
  H. P. (T. Humphrey Paget)   W. P. (Wilson Parker)

GOLD

4074   4076

	FDC £
4074 Five pounds. Bare head l. R. St. George, 1937. Proof	550
4075 Two pounds. Similar, 1937. Proof	325
4076 Sovereign. Similar, 1937. Proof	400
4077 Half-sovereign. Similar, 1937. Proof	150

SILVER

First coinage. Silver, .500 fine, with title IND:IMP

4078

	VF £	EF £	UNC £

4078 Crown. Coronation commemorative, 1937. R. Arms and supporters 10 15 22
4079 — — Proof *FDC* £35

4080   4081

	EF £	UNC £			UNC £

4080 Halfcrown. R. Shield
1937 7
— Proof *FDC* £10
1938 .... 4 18
1939 7
1940 7
1941 7

1942 6
1943 7
1944 5
1945 5
1946 5

4081 Florin. R. Crowned rose, etc.
1937 6
— Proof *FDC* £10
1938 .... 4 15
1939 5
1940 5
1941 5

1942 5
1943 5
1944 5
1945 5
1946 5

4082   4083

4082 Shilling. 'English'. R. Lion rampant on large crown
1937 5
— Proof *FDC* £8
1938 .... 3 15
1939 5
1940 5
1941 5

1942 5
1943 5
1944 5
1945 4
1946 4

	EF	UNC		VF	EF	UNC
	£	£		£	£	£

4083 Shilling. 'Scottish'. R. Lion seated facing on crown, etc.

1937		5	1942			5
— Proof *FDC* £8			1943			5
1938	3	15	1944			5
1939		5	1945			4
1940		6	1946			4
1941		6				

4084   4085

4084 Sixpence. R. GRI crowned

1937		4	1942		3
— Proof *FDC* £5			1943		3
1938	2	6	1944		3
1939		4	1945		3
1940		4	1946		3
1941		4			

4085 Threepence. R. Shield on rose

1937		3	1941		1	4
— Proof *FDC* £5			1942*	3	10	18
1938		3	1943*	3	10	20
1939	3	10	1944*	8	20	35
1940		4	1945*		*Extremely rare*	

*For colonial use only.

4086

	FDC		FDC
	£		£

4086 Maundy Set. Silver, .500 fine. Uniform dates

1937	60	1942	60
— Proof *FDC* £65		1943	60
1938	60	1944	60
1939	70	1945	60
1940	60	1946	60
1941	60		

	FDC		*FDC*
	£		£

4087 — fourpence, 1937-46 .... *from*   10
4088 — threepence, 1937-46 .... *from*   10
4089 — twopence, 1937-46 .... *from*   10
4090 — penny, 1937-46 .... *from*   14

Second coinage. Silver, .925 fine, with title IND.IMP (Maundy only)
4091 Maundy Set (4d., 3d., 2d. and 1d.). Uniform dates

1947	60	1948	60

4092 — fourpence, 1947-8 10
4093 — threepence, 1947-8 10
4094 — twopence, 1947-8 10
4095 — penny, 1947-8 14

Third coinage. Silver, .925 fine, but omitting IND.IMP. (Maundy only)
4096 Maundy Set (4d., 3d., 2d. and 1d.). Uniform dates

1949	70	1951	60
1950	60	1952	60

The 1952 Maundy was distributed by Queen Elizabeth II.

4097 — fourpence, 1949-52 .... *from*   10
4098 — threepence, 1949-52 .... *from*   10
4099 — twopence, 1949-52 .... *from*   10
4100 — penny, 1949-52 .... *from*   14

CUPRO-NICKEL

Second coinage. Types as first (silver) coinage, IND.IMP.

	UNC		*UNC*
	£		£

4101 Halfcrown. R. Shield
1947 5   1948 5

4102 Florin. R. Crowned rose
1947 5   1948 5

4103 Shilling. 'English' type
1947 5   1948 4

4104 — 'Scottish' type
1947 5   1948 4

4105 Sixpence. GRI crowned
1947 4   1948 3

Third coinage. Types as before but title IND.IMP. omitted

4106

	UNC £		VF £	EF £	UNC £
4106 Halfcrown					
1949	6	1951			8
1950	7	— Proof *FDC* £10			
— Proof *FDC* £10		1952			*Extremely rare*
4107 Florin					
1949	8	1951			8
1950	8	— Proof *FDC* £10			
— Proof *FDC* £10					
4108 Shilling. 'English' type					
1949	7	1951			7
1950	7	— Proof *FDC* £7			
— Proof *FDC* £6					
4109 — 'Scottish' type					
1949	9	1951			8
1950	8	— Proof *FDC* £8			
— Proof *FDC* £8					

4110

4110 Sixpence. As illustration					
1949	5	1951			5
1950	5	— Proof *FDC* £5			
— Proof *FDC* £5		1952 2		12	35

Festival of Britain issue

4111

	EF	UNC
	£	£
4111 Crown. R. St. George, 1951. *Proof-like*	4	8

NICKEL BRASS

First issue, with title IND.IMP.

4112   4113

	VF	EF	UNC			VF	EF	UNC
	£	£	£			£	£	£
4112 Threepence (dodecagonal). R. Thrift								
1937			3		1942			2
—Proof *FDC* £6					1943			2
1938		3	8		1944			3
1939		4	18		1945			5
1940			5		1946 5		40	125
1941			3		1948		3	18

Second issue, omitting IND.IMP.
4113 Threepence. Similar

	VF	EF	UNC			VF	EF	UNC
1949 5		45	150		1951		8	35
1950		8	30		— Proof *FDC* £30			
— Proof *FDC* £30					1952			3

BRONZE

First issue, with title IND.IMP.

4114

	UNC £			UNC £
4114 Penny. R. Britannia				
1937	2		1944	7
— Proof *FDC* £8			1945	5
1938	2		1946	2
1939	5		1947	2
1940	6		1948	2

4115   4116

	UNC £			UNC £
4115 Halfpenny. R. Ship				
1937	2		1943	2
— Proof *FDC* £5			1944	2
1938	3		1945	3
1939	4		1946	6
1940	6		1947	3
1941	5		1948	2
1942	2			
4116 Farthing. R. Wren				
1937	1		1943	0.65
— Proof *FDC* £5			1944	0.65
1938	2		1945	0.65
1939	0.65		1946	0.65
1940	1		1947	0.65
1941	0.75		1948	0.75
1942	0.75			

Second issue, without IND.IMP. Types as before

	VF £	EF £	UNC £		VF £	EF £	UNC £
4117 Penny							
1949			2	1951 6	12	18
1950 4	10	20	— Proof *FDC* £18			
— Proof *FDC* £18						

4118

4119

4118 Halfpenny

1949	5	1951	5
1950	4	— Proof *FDC* £5	
— Proof *FDC* £5		1952	3

4119 Farthing

1949	1	1951	0.70
1950	0.70	— Proof *FDC* £5	
— Proof *FDC* £5		1952	0.80

The coins dated 1952 were issued during the reign of Elizabeth II.

Proof Sets

PS15 Coronation, **1937.** Five pounds to Half-sovereign (4 coins)..........................*FDC*   £1450
PS16 — **1937.** Crown to Farthing, including Maundy Set (15 coins) ....*FDC*   £125
PS17 Mid-Century, **1950.** Halfcrown to Farthing (9 coins)..................................*FDC*   £50
PS18 Festival of Britain, **1951.** Crown to Farthing (10 coins)..............................*FDC*   £60

ELIZABETH II, acc. 1952

The earliest coins of this reign have the title BRITT.OMN, but in 1954 this was omitted from the Queen's titles owing to the changing status of so many Commonwealth territories. The minting of 'English' and 'Scottish' shillings was continued. A Coronation commemorative crown was issued in 1953, another crown was struck on the occasion of the 1960 British Exhibition in New York and a third was issued in honour of Sir Winston Churchill in 1965. A very small number of proof gold coins were struck in 1953 for the national museum collections, but between 1957 and 1968 gold sovereigns were minted again in quantity for sale in the international bullion market and to counteract the activities of counterfeiters.

Owing to inflation the farthing had now become practically valueless; production of these coins ceased after 1956 and the coins were demonetized at the end of 1960. In 1965 it was decided to change to a decimal system of coinage in the year 1971. As part of the transition to decimal coinage the halfpenny was demonetized in August 1969 and the halfcrown in January 1970. (See also introduction to Decimal Coinage.

Designer's initials:

B. P. (Benedetto Pistrucci, D. 1855)
J. M. M. (John Mills)
B. R. (Bruce Rushin)
I. R. B. (Ian Rank-Broadley)
M. M. D. (Mary Milner Dickens)
M. R. (Michael Rizzello)
R. E. (Robert Elderton)
A. V. (Avril Vaughan)
M. N. (Michael Noakes)
D. C. (David Cornell)
G. L. (Gilbert Ledward)
W. P. (Wilson Parker)
M. G. (Mary Gillick)
W. G. (William Gardner)
E. F. (Edgar Fuller)

C. T. (Cecil Thomas)
P. N. (Philip Nathan)
R. D. M. (Raphael David Maklouf)
N. S. (Norman Sillman)
I. R. B. (Ian Rank-Broadley)

Other designers whose initials do not appear
on the coins:
Christopher Ironside
Arnold Machin
David Wynne
Professor Richard Guyatt
Eric Sewell
Oscar Nemon
Leslie Durbin
Derek Gorringe

PRE-DECIMAL ISSUES

GOLD

First coinage, with title BRITT.OMN, 1953. *Proof only*

4120 Five pounds. R. St. George	....	*None issued for collectors*
4121 Two pounds. Similar	....	*None issued for collectors*
4122 Sovereign. Similar	....	*None issued for collectors*
4123 Half-sovereign. Similar	....	*None issued for collectors*

Second issue, BRITT.OMN omitted

4125

4124 Sovereign. laur l. head r. R. St. George

1957 .... BV

4125 Sovereign. Similar, but coarser graining
on edge

1958	BV	1965	BV
1959	BV	1966	BV
1962	BV	1967	BV
1963	BV	1968	BV
1964	BV		

SILVER

The Queen's Maundy are now the only coins struck regularly in silver.
The location of the Maundy ceremony is given for each year.

First issue, with title BRITT.OMN.   *FDC*

                                                                       £

4126 Maundy Set (4d., 3d., 2d. and 1d.), 1953. St Paul's.   275
4127 — fourpence, 1953   50
4128 — threepence, 1953   50
4129 — twopence, 1953   50
4130 — penny, 1953   100

Second issue, with BRITT.OMN omitted

4131

FDC
£

4131 Maundy Set (4d., 3d., 2d. and 1d.). Uniform dates

1954 *Westminster*	60	1963 *Chelmsford*	60
1955 *Southwark*	60	1964 *Westminster*	60
1956 *Westminster*	60	1965 *Canterbury*	60
1957 *St. Albans*	60	1966 *Westminster*	60
1958 *Westminster*	60	1967 *Durham*	60
1959 *Windsor*	70	1968 *Westminster*	60
1960 *Westminster*	60	1969 *Selby*	70
1961 *Rochester*	60	1970 *Westminster*	60
1962 *Westminster*	60		

4132 — fourpence, 1954-70   *from*   10
4133 — threepence, 1954-70   *from*   10
4134 — twopence, 1954-70   *from*   10
4135 — penny, 1954-70   *from*   14

CUPRO-NICKEL

First issue, 1953, with title BRITT.OMN.

4136

	EF	UNC	PROOF FDC
	£	£	£
4136 Crown. Queen on horseback. R. Crown in centre of cross, shield in each angle, 1953	6	7	25

4137   4138

4137 Halfcrown, with title BRITT.OMN. R. Arms, 1953	3	9
4138 Florin. R. Double rose, 1953	3	7

4139   4140   4141

4139 Shilling. 'English'. R. Three lions, 1953	1	6
4140 — 'Scottish'. R. Lion rampant in shield, 1953	1	6
4141 Sixpence. R. Interlaced rose, thistle, shamrock and leek, 1953	0.70	5
4142 Set of 9 uncirculated cu-ni, ni-br and Æ coins (2/6 to 1/4d.) in Royal Mint plastic envelope		15

Second issue, similar types but omitting BRITT.OMN.

4143   4144

	EF	UNC
	£	£
4143 Crown, 1960. Bust r. R. As 4136	4	7
— — Similar, from polished dies (New York Exhibition issue)	6	18
— — 'VIP' *proof,* frosted design *FDC* £300		
4144 — Churchill commemorative, 1965. As illustration. R. Bust of Winston Churchill r.		1
— — Similar, satin- finish. *Specimen*		300

4145 Halfcrown. R. As 4137

	EF	UNC		EF	UNC		EF	UNC
	£	£		£	£		£	£
1954	3	15	1960		3	1965		1
1955		4	1961		1	1966		0.60
1956		5	1961 Polished die		5	1967		0.60
1957		2	1962		1	1970 Proof *FDC* £3		
1958	3	12	1963		1			
1959	3	15	1964		3			

4146

4146 Florin. R. As 4138

	EF	UNC				EF	UNC
1954	4	30		1962			1
1955		3		1963			1
1956		3		1964			1
1957	3	20		1965			1
1958	2	10		1966			1
1959	3	25		1967			1
1960		2		1970 Proof *FDC* £3			
1961		2					

	EF	UNC			UNC
	£	£			£

4147 Shilling. 'English' type. R. As 4139

1954		2	1961		0.75
1955		2	1962		0.50
1956		7	1963		0.25
1957		1	1964		0.30
1958	3	15	1965		0.30
1959		1	1966		0.30
1960		1	1970 Proof *FDC* £3		

4148 — 'Scottish' type. R. As 4140

1954		2	1961		5
1955		3	1962		1
1956		7	1963		0.25
1957	3	15	1964		0.50
1958		1	1965		0.50
1959	3	15	1966		0.30
1960		1	1970 Proof *FDC* £3		

4149 Sixpence. R. As 4141

1954		3	1962		0.30
1955		1	1963		0.25
1956		1	1964		0.20
1957		0.65	1965		0.15
1958		4	1966		0.15
1959		0.35	1967		0.15
1960		4	1970 Proof *FDC* £2		
1961		3			

NICKEL BRASS

First issue, with title BRITT.OMN.

4152　　　　　　　　　　4153

4152 Threepence (dodecagonal). R. Crowned portcullis, 1953 1
— Proof *FDC* £5

Second issue (omitting BRIT.OMN)

4153 Similar type

1954		4	1962	0.30
1955		5	1963	0.20
1956		5	1964	0.20
1957		3	1965	0.20
1958		6	1966	0.15
1959		3	1967	0.15
1960		3	1970 Proof *FDC* £2	
1961		0.35		

BRONZE

First issue, with title BRITT.OMN.

4154   4155

	VF £	EF £	UNC £	Proof FDC £
4154 Penny. R. Britannia (only issued with Royal Mint set in plastic envelope), 1953	0.60	2	5	6
4155 Halfpenny. R. Ship, 1953			2	4
4156 Farthing. R. Wren, 1953			0.75	3

Second issue, omitting BRITT.OMN.

4157 Penny. R. Britannia (1954-60 *not issued*)

	UNC £		UNC £
1954	*Unique*	1965	0.10
1961	0.50	1966	0.10
1962	0.15	1967	0.10
1963	0.15	1970 Proof *FDC £3*	
1964	0.10		

4158 Halfpenny. R. Ship (1961 *not issued*)

	£		£
1954	4	1962	0.10
1955	4	1963	0.10
1956	4	1964	0.10
1957	0.60	1965	0.10
1958	0.35	1966	0.10
1959	0.20	1967	0.10
1960	0.10	1970 Proof *FDC £2*	

4156   4159

4159 Farthing. R. Wren

	EF £		EF £	UNC £
1954	0.80	1956	0.55	2
1955	0.75			

Proof Sets

PS19 Coronation, **1953.** Crown to Farthing (10 coins) ....*FDC*   55
PS20 'Last Sterling', **1970.** Halfcrown to Halfpenny plus medallion ....*FDC*   15

All prices quoted assume coins are in their original case. Issued by the Royal Mint in official case from 1887 onwards, but earlier sets were issued privately by the engraver. All pieces have a superior finish to that of the current coins.

		No. of coins	FDC £
PS1	**George IV, 1826**. New issue, Five Pounds to Farthing ....(11)		18,000
PS1A	— — Similar to above, including Maundy Set ....(15)		18,500
PS2	**William IV, 1831.** Coronation, Two Pounds to Farthing ....(14)		16,000
PS3	**Victoria, 1839.** Young head. "Una and the Lion" Five Pounds and Sovereign to Farthing..(15)		27,500
PS4	— **1853.** Sovereign to Farthing, including Gothic type Crown.........(16)		22,500
PS5	— **1887.** Jubilee bust for Golden Jubilee, Five Pounds to Threepence ....(11)		5,500
PS6	— **1887.** Silver Crown to Threepence ....(7)		950
PS7	— **1893.** Old bust, Five Pounds to Threepence ....(10)		6,500
PS8	— **1893.** Silver Crown to Threepence ....(6)		1,000
PS9	**Edward VII, 1902.** Coronation, Five Pounds to Maundy Penny. Matt finish to surfaces..(13)		1,450
PS10	— **1902.** Sovereign to Maundy Penny. Matt finish ....(11)		475
PS11	**George V, 1911.** Coronation, Five Pounds to Maundy Penny..........(12)		2,500
PS12	— **1911.** Sovereign to Maundy Penny..(10)		600
PS13	— **1911.** Silver Halfcrown to Maundy Penny ....(8)		300
PS14	— **1927.** New Coinage. Wreath type Crown to Threepence ....(6)		225
PS15	**George VI, 1937.** Coronation. Five Pounds to Half-Sovereign..........(4)		1,450
PS16	— **1937.** Coronation. Crown to Farthing, including Maundy Set .....(15)		125
PS17	— **1950.** Mid-Century, Halfcrown to Farthing...................................(9)		50
PS18	— **1951.** Festival of Britain, Crown to Farthing...............................(10)		60
PS19	**Elizabeth II, 1953.** Coronation. Crown to Farthing ....(10)		55
PS20	— **1970.** "Last Sterling" set. Halfcrown to Halfpenny plus medallion..(8)		15

DECIMAL COINAGE

A decision to adopt decimal currency was announced in March 1966 following the recommendation of the Halsbury Committee of Enquiry which had been appointed in 1961. The date for the introduction of the new system was 15 February 1971 and it was evident that the Royal Mint facilities which had been located on Tower Hill for more than 150 years would be unable to strike the significant quantities of coins required on that site. The Government therefore decided to build a new mint at Llantrisant in South Wales.

The new system provided for three smaller bronze coins and very large numbers were struck and stock piled for D-Day but the five and ten new pence denominations with the same specifications as the former shilling and florin were introduced in 1968. A further change was the introduction of a 50 new pence coin to replace the ten shilling banknote.

In 1982 and 1983 two more new coins were introduced; the 20 pence which helped to reduce demand for five and ten pence pieces, and the first circulating non-precious metal £1 coin which replaced the bank note of the same value.

Increasing raw material costs, and inflation also play a part in the development of a modern coinage system and a smaller 50 pence was introduced in the autumn of 1997. The bimetallic circulating £2 was postponed due to some technical problems associated with vending and similar machines. It is planned to release the coin this year.

For the collector, many of these changes have been accompanied by special issues often in limited editions struck in precious metal. New designs, particularly on the £1 coins, have added interest to the coins that circulate, and may hopefully stimulate new collectors.

In the period since decimalisation there has been a marked increase in the issue of commemorative coins. The crown size pieces, which by virtue of their size allow much scope for interesting designs seem to be reserved for the commemoration of Royal events or anniversaries, and other denominations such as the £2 and the 50 pence have honoured other interesting themes.

The major change in the coinage in 1998 is the new, and fourth, portrait of H. M. The Queen. Designed by Ian Rank-Broadley, a whole new series has started which will stimulate interest among collectors everywhere.

GOLD

4201   4204

4201   **Five pounds.** As illustration
    1980 Proof *FDC** £425
    1981 Proof *FDC* (Issued: 5,400)** £450
4202   As 4201 but, 'U' in a circle to left of date
    1984 (Issued: 15,104) *Unc* £400
4203   **Two pounds**
    1980 Proof *FDC** £225
    1982 Proof *FDC** £225

1982 Proof *FDC** £450
1984 Proof *FDC* (Issued: 905) £450

1983 Proof *FDC* (Issued: 12,500)** £200

* *Coins marked thus were originally issued in Royal Mint Sets.*
** *Numbers include coins sold in sets.*

4204 Sovereign. As illustration

1974	Unc BV		1981	Unc BV	
1976	Unc BV		— Proof *FDC* (Issued: 32,960) £95		
1978	Unc BV		1982	Unc BV	
1979	Unc BV		— Proof *FDC* (Issued: 20,000) £95		
— Proof *FDC* (Issued: 50,000) £95			1983 Proof *FDC* (Issued: 21,250)** £95		
1980	Unc BV		1984 Proof *FDC* (Issued: 12,880) £95		
— Proof *FDC* (Issued: 81,200) £95					

4205 Half-sovereign

1980 Proof *FDC* (Issued: 76.700) £60		1983 Proof FDC (Issued: 19,710)** £60
1982	Unc BV	1984 Proof FDC (Issued: 12,410) £60
— Proof FDC (Issued: 19,090) £60		

* Coins marked thus were originally issued in Royal Mint sets
** numbers include coins sold in sets

SILVER

	FDC		FDC
	£		£

4211 Maundy Set (4p, 3p, 2p and 1p). Uniform dates. Types as 4131

1971 *Tewkesbury Abbey*	55	1985 *Ripon Cathedral*	55	
1972 *York Minster*	55	1986 *Chichester Cathedral*	55	
1973 *Westminster Abbey*	55	1987 *Ely Cathedral*	75	
1974 *Salisbury Cathedral*	55	1988 *Lichfield Cathedral*	75	
1975 *Peterborough Cathedral*	55	1989 *Birmingham Cathedral*	75	
1976 *Hereford Cathedral*	55	1990 *Newcastle Cathedral*	75	
1977 *Westminster Abbey*	65	1991 *Westminster Abbey*	75	
1978 *Carlisle Cathedral*	55	1992 *Chester Cathedral*	75	
1979 *Winchester Cathedral*	55	1993 *Wells Cathedral*	75	
1980 *Worcester Cathedral*	55	1994 *Truro Cathedral*	75	
1981 *Westminster Abbey*	55	1995 *Coventry Cathedral*	80	
1982 *St. David's Cathedral*	55	1996 *Norwich Cathedral*	85	
1983 *Exeter Cathedral*	55	1997 *Bradford Cathedral*	90	
1984 *Southwell Minster*	55	1998 *Portsmouth Cathedral*	95	

4212	**— fourpence,** 1971-96	*from*	13
4213	**— threepence,** 1971-96	*from*	13
4214	**— twopence,** 1971-96	*from*	13
4215	**— penny,** 1971-96	*from*	15

The place of distribution is shown after each date.

NICKEL-BRASS

| | 4221 | 4222 | |

UNC
£

4221 **One pound** (Royal Arms design). Edge DECUS ET TUTAMEN

1983 3

— Specimen in presentation folder (issued: 484,900) 5

— Proof *FDC** £5 — Proof piedfort in silver *FDC* (Issued: 10,000) £115

— Proof in silver *FDC* (Issued: 50,000) £25

4222 **One pound** (Scottish design). Edge NEMO ME IMPUNE LACESSIT

1984 2

— Specimen in presentation folder (Issued: 27,960) 5

— Proof *FDC** £5 — Proof piedfort in silver *FDC* (Issued: 15,000) £45

— Proof in silver *FDC* (Issued: 44,855) £21

CUPRO-NICKEL

| | 4223 | 4224 |

	UNC £		*UNC* £		*UNC* £

4223 **Fifty new pence** (seven-sided). R. Britannia r.

1969	2	1976	2	1979	2
1970	4	— Proof *FDC** £2		— Proof *FDC** £3	
1971 Proof *FDC** £4		1977	2	1980	2
1972 Proof *FDC** £5		— Proof *FDC** £2		— Proof *FDC** £2	
1974 Proof *FDC** £3		1978	2	1981	2
1975 Proof *FDC** £3		— Proof *FDC** £3		— Proof *FDC** £2	

4224 Accession to European Economic Community. R. Clasped hands, 1973 .... 1.50

— Proof *FDC*** £3

* *Coins marked thus were originally issued in Royal Mint sets as shown on page 457.*

** *Issued as an individual proof coin and in the year set shown on page 457.*

4225

4225 Fifty (50) pence. 'New' omitted. As illustration

1982   2   1983...........................   2   1984*........................   3
— Proof *FDC** £2   — Proof *FDC** £2   — Proof *FDC** £2

4226

4226 Twenty-five pence. Silver Wedding Commemorative, 1972 .... 1.25
— Proof *FDC** (in 1972 Set, See PS48) £4
— Silver proof in case *FDC* (Issued: 100,000) £24

4227

	UNC £

4227 Twenty-five pence Silver Jubilee Commemorative, 1977 .... 0.75
— Specimen in presentation folder.. 2
— Proof *FDC** (in 1977 Set, See PS53) £4
— Silver proof in case *FDC* (Issued: 377,000) £22

* Coins marked thus were originally issued in Royal Mint sets

4228

4228 Twenty-Five pence Queen Mother 80th Birthday Commemorative, 1980 .... 1.25
         — Specimen in presentation folder... 2
         — Silver proof in case *FDC* (issued: 83,672) £32.50

4229

4229 Twenty-five pence. Royal Wedding Commemorative, 1981 .... 1.25
         — Specimen in presentation folder... 2
         — Silver proof in case *FDC* (Issued: 218,142) £30

4230

	UNC		*UNC*		*UNC*
	£		£		£

4230 Twenty (20) pence. R crowned rose
         1982 .... 0.40   1983......................... 0.40   1984......................... 0.40
         — Proof *FDC** £2   — Proof *FDC** £1   — Proof *FDC** £1
         — Proof piedfort
              in silver *FDC* (Issued: 10,000) £40
* *Coins marked thus were originally issued in Royal Mint sets*

4231

4232

4231 Ten new pence. R. Lion passant guardant.

1968	0.30	1974	0.40	1978 Proof *FDC** £4	
1969	0.30	— Proof *FDC** £1		1979	0.50
1970	0.30	1975	0.50	— Proof *FDC** £2	
1971	0.40	— Proof *FDC** £1		1980	0.75
— Proof *FDC** £2		1976	0.50	— Proof *FDC** £1	
1972 Proof *FDC** £3		— Proof *FDC** £1		1981	0.75
1973	0.40	1977	0.50	— Proof *FDC** £1	
— Proof *FDC** £2		— Proof *FDC** £2			

4232 Ten (10) pence. As illustration

1982*	3	1983*	3	1984*	2
— Proof *FDC** £1		— Proof *FDC** £2		— Proof *FDC** £1	

4233

4234

4233 Five new pence. R. Crowned thistle

1968	0.20	1974 Proof *FDC** £2		— Proof *FDC** £1	
1969	0.30	1975	0.20	1979	0.20
1970	0.30	— Proof *FDC** £1		— Proof *FDC** £1	
1971	0.20	1976 Proof *FDC** £2		1980	0.20
— Proof *FDC** £2		1977	0.20	— Proof *FDC** £1	
1972 Proof *FDC** £2		— Proof *FDC** £1		1981 Proof *FDC** £1	
1973 Proof *FDC** £2		1978	0.20		

4234 Five (5) pence. As illustration

1982*	2	1983*	2	1984*	2
— Proof *FDC** £2		— Proof *FDC** £2		— Proof *FDC** £1	

* *Coins marked thus were originally issued in Royal Mint sets.*

BRONZE

	4235			4236	
	UNC		UNC		UNC
	£		£		£

4235 Two new pence. R. Plumes

1971	0.10	1976	0.20	— Proof *FDC** £1	
— Proof *FDC** £1		— Proof *FDC** £1		1980	0.15
1972 Proof *FDC** £2		1977	0.10	— Proof *FDC** £1	
1973 Proof *FDC** £2		— Proof *FDC** £1		1981	0.15
1974 Proof *FDC** £2		1978	0.30	— Proof *FDC** £1	
1975	0.20	— Proof *FDC** £1			
— Proof *FDC** £1		1979	0.15		

4236 Two (2) pence. As illustration

1982*	1	— Error. R. as 4235	£250	1984*	1
— Proof *FDC** £1		— Proof *FDC** £1..		— Proof *FDC** £1	
1983*	1				

	4237		4238	4239	4240

4237 One new penny. R. Crowned portcullis

1971	0.10	1975	0.20	— Proof *FDC** £1	
— Proof *FDC** £1		— Proof *FDC** £1		1979	0.10
1972 Proof *FDC**£2		1976	0.20	— Proof *FDC** £1	
1973	0.20	— Proof *FDC** £1		1980	0.10
— Proof *FDC** £1		1977	0.10	— Proof *FDC** £1	
1974	0.20	— Proof *FDC** £1		1981	0.20
— Proof *FDC** £1		1978	0.20	— Proof *FDC** £1	

4238 One (1) penny. As illustration

1982	0.10	1983	0.20	1984*	1
— Proof *FDC** £1		— *FDC** £1		— Proof *FDC** £1	

4239 Half new penny. R. Crown

1971	0.10	1975	0.25	— Proof *FDC** £1	
— Proof *FDC** £1		— Proof *FDC** £1..		1979	0.10
1972 Proof *FDC** £2		1976	0.20	— Proof *FDC** £1	
1973	0.20	— Proof *FDC** £1..		1980	0.10
— Proof *FDC** £1		1977	0.10	— Proof *FDC** £1	
1974	0.20	— Proof *FDC** £1..		1981	0.20
— Proof *FDC** £1		1978	0.10	— Proof *FDC** £1	

4240 Half (1/2) penny. As illustration

1982	0.10	1983	0.25	1984*	2.00
— Proof *FDC** £1		— Proof *FDC** £1..		— Proof *FDC** £2	

* *Coins marked thus were originally issued in Royal Mint sets.*

The new effigy was designed by Raphael David Maklouf, FRSA. It is the third portrait of the Queen to be used on UK coinage, the previous change of portrait being in 1968 with the introduction of decimal coins. The designer's initials R.D.M. appear on the truncation. There is no portrait change on the Maundy coins (see 4211-4215).

GOLD

4251 4253

4251 Five pounds. R. St. George
1985 Proof *FDC* (Issued: 281) £500
1990 Proof *FDC** £500	1993 Proof *FDC** £500	1996 Proof *FDC** £500
1991 Proof *FDC** £500	1994 Proof *FDC** £500	1997 Proof *FDC** £600
1992 Proof *FDC** £500	1995 Proof *FDC** £500	

4252 Five pounds R. St George, 'U' in a circle to left of date.

	UNC		*UNC*
1985 (Issued: 13,626)..............	£400	1993 (Issued: 906)	£450
1986 (Issued: 7,723)................	£400	1994 (Issued: 1,000)	£500
1990 (Issued: 1,226)................	£425	1995 (Issued: 1,000)	£500
1991 (Issued: 976)...................	£450	1996 (Issued: 901)	£500
1992 (Issued: 797)...................	£450	1997 (Edition: 1,000).................	£500

4253 Five pounds Uncouped portrait of Queen Elizabeth II. As illustration. R. St. George, 'U' in a circle to left of date.
1987 (Issued: 5,694)...............	£425	1988 (Issued: 3,315)	£425

4254 Five pounds 500th Anniversary of Sovereign. As illustration 4277
1989 (Issued: 2,937)...............	£450	— — Proof *FDC** £500	

4261 Two pounds. R. St. George
1985 Proof *FDC** £200	1991 Proof *FDC* (Issued: 620) £225
1987 Proof *FDC* (Issued: 1,801) £175	1992 Proof *FDC* (Issued: 476) £225
1988 Proof *FDC* (Issued: 1,551) £175	1993 Proof *FDC* (Issued: 414) £225
1990 Proof *FDC* (Issued: 716) £200	1996 Proof *FDC* £250

4263 Two pounds 500th Anniversary of Sovereign. As illustration 4277
1989 Proof *FDC* (Issued: 2,000) £250

The 1986 £2, 1994 £2 and two types of 1995 £2 commemorative coins in gold previously listed as 4262, 4264, 4265 & 4266 respectively are now shown in the section commencing 4311 with their respective types in other metals.

4271 Sovereign. R. St. George
1985 Proof FDC (Issued: 11,393) £105	1992 Proof FDC (Issued: 4,772) £160
1986 Proof FDC (Issued: 5,079) £110	1993 Proof FDC (Issued: 4,349) £160
1987 Proof FDC (Issued: 9,979) £110	1994 Proof FDC (Issued: 4,998) £160
1988 Proof FDC (Issued: 7,670) £110	1995 Proof FDC (Issued: 7,500) £160
1990 Proof FDC (Issued: 4,767) £140	1996 Proof FDC (Issued: 7,500) £160
1991 Proof FDC (Issued: 4,713) £140	1997 Proof FDC (Edition: 7,500) £155

* Coins marked thus were originally issued in Royal Mint sets. Where numbers of coins issued or the Edition limit is quoted, these refer to individual coins. Additional coins were included in sets which are listed in the appropriate section.

4272 Sovereign. 500th Anniversary of Sovereign. As illustration 4277
1989 Proof *FDC* (Issued: 10,535) £175

4277

4276 Half-sovereign. R. St. George

1985 Proof *FDC* (Issued: 9,951) £65	1992 Proof *FDC* (Issued: 3,783) £80
1986 Proof *FDC* (Issued: 4,575) £65	1993 Proof *FDC* (Issued: 2,910) £85
1987 Proof *FDC* (Issued: 8,187) £65	1994 Proof *FDC* (Issued: 5,000) £85
1988 Proof *FDC* (Issued: 7,074) £65	1995 Proof *FDC* (Issued: 4,900) £85
1990 Proof *FDC* (Issued: 4,231) £80	1996 Proof *FDC* (Issued: 5,730) £85
1991 Proof *FDC* (Issued: 3,588) £80	1997 Proof *FDC* (Issued: 7,500) £85

4277 Half-sovereign 500th Anniversary of Sovereign. As illustration 4277
1989 Proof *FDC* (Issued: 8,888) £80

4281

	UNC		*UNC*
	£		£

4281 Britannia. One hundred pounds. (1oz of fine gold) R. Britannia standing.

1987....................................	BV	— Proof *FDC* (Issued: 626) £350	
— Proof *FDC* (Issued: 2,486) £350		1989	BV
1988....................................	BV	— Proof *FDC* (Issued: 338) £350	

4282 Britannia. One hundred pounds. (1oz of fine gold alloyed with silver) R. Britannia standing.

1990....................................	BV	— Proof *FDC** £450	
— Proof *FDC* (Issued: 262) £350		1994	BV
1991....................................	BV	— Proof *FDC** £450	
— Proof *FDC* (Issued: 143) £400		1995	BV
1992....................................	BV	— Proof *FDC** £500	
— Proof *FDC** £450		1996	BV
1993....................................	BV	— Proof *FDC** £500	

Where numbers of coins are quoted, these refer to individual coins. Additional coins were included in sets which are listed in the appropriate section.

* Coins marked thus were originally issued in Royal Mint sets.

4283

4283 **Britannia. One Hundred pounds.** (1 oz of fine gold, alloyed with silver) R. Standing figure of Britannia in horse drawn chariot. 10th Anniversary of Britannia issue
1997 Proof *FDC* (Edition: 1,000) £545

4286

4286 **Britannia. Fifty pounds.** (1/2oz of fine gold). R. Britannia standing.

1987..	BV	— Proof *FDC** £160	
— Proof *FDC* (Issued: 2,485) £160		1989	BV
1988..	BV	— Proof *FDC** £175	

4287 **Britannia. Fifty pounds.** (1/2oz of fine gold, alloyed with Silver)
R. Britannia standing.

1990..	BV	— Proof *FDC** £250	
— Proof *FDC** £200		1994	BV
1991..	BV	— Proof *FDC** £250	
— Proof *FDC** £200		1995	BV
1992..	**	— Proof *FDC** £250	
— Proof *FDC** £250		1996	BV
1993..	BV	— Proof *FDC** £250	

4288

4288 **Britannia. Fifty pounds.** (1/2 oz fine gold, alloyed with silver) R. Standing figure of Britannia in horse drawn chariot 10th Anniversay of Britannia issue
1997 Proof *FDC** £300

4291   4296

4291 Britannia. Twenty five pounds. (1/4oz of fine gold). R. Britannia standing.

1987....................................... BV   — Proof *FDC** £85
— Proof *FDC* (Issued: 3,500) £85   1989 .... BV
1988....................................... BV   — Proof *FDC** £100

4292 Britannia. Twenty five pounds. (1/4oz of fine gold alloyed with silver).
R. Britannia standing.

1990.. BV   — Proof *FDC** £135
— Proof *FDC** £120   1994 .... BV
1991.. BV   — Proof *FDC** £135
— Proof *FDC** £135   1995 .... BV
1992.. BV   — Proof *FDC** £135
— Proof *FDC** £135   1996 .... BV
1993.. ***   — Proof *FDC** £135

4293

4293 Britannia. Twenty five pounds. (1/4 oz fine gold, alloyed with silver) R. Standing figure of
Britannia in horse drawn chariot. 10th Anniversary of Britannia issue
1997 Proof *FDC* (Edition: 2,500) £135

4296 Britannia. Ten pounds. (1/10oz of fine gold). R. Britannia standing.

1987....................................... BV   — Proof *FDC* (Issued: 2,694) £50
— Proof *FDC* (Issued: 3,500) £50   1989 .... BV
1988....................................... BV   — Proof *FDC* (Issued: 1,609) £55

4297 Britannia. Ten pounds. (1/10oz of fine gold alloyed with silver). R. Britannia standing.

1990.. BV   — Proof *FDC* (Issued: 997)   £65
— Proof *FDC* (Issued: 1,571) £65   1994 .... **
1991.. BV   — Proof *FDC* (Issued: 994)   £65
— Proof *FDC* (Issued: 954)   £65   1995 .... BV
1992.. *   — Proof *FDC* (Issued: 1,500) £65
— Proof *FDC* (Issued: 1,000) £65   1996 .... BV
1993....................................... BV   — Proof *FDC* (Issued: 2,379) £65

* Coins marked thus were originally issued in Royal Mint sets.
** Issues of bullion quality coins of these years were modest and coins should command a premium
*** Extremely small numbers issued.

4298

4298   Britannia. Ten pounds. (1/10 oz fine gold, alloyed with silver) R. Standing figure of
Britannia in horse drawn chariot. 10th Anniversary of Britannia issue
1997 Proof *FDC* (Edition: 5,000) £65

SILVER

4300

4300   Britannia. Two pounds. (1 oz fine silver) R. Standing figure of Britannia in horse drawn
chariot. 10th Anniversary of Britannia issue
1997 Proof *FDC* (Edition: 20,000) £35

4300A

4300A Britannia. One pound. (1/2 oz of fine silver) R. Standing figure of Britannia in horse
chariot. 10th Anniversary of Britannia issue
1997 Proof *FDC** £25

* Coins marked thus were originally issued in Royal Mint Sets.

4300B

4300B Britannia. Fifty pence. (1/4 oz of fine silver) R. Standing figure of Britannia in horse drawn
chariot. 10th Anniversary of Britannnia issue
1997 Proof *FDC** £20

4300C

4300C Britannia. Twenty pence. (1/4 oz of fine silver) R. Standing figure of Britannia in horse
drawn chariot. 10th Anniversary of Britannia issue
1997 Proof *FDC* (Edition: 50,000) £15

CUPRO-NICKEL

4301

	UNC
	£
4301 Five pounds (crown). Queen Mother 90th birthday commemorative. 1990	8
— Specimen in presentation folder (Issued: 45,250)	10
— Proof in silver *FDC* (Issued: 56,102) £38	
— Proof in gold FDC (Issued: 2,500) £600	

* Coins marked thus were originally issued in Royal Mint Sets.

4302

4302 **Five pounds (crown).** 40th Anniversary of the Coronation. 1993 7
— Specimen in presentation folder.. 9
— Proof *FDC* (in 1993 set, see PS77)* £9
— Proof in silver *FDC* (Edition: 100,000) £32
— Proof in gold *FDC* (Edition: 2,500) £650

4303

4303 **Five pounds (crown).** 70th Birthday of Queen Elizabeth II. R. The Queen's personal flag, the
Royal Standard, the Union Flag, two pennants bearing the dates '1926' and '1996' all against
a backdrop of Windsor Castle. Edge: VIVAT REGINA ELIZABETHA.
1996... 7
— Specimen in presentation folder.. 9
— Proof (in 1996 set, See PS83) *FDC** £12
— Proof in silver *FDC* (Edition: 70,000) £32
— Proof in gold *FDC* (Issued: 2,127) £650

* *Coins marked thus were originally issued in Royal Mint Sets.*

4304

4304 Five pounds (crown). Golden Wedding of Queen Elizabeth II and Prince Philip. Conjoint
portraits of The Queen and Prince Philip. R. Royal Arms and Arms of Prince Philip surmounted by St. Edward's crown which divides the dates 1947 and 1997 20 November, and an
anchor below with the denomination.

1997 7
— Specimen in presentation folder... 9
— Proof *FDC* (in 1997 set, See PS85)* £12
— Proof in silver *FDC* (Edition: 75,000) £32
— Proof in gold *FDC* (Edition: 2,750) £650

NICKEL-BRASS

4311

	UNC		*UNC*
	£		£

4311 Two pounds. R. St. Andrew's cross surmounted by a thistle of Scotland. Edge XIII
COMMONWEALTH GAMES SCOTLAND 1986 3
— Specimen in presentation folder   5   — Proof in silver *FDC* (Issued: 59,779) £20
— .500 silver (Issued: 58,881)   12   — Proof in gold *FDC* (Issued: 3,277) £200
— Proof *FDC** £6

* *Coins marked thus were originally issued in Royal Mint Sets.*

4312   4313

4312 Two pounds 300th Anniversary of Bill of Rights. R Cypher of William and Mary, House of Commons mace and St. Edward's crown.

1989......................................   4   — Proof in silver *FDC* (Issued: 25,000) £23
— Specimen in presentation folder   5   — Proof piedfort in silver *FDC** £45
— Proof *FDC** £6

4313 Two pounds 300th Anniversary of Claim of Right (Scotland). R. As 4312, but with crown of Scotland.

1989......................................   8   — Proof in silver *FDC* (Issued: 24,852) £23
— Specimen in presentation folder 10   — Proof piedfort in silver *FDC** £45
— Proof *FDC** £10

4314

4314 Two pounds 300th Anniversary of the Bank of England. R: Bank's original Corporate Seal, with Crown & Cyphers of William III & Mary II. Edge SIC VOC NON VOBIS.

1994......................................   3   — Proof piedfort in silver *FDC* (Issued: 9,569) £50
— Specimen in presentation folder   5   — Proof in gold *FDC* (Issued: 1,000) £400
— Proof *FDC** £6..................   — gold error. Obverse as 4251 (Included in
— Proof in silver *FDC* (Issued: 27,957) £30   above) £550

* Coins marked thus were originally issued in Royal Mint sets.

4315

4315   Two pounds 50th Anniversary of the End of World War II. R: A Dove of Peace.
Edge 1945 IN PEACE GOODWILL 1995

1995   3
— Specimen in presentation folder   4
— Proof *FDC* *£6 ....   — Proof piedfort in silver *FDC* (Edition: 10,000) £50
— Proof in silver *FDC* (Edition: 50,000) £30 — Proof in gold *FDC* (Edition: 2,500) £375

4316

4316   Two pounds 50th Anniversary of the Establishment of the United Nations. R: 50th
Anniversary symbol and an array of flags. Edge NATIONS UNITED FOR PEACE
1945-1995.

1995   3
— Specimen in presentation folder...   4
— Proof in silver *FDC* (Edition: 175,000) £30   — Proof in gold *FDC* (Edition: 17,500) £350
— Proof piedfort in silver *FDC* (Edition: 10,000) £50

4317

4317   Two pounds European Football Championships. R: A stylised representation of a football.
Edge: TENTH EUROPEAN CHAMPIONSHIP.

1996   3
— Specimen in presentation folder...   4
— Proof *FDC** £6 ....   — Proof piedfort in silver *FDC* (Edition: 10,000) £55
— Proof in silver *FDC* (Edition: 50,000) £26 — Proof in gold *FDC* (Issued: 2,098) £295

* Coins marked thus were originally issued in Royal Mint Sets.

4318

UNC   *UNC*
£   £

4318 **Two pounds** Bimetallic currency issue. **R.** Four concentric circles representing the Iron Age, 18th century industrial development, silicon chip, and Internet. Edge: STANDING ON THE SHOULDERS OF GIANTS

1997 3

— Specimen in presentation folder 6

— Proof *FDC** £6

— Proof in silver FDC (Edition: 30,000) £29

— Proof piedfort in silver *FDC* (Edition: 10,000) £50

— Proof in gold *FDC* (Edition: 2,500) £325

4331   4332

4331 **One pound** (Welsh design). Edge PLEIDIOL WYF I'M GWLAD

1985 2

— Specimen in presentation folder (Issued: 24,850)

— Proof *FDC** £5

— Proof in silver *FDC* (Issued: 50,000) £21

— Proof piedfort in silver *FDC* (Issued: 15,000) £45

1990 3

— Proof *FDC** £6

— Proof in silver *FDC* (Issued: 23,277) £21

4332 **One pound** (Northern Irish design). Edge DECUS ET TUTAMEN

1986 2

— Specimen in presentatioon folder (Issued: 19,908) 4

— Proof *FDC** £4

— Proof in silver *FDC* (Issued: 37, 958) £20

— Proof piedfort in silver *FDC* (Issued: 15,000) £45

1991 3

— Proof *FDC** £6

— Proof in silver *FDC* (Issued: 22,922) £20

* Coins marked thus were originally issued in Royal Mint sets.

4333								4334

**4333	One pound** (English design). Edge DECUS ET TUTAMEN
	1987..	2
	— Specimen in presentation folder (Issued: 72,607)
	— Proof *FDC** £6
	— Proof in silver *FDC* (Issued: 50,000) £20
	— Proof piedfort in silver *FDC* (Issued: 15,000) £45
	1992..	3
	— Proof *FDC** £6
	— Proof in silver *FDC* (Issued: 13,065) £21
**4334	One pound** (Royal Shield). Edge DECUS ET TUTAMEN
	1988..	3
	— Specimen in presentation folder (Issued: 29,550)..................................	5
	— Proof *FDC** £6
	— Proof in silver *FDC* (Issued: 50,000) £25
	— Proof piedfort in silver *FDC* (Issued: 10,000) £45
**4335	One pound** (Scottish design). Edge NEMO ME IMPUNE LACESSIT (Illus. as 4222)
	1989.......................................	3	— Proof in silver *FDC* (Issued: 22,275) £20
	— Proof FDC* £6			— Proof piedfort in silver *FDC* (Issued: 10,000) £50
**4336	One pound** (Royal Arms design). Edge DECUS ET TUTAMEN (Illus. as 4221)
	1993.......................................	3	— Proof in silver *FDC* (Issued: 16,526) £30
	— Proof FDC* £6			— Proof piedfort in silver *FDC* (Edition: 12,500) £50

				4337					4338					4339					4340

**4337	One pound** (Scottish design). R: Lion rampant within a double tressure. Edge NEMO ME
	IMPUNE LACESSIT
	1994.......................................	2	— Proof in silver *FDC* (Issued: 25,000) £50
	— Specimen in presentation folder	3	— Proof piedfort in silver *FDC* (Edition: 11,722) £50
	— Proof *FDC** £6
**4338	One pound** (Welsh design). R. Heraldic dragon Edge PLEIDIOL WYF I'M GWLAD
	1995.......................................	2	— Proof in silver *FDC* (Issued: 27,445) £23
	— Specimen in presentation folder	3	— Proof in piedfort in silver *FDC* (Issued: 8,458) £50
	— Proof *FDC** £5

* Coins marked thus were originally issued in Royal Mint sets.

4339 **One pound** (Northern Irish design). R. A Celtic cross incorporating a pimpernel at its centre. Edge DECUS ET TUTAMEN

1996...	2	— Proof in silver *FDC* (Issued: 25,000) £24	
— Specimen in presentation folder	3	— Proof piedfort in silver *FDC* (Issued: 10,000) £50	
— Proof *FDC** £6			

4340 **One pound** (English design) R. Three lions. Edge: DECUS ET TUTAMEN.

1997...	2	— Proof in silver *FDC* (Edition: 30,000) £25	
— Specimen in presentation folder	5	— Proof piedfort in silver *FDC* (Edition: 10,000) £45	
— Proof *FDC** £6			

4351

4351 **Fifty pence.** R. Britannia r. (4341)

1985	3	— Proof *FDC** £3		1995*.........................	3		
— Proof *FDC** £3		1990*.........................	4	— Proof *FDC** £4			
1986*	3	1991*.........................	4	1996*.........................	3		
— Proof *FDC** £3		— Proof *FDC** £5		— Proof *FDC** £4			
1987*	3	1992*.........................	4	— Proof in silver *FDC** £15			
— Proof *FDC** £3		— Proof *FDC** £5		1997.........................	3		
1988*	3	1993*.........................	4	— Proof *FDC** £4			
— Proof *FDC** £4		— Proof *FDC** £4		— Proof in silver *FDC** £24			
1989*	4						

1990* column also shows "— Proof *FDC** £5 ...." and 1991* shows "— Proof *FDC** £5 ...." and 1992* shows "— Proof *FDC** £5 ...."

4352

4352 **Fifty pence** Presidency of the Council of European Community Ministers and completion of the Single Market. R Conference table top and twelve stars

1992-1993	5	— Proof piedfort in silver *FDC* (Issued: 10,993) £45	
— Proof *FDC** £5		— Proof in gold *FDC* (Issued: 1,864) £400	
— Proof in silver *FDC** (Issued: 26,890) £24			

4352A — Specimen in presentation folder with 1992 date 4351 5

* Coins marked thus were originally issued in Royal Mint sets.

4353

4353 **Fifty pence** 50th Anniversary of the Normandy Landings on D-Day. R: Allied Invasion Force.

1994... 1   — Proof in silver *FDC* (Issued: 40,000) £30
— Specimen in presentation folder 2   — Proof piedfort in silver *FDC* (Issued: 10,000) £50
— Proof *FDC** £5   — Proof in gold *FDC* (Issued: 1,877) £375

4354 **Fifty penc**e R. Britannia: diam 27.3mm

1997... 1   — Proof in silver *FDC* £27
— Proof *FDC** £4   — Proof piedfort in silver *FDC* (Edition: 10,000) £46

4361

4361 **Twenty pence.** R. Crowned double rose

1985	— Proof *FDC** £3.....	1994..........................
— Proof *FDC** £2	1990..........................	— Proof *FDC** £3
1986*	— Proof *FDC** £3.....	1995..........................
1		— Proof *FDC** £3
— Proof *FDC** £2	1991..........................	1996..........................
1987	— Proof *FDC** £3.....	— Proof *FDC** £3
— Proof *FDC** £2	1992..........................	— Proof in silver *FDC** £15
1988	— Proof *FDC** £3.....	1997..........................
— Proof *FDC** £3	1993..........................	— Proof *FDC** £3
1989	— Proof *FDC** £3.....	

4366

	UNC		*UNC*		*UNC*
	£		£		£

4366 **Ten pence.** R. Lion passant guardant

1985*	3	1988*..........................	3	1991*.........................	4
— Proof *FDC* * £2		— Proof *FDC** £3....		— Proof *FDC** £3	
1986*	2	1989*..........................	4	1992*.........................	3
— Proof *FDC** £2		— Proof *FDC** £3.....		— Proof *FDC** £4	
1987*	3	1990*..........................	4	— Proof in silver *FDC** £14	
— Proof *FDC** £3		— Proof *FDC** £3			

* Coins marked thus were originally issued in Royal Mint sets.

4367

4367 **Ten pence** R Lion passant guardant: diam. 24.5mm
1992...
— Proof *FDC** £3 ....
— Proof in silver *FDC** £14 ..
— Proof piedfort in silver *FDC** (Issued: 14,167) £30
1993*.......................................
— Proof *FDC** £2 ....
1994*.......................................
— Proof *FDC** £2 ....

1995 ....
— Proof *FDC** £2
1996 ....
— Proof *FDC** £2
— Proof in silver *FDC** £15
1997 ....
— Proof *FDC** £2

4371

4371 **Five pence.** R. Crowned thistle
1985*   1
— Proof *FDC** £1
1986*   1
— Proof *FDC** £1
1987 ....

— Proof *FDC** £2 ....
1988..........................
— Proof *FDC** £2 ....
1989..........................
— Proof *FDC** £2

1990*   2
— Proof *FDC** £3
— Proof in silver *FDC** £12

4372

4372 **Five pence.** R. Crowned thistle: diam 18mm
1990 ....
— Proof *FDC** £2
— Proof in silver *FDC** £12
— Proof piedfort in silver
   FDC (Issued: 20,000) £25
1991 ....
— Proof *FDC** £2

1992 ....
— Proof *FDC** £2 ....
1993* ....
— Proof *FDC** £2 ....
1994 ....
— Proof *FDC** £2 ....
1995 ....

— Proof *FDC** £2
1996..........................
— Proof *FDC** £2
— Proof in silver *FDC** £15
1997 ....
— Proof *FDC** £2

* Coins marked thus were originally issued in Royal Mint sets.

BRONZE

4376   4381

4376 Two pence. R. Plumes
   1985 ....   1988.........................   1991.........................
   — Proof *FDC** £1   — Proof *FDC** £1 ....   — Proof *FDC** £1
   1986 ....   1989.........................   1992* ....
   — Proof *FDC** £1   — Proof *FDC** £1 ....   — Proof *FDC** £1
   1987 ....   1990.........................
   — Proof *FDC** £1   — Proof *FDC** £1
4381 One penny. R. Portcullis with chains
   1985 ....   1988.........................   1991.........................
   — Proof *FDC** £1   — Proof *FDC** £1 ....   — Proof *FDC** £1
   1986 ....   1989.........................   1992*.........................
   — Proof *FDC** £1   — Proof *FDC** £1 ....   — Proof *FDC** £1
   1987 ....   1990.........................
   — Proof *FDC** £1   — Proof *FDC** £1

COPPER PLATED STEEL

4386 Two pence R. Plumes
   1992 ....   — Proof *FDC** £1 ....   — Proof *FDC** £1
   1993 ....   1995.........................   — Proof in silver *FDC** £15
   — Proof *FDC** £1   — Proof *FDC** £1 ....   1997.........................
   1994 ....   1996.........................   — Proof *FDC** £1
4391 One penny R. Portcullis with chains
   1992 ....   — Proof *FDC** £1 ....   — Proof *FDC** £1
   1993 ....   1995.........................   — Proof in silver *FDC** £15
   — Proof *FDC** £1   — Proof *FDC** £1 ....   1997.........................
   1994 ....   1996.........................   — Proof *FDC** £1

* Coins marked thus were originally issued in Royal Mint sets.

GOLD

4400

4400 Five pounds. R. St George
1998 Proof *FDC** £650

4410 Five pounds. R. St. George, 'U' in a circle to left of date
1998 £300

4420 Two pounds. R. St. George
1998 Proof *FDC** £300

4430 Sovereign. R. St. George
1998 Proof *FDC* (Edition: 10,000) £150

4440 Half sovereign. R. St. George
1998 Proof *FDC* (Edition: 7,500) £85

4450

4450 Britannia. One Hundred pounds. (1oz fine gold, alloyed with silver) R. Standing figure of
Britannia
1998 Proof *FDC** £550

4460

4460 Britannia. Fifty pounds. (1/2 oz of fine gold, alloyed with silver) R. Standing figure of
Britannia
1998 Proof *FDC** £300

* Coins marked thus were originally issued in Royal Mint sets.

4470

4470 Britannia. Twenty five pounds. (1/4 oz of fine gold, alloyed with silver) R. Standing figure of Britannia
1998 — Proof *FDC* (Edition: 1,000) £135

4480 Britannia. Ten pounds. (1/10 oz of fine gold, alloyed with silver) R. Standing figure of Britannia
1998 — Proof *FDC* (Edition: 5,000) £65

SILVER

4500

4500 Britannia. Two pounds. (1 oz of fine silver) R. Standing figure of Britannia
1998 .... £10
— Proof *FDC* (Edition: 20,000) £35

4510

4510 Britannia. One pound. (1/2 oz of fine silver) R. Standing figure of Britannia
1998 — Proof *FDC** £25

4520

4520 Britannia. Fifty pence. (1/4 oz of fine silver) R. Standing figure of Britannia
1998 — Proof *FDC** £20

4530

4530 Britannia. Twenty pence. (1/10 oz of fine silver) R. Standing figure of Britannia
1998 — Proof *FDC* (Edition: 10,000) £15

* Coins marked thus were originally issued in Royal Mint sets.

CUPRO-NICKEL

4550

4550 Five pounds (crown). Prince of Wales 50th Birthday. R. Portrait of The Prince of Wales with
the inscriptions 'The Prince's Trust' and 'Helping young people to succeed' on a ribbon at the
base of the portrait with the denomination 'Five Pounds' and the dates 1948 and 1998.
1998 ....   £7
— Specimen in presentation folder £10
— Proof *FDC* (in 1998 set, see PS 87)* £12
— Proof in silver *FDC* (Edition: 35,000) £33
— Proof in gold *FDC* (Edition: 2,000) £600

NICKEL-BRASS

4570

4570 **Two pounds.** Bimetallic currency issue. R. Four concentric circles, representing the Iron Age, 18th century industrial development, silicon chip and Internet. Edge: STANDING OF THE SHOULDERS OF GIANTS
1998
— Proof *FDC** £6
— Proof in silver *FDC* (Edition: 25,000) £29
— Proof PIEDFORT in silver *FDC* (Edition: 10,000) £50

* Coins marked thus were originally issued in Royal Mint sets.

4590

4590 **One pound** (Royal Arms design). Edge: DECUS ET TUTAMEN (Illus. as 4221)
1998
— Proof *FDC** £6
— Proof in silver *FDC* (Edition: 25,000) £25
— Proof piedfort in silver *FDC* (Edition: 10,000) £45
4610 **Fifty pence.** R. Britannia. (Illus. as 4351)
1998
— Proof *FDC** £3

* Coins marked thus were originally issued in Royal Mint sets.

4611

4611 **Fifty pence.** R. Celebratory pattern of twelve stars reflecting the European flag with the dates 1973 and 1998 commemorating the 25th Anniversary of the United Kingdom's membership of the European Union and Presidency of the Council of Ministers.
1998
— Proof *FDC** £5
— Proof in silver *FDC* (Edition: 25,000) £25
— Proof piedfort in silver *FDC* (Edition: 10,000) £45
— Proof in gold *FDC* (Edition: 1,500) £250

4612

4612 **Fifty pence.** R. A pair of hands set against a pattern of radiating lines with the words Fiftieth Anniversary and the value 50 pence with the initials NHS.
1998
— Specimen in presentation folder £3
— Proof *FDC** £5
— Proof in silver *FDC* (Edition: 25,000) £25
— Proof piedfort in silver *FDC* (Edition: 10,000) £45
— Proof in gold *FDC* (Edition: 1,500) £250

4630 **Twenty pence.** R. Crowned double rose. (Illus. as 4230)
1998
—Proof *FDC** £3

4650 **Ten pence.** R. Lion passant guardant. (Illus. as 4232)
1998
— Proof *FDC** £3

4670 **Five pence.** R. Crowned thistle. (Illus. as 4234)
1998
— Proof *FDC** £3

* *Coins marked thus were originally issued in Royal Mint sets.*

COPPER PLATED STEEL

4690 **Two pence.** R. Plumes. (Illus. as 4376)
1998
— Proof *FDC** £3
4710 **One pence.** R. Portcullis with chains. (Illus. as 4381)
1998
— Proof *FDC** £3

* Coins marked thus were originally issued in Royal Mint sets

Uncirculated Sets

PS21 — **1982**	Uncirculated (specimen) set in Royal Mint folder, 50p to $^1/_2$p, new reverse type, including 20 pence (Issued: 205,000)	(7)	9
PS22 — **1983**	'U.K.' £1 (4221) to $^1/_2$p (Issued: 637,100)	(8)	15
PS23 — **1984**	'Scottish' £1 (4222) to $^1/_2$p (Issued: 158,820)	(8)	13
PS24 — **1985**	'Welsh' £1 (4331) to 1p, new portrait of The Queen (Issued: 102,015)	(7)	13
PS25 — **1986**	Commonwealth Games £2 (4311) plus 'Northern Irish' £1 (4332) to 1p, ((Issued: 167,224)	(8)	14
PS26 — **1987**	'English' £1 (4333) to 1p, (Issued: 172,425)	(7)	12
PS27 — **1988**	'Arms' £1 (4334) to 1p, (Issued: 134,067)	(7)	15
PS28 — **1989**	'Scottish' £1 (4335) to 1p, (Issued: 77,569)	(7)	15
PS29 — **1989**	Bill of Rights and Claim of Right £2s (4312 and 4313) in Royal Mint folder (Issued: not known)...................................	(2)	9
PS30 — **1990**	'Welsh' £1 (4331) to 1p plus new 5p, (Issued: 102,606)..........	(8)	15
PS31 — **1991**	'Northern Irish' £1 (4332) to 1p, (Issued: 74,975)	(7)	15
PS32 — **1992**	'English' £1 (4333), 'European Community' 50p (4352) and Britannia 50p, 20p to 1p plus new 10p (Issued: 78,421)	(9)	15
PS33 — **1993**	'UK' £1 (4336), 'European Community' 50p to 1p ((Issued: 56,945)	(8)	12
PS34 — **1994**	'Bank' £2 (4314), 'Scottish' £1 (4337) and 'D-Day' 50p (4353) to 1p, (Issued: 177,971)	(8)	12
PS35 — **1995**	'Peace' £2 (4315) and 'Welsh' £1 (4338) to 1p (Issued: 105,647)	(8)	12
PS36 — **1996**	'Football' £2 (4317) and 'Northern Irish' £1 (4339) to 1p (Issued: 86,501)..	(8)	11
PS37 — **1997**	'Bimetallic' £2 (4318), 'English' £1 (4340) to 1p plus new 50p (Issue figure not yet available)..	(9)	11
PS38 — **1998**	'Bimetallic' £2 (4570), 'UK' £1 (4590) and 'EU' 50 pence (4611) to 1 pence	(9)	11
PS39 — **1998**	'EU' and Britannia 50 pence (4611 and 4610) in Royal Mint folder.	(2)	6

Proof Sets

PS47 — **1971**	Decimal coinage set, 50 new pence ('Britannia' to $^1/_2$ new pence, plus medallion in sealed plastic case with card wrapper (Issued: 350,000)..	(6)	10
PS48 — **1972**	Proof 'Silver Wedding' Crown struck in c/n (4226) plus 50p to $^1/_2$p (Issued: 150,000)	(7)	12
PS49 — **1973**	'EEC' 50p (4224) plus 10p to $^1/_2$p, (Issued: 100,000)..............	(6)	10
PS50 — **1974**	Britannia 50p to $^1/_2$p, as 1971 (Issued: 100,000)	(6)	8
PS51 — **1975**	50p to $^1/_2$p (as 1974), (Issued: 100,000)	(6)	8
PS52 — **1976**	50p to $^1/_2$p, as 1975, (Issued: 100,000)...................................	(6)	8
PS53 — **1977**	Proof 'Silver Jubilee' Crown struck in c/n (4227) plus 50p to $^1/_2$p, (Issued: 193,000)	(7)	10
PS54 — **1978**	50p to $^1/_2$p, as 1976, (Issued: 86,100).....................................	(6)	12
PS55 — **1979**	50p to $^1/_2$p, as 1978, (Issued: 81,000)....................................	(6)	10
PS56 — **1980**	50p to $^1/_2$p, as 1979, (Issued: 143,000)..................................	(6)	9
PS57 — **1981**	50p to $^1/_2$p, as 1980, (Issued: 100,300)..................................	(6)	9
PS58 — **1982**	50p to $^1/_2$p including 20 pence (Issued: 106,800)....................	(7)	10
PS59 — **1983**	'U.K.' £1 (4221) to $^1/_2$p in new packaging (Issued: 107,800)..	(8)	17
PS60 — **1984**	'Scottish' £1 (4222) to $^1/_2$p, (Issued: 106,520)........................	(8)	15
PS61 — **1985**	'Welsh' £1 (4331) to 1p, (Issued: 102,015).............................	(7)	15
PS62 — **1985**	As last but packed in deluxe red leather case (Included above)	(7)	20
PS63 — **1986**	Commonwealth games £2 (4311) plus 'Northern Irish' £1 (4332) to 1p, (Issued: 104,597)	(8)	18
PS64 — **1986**	As last but packed in deluxe red leather case (Included above)	(8)	23
PS65 — **1987**	'English' £1 (4333) to 1p, (Issued: 88,659)	(7)	20

PS66 — **1987**	As last but packed in deluxe leather case (Included above)	(7)	24
PS67 — **1988**	'Arms' £1 (4334) to 1p, (Issued: 79,314)	(7)	25
PS68 — **1988**	As last but packed in deluxe leather case (Included above)	(7)	29
PS69 — **1989**	Bill of Rights and Claim of Right £2s (4312 and 4313), 'Scottish' £1 (4335) to 1p, (Issued: 85,704)...	(9)	28
PS70 — **1989**	As last but packed in red leather case, (Included above)	(9)	32
PS71 — **1990**	'Welsh' £1 (4331) to 1p plus new 5p, (Issued: 79,052)............	(8)	27
PS72 — **1990**	As last but packed in red leather case (Included above)	(8)	32
PS73 — **1991**	'Northern Irish' £1 (4332) to 1p, (Issued: 55,144)	(7)	27
PS74 — **1991**	As last but packed in red leather case (Included above)	(7)	33
PS75 — **1992**	'English' £1 (4333), 'European community' 50p (4352) and Britannia 50p, 20p to 1p plus new 10p, (Issued: 44,337)	(9)	28
PS76 — **1992**	As last but packed in red leather case (Issued: 17,989)	(9)	33
PS77 — **1993**	'Coronation Anniversary' £5 struck in c/n (4302), 'U.K.' £1 (4336), 50p to 1p, (Issued: 43,509)...	(8)	30
PS78 — **1993**	As last but packed in red leather case (Issued: 22,571)	(8)	35
PS79 — **1994**	'Bank' £2 (4314), 'Scottish' £1 (4337), 'D-Day' 50p (4353) to 1p, (Issued: 44,643)..	(8)	28
PS80 — **1994**	As last but packed in red leather case (Issued: 22,078)	(8)	34
PS81 — **1995**	'Peace' £2 (4315), 'Welsh' £1 (4338) to 1p, (Issued: 42,842) .	(8)	29
PS82 — **1995**	As last but packed in red leather case (Issued: 17,797)	(8)	35
PS83 — **1996**	Proof '70th Birthday' £5 struck in c/n (4303), 'Football' £2 (4317), 'Northern Irish' £1 (4339) to 1p, (Issued: 46,295).......	(9)	30
PS84 — **1996**	As last but packed in red leather case (Issued: 21,286)	(9)	35
PS85 — **1997**	Proof 'Golden Wedding' £5 struck in c/n (4304), 'Bimetallic' £2 (4318), 'English' £1 (4340) to 1p plus new 50p (Edition: 100,000)	(10)	33
PS86 — **1997**	As last but packed in red leather case (Included above)	(10)	40
PS87 — **1998**	Proof £5 'Prince of Wales 50th Birthday', struck in CN (4550), 'Bimetallic' £2 (4570), 'UK'. £1 (4590); 'EU' 50 pence (4611) to 1 pence. (Edition: 100,000)...	(10)	33
PS88 — **1998**	As last, but packed in red leather case. (Edition – included in above)	(10)	40

Silver Sets

PS96 — **1989**	Bill of Rights and Claim of Right £2s (4312 and 4313), Silver piedfort proofs (Issued: 10,000)..	(2)	85
PS97 — **1989**	As last but Silver proofs (Issue figure not known)	(2)	42
PS98 — **1990**	2 x 5p Silver proofs (4371 and 4372), (Issued: 35,000)	(2)	24
PS99 — **1992**	2 x 10p Silver proofs (4366 and 4367), (Not known)..............	(2)	28
PS100 — **1996**	25th Anniversary of Decimal Currency (4339, 4351, 4361, 4367, 4372, 4386, 4391) in Silver proof (Edition: 15,000)	(7)	100
PS101 — **1997**	2 x 50p silver proofs (4351 and 4354) (Edition: 25,000)	(2)	48
PS102 — **1997**	Britannia proofs, £2 – 20 pence (4300, 4300A, 4300B, 4300C) (Edition: 15,000)..	(4)	85
PS103 — **1998**	Britannia proofs, £2 – 20 pence (4500, 4510, 4520, 4530) (Edition: 10,000)..	(4)	85
PS104 — **1998**	'EU' and 'NHS' Silver proofs (4611 and 4612)......................	(2)	50

Gold Sovereign Proof Sets

PS111 — **1980**	Gold £5 to half-sovereign (4201, 4203-4205) (Issued: 10,000)	(4)	700
PS112 — **1981**	U.K. Proof coin Commemorative collection. (Consists of £5, sovereign, 'Royal Wedding' Crown (4229) in silver, plus base metal proofs 50p to 1/2p), (Not known)	(9)	600
PS113 — **1982**	Gold £5 to half-sovereign (Issued: 2,500)	(4)	750

PS114 — **1983**	Gold £2, sovereign and half-sovereign, (Not known)...............	(3)	325
PS115 — **1984**	Gold £5, sovereign and half-sovereign, (Issued: 7,095)	(3)	600
PS116 — **1985**	Gold £5 to half-sovereign (4251, 4261, 4271, 4276) (Issued: 5,849)	(4)	750
PS117 — **1986**	Gold Commonwealth games £2, (4311) sovereign and half-sovereign (Issued: 12,500)	(3)	325
PS118 — **1987**	Gold £2 (4261), sovereign and half-sovereign (Issued: 12,500)	(3)	325
PS119 — **1988**	Gold £2 to half-sovereign (Issued: 11,192)	(3)	325
PS120 — **1989**	Sovereign Anniversary Gold £5 to half-sovereign (4254, 4263, 4272, 4277), (Issued: 5,000)	(4)	900
PS121 — **1989**	Gold £2 to half-sovereign (Issued: 7,936)	(3)	450
PS122 — **1990**	Gold £5 to half-sovereign (as 1985 issue), (Issued: 1,721)	(4)	775
PS123 — **1990**	Gold £2 to half-sovereign (as 1988 issue), (Issued: 1,937)	(3)	375
PS124 — **1991**	Gold £5 to half-sovereign (Issued: 1,336)	(4)	850
PS125 — **1991**	Gold £2 to half-sovereign (Issued: 1,152)	(3)	400
PS126 — **1992**	Gold £5 to half-sovereign (Issued: 1,165)	(4)	875
PS127 — **1992**	Gold £2 to half-sovereign (Issued: 967)	(3)	425
PS128 — **1993**	Gold £5 to half-sovereign with silver Pistrucci medal in case (Issued: 1,078)...	(5)	900
PS129 — **1993**	Gold £2 to half-sovereign (Issued: 663)	(3)	425
PS130 — **1994**	Gold £5, £2 (as 4314), sovereign and half-sovereign (Issued: 918)	(4)	1050
PS131 — **1994**	Gold £2, (as 4314), sovereign and half-sovereign (Issued: 1,249)	(3)	500
PS132 — **1995**	Gold £5, £2 (as 4315), sovereign and half-sovereign (Issued: 718)	(4)	1100
PS133 — **1995**	Gold £2 (as 4315), sovereign and half-sovereign (Issued: 1,112)	(3)	500
PS134 — **1996**	Gold £5 to half-sovereign (as 1992 issue) (Issued: 742)	(4)	1100
PS135 — **1996**	Gold £2 to half-sovereign (as 1992 issue) (Issued: 868)	(3)	500
PS136 — **1997**	Gold £5, £2 (as 4318), sovereign and half-sovereign (Edition: 1,000)	(4)	1175
PS137 — **1997**	Gold £2 (as 4318) to half-sovereign (Edition: 1,250)...............	(3)	500
PS138 — **1998**	Gold £5 to half sovereign (4400, 4420, 4430, 4440) (Edition: 1,500)	(4)	1175
PS139 — **1998**	Gold £2 to half sovereign (4420, 4430, 4440) (Edition: 2,000)	(3)	495

Britannia Series

PS147 — **1987**	Britannia Gold Proofs £100, £50, £25, £10 (4281, 4286, 4291, 4296), (Issued: 10,000)	(4)	625
PS148 — **1987**	Britannia Gold Proofs £25, £10 (4291 and 4296) (Issued: 11,100)	(2)	125
PS149 — **1988**	Britannia Proofs £100 – £10 (as 1987 issue) (Issued: 3,505) ...	(4)	625
PS150 — **1988**	Britannia Proofs £25, £10 (as 1987 issue) (Issued: 894)	(2)	125
PS151 — **1989**	Britannia Proofs £100 – £10 (as 1987) (Issued: 2,268)	(4)	675
PS152 — **1989**	Britannia Proofs £25, £10 (as 1987 issue) (Issued: 451)	(2)	150
PS153 — **1990**	Britannia Proofs, £100-£10, gold with the addition of silver alloy (4282, 4287, 4292, 4297) (Issued: 527)	(4)	775
PS154 — **1991**	Britannia Proofs, as PS153 (Issued: 509)	(4)	775
PS155 — **1992**	Britannia Proofs, as PS153 (Issued: 500)	(4)	900
PS156 — **1993**	Britannia Proofs, as PS153 (Issued: 462)	(4)	900
PS157 — **1994**	Britannia Proofs, as PS153 ((Issued: 435)	(4)	900
PS158 — **1995**	Britannia Proofs, as PS153 (Issued: 500)	(4)	1000
PS159 — **1996**	Britannia Proofs, as PS153 (Issued: 483)	(4)	1000
PS160 — **1997**	Britannia proofs £100, £50, £25, £10 (4283, 4288, 4293, 4298) (Edition: 1,500)	(4)	1045
PS161 — **1998**	Britannia proofs £100, £50, £25, £10 (4450, 4460, 4470, 4480) (Edition: 750)	(4)	1045

SOME COIN DENOMINATIONS

Gold

Angel	Eighty pence (6s. 8d.) from 1464; later 7s. 6d., 8s., 10s. and 11s.
Angelet or 1/2 Angel	Forty pence (3s. 4d.) from 1464, later 3s. 9d., 4s., 5s., 5s. 6d.
Aureus	Roman currency unit (originally 1/60th lb), discontinued A.D. 324 and superceded by the Solidus.
Britain Crown	Five shillings, 1604-12; 5s. 6d. (66d.) 1612-19.
Broad	Twenty shillings, Cromwell, 1656.
Crown	Five shillings, from 1544 (and see below and Britain Crown above).
Crown of the Rose	Four shillings and six pence, 1526.
Crown of the Double Rose	Five shillings, 1526-44.
Florin (Double Leopard)	Six shillings, Edward III.
George Noble	Eighty pence (6s. 8d.) 1526.
Gold 'Penny'	Twenty to twenty-four pence, Henry III.
Guinea	Pound (20s.) in 1663, then rising to 30s. in 1694 before falling to 21s. 6d., 1698-1717; 21s., 1717-1813.
Halfcrown	Thirty pence, 1526 intermittently to 1612; 2s. 9d. (33d.), 1612-19.
Helm (Quarter Florin)	Eighteen pence, Edward III.
Laurel	Twenty shillings, 1619-25.
Leopard (Half Florin)	Three shillings, Edward III.
Noble	Eighty pence (6s. 8d., or half mark), 1344 -1464.
Pound	Twenty shillings, 1592-1600 (see also Unite, Laurel, Broad, Guinea and Sovereign).
Quarter Angel	Two shillings, 1544 -7 and later 2s. 6d.
Rose Noble (Ryal)	Ten shillings, 1464 -70.
Rose-Ryal	Thirty shillings, 1604 -24.
Ryal	Ten shillings, Edward IV and Henry VII; fifteen shillings under Mary and Elizabeth I (see also Spur Ryal).
Solidus	Roman currency unit (1/72nd lb) from A.D. 312; it superceded the Aureus and is the 's' of the £.s.d.
Sovereign	Twenty shillings or pound, 1489-1526 (22s. 6d., 1526-44), 1544-53, 1603-04 and from 1817 (see also Pound, Unite, Laurel, Broad and Guinea, and Fine Sovereign below).
'Fine' Sovereign	Thirty shillings, 1550-96 (see also Rose-Ryal).
Spur-Ryal	Fifteen shillings, 1605-12; 16s. 6d., 1612-25.
Stater	Name commonly given to the standard Celtic gold coin.
Third-Guinea	Seven shillings, 1797-1813.
Thistle Crown	Four shillings, 1604-12; 4s. 5d., 1612-19.
Thrymsa	Early Anglo-Saxon version of the late Roman tremissis (one-third solidus).
Triple Unite	Three pounds, Charles I (Shrewsbury and Oxford only, 1642-4).
Unite	Twenty shillings, 1604-12 and 1625-62; 22s., 1612-19.

Silver (and Cupro-Nickel)

Antoninianus	Roman, 2 denarii in A.D. 214 (later debased to bronze).
Argenteus	Roman, a revived denarius.
Crown	Five shillings, 1551-1965.
Denarius	Roman, originally 10 then 16 asses (25 to the Aureus), later debased: the 'd' of the £.s.d.
Double Florin	Four shillings from 1887-1890.
Farthing	Quarter penny, 1279-1553.
Florin	Two shillings, from 1849-1967.
Groat	Four pence, 1279 – c. 1300 and 1351-1662 (Halfgroat from 1351). 'Britannia' groat, 1836-55 (and 1888 for Colonial use only). See also Maundy money.
Halfcrown	Thirty pence (2s. 6d.), 1551-1967.
Halfpenny	Intermittently, c. 890-c. 970, c. 1108, short cross and, more generally, 1279-1660.
Maundy money	Four, three, two and one penny pieces, from 1660.
New pence	Decimal coinage: 50p from 1969, 25p. (crown) 1972 and 1977, 1980, 1981, 10p. and 5p. from 1968. 'New' removed in 1982.
Quinarius	Roman, half denarius or 8 asses; later debased.
Penny (pl. pence)	Standard unit of currency from c. 775/780 A.D until 1800.
Sceat	Early Anglo-Saxon, small, thick penny.
Shilling	Twelve pence, 1548-1966.
Siliqua	Roman, 1/24th solidus.
Sixpence	From 1551-1967.
Testern (Portcullis money)	One, two, four and eight testerns for use in the Indies (and equal to the Spanish 1, 2, 4 and 8 reales); 1600 only.
Testoon	Shilling, Henry VII and VIII.
Threefarthings	Elizabeth I, 1561-82.
Threehalfpence	Elizabeth I, 1561-82, and for Colonial use, 1834-62.
Threepence	From 1551-1944 (then see Maundy money).
Twenty pence	Decimal coinage from 1982.

Copper, Bronze, Tin, Nickel-Brass, etc.

As	Roman, an early unit of currency; reduced in size and equal to 1/16th of a denarius in Imperial times.
Centenionalis	Roman, replaced the depleted follis in A.D. 346.
Dupondius	Roman, brass two asses or one-eighth of a denarius.
Farthing	Quarter penny: Harrington, Lennox, Richmond, Maltravers and 'rose' farthings, 1613-49; regal issues, 1672-1956 (tin, 1684-92).
Follis	Roman, silver-washed bronze coin, 1/5th an argenteus, introduced c. A.D. 290, later debased.
Half Farthing	Victoria, 1842-56 (and for Colonial use 1828-39).
Halfpenny	From 1672 to 1967 (tin, 1685-92).

New Pence	Decimal coinage; 2p., 1p. and 1/2p. from 1971. 'New' removed from 1982.
Penny	From 1797 to 1967 (previously a silver coin).
Pound	Decimal coin from 1983.
Quadrans	Roman, quarter as or 1/64th of a denarius.
Quarter Farthing	For Colonial use only, 1839-53.
Semis	Roman, half as or 1/32nd of a denarius.
Sestertius	Roman, brass four asses or a quarter denarius.
Third Farthing	For Colonial use only, 1827-1913.
Threepence	Nickel-brass, 1937-67.
Twopence	George III, 'Cartwheel' issue, 1797 only. From 1971 Decimal only.
Mark	Various denominations have been used as moneys of account for which no actual coin existed e.g. the 'mark' was 160 pennies or two thirds of a pound.

APPENDIX II

A SELECT NUMISMATIC BIBLIOGRAPHY

Listed below is a selection of general books on British numismatics and other works that the specialist collector will need to consult.

General Books:

BROOKE, G. C. *English Coins*. 3rd ed., 1966.

CHALLIS, C. E. (ed.) *A New History of the Royal Mint*. 1992

GRUEBER, H. A. *Handbook of the Coins of Great Britain and Ireland*. Revised 1970

KENYON, R. Ll. *Gold Coins of England*. 1884

NORTH, J. J. *English Hammered Coinage*, Vol. I, c. 650-1272; 1994 Vol. II, 1272-1662. 1991

PECK, C. W. *English Copper, Tin and Bronze Coins in the British Museum, 1558-1958*. 1970

SUTHERLAND, C. H. V. *English Coinage, 600-1900*. 1972

Specialist Works:

ALLEN, D. *The Origins of Coinage in Britain: A Reappraisal*. Reprint 1978

ALLEN, D. F. *English Coins in the British Museum: The Cross-and-Crosslets ('Tealby') type of Henry II*. 1951

ARCHIBALD, M. M. and BLUNT, C. E. *British Museum. Anglo-Saxon Coins. Athelstan to the reform of Edgar. 924-c 973*. 1986

ASKEW, G. *The Coinage of Roman Britain*. (1951) Reprinted 1980.

BLUNT, C. E. and WHITTON, C. A. *The Coinages of Edward IV and of Henry VI (Restored)*.

BLUNT, C. E., STEWART, B.H.I.H. and LYON, C.S.S. *Coinage in Tenth-Century England. From Edward the Elder to Edgar's Reform*. 1989

BRAND, J.D. *The English Coinage 1180-1247: Money, Mints and Exchanges* 1994

BROOKE, G. C. *English Coins in the British Museum: The Norman Kings*. 1916

DOLLEY, R. H. M. (ed.). *Anglo-Saxon Coins; studies presented to Sir Frank Stenton*. 1964

HOBBS, R. *British Iron Age Coins in the British Museum*. 1996

KEARY, C. and GREUBER, H. *English Coins in the British Museum: Anglo-Saxon Series*. 1887, reprinted, 1970, 2 volumes.

LAWRENCE, L. A. *The Coinage of Edward III from 1351*.

MANVILLE, H. E. *Encyclopedia of British Numismatics. Numismatic Guide to British and Irish Periodicals 1731-1991*. 1993

MANVILLE, H. E. and ROBERTSON, T. J. *An Annotated Bibliography of British Numismatic Auction Catalogues from 1710 to the Present*. 1986

MARSH, M. A. *The Gold Sovereign, The Gold Half Sovereign*. 1982

NORTH, J. J. *Edwardian English Silver Coins 1279-1351. (SCBI 39)* 1989

NORTH, J. J. and PRESTON-MORLEY, P. J. *The John G. Brooker Collection: Coins of Charles I. (SCBI 33)* 1984

RAYNER, P.A. *The English Silver Coinage from 1649*. 5th ed. 1992

REECE, R. *Coinage in Roman Britain,* 1987.

ROBINSON, Dr. B. *The Royal Maundy.* 1992

SEAR, D. R. *Roman Coins and their Values. 3rd Edition* (1988) Reprinted 1997

VAN ARSDELL, R. *Celtic Coinage of Britain.* 1989.

WHITTON, C. A. *The Heavy Coinage of Henry VI.*

WOODHEAD, P. *English Gold Coins 1257-1603. The Herbert Schneider Collection, vol. 1 (SCBI 47)* 1996

For further references to British hammered coinage see Sylloge of Coins of the British Isles, a serial publication now comprising 47 volumes cataloguing collections in private hands and institutions.

Other authoritative papers are published in the *Numismatic Chronicle, British Numismatic Journal and Spink's Numismatic Circular.* A complete book list is available from Spink & Son Ltd., Book Department, 5 King Street, St James's, London SW1Y 6QS. Tel: 0171 930 7888

LATIN OR FOREIGN LEGENDS ON ENGLISH COINS

A DOMINO FACTUM EST ISTUD ET EST MIRABILE IN OCULIS NOSTRIS.
(This is the Lord's doing and it is marvellous in our eyes: *Psalm 118.23.*) First used on
'fine' sovereign of Mary.

AMOR POPULI PRAESIDIUM REGIS. (The love of the people is the King's
protection.) Reverse legend on angels of Charles I.

ANNO REGNI PRIMO, etc. (In the first year of the reign, etc.) Used around the edge of
many of the larger milled denominations.

CHRISTO AUSPICE REGNO. (I reign under the auspice of Christ.) Used extensively in
the reign of Charles I.

CIVIUM INDUSTRIA FLORET CIVITAS. (By the industry of its people the State
flourishes.) On the 1951 Festival Crown of George VI.

CULTORES SUI DEUS PROTEGIT. (God protects His worshippers.) On gold double
crowns and crowns of Charles I.

DECUS ET TUTAMEN. (An ornament and a safeguard: Virgil, *Aenid*, v.262.) This
inscription on the edge of all early large milled silver was suggested by Evelyn, he
having seen it on the vignette in Cardinal Richelieu's Greek Testament, and of course
refers to the device as a means to prevent clipping. This legend also appears on the edge
of U.K. and Northern Ireland one pound coins.

DIEU ET MON DROIT. (God and my right.) On halfcrowns of George IV and later
monarchs

DIRIGE DEUS GRESSUS MEOS. (May the Lord direct my steps.) On the 'Una' Five
pounds of Queen Victoria.

DOMINE NE IN FURORE TUO ARGUAS ME. (O Lord, rebuke me not in Thine anger:
Psalm 6, 1.). First used on the half-florin of Edward III and then on all half-nobles.

DomiNus Deus Omnipotens REX. (Lord God, Almighty King.) Viking coins.

DUM SPIRO SPERO. (Whilst I live, I hope.) On the coins struck at Pontefract Castle
during the Civil War after Charles I had been imprisoned.

EXALTABITUR IN GLORIA. (He shall be exalted in glory.) On all quarter-nobles.

EXURGAT DEUS ET DISSIPENTUR INIMICI EIUS. (Let God arise and let His
enemies be scattered: *Psalm* 68, 1.) On the Scottish ducat and early English coins of
James I (VI) and was chosen by the King himself. Also on Charles I, civil war, and
Declaration coins,

FACIAM EOS IN GENTEM UNAM. (I will make them one nation: *Ezekiel, 37, 22.)* On
unites and laurels of James I.

FLORENT CONCORDIA REGNA. (Through concord kingdoms flourish.) On gold unite
of Charles I and broad of Charles II.

HANC DEUS DEDIT. (God has given this, i.e. the crown .) On siege-pieces of Pontefract
struck in the name of Charles II.

HAS NISI PERITURUS MIHI ADIMAT NEMO. (Let no one remove these [letters] from
me under penalty of death.) On the edge of crowns and half-crowns of Cromwell.

HENRICUS ROSAS REGNA JACOBUS. (Henry united the roses, James the kingdoms.)
On English and Scottish gold coins of James I (VI).

HONI SOIT QUI MAL Y PENSE. (Evil to him who evil thinks.) The Motto of the Order
of the Garter, first used on the Hereford (?) halfcrowns of Charles I. It also occurs on
the Garter Star in the centre of the reverse of the silver coins of Charles II, but being so
small it is usually illegible; it is more prominent on the coinage of George III.

ICH DIEN. (I serve.) Aberystwyth Furnace 2d, and Decimal 2p. The motto of The Prince
of Wales.

INIMICOS EJUS INDUAM CONFUSIONE. (As for his enemies I shall clothe them with shame: *Psalm* 132, 18.) On shillings of Edward VI struck at Durham House, Strand.

JESUS AUTEM TRANSIENS PER MEDIUM ILLORUM IBAT. (But Jesus, passing through the midst of them, went His way: *Luke iv. 30.)* The usual reverse legend on English nobles, ryals and hammered sovereigns before James I; also on the very rare Scottish noble of David II of Scotland and the unique Anglo-Gallic noble of Edward the Black Prince.

JUSTITIA THRONUM FIRMAT. (Justice strengthens the throne.) On Charles I half-groats and pennies and Scottish twenty-penny pieces.

LUCERNA PEDIBUS MEIS VERBUM EST. (Thy word is a lamp unto my feet: *Psalm 119, 105.)* Obverse legend on a rare half-sovereign of Edward VI struck at Durham House, Strand.

MIRABILIA FECIT. (He made marvellously.) On the Viking coins of (?) York.

NEMO ME IMPUNE LACESSIT. (No-one provokes me with impunity.) On the 1984 Scottish one pound. Motto of The Order of the Thistle.

NUMMORUM FAMULUS. (The servant of the coinage.) The legend on the edge of the English tin coinage at the end of the seventeenth century.

O CRUX AVE SPES UNICA. (Hail! O Cross, our only hope.) On the reverse of all half-angels.

PAX MISSA PER ORBEM. (Peace sent throughout the world.) The reverse legend of a pattern farthing of Anne.

PAX QUÆRITUR BELLO. (Peace is sought by war.) The reverse legend of the Cromwell broad.

PER CRUCEM TUAM SALVA NOS CHRISTE REDEMPTOR. (By Thy cross, save us, O Christ, our Redeemer.) The normal reverse of English angels.

PLEIDIOL WYF I'M GWLAD. (True am I to my country.) Used on the 1985 Welsh one pound. Taken from the Welsh National Anthem.

POST MORTEM PATRIS PRO FILIO. (After the death of the father for the son.) On siege-pieces struck at Pontefract in 1648 (old style) after the execution of Charles I.

POSUI DEUM ADJUTOREM MEUM. (I have made God my Helper: *comp. Psalm* 54, 4.) Used on many English and Irish silver coins from Edward III until 1603. Altered to POSUIMUS and NOSTRUM on the coins of Philip and Mary.

PROTECTOR LITERIS LITERÆ NUMMIS CORONA ET SALUS. (A protection to the letters [on the face of the coin], the letters [on the edge] are a garland and a safeguard to the coinage.) On the edge of the rare fifty-shilling piece of Cromwell.

QUÆ DEUS CONJUNXIT NEMO SEPARET. (What God hath joined together let no man put asunder: *Matthew 19, 6.)* On the larger silver English and Scottish coins of James I after he succeeded to the English throne.

REDDE CUIQUE QUOD SUUM EST. (Render to each that which is his own.) On a Henry VIII type groat of Edward VI struck by Sir Martin Bowes at Durham House, Strand.

RELIGIO PROTESTANTIVM LEGES ANGLIÆ LIBERTAS PARLIAMENTI. (The religion of the Protestants, the laws of England, the liberty of the Parliament.) This is known as the 'Declaration' and refers to Charles I's declaration to the Privy Council at Wellington, 19 September, 1642; it is found on many of his coins struck at the provincial mints during the Civil War. Usually abbreviated to REL:PROT:LEG: ANG:LIB:PAR: ROSA SINE SPINA. (A rose without a thorn.) Found on some gold and small coins of Henry VIII and later reigns.

RUTILANS ROSA SINE SPINA. (A dazzling rose without a thorn.) As last but on small gold only.

SCUTUM FIDEI PROTEGET EUM or EAM. (The shield of faith shall protect him, or her.) On much of the gold of Edward VI and Elizabeth.

SIC VOC NON VOBIS (Thus we labour but not for ourselves). 1994 £2 Bank of England.

TALI DICATA SIGNO MENS FLUCTUARI NEQUIT. (Consecrated by such a sign the mind cannot waver: from a hymn by Prudentius written in the fourth century, entitled 'Hymnus ante Somnum'.) Only on the gold 'George noble' of Henry VIII.

TIMOR DOMINI FONS VITÆ. (The fear of the Lord is a fountain of life: *Proverbs, 14, 27.)* On many shillings of Edward VI.

TVAETUR UNITA DEUS. (May God guard these united, i.e. kingdoms.) On many English Scottish and Irish coins of James I.

VERITAS TEMPORIS FILIA. (Truth, the daughter of Time.) On English and Irish coins of Mary Tudor.

Some Royal Titles:

REX ANGL*orum*—King of the English.

REX SAXONUM OCCIDENTA LIM —King of the West Saxons.

DEI GRA*tia ANGLiae ET FRANCiae DomiNus HYBerniae ET AQVITaniae*—By the Grace of God, King of England and France, Lord of Ireland and Aquitaine.

D*ei GRAtia Magnae Britanniae, FRanciae ET Hiberniae REX Fidei Defensor BRunsviciensis ET Luneburgen-sis Dux, Sacri Romani Imperii Archi-THesaurarius ET ELector*=By the Grace of God, King of Great Britain, France and Ireland, Defender of the Faith, Duke of Brunswick and Luneburg, High Treasurer and Elector of the Holy Roman Empire.

BRITANNIARUM REX —King of the Britains (i.e. Britain and British territories overseas).

BRITT:OMN:REX:FID:DEF:IND:IMP: —King of all the Britains, Defender of the Faith, Emperor of India.

VIVAT REGINA ELIZABETHA — Long live Queen Elizabeth. On the 1996 £5 Queen's 70th birthday £5 crown.

APPENDIX IV

NUMISMATIC CLUBS AND SOCIETIES

Coins News is the major monthly numismatic magazine. Spink's *Numismatic Circular* is long established, its first issue appeared in December 1892, and is now published 10 times a year. There are many numismatic magazines which carry articles of interest, such as the *CNG Review* and the *S & B Bulletin.* Many local clubs and societies are affiliated to the British Association of Numismatic Societies, (B.A.N.S) which holds an annual Congress. Details of your nearest numismatic club can be obtained from the Hon. Secretary, Philip Mernick, British Association of Numismatic Societies, c/o Bush, Boake Allen Ltd. Blackhorse Lane, London E17 5QP.

The two principal learned societies are the Royal Numismatic Society, c/o Department of Coins and Medals, the British Museum, Great Russell Street, Bloomsbury, London WC1 3DG, and the British Numismatic Society, c/o Graham Dyer, The Royal Mint, Llantrisant, Pontyclun, mid Glamorgan, Wales. Both these societies publish an annual journal.

MINTMARKS AND OTHER SYMBOLS ON ENGLISH COINS

A Mintmark (*mm.),* is a term borrowed from Roman and Greek numismatics where it showed the place of mintage; it was generally used on English coins to show where the legend began (a religious age preferred a cross for the purpose). Later, this mark, since the dating of coins was not usual, had a periodic significance, changing from time to time. Hence it was of a secret or 'privy' nature; other privy marks on a coin might be the code-mark of a particular workshop or workman. Thus a privy mark (including the *mintmark.)* might show when a coin was made, or who made it. In the use of precious metals this knowledge was necessary to guard against fraud and counterfeiting.

Mintmarks are sometimes termed 'initial marks' as they are normally placed at the commencement of the inscription. Some of the symbols chosen were personal badges of the ruling monarch, such as the rose and sun of York, or the boar's head of Richard III, the dragon of Henry Tudor or the thistle of James I; others are heraldic symbols or may allude to the mint master responsible for the coinage, e.g. the *mm.* bow used on the Durham House coins struck under John Bowes and the WS mark of William Sharrington of Bristol.

A table of mintmarks is given on the next page. Where mintmarks appear in the catalogue they are sometimes referred to only by the reference number, in order to save space, i.e. *mm. 28* (=mintmark Sun), *mm.28/74 (=mm.* Sun on obverse, *mm.* Coronet on reverse), *mm. 28/-* (=*mm.* Sun on obverse only).

MINTMARKS AND OTHER SYMBOLS

1 Edward III, Cross 1 (Class B+C).
2 Edward III, broken Cross 1 (Class D).
3 Edward III, Cross 2 (Class E)
4 Edward III, Cross 3 (Class G)
5 Cross Potent (Edw. III Treaty)
6 Cross Pattee (Edw. III Post Treaty Rich. III).
7 (a) Plain of Greek Cross.
   (b) Cross Moline.
8 Cross Patonce.
9 Cross Fleuree.
10 Cross Calvary (Cross on steps).
11 Long Cross Fitchee.
12 Short Cross Fitchee.
13 Restoration Cross (Hen. VI).
14 Latin Cross.
15 Voided Cross (Henry VI).
16 Saltire Cross.
17 Cross and 4 pellets.
18 Pierced Cross.
19 Pierced Cross & pellet.
20 Pierced Cross & central pellet.
21 Cross Crosslet.
22 Curved Star (rayant).
23 Star.
24 Spur Rowel.
25 Mullet.
26 Pierced Mullet.
27 Eglantine.
28 Sun (Edw. IV).
29 Mullet (Henry V).
30 Pansy.
31 Heraldic Cinquefoil (Edw. IV).
32 Heraldic Cinquefoil (James I).
33 Rose (Edw. IV).
34 Rosette (Edw. IV).
35 Rose (Chas. I).
36 Catherine Wheel.
37 Cross in circle.
38 Halved Sun (6 rays) & Rose.
39 Halved Sun (4 rays) & Rose.
40 Lis-upon-Half-Rose.
41 Lis-upon-Sun & Rose.
42 Lis-Rose dimidiated.
43 Lis-issuant-from-Rose.
44 Trefoil.

45 Slipped Trefoil, James I (1).
46 Slipped Trefoil, James I (2).
47 Quatrefoil.
48 Saltire.
49 Pinecone.
50 Leaf (-mascle, Hen. VI).
51 Leaf (-trefoil, Hen. VI).
52 Arrow.
53 Pheon.
54 A.
55 Annulet.
56 Annulet-with-pellet.
57 Anchor.
58 Anchor & B.
59 Flower & B.
60 Bell.
61 Book.
62 Boar's Head (early Richard III).
63 Boar's Head (later Richard III).
64 Boar's Head, Charles I.
65 Acorn   (a) Hen. VIII
                   (b) Elizabeth.
66 Bow.
67 Br. (Bristol, Chas. I).
68 Cardinal's Hat.
69 Castle (Henry VIII).
70 Castle with H.
71 Castle (Chas. I).
72 Crescent   (a) Henry VIII
                   (b) Elizabeth.
73 Pomegranate. (Mary; Henry VIII's is broader).
74 Coronet.
75 Crown.
76 Crozier   (a) Edw. III
                   (b) Hen. VIII.
77 Ermine.
78 Escallop (Hen. VII).
79 Escallop (James I).
80 Eye (in legend Edw. IV).
81 Eye (Parliament).
82 Radiate Eye (Hen. VII).
83 Gerb.
84 Grapes.
85 Greyhound's Head.
86 Hand.
87 Harp.
88 Heart.
89 Helmet.
90 Key.
91 Leopard's Head.

91A Crowned Leopard's Head with collar (Edw. VI).
92 Lion.
93 Lion rampant.
94 Martlet.
95 Mascle.
96 Negro's Head.
97 Ostrich's Head.
98 P in brackets.
99 Pall.
100 Pear.
101 Plume.
102 Plume. Aberystwyth and Bristol.
103 Plume. Oxford.
104 Plume. Shrewsbury.
105 Lis.
106 Lis.
107 Portcullis.
108 Portcullis, Crowned.
109 Sceptre.
110 Sunburst.
111 Swan.
112 R in brackets.
113 Sword.
114 T (Henry VIII).
115 TC monogram.
116 WS monogram.
117 y or Y.
118 Dragon (Henry VII).
119 (a) Triangle
     (b) Triangle in Circle.
120 Sun (Parliament).
121 Uncertain mark.
122 Grapple.
123 Tun.
124 Woolpack.
125 Thistle.
126 Figure 6 (Edw. VI).
127 Floriated cross.
128 Lozenge.
129 Billet.
130 Plume. Bridgnorth or late declaration
131 Two lions.
132 Clasped book.
133 Cross pomee.
134 Bugle.
135 Crowned T (Tournai, Hen VIII)
136 An incurved pierced cross

The reign listed after a mintmark indicates that from which the drawing is taken. A similar mm. may have been used in another reign and will be found in the chronological list at the beginning of each reign.

1	2	3	4	5	6	7a	7b	8	9
10	11	12	13	14	15	16	17	18	19
20	21	22	23	24	25	26	27	28	29
30	31	32	33	34	35	36	37	38	39
40	41	42	43	44	45	46	47	48	49
50	51	52	53	54	55	56	57	58	59
60	61	62	63	64	65a	65b	66	67	68
69	70	71	72a	72b	73	74	75	76	77
78	79	80	81	82	83	84	85	86	87
88	89	90a	90b	90c	91	92	93	94	95
96	97	98	99	100	101	102	103	104	105
106	107	108	109	110	111	112	113	114	115
116	117a	117b	118	119a	119b	120	121	122	123
124	125	126	127	128	129	130	131	132	133
134	135	136							

ALPHABETICAL INDEX
OF RULERS AND COIN ISSUES